ADOBE® ILLUSTRATOR® 7.0

Advanced Digital Illustration

PRENTICE HALL
Upper Saddle River, NJ 07458

Library of Congress Cataloging-in-Publication Data

Adobe Illustrator 7.0: advanced digital illustration.
p. cm. -- (Against the clock)
Includes Index.
ISBN 0-13-080506-8
1. Computer graphics. 2. Adobe Illustrator (Computer file)
I. Series.
T385.A358125 1998
006.6' 869 -- dc21

98-14260
CIP

Acquisitions Editor: *Elizabeth Sugg*
Developmental Editor: *Judy Casillo*
Supervising Manager: *Mary Carnis*
Production Editor: *Denise Brown*
Director of Manufacturing & Production: *Bruce Johnson*
Manufacturing Buyer: *Ed O'Dougherty*
Editorial Assistant: *Leanne Nieglos*
Formatting/page make-up: *Against The Clock, Inc.*
Printer/Binder: *Banta/Harrisonburg*
Cover Design: *Joe Sengotta*
Icon Design: *James Braun*
Creative Director: *Marianne Frasco*
Marketing Manager: *Danny Hoyt*

Printed in the United States of America

10 9 8 7 6 5 4 3

ISBN 0-13-080506-8

Prentice Hall International (UK) Limited, London
Prentice Hall of Australia Pty. Limited, Sydney
Prentice Hall Canada Inc., Toronto
Prentice Hall Hispanoamericana, S.A., Mexico
Prentice Hall of India Private Limited, New Delhi
Prentice Hall of Japan, Inc., Tokyo
Simon & Schuster Asia Pte. Ltd., Singapore
Editora Prentice Hall do Brasil, Ltda., Rio de Janeiro

Contents

PURPOSE

The Against The Clock series has been developed specifically for those involved in the field of graphic arts.

Welcome to the world of electronic design and prepress. Many of our readers are already involved in the industry — in advertising and design companies, in prepress and imaging firms, and in the world of commercial printing and reproduction. Others are just now preparing themselves for a career somewhere in the profession.

This series of courses will provide you with the skills necessary to work in this fast-paced, exciting, and rapidly expanding business. Many people feel that they can simply purchase a computer, the appropriate software, a laser printer, and a ream of paper, and begin designing and producing high-quality printed materials. While this might suffice for a barbecue announcement or a flyer advertising a local hair salon, the real world of four-color printing and professional communications requires a far more serious commitment.

THE SERIES

The applications presented in the Against The Clock series stand out as the programs of choice in professional graphic arts environments.

We've used a modular design for the Against The Clock series, allowing you to mix and match the drawing, imaging, and page layout applications that exactly suit your specific needs.

Titles available in the Against The Clock series include:

Macintosh: Basic Operations
Windows: Basic Operations
Adobe Illustrator: An Introduction to Digital Illustration
Adobe Illustrator: Advanced Digital Illustration
Freehand: An Introduction to Digital Illustration
Freehand: Advanced Digital Illustration
Adobe PageMaker: An Introduction to Electronic Mechanicals
Adobe PageMaker: Advanced Electronic Mechanicals
QuarkXPress: An Introduction to Electronic Mechanicals
QuarkXPress: Advanced Electronic Mechanicals
Adobe Photoshop: An Introduction to Digital Images
Adobe Photoshop: Advanced Digital Images
File Preparation: The Responsible Electronic Page
Preflight: An Introduction to File Analysis and Repair
TrapWise: Trapping
PressWise: Imposition

We've designed our courses to be "cross-platform." While many sites use Macintosh computers, there is an increasing number of graphic arts service providers using Intel-based systems running Windows (or Windows NT). The books in this series are applicable to either of these systems.

All of the applications that we cover in the Against The Clock series are similar in operation and appearance whether you're working on a Macintosh or a Windows system. When a particular function does differ from machine to machine, we present both.

ICONS AND VISUALS

Pencil icon indicates a comment from an experienced operator. Whenever you see the pencil icon, you'll find corresponding sidebar text that augments or builds upon the subject being discussed at the time.

Bomb icon indicates a potential problem or difficulty. For instance, a certain technique might lead to pages that prove difficult to output. In other cases, there might be something that a program cannot easily accomplish, so we might present a workaround.

Pointing Finger indicates a hands-on activity — whether a short exercise or a complete project. This will be the icon you'll see the most throughout the course.

Key icon is used to point out that there is a keyboard equivalent to a menu or dialog-box option. Key commands are often faster than using the mouse to select a menu option. Experienced operators often mix the use of keyboard equivalents and menu/dialog box selections to arrive at their optimum speed.

If you are a Windows user, be sure to refer to the corresponding text or images whenever you see this **Windows** icon. Although there isn't a great deal of difference between using these applications on a Macintosh and using them on a Windows-based PC, there are certain instances where there's enough of a difference for us to comment.

Course Walkthrough

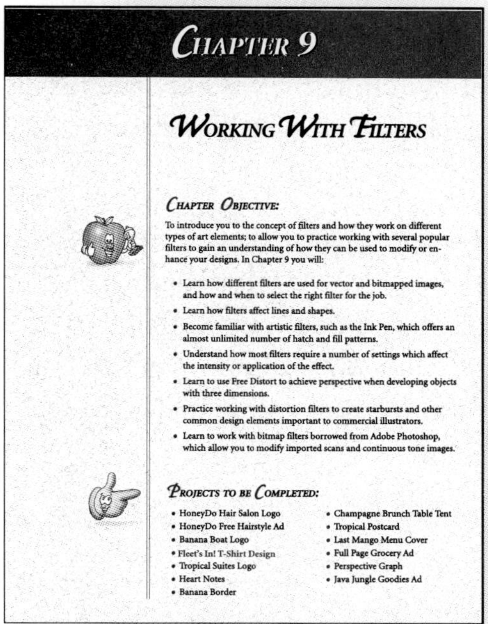

Chapter 9

Working With Filters

Chapter Objective:

To introduce you to the concept of filters and how they work on different types of art elements; to allow you to practice working with several popular filters to gain an understanding of how they can be used to modify or enhance your designs. In Chapter 9 you will:

- Learn how different filters are used for vector and bitmapped images, and how and when to select the right filter for the job.
- Learn how filters affect lines and shapes.
- Become familiar with artistic filters, such as the Ink Pen, which offers an almost unlimited number of hatch and fill patterns.
- Understand how most filters require a number of settings which affect the intensity or application of the effect.
- Learn to use Free Distort to achieve perspective when developing objects with three dimensions.
- Practice working with distortion filters to create starbursts and other common design elements important to commercial illustrators.
- Learn to work with bitmap filters borrowed from Adobe Photoshop, which allow you to modify imported scans and continuous tone images.

Projects to be Completed:

- HoneyDo Hair Salon Logo
- HoneyDo Free Hairstyle Ad
- Banana Boat Logo
- Fleet's In! T-Shirt Design
- Tropical Suites Logo
- Heart Notes
- Banana Border
- Champagne Brunch Table Tent
- Tropical Postcard
- Last Mango Menu Cover
- Full Page Grocery Ad
- Perspective Graph
- Java Jungle Goodies Ad

***CHAPTER OPENINGS** provide the reader with specific objectives.*

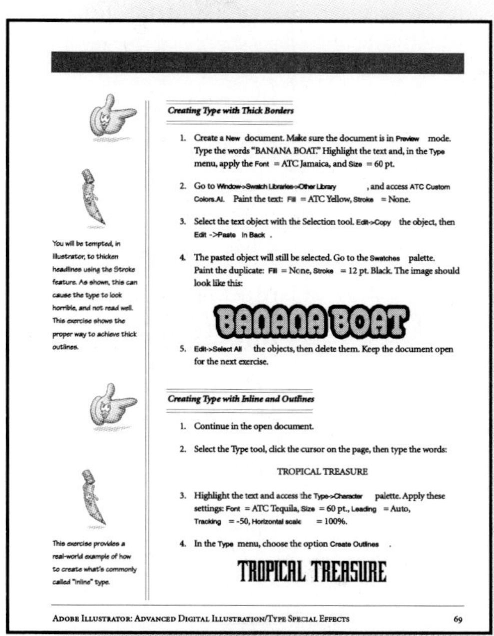

Creating Type with Thick Borders

1. Create a New document. Make sure the document is in Preview mode. Type the words "BANANA BOAT." Highlight the text and, in the Type menu, apply the Font = ATC Jamaica, and Size = 60 pt.
2. Go to Window->Swatch Libraries->Other Library, and access ATC Custom Colors.AI. Paint the text: Fill = ATC Yellow, Stroke = None.
3. Select the text object with the Selection tool. Edit->Copy the object, then Edit ->Paste In Back.
4. The pasted object will still be selected. Go to the Swatches palette. Paint the duplicate: Fill = None, Stroke = 12 pt. Black. The image should look like this:

BANANA BOAT

5. Edit->Select All the objects, then delete them. Keep the document open for the next exercise.

You will be tempted, in Illustrator, to thicken headlines using the Stroke feature. As shown, this can cause the type to look horrible, and not read well. This exercise shows the proper way to achieve thick outlines.

Creating Type with Inline and Outlines

1. Continue in the open document.
2. Select the Type tool, click the cursor on the page, then type the words:

TROPICAL TREASURE

3. Highlight the text and access the Type->Character palette. Apply these settings: Font = ATC Tequila, Size = 60 pt., Leading = Auto, Tracking = -50, Horizontal scale = 100%.
4. In the Type menu, choose the option Create Outlines.

TROPICAL TREASURE

This exercise provides a real-world example of how to create what's commonly called "inline" type.

Adobe Illustrator: Advanced Digital Illustration/Type Special Effects 69

***SIDEBARS and HANDS-ON ACTIVITIES** supplement concepts presented in the material.*

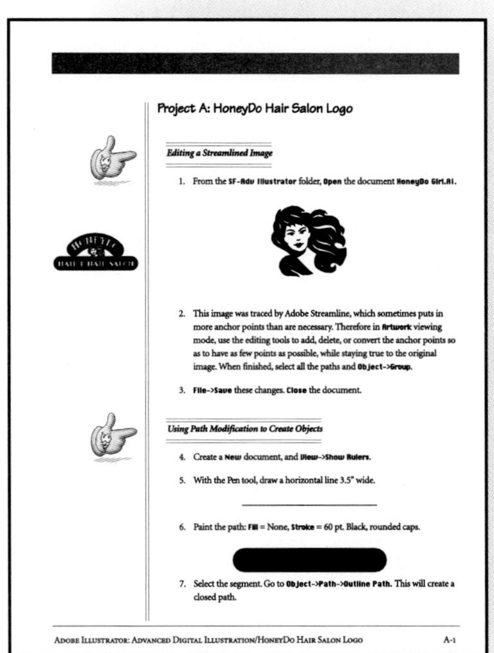

Project A: HoneyDo Hair Salon Logo

Editing a Streamlined Image

1. From the **SF-Adv Illustrator** folder, **Open** the document **HoneyDo Girl.AI**.
2. This image was traced by Adobe Streamline, which sometimes puts in more anchor points than are necessary. Therefore in **Artwork** viewing mode, use the editing tools to add, delete, or convert the anchor points so as to have as few points as possible, while staying true to the original image. When finished, select all the paths and **Object->Group**.
3. **File->Save** these changes. **Close** the document.

Using Path Modification to Create Objects

4. Create a **New** document, and **View->Show Rulers**.
5. With the Pen tool, draw a horizontal line 3.5" wide.
6. Paint the path: **Fill** = None, **Stroke** = 60 pt. Black, rounded caps.
7. Select the segment. Go to **Object->Path->Outline Path.** This will create a closed path.

Adobe Illustrator: Advanced Digital Illustration/HoneyDo Hair Salon Logo A-1

***SUPPLEMENTAL PROJECTS** offer practice opportunities in addition to the exercises.*

***PROJECT ASSIGNMENTS** will result in finished artwork — with an emphasis on proper file construction methods.*

The Projects You Will Work On

The Against The Clock course materials have been constructed with two primary building blocks: exercises and projects. Projects always result in a finished piece of work — digital imagery built from the ground up, utilizing photographic-quality images, vector artwork from Adobe Illustrator, and type elements from the library supplied on your student CD-ROM.

This course, *Adobe Illustrator: Advanced Digital Images*, is no exception; the material includes plenty of project assignments. Each will strengthen your understanding and experience with Adobe Illustrator. You will find the projects displayed on the inside front cover of the book. At the end of certain chapters in the book, you will be referred to specific projects and asked to complete them before moving on to the next section.

Here's a brief overview of each.

Project A: HoneyDo Hair Salon Logo

Type on a partial circle is required for the *HoneyDo Hair Salon* job, and both the banner type at the top and the "deck" copy at the bottom are reversed from a black background. The woman's head element is refined using path editing techniques studied in the course. Inline effects are used throughout the piece.

Project B: HoneyDo Free Hairstyle Ad

The *HoneyDo Free Hairstyle Ad* calls upon the designer to use elements created in several other projects to build a display ad that could be resized for many different mechanical applications. You're required to apply text wrap to make sure that the copy fits properly around the imported EPS file of the woman's head.

Project C: Banana Boat Logo

Starting with a template supplied on your CD-ROM, completing the *Banana Boat Logo* requires that you hand-sketch the primary logo shape, using the path editing techniques you've learned to refine it to meet the original. The Pathfinder filters come into play to create the placard in which some of the type elements fit. The creation and positioning of the type elements complete the logo.

Project D: Fleet's In! T-Shirt Design

T-Shirt Design makes extensive use of type on paths to create the banner that's displayed at the bottom of the graphic. Illustrator is used extensively in the textile silkscreening industry, and this is a good example of the kind of complex, multi-colored artwork that's popular in that genre. Transformations are used throughout the work, to create the waves, duplicate them in rows, and create the shadows that appear under each.

Project E: Tropical Suites Logo

The *Tropical Suites Logo* relies on the use of transformation tools — specifically the reflection function — to create the symmetrical palm trees that frame the inline type elements. Proper placement of the origin point demonstrates the importance of accurate reflections; you can see this technique in commercial artwork almost everywhere you look. The project also requires that you join points, and utilizes stacked type elements to create the inline effect you see in the main logotype.

Project F: Heart Notes

Heart Notes is a graphic meant to be used as notepaper or the border for a friendship or holiday card. Once again, the concepts of using multiple transforms come into play, and you're required to build the card on a single axis, with reflection and cloning evident in the rules and border graphics. The heart itself is skewed and shaped with Free Distort to add flavor to the design. Type is added to the object, and Pathfinder used to create the drop shadow that's positioned behind the note border.

Project G: Banana Border

This is a simple example of using a hand-drawn element to create an elegant but fun *Banana Border*, which could be used for a wide range of applications. The project relies on the use of multiple duplications (really a type of transformation), reflections, and the Align and Distribute tools. Rotation is used to ensure that the elements remain consistently positioned around the border.

Project H: Champagne Brunch Table Tent

The *Champagne Brunch Table Tent* relies on advanced image compositing features, including masking continuous-tone visuals that you import from the student files supplied on your CD-ROM. Careful stacking and positioning is required to create and layer the drop shadows contained on some of the images. Type is created directly on the page, and an imported EPS logo used to complete the complex layout.

PROJECT I: TROPICAL POSTCARD

The *Tropical Postcard* project also utilizes advanced functions. The palm tree and sun images are imported as continuous-tone graphics (grayscale) and then rasterized to a bitmap in Illustrator to achieve a high-contrast look. Type fitting is required as well, to ensure balance and impact from the copy on the upper left and lower right corners. The final images are positioned at an angle using the rotate function.

PROJECT J: LAST MANGO MENU COVER

The use of patterns — from simple geometric shapes to complex and seemingly random textures — is evident in a large percentage of commercial work. The *Last Mango Menu Cover* is an example of a subtle pattern applied as a background element that bleeds off the page. The design also calls for the creation of an embossed effect on the primary type at the bottom of the page.

PROJECT K: FULL PAGE GROCERY AD

In *Full Page Grocery Ad*, you really see the capacity of Illustrator to stand alone as a full-blown page layout tool. Most designers would build a page like this in a program like PageMaker or QuarkXPress, using dozens of imported elements and resulting in an overly-complex file. Here, the entire project is done using a structured grid, imported scans, and a host of Illustrator functions. The result is a self-contained ad ready for any newspaper.

PROJECT L: PERSPECTIVE GRAPH

The *Perspective Graph* requires the use of several advanced features. The graphic displays statistical data using custom icons of palm trees that you build yourself and then use to graph the data. Depth is added to the graph, giving it a really professional look, using a perspective grid — something you will learn about in the course.

PROJECT M: JAVA JUNGLE GOODIES AD

In *Java Jungle* you begin to see Illustrator's capacity as a layout program. This single-page display ad requires the placement of art elements to create a balanced design. While the ad seems very simple, the project makes use of some very advanced features, including the creation of a knock-out mask that silhouettes the imported scan in the center of the ad. The techniques used to create this job are critical in a great deal of commercial work.

Support Materials

For the Student

On the CD-ROM, you will find a complete set of Against The Clock (ATC) fonts, as well as a collection of data files used to construct the various exercises and projects.

The ATC fonts are solely for use while you are working with the Against The Clock materials. These fonts will be used throughout both the exercises and projects and are provided in both Macintosh and Windows format.

A variety of student files has been included. These files, necessary to complete both the exercises and projects, are also provided in both Macintosh and Windows formats.

For the Instructor

The Instructor Kit consists of an Instructor's manual and an Instructor's CD-ROM. It includes various testing and presentation materials in addition to the files that come standard with the student books.

- **Overhead Presentation Materials** are provided and follow along with the course. These presentations are prepared using Microsoft PowerPoint and are provided in both "native" PowerPoint format as well as Acrobat Portable Document Format (PDF).
- **Extra Projects** are provided along with the data files required for completion. These projects may be used to extend the course, or may be used to test the student.
- **A Test Bank of Questions** is included within the instructor kit. These questions may be modified, reorganized, and administered throughout the delivery of the course.
- Halfway through the course is a **Review** of material covered to that point, with a **Final Review** at the end.

Acknowledgments

I would like to give special thanks to the writers, editors, and others who have worked long and hard to complete the Against The Clock series. Foremost among them are Dean Bagley, Gavin Nagatomo, Gary Poyssick, Jim Wheaton, Gary Paul Howland, Tyler Robinson, and Don Poyssick, whom I thank for their long nights, early mornings, and their seemingly endless patience.

Thanks to the dedicated teaching professionals whose comments and expertise contributed to the success of these products, including Renée Prim of Central Piedmont Community College, Ron Bertolina of The Graphic Arts Technical Foundation, and Dr. Mitchell Henke of Bemidji State University.

A big thanks to Judy Casillo, Developmental Editor, for her guidance, patience, and attention to detail.

A special thanks to my husband for his unswerving support and for living in a publishing studio and warehouse during the three years it took to develop the ATC series of courses.

Thanks to my original partner and friend Steve Tripp, for his faith and patience in the early days. Thanks, too, to Jung Mills, who was with me each and every day — making Against The Clock a household name.

Thanks to my "Fishin' Buddies" EW Spencer and Jeannie Pugh. And special thanks to my dogs, Spike (who left for the big rawhide factory in the sky before the project was completed), Boda, and Chase.

Ellenn Behoriam, January 1998

Against The Clock

Against The Clock (ATC) was founded in 1990 as a part of Lanman Systems Group, one of the nation's leading systems integration and training firms. The company specialized in developing custom training materials for such clients as *L.L. Bean,* The *New England Journal of Medicine, Smithsonian,* the *National Education Association, Air & Space Magazine, Publishers Clearing House,* The *National Wildlife Society, Home Shopping Network,* and many others. The integration firm was among the most highly respected in the graphic arts industry.

To a great degree, the success of Systems Group can be attributed to the thousands of pages of course materials developed at the company's demanding client sites. Throughout the rapid growth of Systems Group, founder and General Manager Ellenn Behoriam developed the expertise necessary to manage technical experts, content providers, writers, editors, illustrators, designers, layout artists, proofreaders, and the rest of the chain of professionals required to develop structured and highly effective training materials.

Following the sale of the Lanman Companies to World Color, one of the nation's largest commercial printers, Ellenn embarked on a three-year project to fully redevelop a library of training materials engineered specifically for the professional graphic artist. The result of this effort is the ATC training library.

Ellenn lives in Tampa, Florida with her husband and her dogs, Boda and Chase.

About the Authors

Every one of the Against The Clock course books was developed by a group of people working as part of a design and production team. In all cases, however, there was a primary author who assumed the bulk of the responsibility for developing the exercises, writing the copy, and organizing the illustrations and other visuals.

In the case of *Adobe Illustrator: Advanced Digital Illustration,* that author was **Dean Bagley**. Dean is an experienced marketing and advertising expert. One of Dean's most effective skills is the development of hands-on activities, which, as you'll see, is the foundation of the ATC series.

Dean is a professional cartoonist, well-known for his imaginative and entertaining "Baggy Gator" series of comic characters. Dean lives in Winter Haven, Florida with his cat Nuci.

Platform

The Against The Clock series is specifically designed to apply to both Macintosh and Windows systems — the courses will work for you no matter what environment you find yourself in. There are some slight differences in the two, but when you're working in an actual application, these differences are limited to certain types of functions and actions.

Naming Conventions

In the old days of MS-DOS systems, file names on the PC were limited to something referred to as "8.3," which meant that you were limited in the number of characters you could use to an eight-character name (the "8") and a three-character suffix (the "3"). Text files, for example, might be called *myfile.txt*, while a document file from a word processor might be called *myfile.doc* (for document). On today's Windows-based systems, these limitations have been somewhat overcome. Although you can use longer file names, suffixes still exist. Whether or not you see them is another story.

When your system is first configured, the Views are normally set to a default that hides these extensions. This means that you might have a dozen different files named *myfile*, all of which may have been generated by different applications and be completely different types of files.

On a Windows system, you can change this view by clicking on *My Computer* (the icon is on your desktop) with the right button, and choosing View ->Options. From this dialog box you may choose whether or not to display these older, MS-DOS file extensions. In some cases, it's easier to know what you're looking at if they're visible. This is a personal choice.

To ensure that the supplied student files are fully compatible with both operating systems, we've named all the files using the three-character suffix — even those on the Macintosh.

Key Commands

Key commands are fairly consistent between the Macintosh and the Windows versions of Adobe Illustrator. The major difference lies in the names of special function keys. The Macintosh has a key marked with an Apple and an icon that looks like a clover leaf. This is called the Command key. Whenever you see this icon, you will need to hold this key down. The Command key is a *modifier* key; that is, it doesn't do anything by itself, but changes the function of a key pressed while it's being held down. A good example is holding Command while pressing the "S" key: this Saves your work. The same thing applies to the "P" key; hold down Command and press it to Print your work.

On Windows-based systems, the Control key is almost always the equivalent of the Command key on the Macintosh. (This is sometimes confusing to new users, since the Macintosh also has a Control key, although, on the Macintosh, it's hardly ever used in popular applications).

Another special function key on the Macintosh is the Option key. It's also a modifier key, and you'll need to hold it down along with whatever other key is required for a specific function. The equivalent modifier key on a Windows system is called the ALT key (for alternative). Besides these two nomenclature issues, there isn't really a lot of difference between using a Windows system and a Macintosh system (particularly when you're within a particular application).

The CD-ROM and Initial Setup Considerations

Before you begin using your Against The Clock course book, you will have to set up your system so that you have access to the various files and tools you'll need to complete your lessons.

Student Files

This course comes complete with a collection of student files. These files are an integral part of the learning experience, as they're used throughout the course to help you construct increasingly complex elements. Having these building blocks available to you throughout your practice and study sessions will ensure that you will be able to experience the exercises and complete the project assignments smoothly and with a minimum of time spent looking for the various components required.

In building the Student Files folders, we've created sets of data for both Macintosh and Windows users. Locate the appropriate version of the "SF-Advanced Illustrator" folder for your platform of choice and simply drag the icon onto your hard disk drive. If you have limited disk space, you may want to copy only the files for one or two lessons at a time.

Creating a Project Folder

We strongly recommend that you work from your hard disk. However, in some cases you might not have enough room on your system for all of the files that we've supplied. If this is the case, you can work directly from the CD-ROM.

Throughout the exercises and projects, you'll be required to save your work. Since the CD-ROM is "read-only," you cannot write information to it. Create a Project Folder on your hard disk and use it to store your work-in-progress. Create your project folder using Command-N (Macintosh) or Control-N (Windows) while you're looking at your desktop. This will create the folder at the highest level of your system, where it will be easy to find.

Fonts

Whatever platform you're working on — Macintosh or Windows — you will have to install the ATC font library to ensure that your lessons and exercises will work as they're described in the course book. These fonts are provided on the student CD-ROM. There is a version for Windows and one for Macintosh.

Instructions for installing fonts are provided in the documentation that came with your computer. If you're using a font utility such as Suitcase or Font Juggler, then be sure to refer to the instructions that came with the font management application for installing your ATC fonts onto your system.

Preferences

We recommend that you throw away your Preferences file before you begin the lessons in this course. The "Illustrator Prefs" file may be found inside your System folder.

Prerequisites

This book assumes that you have a basic understanding of how to use your system. Whether you're working on a Macintosh or a Windows workstation, the skill sets are basically the same.

You should know how to use your mouse to point and click, and how to drag items around the screen. You should know how to resize a window, and how to arrange windows on your desktop to maximize the space you have available. You should know how to access pull-down menus and how check boxes and radio buttons work. Lastly, you should know how to create, open, and save files.

If you're familiar with these fundamental skills, then you know all that's necessary to utilize the Against The Clock courseware library.

Notes:

CHAPTER 2

INITIAL SETUP

CHAPTER OBJECTIVE:

To teach you how proper use of Setup and Preference controls can make you more productive, and help you get work done quicker and more efficiently. As you study Chapter 2, you will:

- Learn that many experienced operators fail to take advantage of features found within Illustrator's "environmental" controls.
- Learn about customizing page and document setup dialogs to maximize the quality and efficiency of output from your drawing files.
- Practice making changes to the way Illustrator displays documents on screen, and how that display affects the output options available to you.
- Understand more about using the keyboard as a tool to move and position objects, and how to change the distance a specific key moves a selection element.
- Learn more about guides and grids, and how to modify the default measurements systems that are used by grids, guides, and snap-to functions.
- Work with the *Startup Document*, a special file that Illustrator uses to set up all of its many defaults — such as colors, patterns, fonts, gradients, and other options.
- Understand more about how Illustrator renders typefaces on screen and during output, and learn more about using Adobe Type Manager.
- Review the Toolbox and learn more about optional tools available to the more advanced and experienced Illustrator user.

Initial Setup

The more familiar you become with an application, the more efficiently you can perform the work. This includes learning the shortcuts that will be discussed in the coming sections, and how to create default settings to coincide with the way you work.

Many otherwise advanced users don't really spend enough time setting up their workspace. These next few pages discuss how settings affect your work environment.

The first two places that affect your working environment can be found under the **File** menu:

- **Document Setup**
- **Preferences**

Document Setup

The **Document Setup** window offers many options that allow you to customize your document.

In a production environment, settings determined early on in the project can have a profound effect on the service provider's ability to output high-quality, accurate film. Incorrect output resolution, flatness, and other settings can result in inaccurate film, or wasted time fixing files when they're already at the printer.

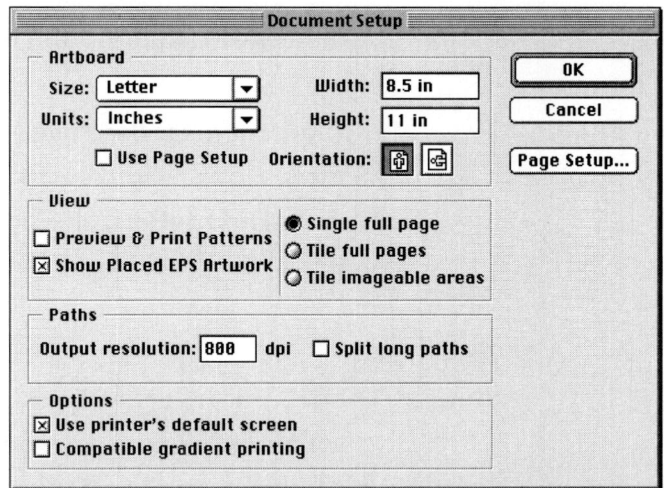

Macintosh

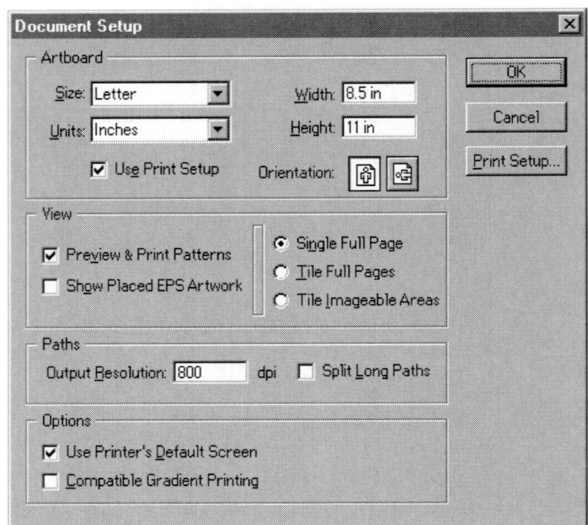

Windows

Artboard

- **Artboard** — This section lets you select the page size and page orientation (portrait or landscape) of the Artboard. New documents default to the letter size in portrait orientation, but you can customize page dimensions in the Width/Height data boxes.

  If you check the **Use Page** (Macintosh) or **Print** (Windows) **Setup** box, the Artboard will accept the settings in the **Page** (Macintosh) **Print** (Windows) **Setup** dialog box. Otherwise, **Size** and **Orientation** options selected in the **Artboard** section will be used as your settings.

  The Artboard is your work area. You should set its size to be larger than your Page Tiling, to give you working room. This is important if you use the Page tool to maneuver the Page Tiling around inside the Artboard. If the Artboard is the same size as the Page Tiling, using the Page tool will move the tiling off the Artboard's view, and you will lose most of the page.

In **Page Setup** (Macintosh only), to use Reduce or Enlarge on an Illustrator document will scale the image, large or small, to better fit your page without having to alter your artwork with the Scale tool. But, this will not affect the image if you **Save As** the file to an Illustrator EPS. The image, when **Placed** in another document, will be the normal size you created it.

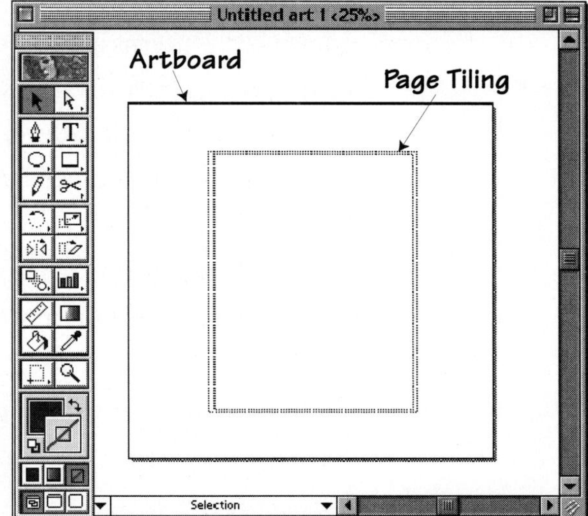

Page Tiling size and orientation is determined by Page Setup only.

When Artboard uses Page Setup, its size and orientation is determined, as well. Select Custom in the Size menu to set your own Artboard size.

If you are creating only a small design that will easily fit on a letter-size page, the default **Letter** size will be sufficient.

Use **Page Setup** to set the Page Tiling to the size and orientation you desire.

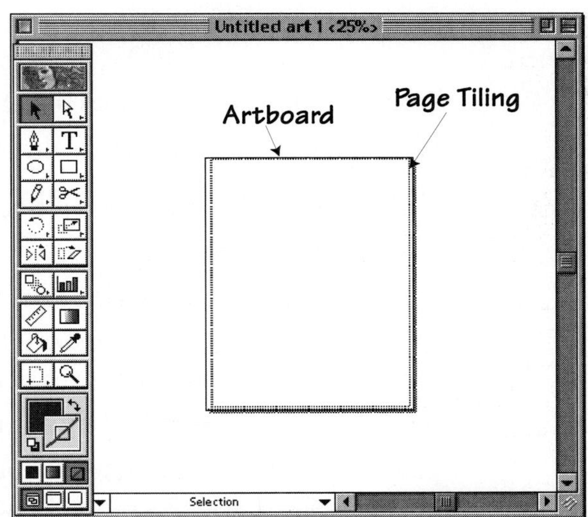

When the Artboard and Page Tiling are the same size, this does not give any room to move the Page Tiling around with the Page Tool, which is a simple way to fine-tune a design's position on the page, without moving the artwork.

If you can grow accustomed to working with your patterns turned off — at least during early development — your system will respond much faster. Even on the most powerful workstations, drawing patterns "on the fly" is very processor-intensive.

Be careful transforming a lot of patterned objects. It takes a lot of printing horsepower to output very complex patterns — especially if there are a dozen variants in a single illustration.

View

- **Preview & Print Patterns** controls whether a pattern can be seen on screen and printed. Patterns are sometimes very slow to preview depending on their complexity and size. You might consider keeping this option turned off as you're developing your artwork, and turning it on towards the end when you need to see the completed art.

- **Show Placed EPS Artwork** is very important to have clicked. This allows you to see a screen representation of the placed EPS in **Artwork** view.

- **Single Full Page** — Good for proofing illustrations smaller than the maximum paper size of your laser printer.

- **Tile Full Pages** — Used when you're creating a multiple page document in Illustrator. The **Artboard** size must be large enough to fit all pages.

- **Tile Imageable Areas** — Used to proof oversized artwork. When printed to the laser printer, the illustration will tile onto multiple pages. Then you will just need to cut and paste the printed pages in the order shown to get a proof of your entire illustration.

Paths

- **Output Resolution** determines the flatness of the file. A higher flatness value requires less memory on the PostScript output device. As with **Split Long Paths**, the most common error that is addressed by increasing flatness is LimitCheck.

- **Split Long Paths** should be used only by those who are familiar with how this option affects the paths of a design. The most common PostScript error that is fixed by this option is LimitCheck, when the path in question has become too complicated. **Split Long Paths** cuts the long paths and **Joins** them into smaller objects that make up the image.

  If you try to use this, do it on a copy of the file in question. Add the word "split" to the name for identification. If your original design gets split up, it will take considerable time to fix it if **Split Long Paths** did not stop the LimitCheck error.

Options

- **Use Printer's Default Screen** — This option should be clicked because it will allow your artwork to print at the DPI set on the final output device. The PPD of the laser printer determines this, if you are printing from Illustrator. If you Save the file as Illustrator EPS, and Place the EPS into a publishing program, the program will allow you set the DPI.

Using **Split Long Paths** can result in your artwork being cut up in some weird, arbitrary way. It happens when you save the document. Sometimes you'll come back and find all sorts of cuts in your artwork. This is why in most cases you should leave this option turned off.

- **Compatible Gradient Printing** — Use this option only with files containing gradients to be printed on imagesetters that have difficulty printing such files. This option can slow printing on printers that don't have problems with gradients.

- **Page Setup** (Macintosh) **Print Setup** (Windows) allows you to select page size and orientation.

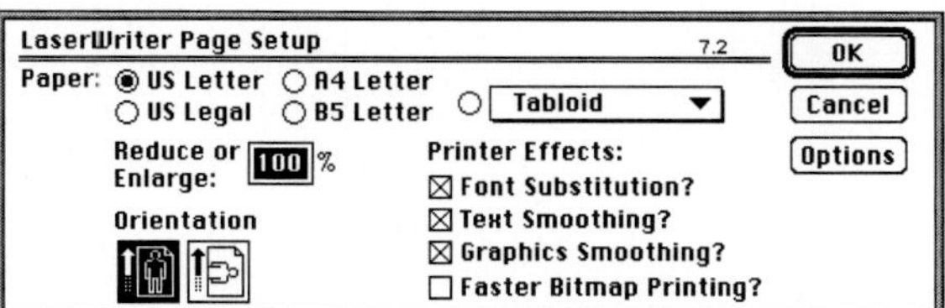

Macintosh

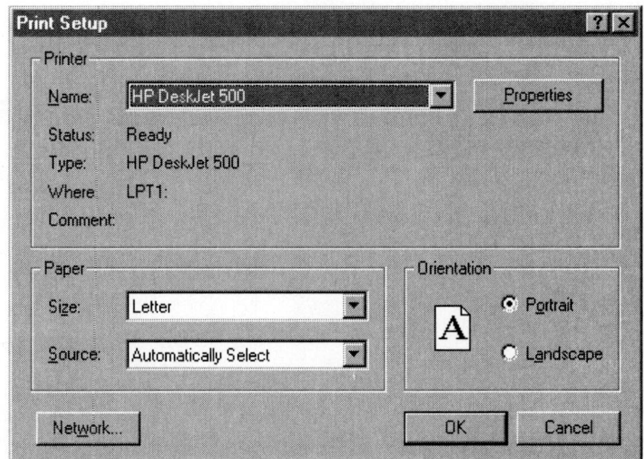

Windows

Preferences

All applications offer the user control over certain aspects of the program's operations. Another way of looking at this ability to modify the way the program works, or looks, is to think of the entire program as an *environment*. There are many different aspects to an environment: how tools look, what units of measurement are available, how layers react when you copy and paste something, or how your tool cursors look on the screen. These are only a few examples — this chapter will explain these and many more.

For the Macintosh, you can make your cursor turn to a Precise Cursor crosshair temporarily by pressing the Caps-Lock key. When this key is pressed, the cursor turns into Precise Cursor mode. When you take Caps-Lock off, the cursor goes back to normal.

General

The **File->Preferences->General** window gives more choices for customizing the tools and the effects they create.

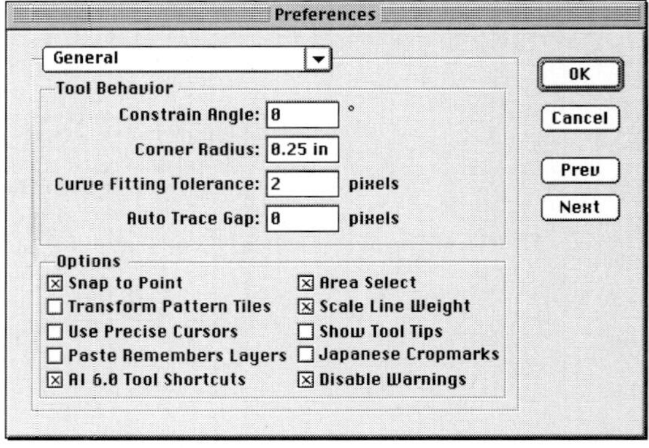

Macintosh

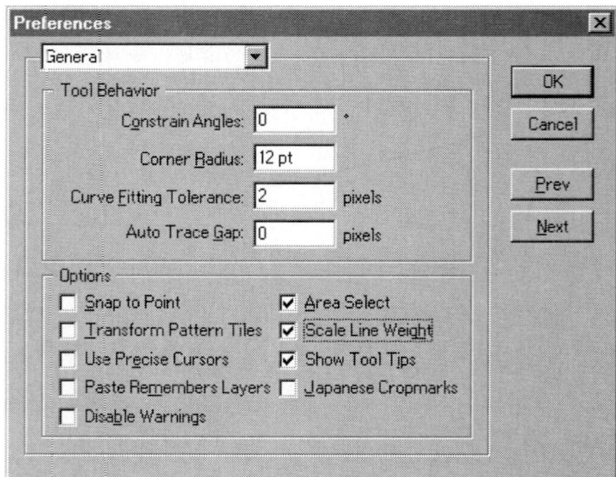

Windows

- **Snap to Point** should not be clicked for now. It interferes when using the Pen tool, by snapping to other close points.

- **Transform Pattern Tiles** should be clicked only with the use of Tiles.

- **Use Precise Cursors** changes the shape of the cursor to a crosshair for more precision when clicking certain areas.

- **Paste Remembers Layers** is helpful when Cutting/Pasting objects to or from different layers. See the chapter on Layers for more detail.

- **AI 6.0 Tool Shortcuts** (for Macintosh only) retains some of the keyboard shortcuts from the previous version, Illustrator 6.0.

- **Area Select** makes it possible to click on a painted object in **Preview** mode and select it. This does not work in **Artwork** mode.

- **Scale Line Weight** automatically adjusts line weights in proportion to the selected scaling factor. This should be clicked because, without it, a small image with 1 pt. Strokes, can be quadrupled in size, and still possess only a 1 pt. Stroke. In most cases, the artist wants the Stroke thickness to scale, uniformly, along with the size of the artwork.

- **Show Tool Tips** turns on balloon tips that explain a tool's functions.

- **Japanese Cropmarks** sets crop marks to the Japanese style, which is different from American crop marks style.

- **Disable Warnings** turns off certain warnings that might affect your work. Keep this unclicked to have the helpful warnings.

Always think about changing the **Constrain Angle** when developing drawings that aren't on the horizontal or vertical. Many designs require a different axis for the creation of objects. Three-dimensional objects are a good example.

No matter what you set this dialog to, you can always enter numbers in other measurement units. You could enter 1p if you needed a Pica, and the program was set to inches, or 1i if you wanted inches from a point-pica measurement system.

Anti-aliasing is a method of softening the edges of line art. The process is accomplished by mixing various shades together at "hard" edges. Rather than the edge of a circle going from black to white, an anti-alias process would begin with black, move to 75% gray, then to 50% gray, then to 25% gray before hitting the white area. The result is a tiny blend, which softens the edge.

Keyboard Increments

The **File->Preferences->Keyboard Increments** window gives more choices for customizing the effects the keyboard shortcuts create.

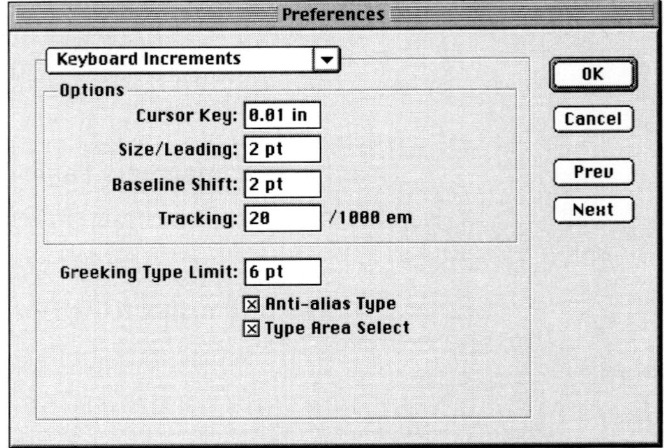

- **Cursor Key** — controls the distance the cursor or a selected object moves when a keyboard Arrow key is pressed.
- **Size/Leading, Baseline Shift, Tracking** — when you use the keyboard shortcuts to control these type settings, this allows you to customize the increments used each time a key is pressed.
- **Greeking Type Limit** — If the size in pixels of the type on the monitor is less than the specified number, the type will appear as gray bars instead of real type. Example: If you set **Greeking Type Limit** to 6, any 10 pt. type will Greek at 50% or less. This feature will speed up redraw time.
- **Anti-alias Type** — will set an Anti-alias exterior to the edges of the type.
- **Type Area Select** — allows selecting text by clicking on any part of the type's painted area. Similar to **Area Select**.

Units & Undo

The **File->Preferences->Units & Undo** window gives more choices for customizing the measuring units and Undo levels.

Set your Undo level to around 10 or so. The more Undo's you require, the more memory the program requires.

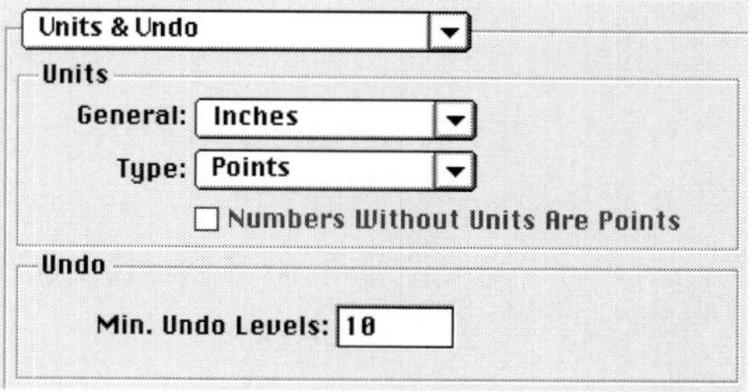

- **General** — sets the unit of measurement of the rulers and the dialog boxes. While you might like the ruler set to Inches, and the Stroke thickness set to Points, you can't have both.
- **Type** — sets the units that type is measured by. You should keep this at Points, which is the typographical standard.
- **Min. Undo Levels** — Lowering the number of available Undo's increases memory for your drawing in Illustrator. Systems with less than optimum RAM configurations may benefit with less Undo's. The maximum number of Undo's is 200, but we advise 5 or 10.

Guides & Grid

The **File->Preferences->Guides & Grid** window gives more choices for customizing the page guides and grid.

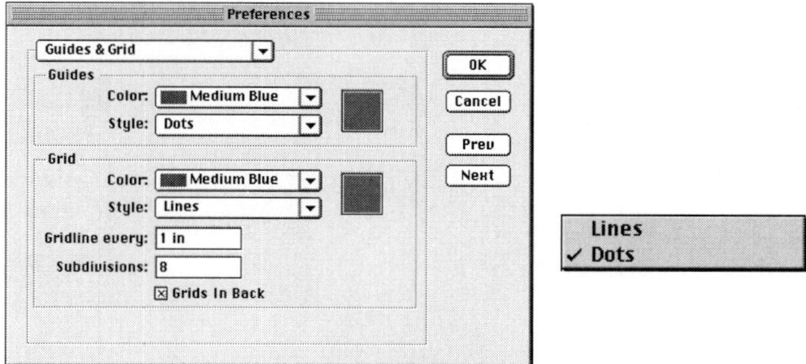

- **Guides** — sets the **Color** and **Style** (**Dots** or **Lines**) of the Guides.
- **Grid** — sets the **Color** and **Style** (**Dots** or **Lines**) of the Grid. **Gridline every** sets the separation between the gridlines. **Subdivisions** is the number of small squares that go between the gridlines.

The Startup Document

There is an entire range of preset conditions that are taken into consideration whenever Illustrator starts up, such as colors in the Swatches palette, page size, orientation, Artboard size, default type specifications, if rulers are on/off.

These settings are stored in a special file called, appropriately, the Startup file. Stored in the **Plug-Ins** folder, the file is called **Adobe Illustrator Startup** on the Macintosh, and **Startup.ai.** on Windows-based systems.

We're surprised at how few experienced operators actually use custom startup documents. It's a super tactic and can really help create a personal workspace, saving time and effort every time you start the program.

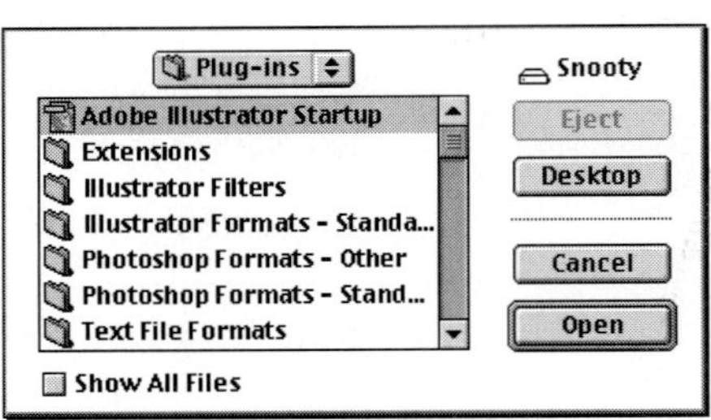

Macintosh

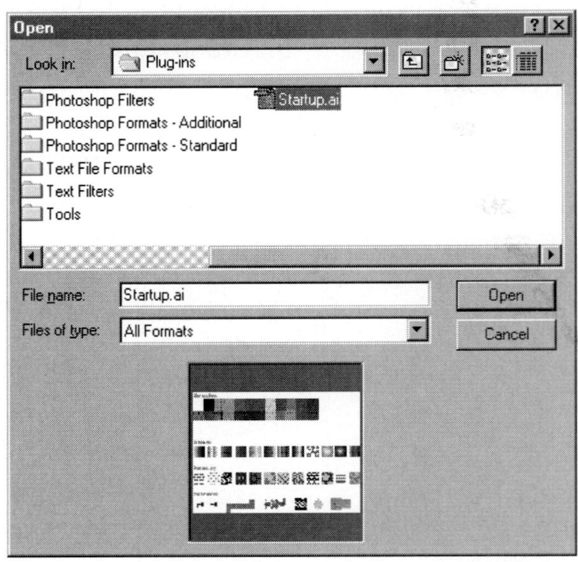

Windows

This is a convenient way for you to customize certain settings that fit the way you work. When you open the Startup document in Illustrator, you will see the colors and patterns that Illustrator already has resident for its default settings.

From **File->Document Setup** access **Page setup** (Macintosh) or **Print setup** (Windows) to set the **Page dimension** and **Orientation.** Any Spot color, Pattern, or Gradient that you like can be copied to this document and will be resident in all documents after you restart Illustrator. You can also set the view percentage and use the Page tool to position the Page tiling where you want the page to appear.

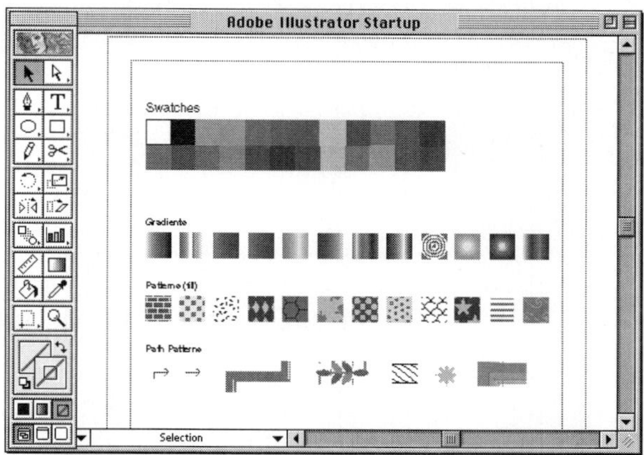

Not all settings or palettes will appear when you set them in the Startup document. You will have to experiment with the settings to see what will work.

Modifying the Startup Document

Note: before doing this exercise, make a duplicate of the Illustrator Startup file and put it aside for use after you finish.

1. Using **File->Open,** go to the **Plug-ins** folder located in the folder that holds the Illustrator application. **Open** the Startup file. For Macintosh, the file is **Adobe Illustrator Startup**. For Windows, the file is called **Startup.ai.**

2. In the **File->Document Setup** menu set the **Artboard** to **Width** =20", **Height** = 15". Make sure **Use Page Setup** (Macintosh) or **Use Print Setup** (Windows) is not clicked.

The actual artboard on which your drawing exists is very large, providing you with lots of room to work. The Page tool is used to move the Page Tiling, determining which area of the board is going to be printed.

You should get used to using the small percentage setting in the lower left corner of the Illustrator window. It lets you select an exact viewing percentage.

3. Click **Page Setup** (Macintosh) or **Print Setup** (Windows) and set the paper size for **US Legal.** Set the **Orientation** for Landscape. Press **OK.** Back in the **Document Setup** dialog box, click **OK.**

4. In the document, use the Page tool to relocate the page to the middle of the Artboard.

5. Press Command-R (Macintosh) or Ctrl-R (Windows) to Show Rulers.

6. Click the view percentage menu in the lower left of the screen to reduce the view to 25%.

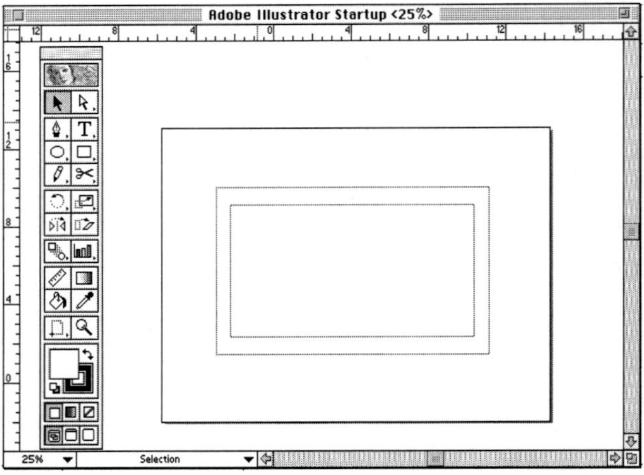

7. Go to **Window->Swatch Libraries->Other Library.** In the following window, go to the Student Folder and **Open** the document **ATC Custom Colors.AI.** A separate swatch palette for these colors will appear.

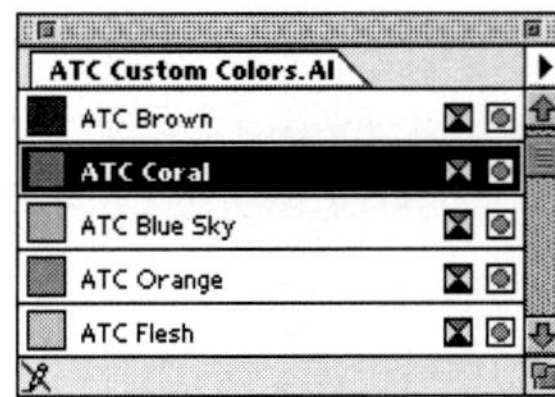

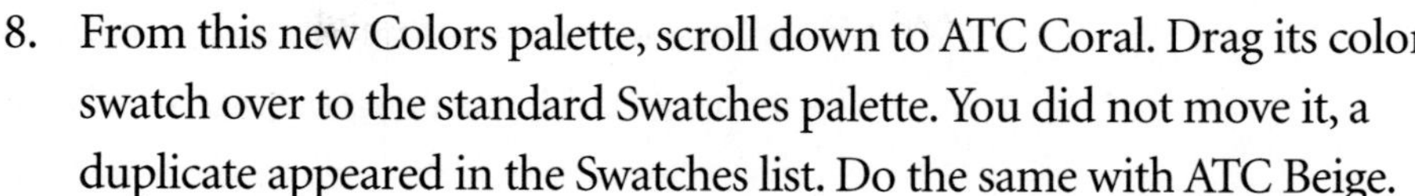

8. From this new Colors palette, scroll down to ATC Coral. Drag its color swatch over to the standard Swatches palette. You did not move it, a duplicate appeared in the Swatches list. Do the same with ATC Beige.

   Because these ATC colors are in the default **Swatches** palette, they will appear in all new documents after Illustrator is restarted. If you do not want certain colors, gradients, or patterns in the **Swatches** palette, delete them using the Trash icon at the bottom of the palette.

9. **Save** the document and **Close**. Press Command-Q (Macintosh) or Alt-Q (Windows) to **Quit** Illustrator.

10. Launch the Illustrator application and observe how the new document window looks. Go to the **Swatches** palette and look for the two ATC colors. **Close** the document without saving.

11. When finished with this exercise, remove the startup file you altered, and put the duplicate back in **Plug-ins**, named as it was before.

Adobe Type Manager (ATM) is a control panel that you can turn on or off.
For the Macintosh, you can set the size of your Font Cache (the more fonts you have the higher it should be), and choose whether to preserve Line spacing or Character shapes. We suggest you keep it set to preserve line spacing. This sometimes causes descenders to be clipped off — but only on-screen. Descenders that appear cut off will still print properly.
For Windows, Font Cache is the only available option ATM offers.

Adobe Type Manager

Adobe Systems, Inc. includes their Adobe Type Manager (ATM) with some, not all, of their product packages. You will have to examine your Illustrator CD to see if it was included. If you do not have Type Manager installed on your computer, you should have it. Type 1 fonts will appear rough and jaggy if Type Manager is not running.

In this example, the B on the left is how Type 1 fonts look without Type Manager. The B on the right is the smooth, normal way a font should look after Type Manager is installed.

You might have some fonts that look jaggy, and others that look good. The reason that certain fonts are displaying properly while others are not may be due to the fact that you probably have both TrueType and Type1 fonts installed at the same time, and ATM isn't running.

TrueType fonts do not need Adobe Type Manager to look smooth. Only Type 1 fonts need ATM, a utility program that "draws" fonts onto your monitor. If it's active, your Type1 fonts will be smooth and attractive, however closely you look at your work. If it's not running, you get the font jaggies.

Keep in mind that there are conflicts that cause printing problems when both TrueType and Type 1 fonts are active in your computer.

Example: you could have a TrueType font in your **System->Font** folder, which would be active upon startup. At the same time, you could have a font of the same name in another folder, made active with a font program such as Suitcase. In short, you actually have the same font name active, in two different locations.

The trouble begins when you are sending your document to the laser printer, which, most likely, will be a PostScript printer. The printer will have both fonts, TrueType and Type 1, downloaded to it and does not know which one to use. Result? Crash or lock-up of your computer.

You should make sure that only one font of a certain name is active. This will take some research and investigation among your fonts, but will eliminate having your computer lock up during a print job, when you least need that problem.

Chapter 3

Toolbox Review

Chapter Objective:

To comprehensively review the Adobe Illustrator 7.0 Toolbox; to explore the optional tools and adaptations of standard tools that extend the program's functionality. As you study the charts provided in Chapter 3, you will:

- Become familiar with the terminology and tool naming conventions used throughout this course.
- Learn to use the toolbox to quickly and easily apply fill and stroke characteristics to an object.
- Learn to change tool defaults.
- Know how to control various viewing methods used by professional artists to maximize their working space.
- Explore pop-up tool options, which dramatically extend the functionality of a great many of Illustrator's tools.
- Analyze the Graphing tool, an important function for artists working to visually present statistical information.
- Have the ability to utilize these charts as reference material as you work through the various exercises and project assignments in the course.

Toolbox Summary

For people who are using this course to learn the differences between Illustrator 7.0 and earlier versions, the Toolbox is one of the most important places to start. There are considerable variations in the Toolbox of this and prior versions. Many drawings are complex, and require the use of many of the tools available to you. Here are the tools you will see in the document window.

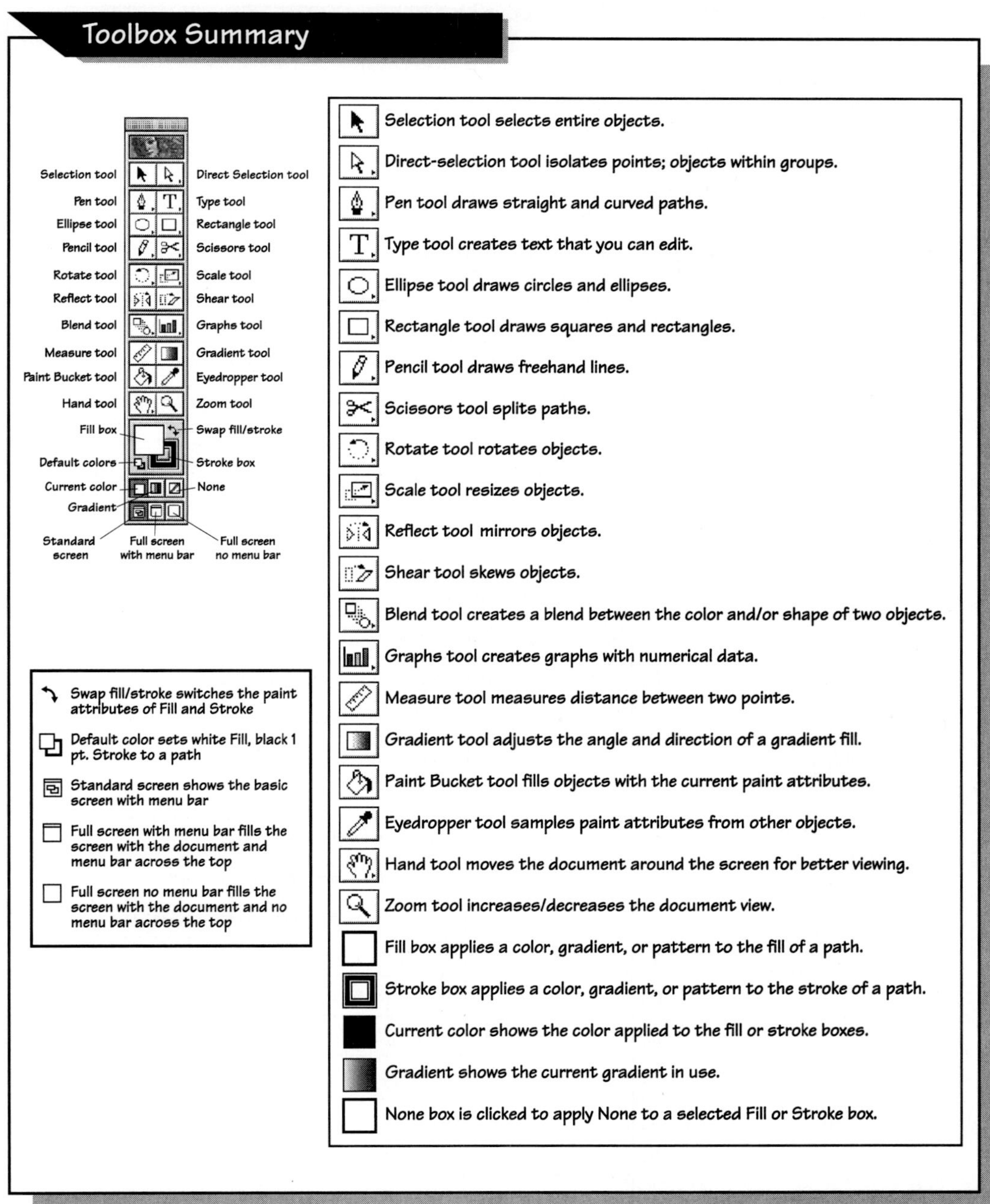

Toolbox Pop up Menus

Many people work with Illustrator for a long time before they realize that there are different aspects to certain tools. For example, the Text tool has five options; the Pen tool, three. There are times when these variations on the original function can streamline certain tasks, such as removing points, or drawing complex shapes. Tool icons with a small triangle-shaped button in the lower right corner indicates that there are optional tools available:

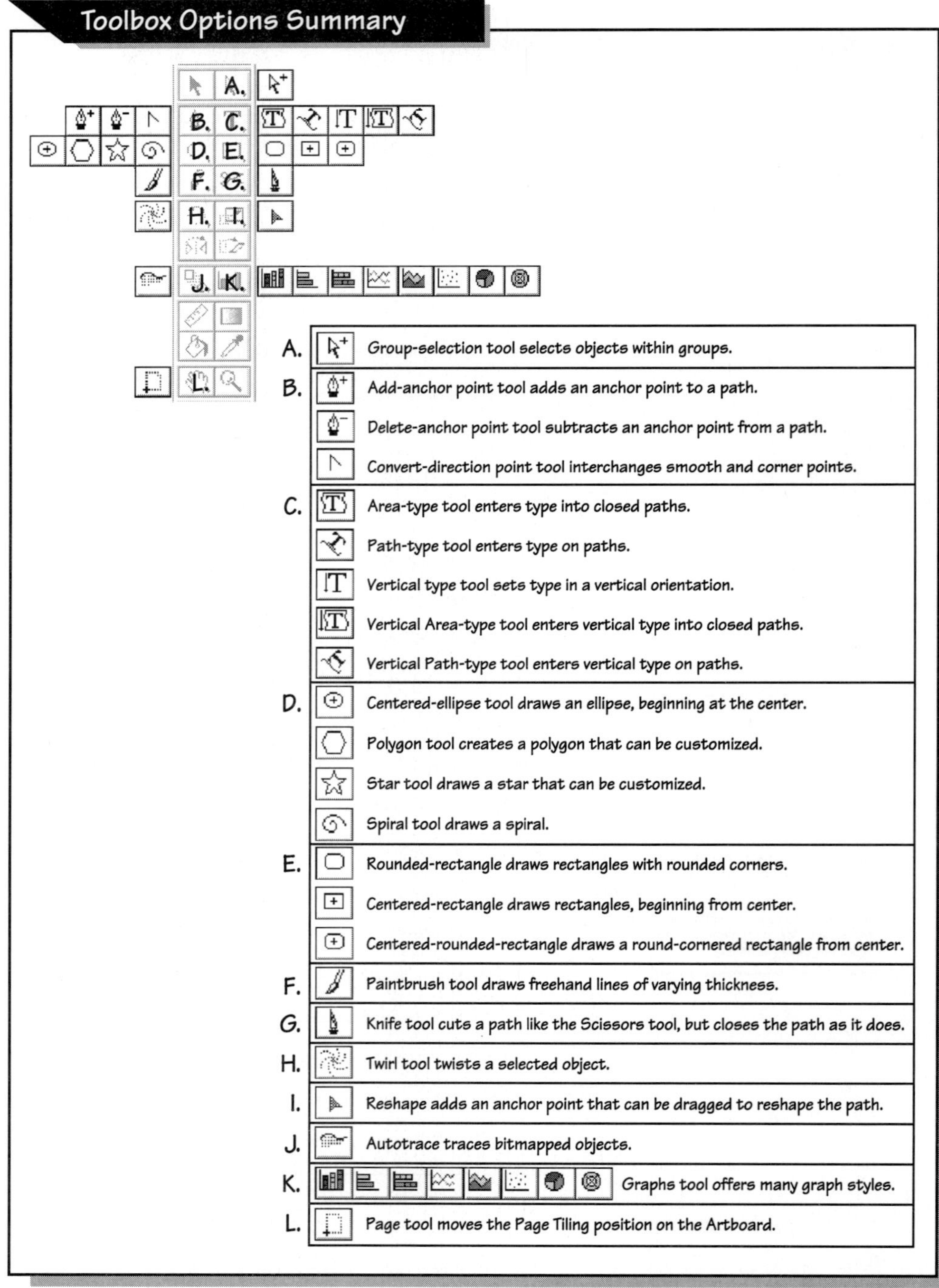

Chapter 4

Working With Layers

Chapter Objective:

To further explore the concept of layers, and particularly how they affect the development of more complex illustrations; to learn more about managing layers in complex documents. In Chapter 4, you will:

- Review the Layers palette and work with the creation and management of multi-layer documents.
- Learn about locking and hiding layers during development, and practice workflows relative to layer management.
- Practice using different views on different layers, and how to recognize which view has been applied to specific layers.
- Work with layer assignment, learning how to rapidly and effectively move elements from one layer to another.
- Learn more about preferences and setup conditions that affect copying, cutting, and pasting elements in multi-layered documents.

Working with Layers

Do you use Photoshop? If so, you probably use layers routinely. Many experienced Photoshop users use layers when they use Photoshop but not when they use Illustrator. Can you think of why that might be?

As we've mentioned in other books, the use of layers is really a thing of personal style. Some people think that you cannot live without them, while others – equally skilled and professional – hardly use them at all. It's a good thing to understand, though, because there are certain times when they're indispensable.

A solid understanding of Layers and how they work is a building block of advanced use of the software. Using layers will allow you to group objects of the same nature, and either lock them all, hide them, or toggle them between artwork and preview modes — all with a click of the mouse. Layers also allow you to isolate a group of items for performing specific operations on them, like locking the background (or any other) layer to prevent accidental tampering, or setting the layer with the gradients or patterns to artwork mode for faster screen redraw.

The Layers Palette

Most of the time you'll find yourself working from the Layers palette. Whenever you create a new document, it starts with a layer called Layer 1; so when you first access the palette you will see Layer 1 already in the list:

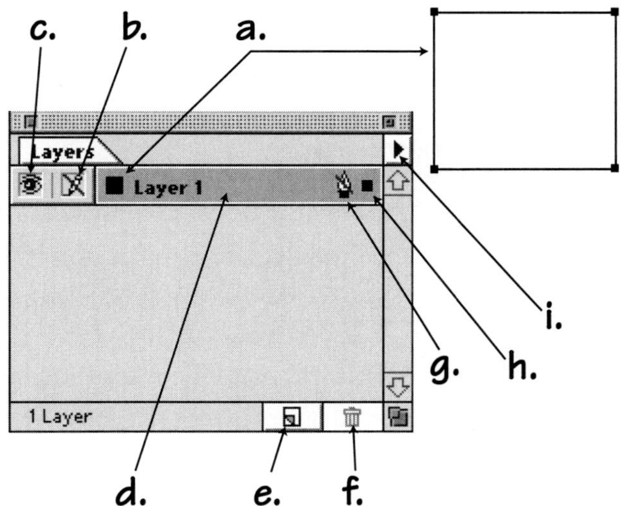

a. The color of each layer will also be the color of the handles and edges of any object assigned to that layer.

b. This is the Lock/Unlock column. When the square is empty, the layer is Unlocked. If you click here to Lock it, a crossed-out pencil icon (shown here) will tell you it is Locked.

c. This is the Show/Hide column. The Eye icon stands for Show, meaning the objects on the layer will be visible. If clicked on, and the eye disappears, the objects are hidden from view.

d. When a layer is highlighted, it is selected and is the working layer.

e. This is the New Item icon to click to create a new layer.

f. This is the Trash icon to click to delete a layer.

g. The pencil icon means that this is the working layer. If the pencil icon has a slash crossed over it, the layer is Locked.

h. A small dot means the selected object is assigned to this layer.

i. The **Layers** palette menu button. Click-hold on this when you want to access the **Layers** palette menu for further options and functions.

Toggling is a common programming technique, again meant to reduce or minimize the number of commands or menu items you need to know. Toggling simply means that the first time you issue a command it turns something on, and the next time you issue the exact same command, it turns that same thing off.

Additional Keyboard Functions

Holding certain keys while you click on an item in the **Layers** palette can do different things.

Artwork View

Pressing the Command (Macintosh) or Control (Windows) key and clicking the Eye icon will turn the objects on that layer to **Artwork** view. When this happens, the eye pupil becomes dilated to show this.

When you press these keys and add the Option (Macintosh) or Alt (Windows) key, all layers except the clicked layer will go to **Artwork** view.

To bring a layer back to **Preview** mode, the dilated Eye icon must toggled while holding the Command (Macintosh) or Control (Windows) key.

Lock/Unlock

Pressing the Option (Macintosh) or Alt (Windows) key and clicking the Lock/ Unlock square will Lock all layers except the clicked layer.

Any layer can then be Unlocked individually by clicking on its Lock square.

The Layers Palette Menu

A new layer can be created and deleted using the **Layers** palette menu. Also, **Hide**, **Lock,** and **Artwork** can be applied to layers other than the highlighted layer.

Paste Remembers Layers will keep objects on a layer, even though they have been Cut & Pasted. This causes problems when using **Paste In Front** or **Paste In Back** between different layers. If **Paste Remembers Layers** is toggled On, **Paste In Front** or **Paste In Back** will not work. It should be toggled Off.

You should always name your layers. It makes them much easier to identify.

When **Paste Remembers Layers** is toggled Off, the object being pasted will be assigned to a different layer (if any) than it is pasted to.

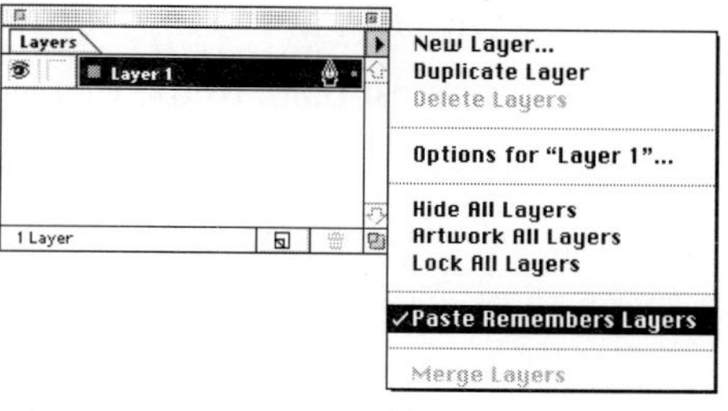

The Layer Options Window

When creating a **New Layer** in the **Layers** palette menu, the **Layer Options** window automatically appears. The desired settings for a layer can be made here. This options window can also be accessed by double-clicking on the desired layer in the **Layers** palette.

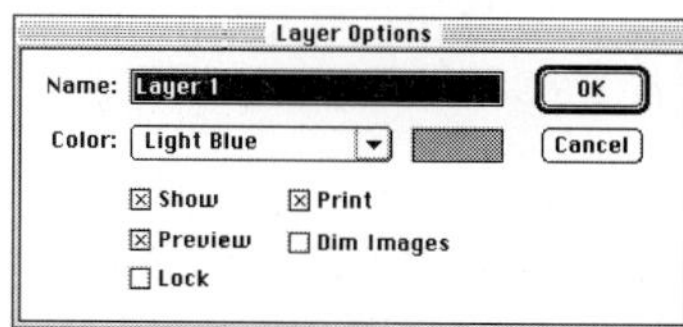

- Give the layer a **Name** for easy identification.

- **Color** assigns the color of the Edges to an object on a layer. Selecting a different color for each layer makes it easier to distinguish between layers in your work.

- **Show** displays the layer objects. If it is not selected, objects will be hidden.

- **Preview** allows the layer objects to be seen in **Preview** mode. If not selected, the layer will display only in **Artwork** mode.

- **Lock** makes the objects on the layer inaccessible to selection.

- **Print** controls whether or not objects on this layer will print.

- **Dim Images** will gray placed images so they can be used as templates.

The Priority of Layer Levels

The layer names we use here are for demonstration purposes only. So, do as we say, not as we do. It is best to name your layers so that they reflect what objects reside on them.

What is the relationship between how the layers are listed in the **Layers** palette and how they appear in your work?

The layer at the top of the list is the frontmost layer. The layer listed last is the furthest back in the order. For example, in this palette window Layer 3 is in front of all others, followed by Layer 2, Layer 1, and Layer 4.

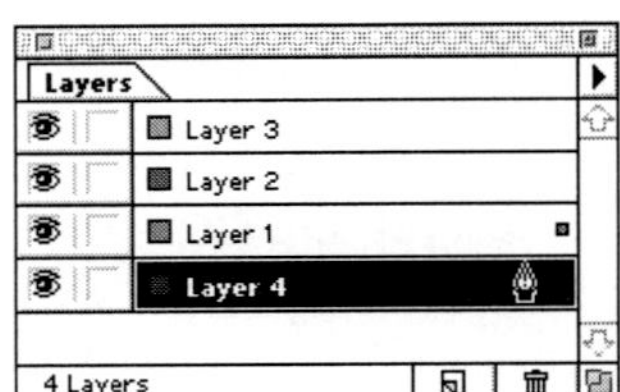

Changing and Reassigning Layer Levels & Objects

There will be times when you may want to move a layer to another level. Simply click on the desired layer and drag it up or down the **Layers** palette list.

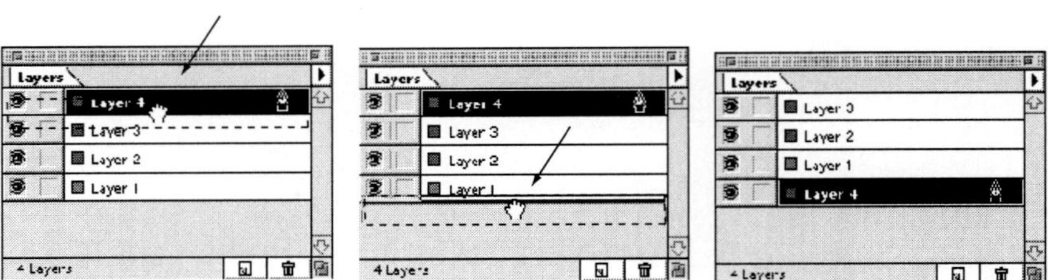

When you click-hold on the layer, the cursor turns into a clenched fist to symbolize that you are grabbing the layer. The layer can then be dragged up or down the layer levels to reassign it.

Reassigning Objects to Other Layers

You can reassign an object from one layer to another in the **Layers** palette. Simply select the object you want to switch, and drag its colored dot to the desired layer.

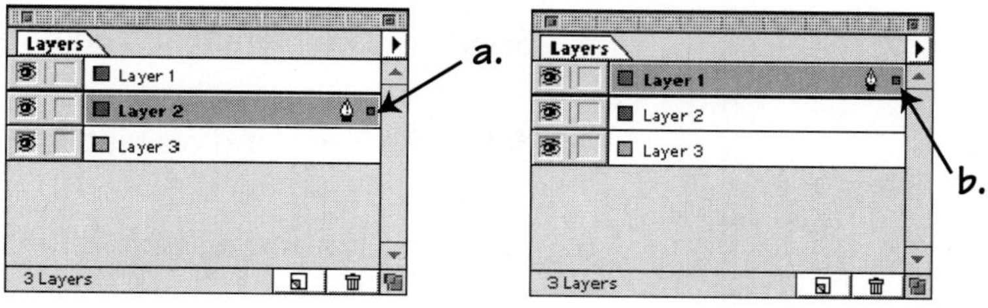

The object's colored dot (a.) is dragged to the target layer (b.)

Creating New Layers

1. Go to the **SF-ADV Illustrator** folder and **Open** the Illustrator document **Tropical Suites Layers.AI.**

2. From the **Window** menu, select **Show Layers.**

3. Double-click on the Layer 1 name.

4. In the **Layer Options** window, rename the layer "Palm Layer." Make the **Color** = Green. Leave all other options as is. Click **OK.**

5. Create three more new layers.

   Name the first "Type Layer" and make **Color:** Yellow.
   Name the second "Sun Layer" and make **Color:** Red.
   Name the third "Beach Layer" and make **Color:** Blue.

6. Keep the document open for the next exercise.

You should pick a color for a layer's anchor points and segments that doesn't conflict with the objects on that layer. For example, setting a layer's color to yellow isn't good if you're drawing a sun.

Reassigning Objects to Other Layers

1. Continue your work in the open document.
2. Select the two type (type outlines) objects and reassign them to the Type layer by dragging their colored dots to this layer.
3. Select the two palm trees and notice that they're on the Palm layer.
4. Select the beach and reassign it to the Beach layer.
5. Select the sun and reassign it to the Sun layer.
6. Press Command-S (Macintosh) or Control-S (Windows) to save the file.
7. Keep the document open.

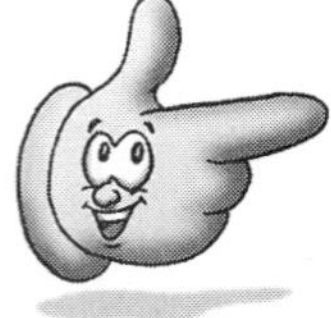

Arranging the Order of Layers

1. In the open document, experiment with reordering the layers.
2. Finish up with the layers stacked in this order:

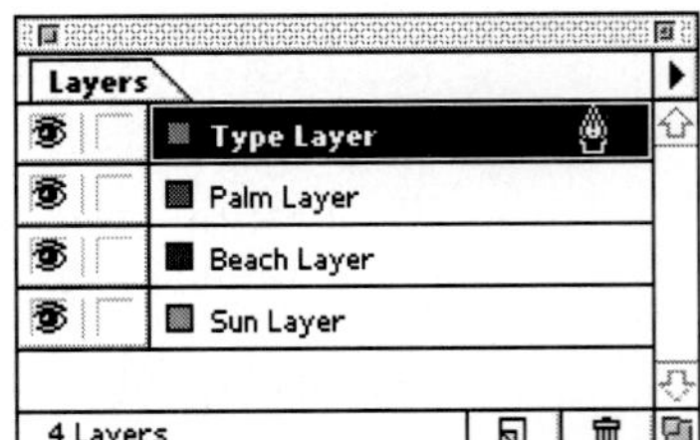

3. Press Command-S (Macintosh) or Ctrl-S (Windows) to save the file.
4. Keep the document open for the next exercise.

Controlling Layers

1. Continue in the open document. Make sure you are in **Preview** mode.

2. Click on the Type layer to select it.

3. Click on the layer's Eye icon (👁); the type outlines become Hidden. Click again on the same space where the eye was located, to bring the objects back to view.

4. Click on the Palm layer Eye icon, while holding the Command (Macintosh) or Ctrl (Windows) key. Observe how the palm tree outlines turn to **Artwork** mode. Hold the same key, and click again on the same Eye icon to bring the layer back to **Preview** mode.

5. Hold the Command (Macintosh) or Ctrl (Windows) key, add the Option (Macintosh) or Alt (Windows) key, and click on the Beach layer Eye icon. Notice how all other layers, except the Beach layer, go to **Artwork** mode. Hold the same keys, and click on the same Eye icon to bring the other layers back to **Preview** mode.

6. Click on the Sun layer to select it.

7. Click the Lock/Unlock square for this layer. You will be Locking the layer. To show that it is Locked, a crossed-out Pencil icon fills the square (✗). Try to click on and move the sun in the design. Observe the success of your efforts. Click on the crossed-out Pen icon, and you toggle back to the layer being Unlocked. Now try to move the sun.

8. Holding the Option (Macintosh) or Alt (Windows) key, click on the Show/Hide Eye icon for the Palm layer. What happened to all the objects except the Palms? Click again on this Eye icon, holding the same key.

9. Holding the Option (Macintosh) or Alt (Windows) key, click on the Lock/Unlock square for the Beach layer. Try to click on and select any objects except the Beach. How successful are your efforts? Holding the Option (Macintosh) or Alt (Windows) key, click again on the Lock/Unlock square for the Beach layer.

10. **Save** and **Close** the document.

Notes:

CHAPTER 5

TEXT ATTRIBUTES

CHAPTER OBJECTIVE:

To improve your understanding of type elements, and how to manage them within your document; to teach you more about the sophisticated typographic features provided by Adobe Illustrator. In Chapter 5 you will work to:

- Fully understand the Type palette; what options it offers, and how to work from within it to change and manage fonts and typographic attributes in your documents.
- Learn about paragraph formatting, a critical skill for individuals who will be working with type-intensive drawings or layouts in Illustrator.
- Learn about case controls, and how to set them for individual type elements or as a default condition of the Type tool.
- Practice working with the powerful spelling tools.
- Learn to use the Find/Change and Find Font functions to assist in the structured development of your drawings.
- Work to develop multi-column documents and learn more about linked text boxes and elements.
- Learn about importing and exporting copy, and how to flow copy from external word processors into your illustrations and layouts.
- Understand text wrap and work through hands-on exercises that place type outside, within, and around various shaped elements.

Text Attributes

Good, solid typography is the cornerstone of many professional designs, and Illustrator certainly provides the tools and functions you will need to create and control type within any design or project. From small, single lines of copy, to text-intensive layouts with linked columns of text, the program can meet almost any imaginable need. This isn't to say that the program is designed for long documents, though. In those cases you will be better served using a page-layout or word-processing application. For really fine typography, you might consider using Illustrator to create graphics of certain type elements and import them into your pages. One example of this is hanging punctuation; a feature that no page layout program currently offers.

You can never know too much about type. Selection, formatting, spacing, leading, color (the density on the page, not the shade you assign from the color palette), and readability are all very important issues to a professional designer. Read everything about type that you can find.

In the **Type** menu, you'll see the various Type selections.

The Type Character Palette

The **Character** option of the **Type** menu shows a dialog box that allows many adjustments to any highlighted text. When any new numbers are typed into a data box, Return (Macintosh) or Enter (Windows) must be pressed to apply this to the highlighted text. However, if you are entering a sequence of data such as weight, scale, and leading, pressing tab to move from field to field will also apply the last entered value.

When the **Character** palette is first accessed from the **Type** menu, only half of the palette will show. **Show Options** must be selected from the submenu to show the full palette.

You can use the Tab key to move around in this (and almost all other) dialog boxes. With experience, you can automatically hit Tab the right number of times to get almost anywhere.

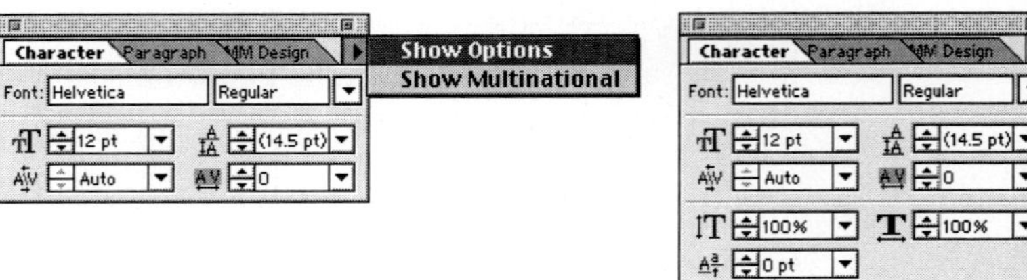

When the full **Character** palette is shown, it will look like this. Here are all the type options and their names.

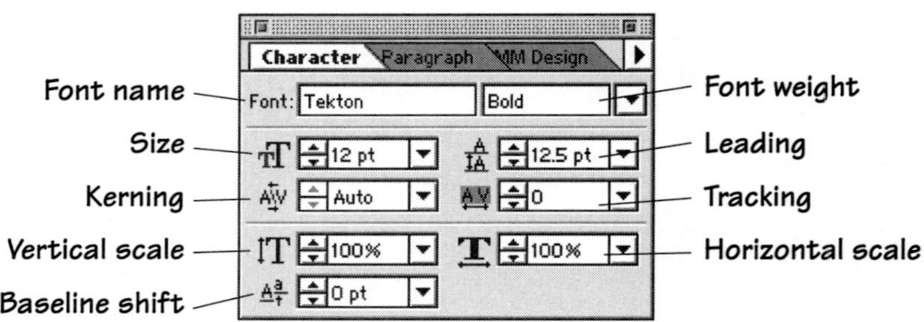

Using the Type Character Palette

1. **File->Open** the file **Text Formatting.AI** from the **SF-ADV Illustrator** folder.

2. Highlight all the text with the Type tool.

3. In the **Type->Character** palette, apply these settings: **Font** = ATC Sands, **Size** = 14 pt., **Leading** = Auto, **Tracking** = 0, **Horizontal scale** = 80%.

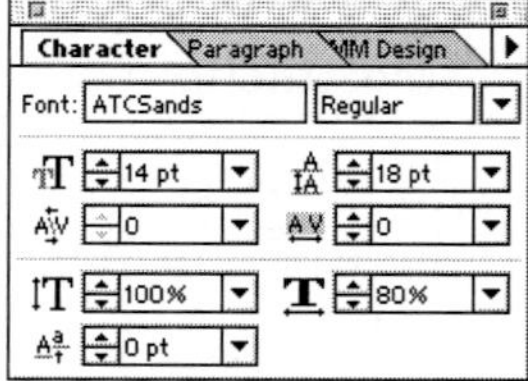

4. **File->Save** the file. Keep the file open for the following exercises.

The Type Paragraph Palette

The **Type->Paragraph** palette shows a dialog box with options that allow many adjustments to any highlighted text.

When any new numbers are typed into a box, Return (Macintosh) or Enter (Windows) must be pressed to apply this to the highlighted text.

The "all lines" justification method will force justify the copy even if there is only one word such as:

R O M A N

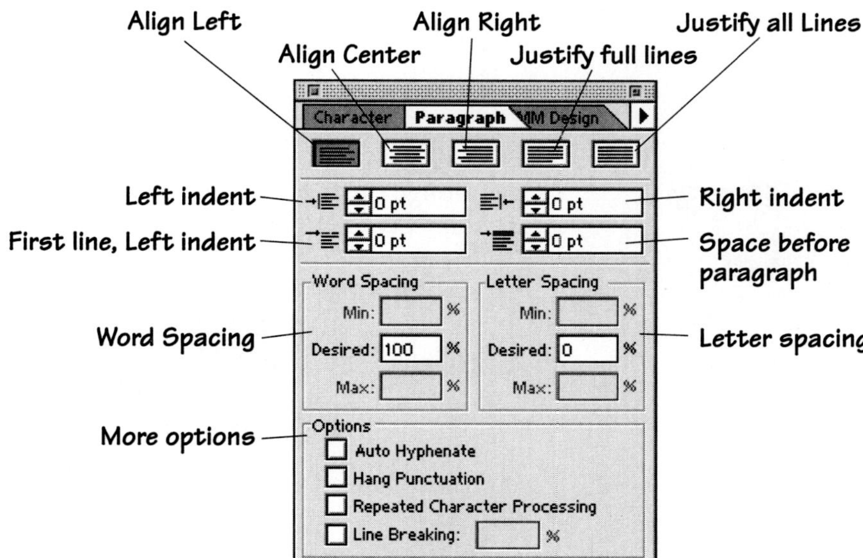

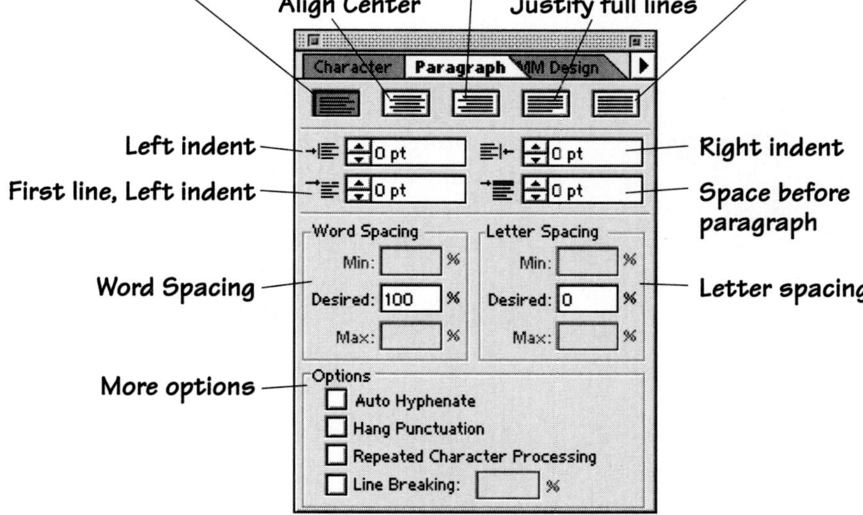

Using the Type Paragraph Palette

1. Continue in the open document, **Text Formatting.AI.**
2. Highlight all the text with the Type tool. Apply these settings: **Alignment** = Justified full lines, **First line indentation** = 10, **Word Spacing Desired** = 130%, **Space before paragraph** = 5 pt.
3. Experiment with other settings and press Return (Macintosh) or Enter (Windows) to apply them to the text. Observe how the text is affected.
4. **File->Save** the file. Keep the document open for the next exercise.

Change Case

In the **Type** menu, **Change Case** allows you to modify the case of the letters. **Upper Case** makes all selected text upper case. **Lower Case** converts any upper case letters to lower case. **Mixed Case** capitalizes the first words of the sentence.

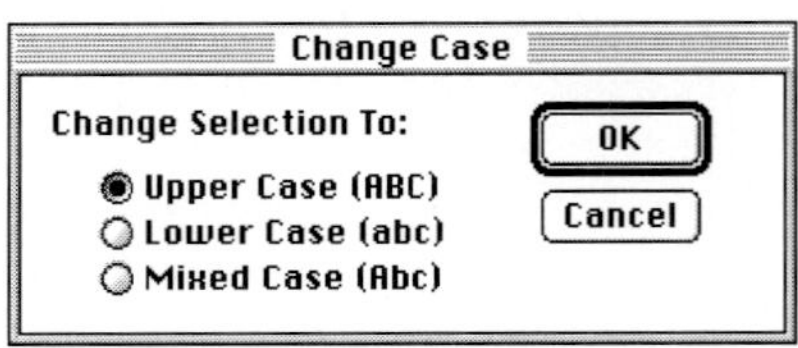

Using Change Case

1. Continue in the open document, **Text Formatting.AI.**
2. Highlight the title "All my troubles seemed so far away." Go to **Type->Change Case**.
3. Select **Upper Case**. Click **OK**. All the letters became upper case.

   ALL MY TROUBLES SEEMED SO FAR AWAY

4. Select **Lower Case.** You will see how all the upper case letters were changed to lower case.

   all my troubles seemed so far away

5. Highlight and capitalize the "a" in "all" to "A." Now, highlight the entire title. Select **Mixed Case.** Observe the initial letter of each word.

   all My Troubles Seemed So Far Away

   Did you notice anything different happening? Yes, the **Mixed Case** reversed all initial letters, including the capital "A." Be aware of this slight mishap. This teaches us to proofread, doesn't it?

6. Capitalize the "a" and leave the title with **Mixed Case** letters.
7. **File->Save** the file. Keep the document open.

Don't ever make the mistake of thinking that a spell checking system is anywhere near as good as a real proofreader. These are simple, basic tools, and don't replace a human in this critical job. Have someone look at all your work – you cannot proofread your own stuff.

Check Spelling

As designers are increasingly finding themselves executing entire projects — writing the copy, doing the layout, and creating the illustrations — the need for proofreading or error-checking functions grows. Fortunately, you're able to check the spelling of items in your illustrations using the **Check Spelling** command. This is another example of a function that many designers simply don't use. It saves a lot of time and money finding simple errors that can ultimately result in extra turnaround time. Don't totally trust spell checkers, though. There are many things, like grammatical errors, that they ignore.

Check Spelling searches the selected text for misspelled words and suggests words for substitution. The various options, such as **Case Sensitive**, allow you to be as specific or as general as you desire.

Spell checkers work about the same in any program where they're found, from word processing programs to drawing programs like Adobe Illustrator.

The neighbors who had called them peered over their wooden fences, gaping and pointing at what was surely the most horrifying spectícle ever to appear in their neighberhood.
Their ajoining neighbor, Walter Melon, had created a blazing bonfire in his backyard that was a veritable funeril pyre of books from his library.

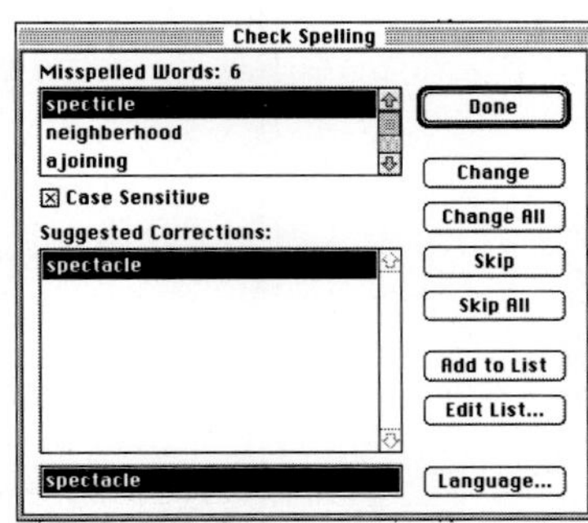

Using Check Spelling

1. Continue in the open document, **Text Formatting.AI.**

2. You do not need to highlight or select any text. Go to **Edit->Select All.** Go to **Type->Check Spelling**. The **Check Spelling** dialog box will show all the words that it thinks are misspelled and the suggested replacements.

3. Click on each word in the **Misspelled Words** list. Click on the appropriate replacement word in **Suggested Corrections**. Click **Change**. If the word needs no replacing, such as the author's name, Bagley, click **Skip**.

4. When finished making corrections, click **Done.**

5. **File->Save** the changes. Keep the document open.

Find Font

Find Font is very useful for changing the fonts in a document. The text doesn't have to be selected. The dialog box will display all the fonts used in the document in the **Current Font List** window.

The replacing font names are shown in the **Replacement Font List** window. If you are only going to swap fonts that are used in the document, leave the **Font List** set for **Document.** To see all the active fonts in your computer system, set the **Font List** to **System.**

When you click a font name in the **Current Font List** window, all text of that typeface in the document will be highlighted. Then, the replacing font name in the **Replacement Font List** window should be clicked. When this is clicked, if there are several text blocks in the document with this typeface, the frontmost block will be selected. If **Change** is pressed, all selected text in this block will be changed. Then, the highlighting moves on to the next block in sequence.

Pressing **Change All** will replace all the text blocks in the document with the font you selected. You can also avoid replacing a selection with **Skip.**

When font replacement is finished, **Done** is clicked to close the window.

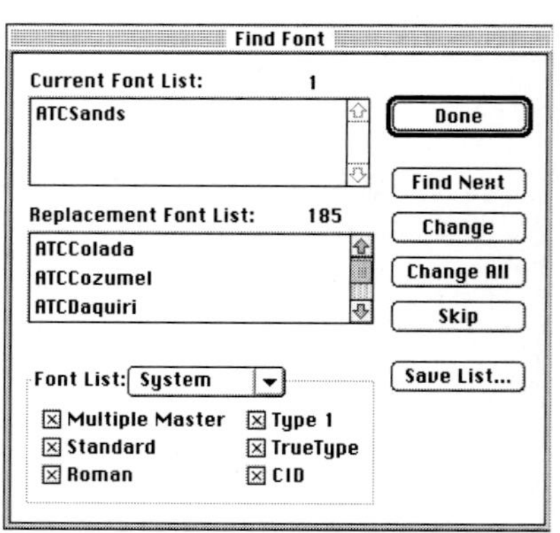

Searching and replacing fonts is sometimes very important when you're getting ready to output a file and you're having a problem. Check here to make sure you're using fonts installed on your system.

Using Find Font

1. Continue in the open document.

2. You do not have to highlight or select any text. Go to **Type->Find Font.** Set the **Font List** to **System.**

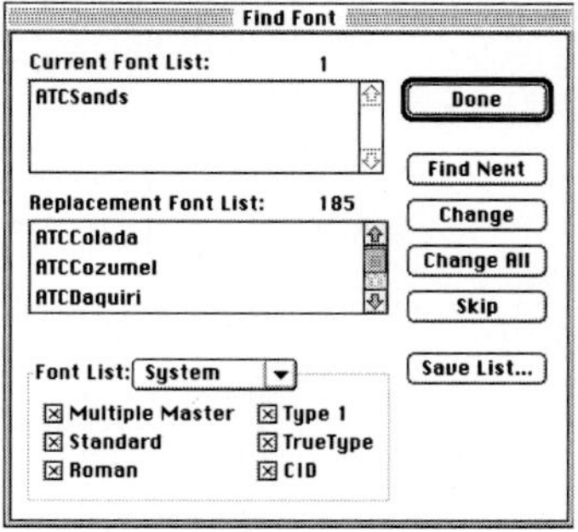

3. Click on ATC Sands in the **Current Font List** window. You will see the text in the text block become highlighted.

4. Click on ATC Colada in the **Replacement Font List** window.

5. To execute this replacement, click **Change.** Select **Done.**

6. Use the Zoom tool to magnify the view of the text to see the typeface change.

7. **File->Save** the file. Keep the document open.

Finding and changing is very useful in documents containing a lot of text, or when you import text from someone else and need to replace things like inch marks or double spaces after a period.

Find/Change

Find/Change lets you find words and replace them. The options allow for whole word searches and case sensitivity. They also allow you to replace one word or to replace all words.

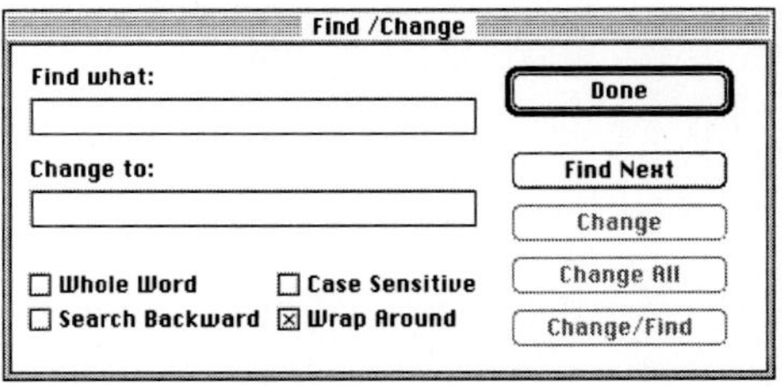

Using Find/Change

1. Continue in the open document.
2. Highlight all the text in the text block with the Type tool.
3. Go to the **Type** menu and select **Find/Change**.

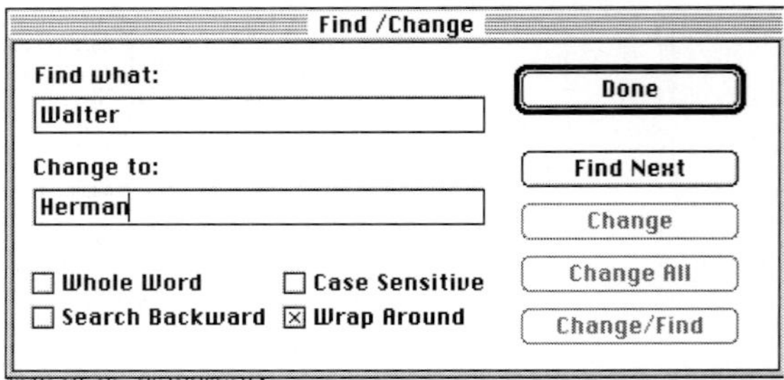

4. In the **Find what** box, type "Walter." In the **Change to** box, type "Herman." You will notice that all buttons, except **Find Next** are grayed out.
5. To activate the buttons, click **Find Next**. Then, click **Change.** Click **Find Next** again.
6. Click **Change All**. Observe how all the "Walter" words became "Herman."
7. Click **Done.**
8. **File->Save** the file. Keep the document open.

Smart Punctuation

Smart Punctuation makes changes to text that needs ligatures, smart quotes, smart spaces, ellipses, en and em dashes, etc. The dialog box allows these changes to be specified for application to either selected text or the whole document. It will also report to you, in a message window, the changes.

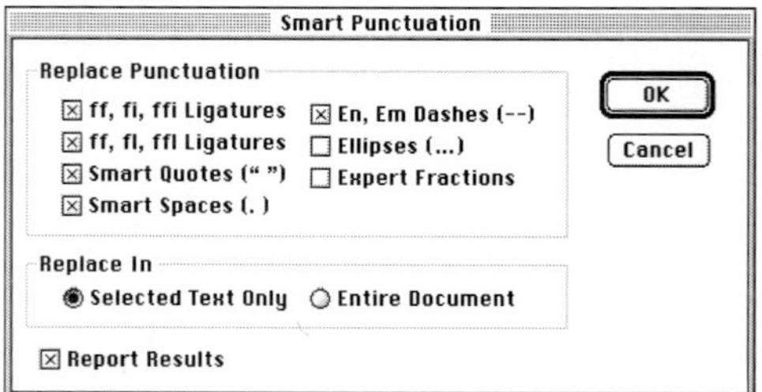

Smart punctuation is one of those features that allow you almost unprecedented control over high-quality typographic options. Hanging punctuation, for example (where any punctuation hangs outside the margins of justified text), isn't available anywhere, as far as we know.

If you use **Smart Punctuation**, there might be times when they don't display properly on screen. Try zooming in and out to force the screen to redraw.

Using Smart Punctuation

1. Continue in the open document. Zoom in on the title of the story. The quotation marks are the common, standard quotes, sometimes called "inch marks."

2. Click the text cursor in the text block. The text must be highlighted.

3. Go to **Edit->Select All.**

4. In the **Type** menu, select **Smart Punctuation.**

5. Make no changes to the selected items in the dialog box.

6. Press **OK**. Observe how the quotation marks of the title were changed to typographer's quotes.

7. **File->Save** the file. **Close** the document.

Rows & Columns

Rows & Columns takes a single text block and splits it into several blocks with user-defined gutters and text flow.

- **Rows** determines the number of rows the columns will divide into.
- **Columns** determines the number of columns that will be created.
- **Preview**, in the dialog box, should be clicked in order to see the result of the settings before **OK** is clicked.
- **Text Flow** gives you four choices to control how the text will flow throughout the **Rows & Columns**.

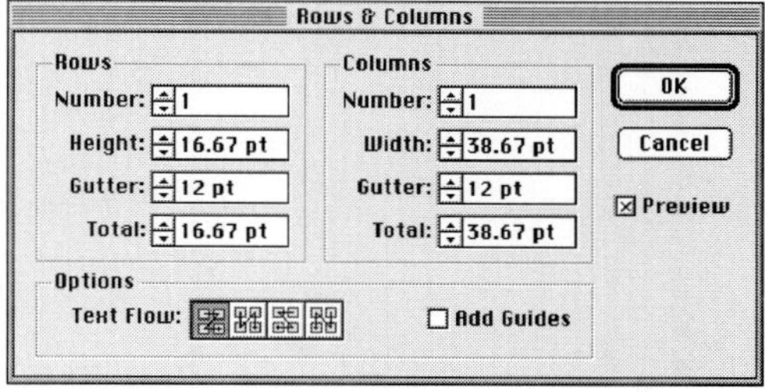

Using Rows & Columns

1. Go to the **SF-ADV Illustrator** folder and **File->Open** the document **All My Troubles.AI.**

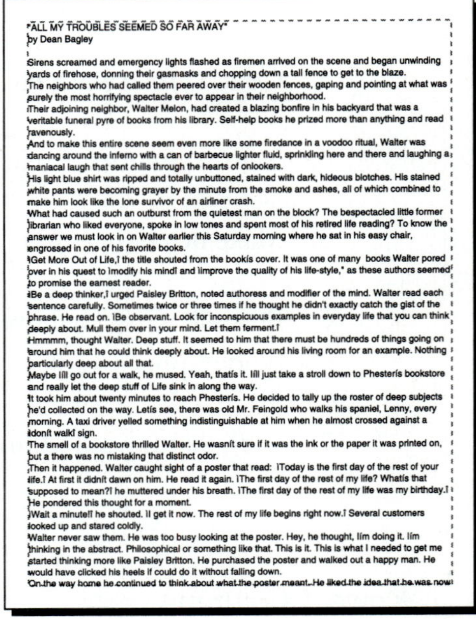

"ALL MY TROUBLES SEEMED SO FAR AWAY"
by Dean Bagley

Sirens screamed and emergency lights flashed as firemen arrived on the scene and began unwinding yards of firehose, donning their gasmasks and chopping down a tall fence to get to the blaze.
The neighbors who had called them peered over their wooden fences, gaping and pointing at what was surely the most horrifying spectacle ever to appear in their neighborhood.
Their adjoining neighbor, Walter Melon, had created a blazing bonfire in his backyard that was a veritable funeral pyre of books from his library. Self-help books he prized more than anything and read ravenously.
And to make this entire scene seem even more like some firedance in a voodoo ritual, Walter was dancing around the inferno with a can of barbecue lighter fluid, sprinkling here and there and laughing a maniacal laugh that sent chills through the hearts of onlookers.
His light blue shirt was ripped and totally unbuttoned, stained with dark, hideous blotches. His stained white pants were becoming grayer by the minute from the smoke and ashes, all of which combined to make him look like the lone survivor of an airliner crash.
What had caused such an outburst from the quietest man on the block? The bespectacled little former librarian who liked everyone, spoke in low tones and spent most of his retired life reading? To know the answer we must look in on Walter earlier this Saturday morning where he sat in his easy chair, engrossed in one of his favorite books.
ìGet More Out of Life,î the title shouted from the bookís cover. It was one of many books Walter pored over in his quest to ìmodify his mindî and ìimprove the quality of his life-style," as these authors seemed to promise the earnest reader.
ìBe a deep thinker,î urged Paisley Britton, noted authoress and modifier of the mind. Walter read each sentence carefully. Sometimes twice or three times if he thought he didn't exactly catch the gist of the phrase. He read on. ìBe observant. Look for inconspicuous examples in everyday life that you can think deeply about. Mull them over in your mind. Let them ferment.î
Hmmmm, thought Walter. Deep stuff. It seemed to him that there must be hundreds of things going on around him that he could think deeply about. He looked around his living room for an example. Nothing particularly deep about all that.
Maybe Iíll go out for a walk, he mused. Yeah, thatís it. Iíll just take a stroll down to Phesterís bookstore and really let the deep stuff of Life sink in along the way.
It took him about twenty minutes to reach Phesterís. He decided to tally up the roster of deep subjects he'd collected on the way. Letís see, there was old Mr. Feingold who walks his spaniel, Lenny, every morning. A taxi driver yelled something indistinguishable at him when he almost crossed against a ìdonít walkî sign.
The smell of a bookstore thrilled Walter. He wasnít sure if it was the ink or the paper it was printed on, but a there was no mistaking that distinct odor.
Then it happened. Walter caught sight of a poster that read: ìToday is the first day of the rest of your life.î At first it didnít dawn on him. He read it again. ìThe first day of the rest of my life? Whatís that supposed to mean?î he muttered under his breath. ìThe first day of the rest of my life was my birthday.î
He pondered this thought for a moment.
ìWait a minute!î he shouted. ìI get it now. The rest of my life begins right now.î Several customers looked up and stared coldly.
Walter never saw them. He was too busy looking at the poster. Hey, he thought, Iím doing it. Iím thinking in the abstract. Philosophical or something like that. This is it. This is what I needed to get me started thinking more like Paisley Britton. He purchased the poster and walked out a happy man. He would have clicked his heels if could do it without falling down.
On the way home he continued to think about what the poster meant. He liked the idea that he was now

Using text in columns is yet another feature that lets you use Illustrator as a full-function page layout program. Again, it's best suited for single-page layouts.

2. Click the Type tool cursor in the text block. Go to **Edit->Select All.** Access the **Type->Character** dialog box. Apply these settings: **Font** = ATC Sands, **Size** = 10 pt., **Leading** = Auto, **Tracking** = 0, **Horizontal scale** = 100%.

3. With the Selection tool, select the text block. Go to **Type->Rows & Columns.**

4. Change the **Number** of **Columns** to 3, then click **OK**.

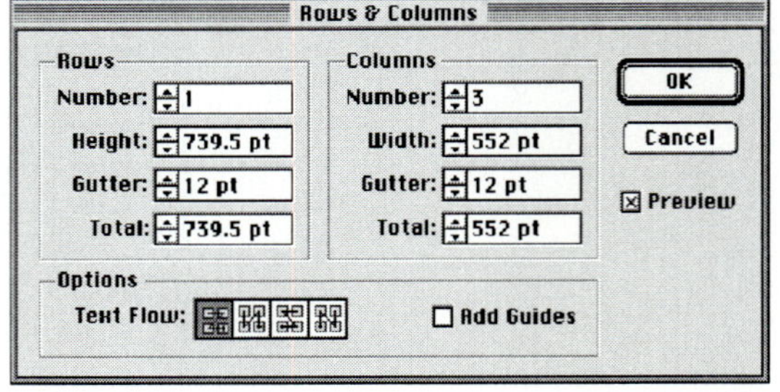

5. Observe how the one text block was divided into three text block columns.

"ALL MY TROUBLES SEEMED SO FAR AWAY"
by Dean Bagley

Sirens screamed and emergency lights flashed as firemen arrived on the scene and began unwinding yards of firehose, donning their gasmasks and chopping down a tall fence to get to the blaze.

The neighbors who had called them peered over their wooden fences, gaping and pointing at what was surely the most horrifying spectacle ever to appear in their neighborhood.

Their adjoining neighbor, Walter Melon, had created a blazing bonfire in his backyard that was a veritable funeral pyre of books from his library. Self-help books he prized more than anything and read ravenously.

And to make this entire scene seem even more like some firedance in a voodoo ritual, Walter was dancing around the inferno with a can of barbecue lighter fluid, sprinkling here and there and laughing a maniacal laugh that sent chills through the hearts of onlookers.

His light blue shirt was ripped and totally unbuttoned, stained with dark, hideous blotches. His stained white pants were becoming grayer by the minute from the smoke and ashes, all of which combined to make him look like the lone survivor of an airliner crash.

What had caused such an outburst from the quietest man on the block? The bespectacled little former librarian who liked everyone, spoke in low tones and spent most of his retired life reading? To know the answer we must look in on Walter earlier this Saturday morning where he sat in his easy chair, engrossed in one of his favorite books.

ìGet More Out of Life,î the title shouted from the bookís cover. It was one of many books Walter pored over in his quest to ìmodify his mindî and ìimprove the quality of his life-style," as these authors seemed to promise the earnest reader.

ìBe a deep thinker,î urged Paisley Britton, noted authoress and modifier of the mind. Walter read each sentence carefully. Sometimes twice or three times if he thought he didn't exactly catch the gist of the phrase. He read on. ìBe observant. Look for inconspicuous examples in everyday life that you can think deeply about. Mull them over in your mind. Let them ferment.î

Hmmmm, thought Walter. Deep stuff. It seemed to him that there must be hundreds of things going on around him that he could think deeply about. He looked around his living room for an example. Nothing particularly deep about all that.

Maybe Iíll go out for a walk, he mused. Yeah, thatís it. Iíll just take a stroll down to Phesterís bookstore and really let the deep stuff of Life sink in along the way.

It took him about twenty minutes to reach Phesterís. He decided to tally up the roster of deep subjects he'd collected on the way. Letís see, there was old Mr. Feingold who walks his spaniel, Lenny, every morning. A taxi driver yelled something indistinguishable at him when he almost crossed against a ìdonít walkî sign.

The smell of a bookstore thrilled Walter. He wasnít sure if it was the ink or the paper it was printed on, but a there was no mistaking that distinct odor.

Then it happened. Walter caught sight of a poster that read: ìToday is the first day of the rest of your life.î At first it didnít dawn on him. He read it again. ìThe first day of the rest of my life? Whatís that supposed to mean?î he muttered under his breath. ìThe first day of the rest of my life was my birthday.î He pondered this thought for a moment.

ìWait a minute!î he shouted. ìI get it now. The rest of my life begins right now.î Several customers looked up and stared coldly.

Walter never saw them. He was too busy looking at the poster. Hey, he thought, Iím doing it. Iím thinking in the abstract. Philosophical or something like that. This is it. This is what I needed to get me started thinking more like Paisley Britton. He purchased the poster and walked out a happy man. He would have clicked his heels if could do it without falling down. On the way home he continued to think about what the poster meant. He liked the idea that he was now a thinking man. An intellectual. A philosopher. He frowned slightly to make people on the streets think he was brooding about something important. He changed his pace to a little faster tempo; like that of one who was marching to the beat of a different drummer, he once heard someone say. He leaned slightly into the wind holding his poster which was

Remember to balance your pages when using columns. Try setting up a page with a half-inch margin and a one-inch space between columns, and you'll get a good visual picture of the concept.

6. With the Selection tool, select the text block. Go to **Type->Rows & Columns**. Change the **Number** of **Rows** to 2, the **Gutter** to 24 pt., then click **OK**.

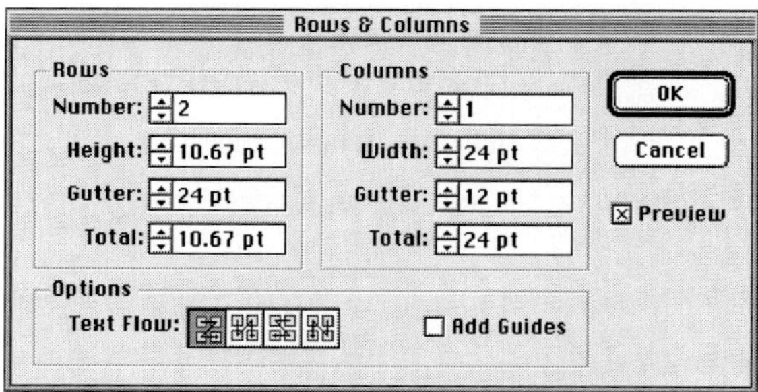

7. Observe how the three columns were cut in half, with a 36 pt. space (gutter) dividing the two rows.

"ALL MY TROUBLES SEEMED SO FAR AWAY"
by Dean Bagley

Sirens screamed and emergency lights flashed as firemen arrived on the scene and began unwinding yards of firehose, donning their gasmasks and chopping down a tall fence to get to the blaze.
The neighbors who had called them peered over their wooden fences, gaping and pointing at what was surely the most horrifying spectacle ever to appear in their neighborhood.
Their adjoining neighbor, Walter Melon, had created a blazing bonfire in his backyard that was a veritable funeral pyre of books from his library. Self-help books he prized more than anything and read ravenously.
And to make this entire scene seem even more like some firedance in a voodoo ritual, Walter was dancing around the inferno with a can of barbecue lighter fluid, sprinkling here and there and laughing a maniacal laugh that sent chills through the hearts of onlookers.
His light blue shirt was ripped and totally unbuttoned, stained with dark, hideous blotches. His stained white pants were becoming grayer by the minute from the smoke and ashes, all of which combined to make him look like the lone survivor of an airliner crash.
What had caused such an outburst from the quietest man on the block? The bespectacled little former librarian who liked everyone, spoke in low tones and spent most of his retired life reading? To know the answer we must look in on Walter earlier this Saturday morning where he sat in his easy chair, engrossed in one of his favorite books.
ìGet More Out of Life,î the title shouted from the bookís cover. It was one of many books Walter pored over in his quest to ìmodify his mindî and ìimprove the quality of his life-style," as these authors seemed to promise the earnest reader.
ìBe a deep thinker,î urged Paisley Britton, noted authoress and modifier of the mind. Walter read each sentence carefully. Sometimes twice or three times if he thought he didn't exactly catch the gist of the phrase. He read on. ìBe observant. Look for inconspicuous examples in everyday life that you can think deeply about. Mull them over in your mind. Let them ferment.î
Hmmmm, thought Walter. Deep stuff. It seemed to him that there must be hundreds of things going on around him that he could think deeply about. He looked around his living room for an example. Nothing particularly deep about all that.
Maybe Iíll go out for a walk, he mused. Yeah, thatís it. Iíll just take a stroll down to Phesterís bookstore and really let the deep stuff of Life sink in along the way.
It took him about twenty minutes to reach Phesterís. He decided to tally up the roster of deep subjects he'd collected on the way. Letís see, there was old Mr. Feingold who walks his spaniel, Lenny, every morning. A taxi driver yelled something indistinguishable at him when he almost crossed against a ìdonít walkî sign.
The smell of a bookstore thrilled Walter. He wasnít sure if it was the ink or the paper it was printed on, but a there was no mistaking that distinct odor.
Then it happened. Walter caught sight of a poster that read: ìToday is the first day of the rest of your life.î At first it didnít dawn on him. He read it again. ìThe first day of the rest of my life? Whatís that supposed to mean?î he muttered under his breath. ìThe first day of the rest of my life was my birthday.î He pondered this thought for a moment.
ìWait a minute!î he shouted. ìI get it now. The rest of my life begins right now.î Several customers looked up and stared coldly.
Walter never saw them. He was too busy looking at the poster. Hey, he thought, Iím doing it. Iím thinking in the abstract. Philosophical or something like that. This is it. This is what I needed to get me started thinking more like Paisley Britton. He purchased the poster and walked out a happy man. He would have clicked his heels if could do it without falling down. On the way home he continued to think about what the poster meant. He liked the idea that he was now a thinking man. An intellectual. A philosopher. He frowned slightly to make people

8. **Close** the document without saving.

Importing text from other applications ensures that you get whatever they entered into the file. Some things to look out for are inch marks (used instead of real typographer's quotes) and double spaces after a period. Both items diminish the quality of your typesetting.

Placing Text

To Place text in your document is to import it from an outside source. In the graphic arts world, it is now most common for a client to hand you a disk with a text file that was created on their computer.

The text will have to be transferred into your document for further formatting and use. To get the external text document into your computer, you must use **Place**, found in the **File** menu.

Placing Text in a Document

1. Create a **New** document. Go to **View->Show Rulers** for measuring.

2. With the Type tool, draw an Area text container 5" x 7" in size. Leave the Type cursor in this block.

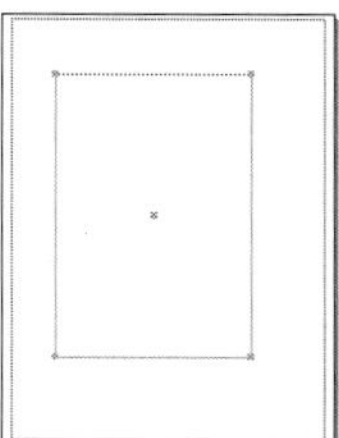

Not many professional designers use fully justified type, except for rare situations where they feel it's needed. Well-hyphenated, left-justified (also called "ragged right") is far more common.

3. Go to **File->Place.**

4. The next window allows you to select the file you want to import.

5. Go to the **SF-ADV Illustrator** folder, and **Place** the file **Import Text.TXT.**

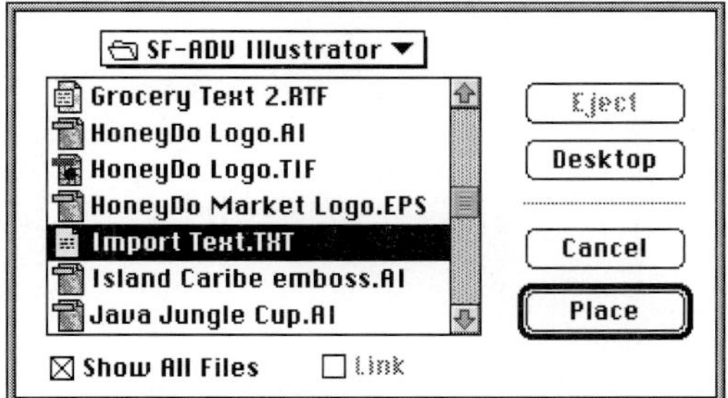

6. With the Selection tool, click on the text container. Press Command-T (Macintosh) or Ctrl-T (Windows) to access the **Type Character** palette.

7. Make these settings: **Font** = ATC Colada, **Size** = 14 pt., **Leading** = 21.

8. With the Type tool, highlight "Gobbledygook Latin Nonsense, by, Oedipus Wrecks." Make the **Font** = ATC Mango, **Size** = 18 pt., **Leading** = 24 pt.

9. With this text still highlighted, access the **Type->Paragraph** palette. Click on the Align Center box.

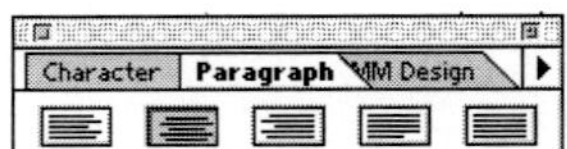

10. Highlight the body text. In the **Paragraph** palette, click on Justify Full Lines, then Justify All Lines. Observe how the spacing between the words is affected.

Lorem ipsum dolor sit amet, consectetuer adipiscing elit, sed diam nonummy nibh euismod tincidunt ut laoreet dolore magna aliquam erat volutpat. Ut wisi enim ad minim veniam, quis nostrud exerci tation ullamcorper suscipit lobortis nisl ut aliquip ex ea commodo consequat. Duis autem vel eum iriure dolor in hendrerit in vulputate.

Lorem ipsum dolor sit amet, consectetuer adipiscing elit, sed diam nonummy nibh euismod tincidunt ut laoreet dolore magna aliquam erat volutpat. Ut wisi enim ad minim veniam, quis nostrud exerci tation ullamcorper suscipit lobortis nisl ut aliquip ex ea commodo consequat. Duis autem vel eum iriure dolor in hendrerit in v u l p u t a t e .
Velit esse molestie consequat, vel illum dolore eu

Click on Align Left, then on Align Right. Observed the difference. Finally, click on Align Center, to make the design uniform.

Remember, you can use the Direct Selection tool to change the size and shape of text blocks.

11. Highlight only the title "Gobbledygook Latin Nonsense." Make the **Size** = 22 pt. You have placed text, and formatted an attractive design.

Gobbledygook Latin Nonsense
by
Oedipus Wrecks

Lorem ipsum dolor sit amet, consectetuer adipiscing elit, sed diam nonummy nibh euismod tincidunt ut laoreet dolore magna aliquam erat volutpat. Ut wisi enim ad minim veniam, quis nostrud exerci tation ullamcorper suscipit lobortis nisl ut aliquip ex ea commodo consequat. Duis autem vel eum iriure dolor in hendrerit in vulputate.
Velit esse molestie consequat, vel illum dolore eu feugiat nulla facilisis at vero eros et accumsan et iusto odio dignissim qui blandit praesent luptatum zzril delenit augue duis dolore te feugait nulla facilisi. Lorem ipsum dolor sit amet, consectetuer adipiscing elit, sed diam nonummy nibh euismod tincidunt ut laoreet dolore magna.
Aliquam erat volutpat. Ut wisi enim ad minim veniam, quis nostrud exerci tation ullamcorper

Linking text blocks can be confusing at times. Just remember to try to link from the left side of the page to the right, top to bottom. If you reduce a linked text block, the type is still there, but hidden.

12. **Close** the file without saving.

Linking Text Blocks

When the text blocks are not big enough to show all of the type, a small box with a "+" in it will appear. This is the *overset text* indicator.

```
Lorem ipsum
dolor sit amet,
consectetuer
adipiscing elit, sed
diam nonummy
nibh euismod
tincidunt ut laor [+]
eet dolore magna
```

This tells you that more type is available. You could choose to enlarge the block with the Direct Selection tool, or make the type smaller. Another feature you could use is to **Link** the text into another text block.

Using Link Blocks with Text

1. Create a **New** document.

2. Select the Type tool and draw a 2" x 3" Area text block. Click the cursor in the text block, and go to **File->Place**. In the **Place** window, go to the **SF-ADV Illustrator** folder and **Place** the file **Import Text.TXT.** You will then have a text block with an overset text indicator.

```
Gobbledygook Latin
Nonsense
by
Oedipus Wrecks


Lorem ipsum dolor
sit amet,
consectetuer
adipiscing elit,
sed diam nonummy
nibh euismod
tincidunt ut
laoreet dolore
```

3. Select the text container with the Selection tool and drag it to the right while holding the Option (Macintosh) or Alt (Windows) key.

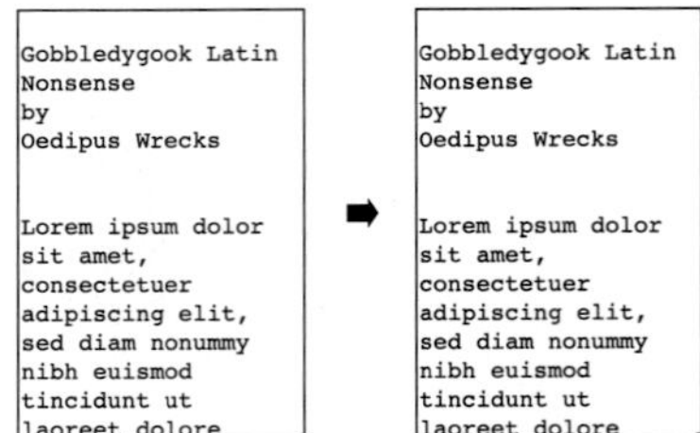

You can export a wide variety of file formats from within Illustrator. As you can see in this section, you can also export just the text elements.

4. Select both text blocks with the Selection tool. From the **Type** menu, choose **Blocks->Link.**

The unseen text will flow into the duplicate text block. To see all of the text, either perform linking further, or use the Direct Selection tool to enlarge the text containers.

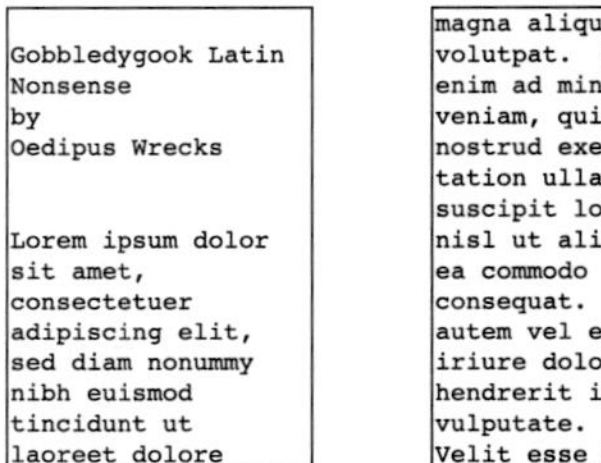

5. Keep the document open for the next exercise.

Fitting headlines is an important skill. Just squishing them until they fit isn't the trick; it's combining size, letter spacing, and possibly a slight horizontal scaling to get them just right. Remember, if you do modify headlines or subheads, do so consistently throughout the illustration.

Export

Export allows you to export selected text to an external text file. The text is highlighted with the Type tool cursor; then, **File->Export** is chosen. A dialog box appears, where you can choose the **Format** of the exported text, name the file, and **Save** it where you want.

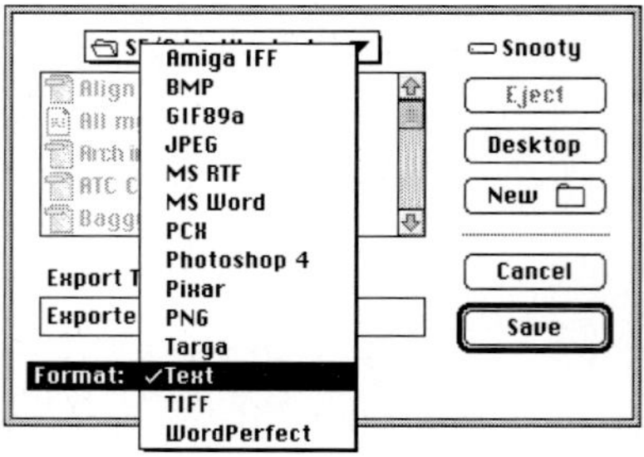

Macintosh

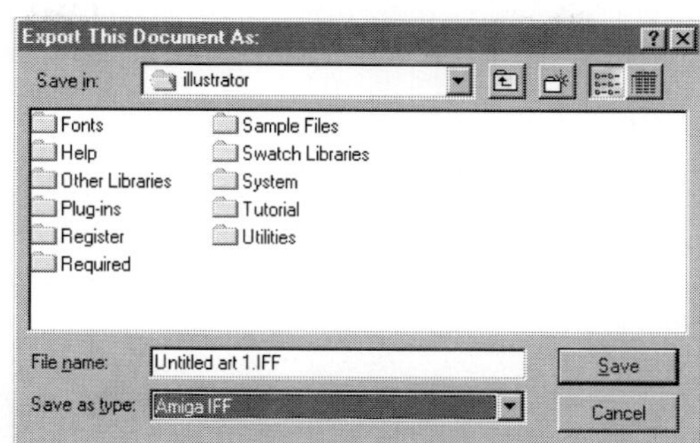

Windows

Using Export

1. Continue in the open document from the previous exercise.

2. Click the Type tool cursor in the text block. Go to **Edit->Select All.** In the **File** menu, select **Export.**

3. In the next window, click-hold on the **Format** menu of choices. For Macintosh, select the **Text** option. This is basic ASCII text format. In Windows, select the **PC ASCII** option. Name the file "Exported Text.TXT."

4. **Close** the file without saving.

Fitting Type to a Required Space

1. Create a **New** document.

2. Click the Type tool on the page, then type the words: TROPICAL SUITES.

3. Highlight the text and access **Type->Character.** Apply these settings: **Font** = ATC Sea Breeze, **Size** = 36 pt., **Leading** = Auto, **Tracking** =0, **Horizontal scale** = 70%.

TROPICAL SUITES

4. Select the Type tool and drag it to create a new text container that is the exact width of the TROPICAL SUITES type.

Start

TROPICAL SUITES

Drag text block

5. Type the phrase: A CARIBBEAN RESORT

TROPICAL SUITES

6. Highlight the text, access **Type->Character**, and make these settings: **Font** = ATC Sunset, **Size** = 12 pt., **Leading** = Auto, **Tracking** = 0, **Horizontal scale** = 100%.

7. Keep the text highlighted, and go to **Type->Fit Headline.** This will extend the tracking of the letters to fit the width of the text block.

TROPICAL SUITES

A CARIBBEAN RESORT

8. **Close** the document without saving.

You can never rely totally on a program to accurately wrap type around the shape of an object. Always be sure to check each line in wrapped type to ensure that you don't have any bad line breaks or hyphenations.

Text Wrap

When a designer is working with both text and path objects, the question of wrapping text around the objects comes up. Creating ads is probably the most common usage of text wrap, but it's also used in package design and magazine page layout.

To wrap text is quite simple, but there are rules. If you adhere to the requirements, you will be wrapping text quite efficiently. The rules are:

- The text must be behind the object(s) you are wrapping around.
- Both the text and the object(s) must be selected before wrapping.
- An Area Text block is required for wrapping.

Again, pay special attention to the spacing in lines where an object is being wrapped. There are times when one line can have a ton of space while the next one is all smashed together. Inspect every wrap.

- Wrapping around several objects, even when grouped, is clumsy and does not give a good wrap. You should draw a separate closed path around the group, then wrap the text around this single object. The offsetting path must be closed and should also be painted with None so as not conflict with the design.

- There is no setting that can be applied to the amount of space the text offsets away from the object. If you requre extra space between the text and the object(s), you should draw a separate closed path, then wrap around this path. You can then use your Direct Selection tool to adjust the single path for a better fit.

- Wrapping text around an object(s) literally groups them together. If you move one, you move the other. You will have to **Type->Wrap ->Release** them to reposition.

Wrapping Text Around Objects

1. Go to the **SF-ADV Illustrator** folder and **File->Open** the document **Text Wrap.AI.**

2. With the Ellipse tool, draw an oval that overlaps the text container.

3. Select the oval and the text container. Go to **Type->Wrap->Make.** Observe how the text wraps around the path of the oval.

4. With the Direct Selection tool, pull down the oval's top anchor point slightly to see how adjusting the wrapping paths will affect the type.

If you're creating artwork that might be moved around a type-intensive page, you might consider saving it with an invisible (no stroke, no fill) line that can later be used to create a text wrap in any application.

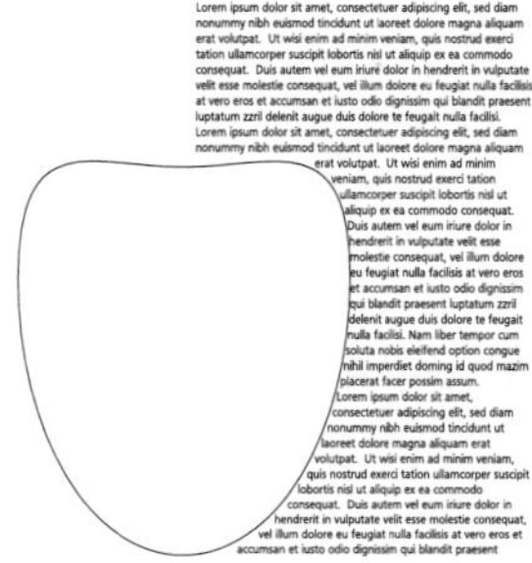

5. Select the oval and text with the selection tool, go to **Type->Wrap->Release.** Then Delete the oval.

6. Select the **Tropical Suites Logo** and position it to overlap the text. Go to **Object->Bring To Front.**

7. Select the logo and the text. Go to **Type->Wrap->Make.** Use the Zoom tool to magnify the area where the text wrapped. Go to **View->Artwork** mode to see how poorly the text offset from the paths.

8. With the logo and text selected, go to **Type->Wrap->Release.** Select the text container and **Object->Hide** it. This is to see the logo paths better. Continue in **Artwork** mode.

9. Use the Pencil tool to draw a simple closed path around the exterior of the logo. Remember, the offsetting objects must be closed paths. Paint this path: **Fill** = None, **Stroke** = None.

10. Go to **Object->Show All** to bring back the text. Select the text block and the new path. Go to **Type->Wrap->Make.** Set the view for **Preview** mode. You will see how your custom path did a good job of offsetting. The Direct Selection tool can fine-tune the path for a better fit.

velit esse molestie consequat, vel illum dc
at vero eros et accumsan et iusto odio di
luptatum zzril del
feugait nulla fa
amet, conse
diam nonum
ut laoreet do
volutpat. Ut v
quis nostrud e
suscipit lobor
commodo co
Duis autem ve
hendrerit in vulp
consequat, vel illum
facilisis at vero eros et ac
dignissim qui blandit praesent luptatum z
dolore te feugait nulla facilisi. Nam liber t

Tropical Suites
A Caribbean Resort

11. **Close** the file without saving.

Chapter 6

Type Special Effects

Chapter Objective:

To instruct you in the creation of professional special effects through the advanced use of type elements; to teach you methods of achieving many effects that you can find in commercial artwork. In Chapter 6, you will:

- Learn about putting type on paths.
- Understand more about fine-tuning spacing in type, both vertically as well as within individual lines of type; learn kerning, or the custom spacing of two or more letters, usually applied when creating headlines.
- Learn more about controlling type elements from the keyboard, to improve your efficiency.
- Learn to use type elements or text to fill irregular shapes.
- Practice methods of putting type around and inside of closed paths.
- Understand a variety of methods used to create custom outline and inline type elements.
- Learn to create popular effects such as embossed, three-dimensional, and shadowed type.

Projects to be Completed:

- **HoneyDo Hair Salon Logo**
- **HoneyDo Free Hairstyle Ad**
- Banana Boat Logo
- Fleet's In! T-Shirt Design
- Tropical Suites Logo
- Heart Notes
- Banana Border
- Champagne Brunch Table Tent
- Tropical Postcard
- Last Mango Menu Cover
- Full Page Grocery Ad
- Perspective Graph
- Java Jungle Goodies Ad

Type Special Effects

The graphic arts, commercially speaking, caters to one main objective — selling products. Whether it be ads, package design, or posters, the designer is challenged with making the design as eye-catching as possible. Knowing how to create special effects with type is a great advantage for the computer artist. Their use in creating attractive headlines is very important, as well for things like "bugs" — those ON SALE!!! and NEW ITEM! elements you sometimes see floating around catalog pages, flyers, newspaper ads, or announcements.

Text and Paths

The term Special Effects can mean almost anything. Suffice it to say that with Illustrator you aren't limited to the original forms supplied by the type manufacturer. The ability to design innovative effects with type often differentiates designers in commercial environments.

Sometimes a square or rectangular boundary for type elements won't meet the requirements of a design; at these times, you may find yourself needing to create a shape into which your text will be constrained. You can accomplish this simply by drawing a shape and using one of the Type tool options.

You can access these optional text tools by click-holding the regular Type tool. Your options are:

- Area-type — when the tool is clicked on a closed path, inserts the cursor inside the path area to fill it with the typed or pasted text.
- Path-type — when the tool is clicked on an open path, the cursor follows the contours of the path's outline.

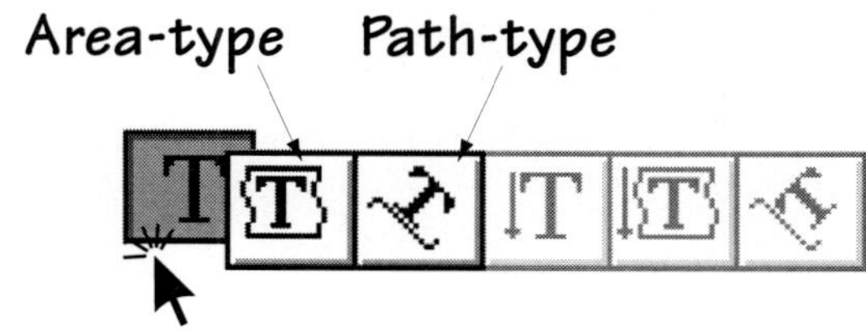

Area-type and Path-type are still text and can have any attributes applied to them.

Typographical Controls

Once text is inside or on the path, it is important that you pay special attention to readability and design aesthetics. To properly fit type into an area (regardless of the shape), you'll need to focus on Leading, Baseline Shift, Kerning, and Tracking.

Leading

Leading is the spacing between two or more lines of type. The line can be a single letter, word, or sentence. Leading is measured from the baselines of two lines.

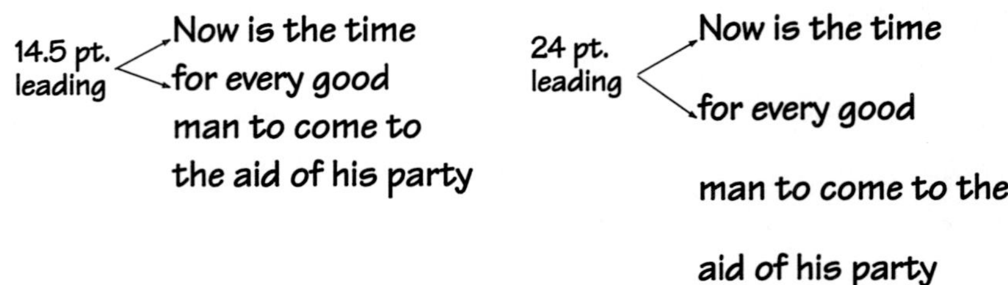

Baseline Shift

Located in the **Type->Character** dialog box in the **Window** menu, Baseline Shift can move type above and below the baseline of the typed text.

Zero (0) is the default setting for all type. When the numbers are increased, the text will rise above the baseline. Negative numbers will lower the letters below the baseline. Baseline Shift adjusts text when setting type around a circle (or other shapes).

You can change leading on the fly by holding down the Option key (Macintosh) or the Alt key (Windows) and using the up or down arrows. Spacing will open or close as you press the arrow. This is a very useful visual leading method.

The imaginary line that letters sit on is called the Baseline. For you to move the baseline of letters up or down is called Baseline Shift.

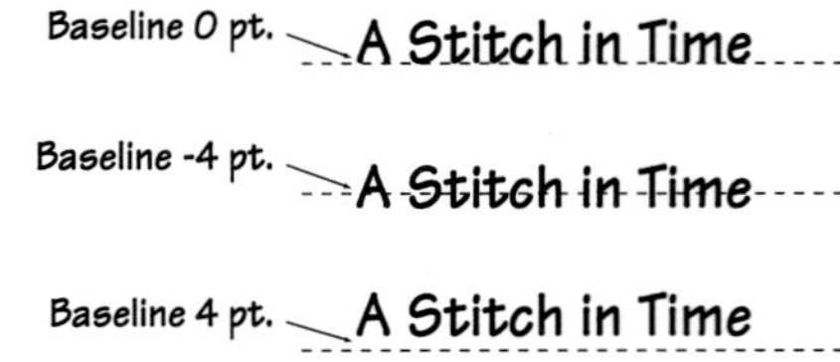

This feature is extremely valuable when creating logos that have certain letters that rise above or go below the Baseline.

Kerning

Kerning is adjusting spacing between two letters. The text cursor is placed between the two letters, then the Tracking keyboard shortcuts are applied.

The term for the two letters is "Kerning Pairs." This is because certain letters do not fit together, unless kerned.

Be careful not to get carried away with kerning. All letters, even the A's and the W's, need some space to look correct. When you do kern, make sure you do it evenly. Not necessarily the same between each character, but not a lot on one set and none on another.

Letter's left/right dimensions butt up to each other.

WAT

This looks bad, and makes reading difficult.

WAT

Kerning makes the letters fit better.

Kerning can be performed on two types of text.

- On a "Kerning Pairs" of two letters. To kern between two letters, the text cursor is placed between them. The keyboard shortcuts are best for kerning, because you can see the letters moving as the keys are pressed.

- On all selected text. For selected text, the type is highlighted with the text cursor (I-beam). Then, when the keyboard shortcuts are applied, all the selected text will respond.

Tracking

Tracking is the spacing between letters. There are several descriptive words often used to describe tracking: loose, normal, tight, or tighter. In Illustrator, the tracking is measured in numeric increments. Zero (0) could be called "normal" and -20 could be called "tight." You adjust the increments to your own liking in the **Type Character** palette. Any type, or text blocks selected can be modified in this palette.

The Tracking Menu

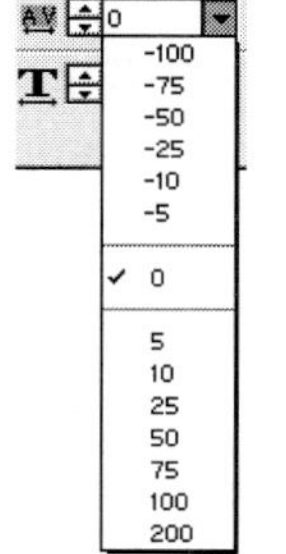

This tracking is set for 0.

This tracking is set for -25.

This tracking is set for -50

This tracking is set for 15.

This tracking is set for 25.

This tracking is set for 50.

Keyboard Shortcuts for Typographical Control

Using keyboard shortcuts is critical to efficient use of any program, and Illustrator is no exception. Particularly when working with text, accessing functions from the keyboard can prove far quicker and more productive than going back and forth to menus or dialog boxes every time you need to tweak type.

One example can be found in the **Preferences->Keyboard Increments** dialog box. Increasing the size of highlighted text can be done using Shift-Command (Macintosh) Control (Windows) -“ >” (the greater-than symbol on the keyboard). Reducing its size can be done with Shift-Command (Macintosh) Control (Windows) -“ <” (the lesser-than symbol.) Exactly how much bigger or smaller highlighted copy becomes when you invoke the command is controlled from **Preferences**.

From the **Preferences-> Keyboard Increments** dialog, you can change the amount of increments a keyboard command (such as arrow keys) has on kerning and leading.

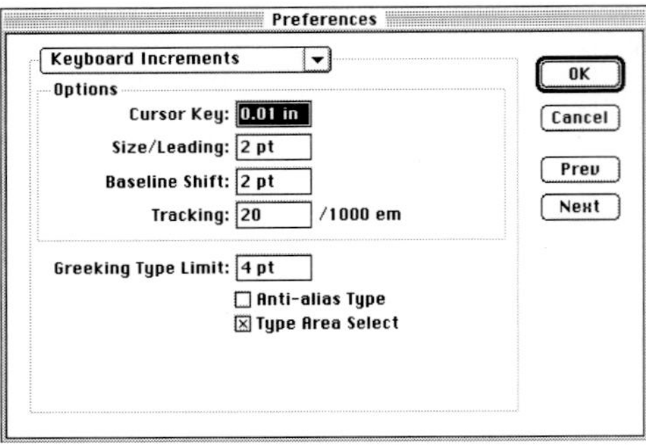

Using the Keyboard Shortcuts

- **Point Size** — Select the text, then hold the Shift key, plus the Command (Macintosh) or Ctrl (Windows) key, and press the Greater-Than (>) or Less-Than (<) key. The Greater-Than key increases the point size in increments; the Less-Than key decreases the point size.

- **Leading** — Select the text, then hold the Option (Macintosh) or Alt (Windows) key and press the Up or Down arrow keys. The Up arrow decreases the leading, and closes up the spaces between lines. The Down arrow key increases the leading, and expands the spacing.

- **Baseline Shift** — Select the text, then hold the Shift key, plus the Option (Macintosh) or Alt (Windows) key and press the Up or Down arrow keys. The Up arrow increases the increments; the Down arrow decreases the increments.

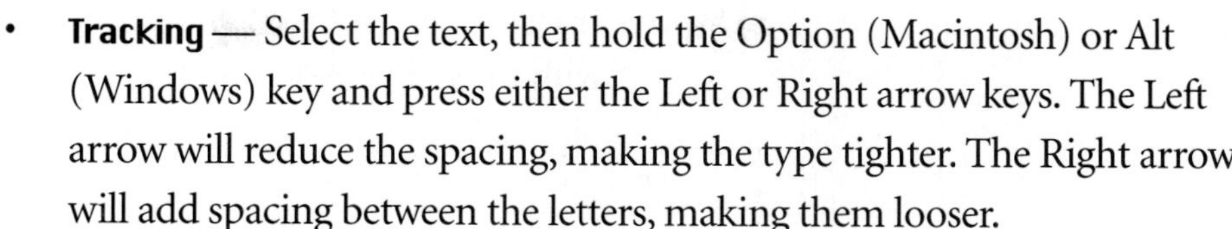

- **Tracking** — Select the text, then hold the Option (Macintosh) or Alt (Windows) key and press either the Left or Right arrow keys. The Left arrow will reduce the spacing, making the type tighter. The Right arrow will add spacing between the letters, making them looser.

- **Kerning** — To kern, click the Type tool cursor between the two characters you are going to kern, then hold the Option (Macintosh) or Alt (Windows) key and press the Left or Right arrow keys. The Left arrow closes up the spacing between the letters. The Right arrow key expands the spacing.

Filling a Path with Text

1. Create a **New** document. With the Ellipse tool, draw an ellipse with the dimensions of **Width** = 1.86 in., **Height** = 2.25 in.

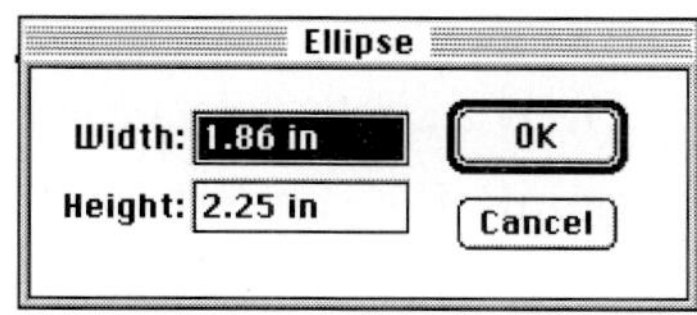

2. With the Area-type tool cursor, click on the top of the path.

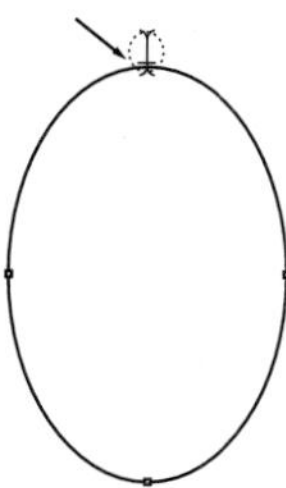

3. Type the phrase: "Browse our wonderful shops for an experience you'll never forget."

4. Highlight all the text. Access the **Type->Character** palette and apply these settings: **Font** = ATC Sands, **Size** = 14 pt., **Leading** = Auto, **Horizontal scale** = 100%. **Alignment** = Center.

5. Keep the text highlighted and use the keyboard shortcuts to adjust the leading, tracking, and baseline shift so that it artistically centers the oval. Experiment with these shortcuts to achieve this image.

Illustrator is excellent for achieving type objects that require precision (or even oddball) spacing or formats. Even if your project is being done in a page layout program, some type elements are better created as graphics and imported into the page layout.

Because the path is now a text container, you will have to select the oval with the Direct Selection tool in order to paint it: **Fill** = None, **Stroke** = 0.5 pt. Black.

6. **Close** the document without saving.

Wrapping Text Around a Circle

1. Create a **New** document. Set the view to **Artwork** mode.

2. Draw a circle. Select the Path-type tool. Click the cursor on the top anchor point of the circle to attach the Path-type tool to the path.

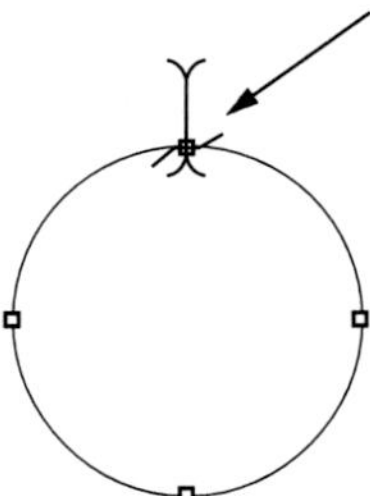

Type the words "TYPE ON TOP."
Apply these settings to the type: **Font** = ATC Sands, **Size** = 9 pt. Click on the path with the Selection tool to see the text cursor. Press Command-Shift-C (Macintosh) or Ctrl-Shift-C (Windows) to center the alignment of the selected text object.

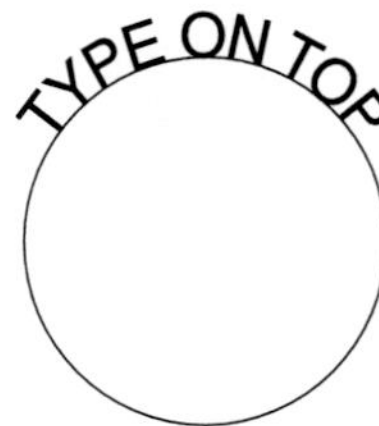

Pay extra attention to the line and letter spacing when you're putting type into a shape. Most fonts are designed to space properly within rectangles, and weird shapes can throw them off somewhat.

3. Click on the I-beam cursor with the Selection tool, then hold down the Option (Macintosh) or Alt (Windows) key and drag the cursor around to the bottom of the circle. This will duplicate the path. If the type inadvertently goes inside the circle, press Command-Z (Macintosh) or Ctrl-Z (Windows) to Undo, then try again.

Text elements wrapped around circles and ovals are very common in logo and retail design. This is another case where you should consider studying around contemporary materials for visuals that employ this technique.

4. With the Selection tool, double-click on the I-beam of the duplicate text, which will send the text inside the circle. Highlight the word TOP with the cursor and type the word BOTTOM.

5. Click on the TYPE ON TOP path with the Selection tool. Press Command-U (Macintosh) or Ctrl-U (Windows) to **Hide** it. Click on the bottom path. Hold down the Shift-Option (Macintosh) or Shift-Alt (Windows) key while pressing the Down arrow key five times. This will apply Baseline Shift to the text, lowering it below the baseline. This moves the text outside of the circle.

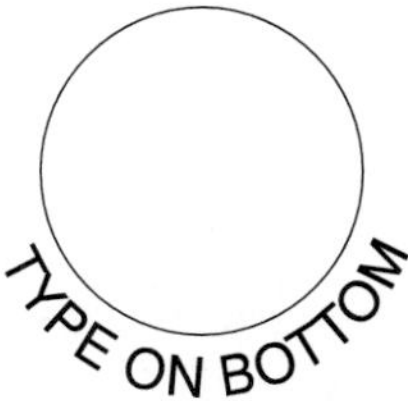

Object->Show All to bring back the top path. Select the bottom text path, and **Object->Hide** it.

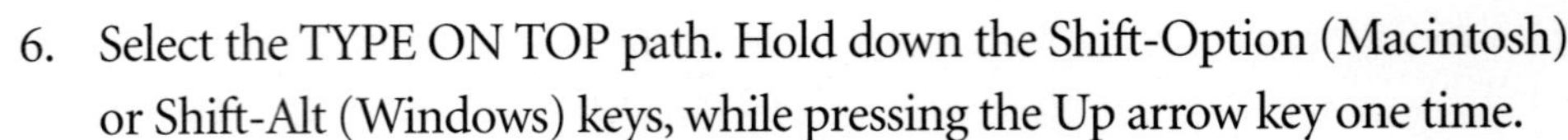

6. Select the TYPE ON TOP path. Hold down the Shift-Option (Macintosh) or Shift-Alt (Windows) keys, while pressing the Up arrow key one time.

Go to **Object->Show All** to bring back the bottom text path. Deselect all objects.

7. **View** the design in **Preview** mode. You have succeeded in fitting text on a circle.

8. **Close** the document without saving.

There's really no limit to the typographic effects that you can achieve with Adobe Illustrator. Outlining and creating bordered or inline type is only one example. This is another very popular and common technique in use today.

Text Outlining Techniques

If you are working with a headline or with logo type that requires a thick outline, simply applying a thick Stroke to the text is not recommended. Because a Stroke's thickness goes halfway inside and outside of the path, a Stroke that is too thick will hurt the appearance of the type.

In this example, the normal type (a.) was **Stroked** with a black 10 pt. rule (b.). The appearance of the type leaves much to be desired. The original was **Copied,** then **Paste In Back** applied to it. The thick Stroke was applied to the duplicate (c.). The unchanged original (shown in gray) rests on top.

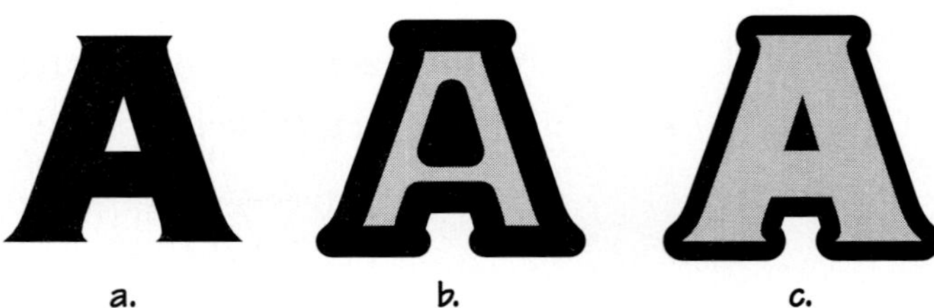

Creating Type with Thick Borders

1. Create a **New** document. Make sure the document is in **Preview** mode. Type the words "BANANA BOAT." Highlight the text and, in the **Type** menu, apply the **Font** = ATC Jamaica, and **Size** = 60 pt.

2. Go to **Window->Swatch Libraries->Other Library**, and access **ATC Custom Colors.AI.** Paint the text: **Fill** = ATC Yellow, **Stroke** = None.

3. Select the text object with the Selection tool. **Edit->Copy** the object, then **Edit->Paste In Back.**

You will be tempted, in Illustrator, to thicken headlines using the Stroke feature. As shown, this can cause the type to look horrible, and not read well. This exercise shows the proper way to achieve thick outlines.

4. The pasted object will still be selected. Go to the **Swatches** palette. Paint the duplicate: **Fill** = None, **Stroke** = 12 pt. Black. The image should look like this:

BANANA BOAT

5. **Edit->Select All** the objects, then delete them. Keep the document open for the next exercise.

Creating Type with Inline and Outlines

1. Continue in the open document.

2. Select the Type tool, click the cursor on the page, then type the words:

TROPICAL TREASURE

3. Highlight the text and access the **Type->Character** palette. Apply these settings: **Font** = ATC Tequila, **Size** = 60 pt., **Leading** = Auto, **Tracking** = -50, **Horizontal scale** = 100%.

This exercise provides a real-world example of how to create what's commonly called "inline" type.

4. In the **Type** menu, choose the option **Create Outlines**.

TROPICAL TREASURE

5. Press Command-G (Macintosh) or Ctrl-G (Windows) to Group the letters into one object. Paint the group: **Fill** = None, **Stroke** =8 pt. Black with rounded caps and joins.

6. **Copy** the grouped object and **Edit->Paste In Front.** Paint the copy: **Fill** = None, **Stroke** =2 pt. White.

7. **Edit->Copy** the duplicate that was **Stroked** with White, then **Edit->Paste In Front**. Paint the copy: **Fill** = Purple, Red, Yellow Gradient, **Stroke** = None.

If you want to find inline type being used, try looking at some older typefaces. Looking at materials designed in the past can give you new insight into modern design. In the words of Goudy, one of the world's greatest type designers, "Those old guys stole all of our best ideas."

8. With this painted object still selected, click on the Gradient tool in the Toolbox. Drag the tool's crosshair from the left side of the object to the right side, at an angle

This will extend the gradient across the entire text from left to right, rather than within each individual letter holding the gradient.

9. **Close** the document without saving.

Adding Embossed Effect to Type

For type to have an embossed (upraised) effect requires four elements: the original type, the light source, the shadow, and a surface with which the embossing is to contrast.

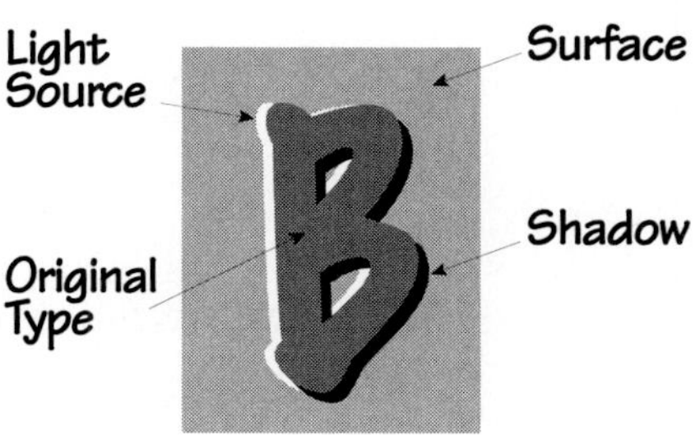

Embossing Headline Type

1. Go to the **SF-ADV Illustrator** folder and **File->Open** the student file **Island Caribe Emboss.AI.**

2. Select the "ISLAND CARIBE" type group. Paint it: **Fill** = ATC Blue, **Stroke** = None.

3. Press Command-C (Macintosh) or Control-C (Windows) to **Copy** it. Press Command-B (Macintosh) or Control-B (Windows) to **Paste In Back** of the selected original. The **Pasted** copy will then be the selected object. Press the keyboard Right Arrow key two times, then the Down Arrow two times. Paint this copy: **Fill** = Black, **Stroke** = None.

If you use a technique that relies on shadows or light sources, be sure that you remain consistent throughout the design. Nothing's worse than a shadow going one way on one element and a different way on another.

4. Select the original type group. Press Command-C (Macintosh) or Ctrl-C (Windows) to **Copy** it. Press Command-B (Macintosh) or Ctrl-B (Windows) to **Paste In Back** of the selected original. Press the keyboard Left Arrow key two times. Paint this copy: **Fill** = White, **Stroke** = None.

5. You have created an embossed effect, based on the light source originating from the left.

6. **File->Save** the document. **Close** the document.

Project A: HoneyDO Hair Salon Logo

Project B: HoneyDO Free Hairstyle Ad

Chapter 7

Editing Paths

Chapter Objective:

To teach you methods of editing and modifying existing paths; to learn how to rough a drawing into shape and fine-tune it to meet your exact specifications as a separate process. In Chapter 7 you'll:

- Learn to reduce the number of paths required to render a perfect curve. This skill ensures that your elements are as efficient as possible.
- Complete hands-on activities designed to familiarize you with the Pen tool's three primary editing options.
- Learn to add and delete specific anchor points and understand the effect such changes will have on common curves.
- Practice working with the Scissors tool.
- Work through a series of exercises meant to familiarize you with advanced path editing techniques.
- Learn to edit paths as a method of fitting elements and shapes to irregular guides.

Projects to be Completed:

- HoneyDo Hair Salon Logo
- HoneyDo Free Hairstyle Ad
- **Banana Boat Logo**
- Fleet's In! T-Shirt Design
- Tropical Suites Logo
- Heart Notes
- Banana Border
- Champagne Brunch Table Tent
- Tropical Postcard
- Last Mango Menu Cover
- Full Page Grocery Ad
- Perspective Graph
- Java Jungle Goodies Ad

Editing Paths

When you add an anchor point to a curved segment, the new point will have the same curve value as the existing curve. Deleting an anchor point can dramatically alter the path.

The philosophy for drawing paths in Illustrator is to click the anchor points and create the paths, but not to be too concerned with the exactness of the paths as you are roughing them in. Once the paths are roughly positioned, you then go back and do the precision adjustments, getting the curves, segments, and anchor points in just the right place.

Fine-tuning the curves, segments, and anchor points is called "editing paths." There's a real art to working with paths, so don't expect to master it overnight. With practice, however, the editing will become second nature to you.

Reducing the Number of Points

The first rule in drawing paths in Illustrator is "use anchor points sparingly."

- Too many anchor points make the art too complicated and increase the risks of getting PostScript errors.
- The file size increases in proportion to the number of anchor points.
- In many cases, the fewer points a curve has, the better (smoother) it appears in the final output.

Here's an example of using the least number of anchor points to achieve the same curving path.

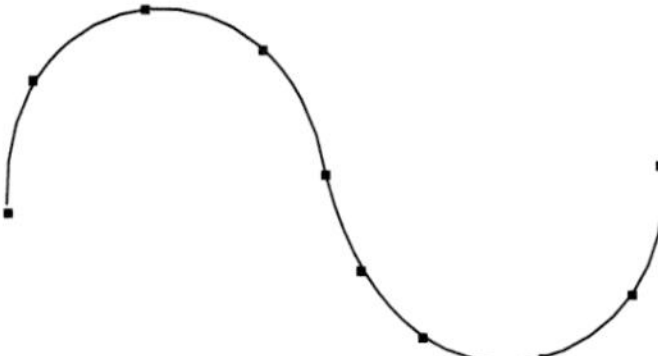

Too many anchor points

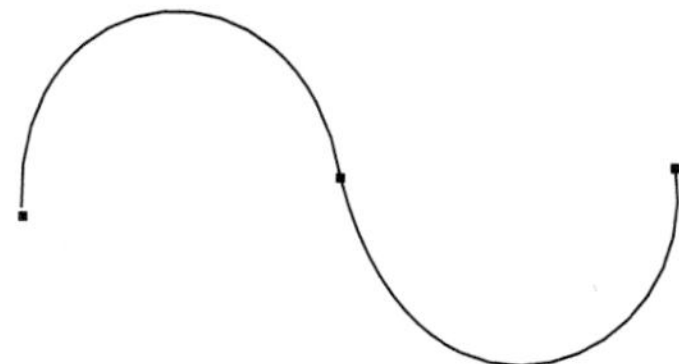

Same curve - 3 anchor points

The Path Editing Tools

Pen Tool Options

Dragging the Convert-direction point cursor on a Smooth Point doesn't have any effect.

Dragging the tool on a Corner Point will turn it into a Smooth Point with two handles.

There are three tools used for editing and modifying anchor points and segments, and they're available underneath the regular Pen tool. Click-hold on the tool's icon and the other tools will reveal themselves.

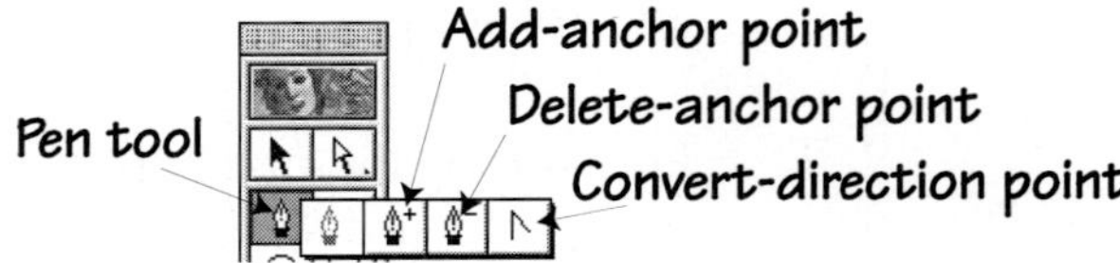

- The Add-anchor point tool inserts an anchor point where it is clicked (a. - b.). These points can then be moved to enhance the design (c.).

- The Delete-anchor point tool removes anchor points from the path (d. - g.).

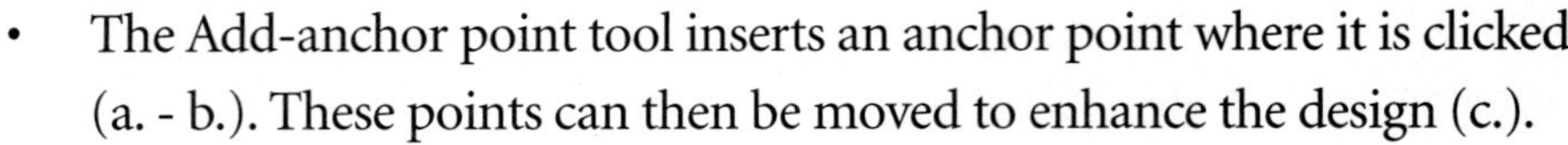

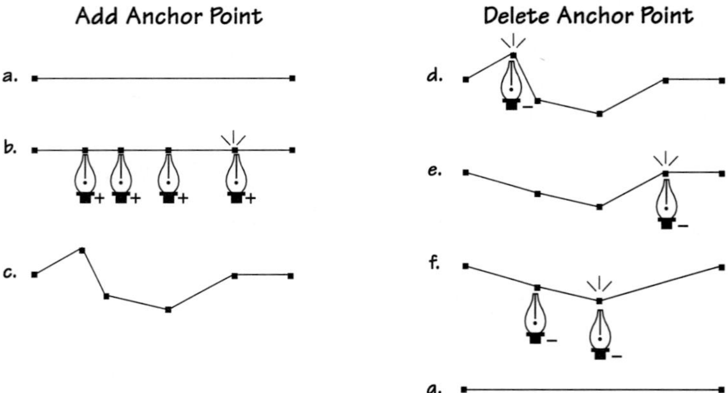

- The Convert-direction point tool will change anchor points that have curves connected to them. The two curve types are the "Smooth Point" and the "Corner Point."

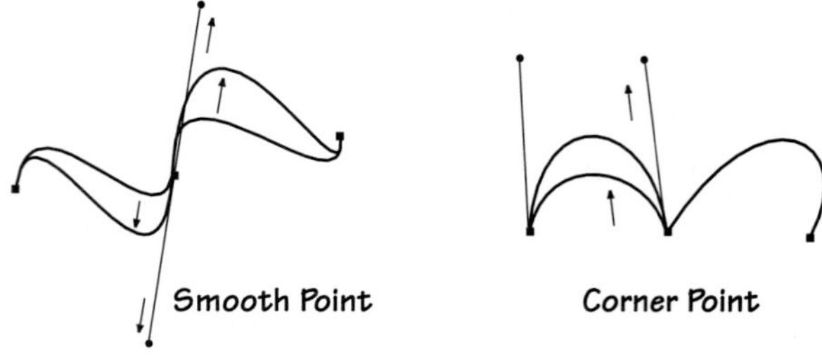

The Effects on a Smooth Point

If a Smooth Point is single-clicked with the Convert-direction cursor (a.), the point loses its handles, making the two segments connected to it independent of each other (b.).

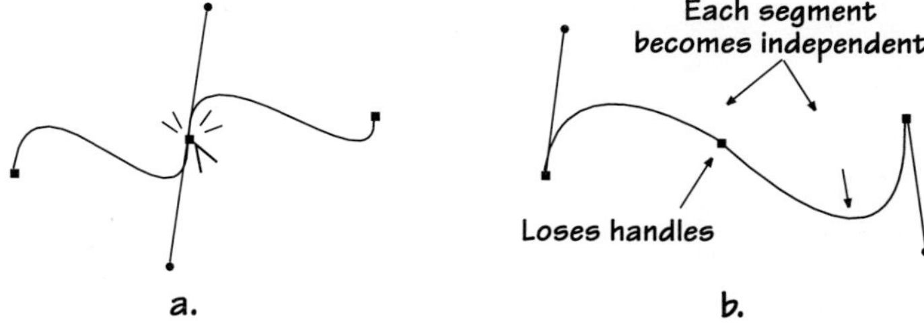

Changing a point from a Corner Point to a Smooth Point is often required when you're cleaning up autotraced paths.

The Effects on a Corner Point

Single-clicking the Convert-direction tool on a Corner Point (a.) removes the curve from the segment, leaving a straight segment.

If the Convert-direction cursor is dragged from a Corner Point, it becomes a Smooth Point (b.).

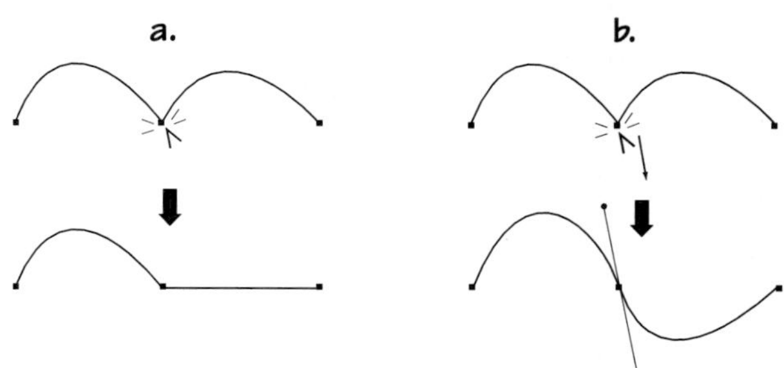

The Scissors Tool

Another path-editing feature is the Scissors tool, which splits a path where it is clicked. The Scissors tool cursor is a crosshair (a.). The crosshair is laid on the path where a split is desired. When the split is made, it is not apparent. The two endpoints are actually on top of each other (b.). They can be moved with the Direct Selection tool to reveal the actual split in the path (c.).

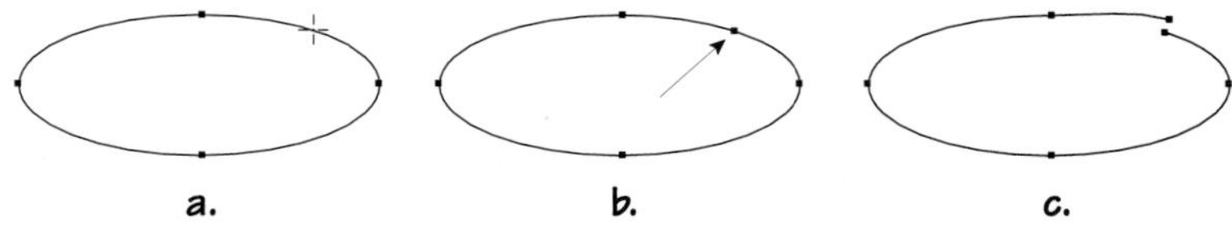

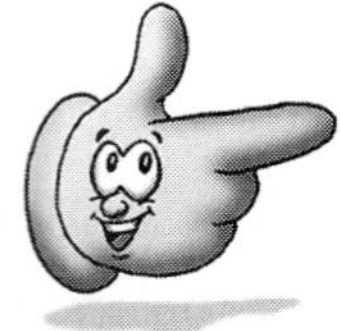

Editing Paths

1. Create a **New** document. Draw a line segment with the Pen tool (a.).

2. With the Add-anchor point tool, add a point in the middle of the segment (b.).

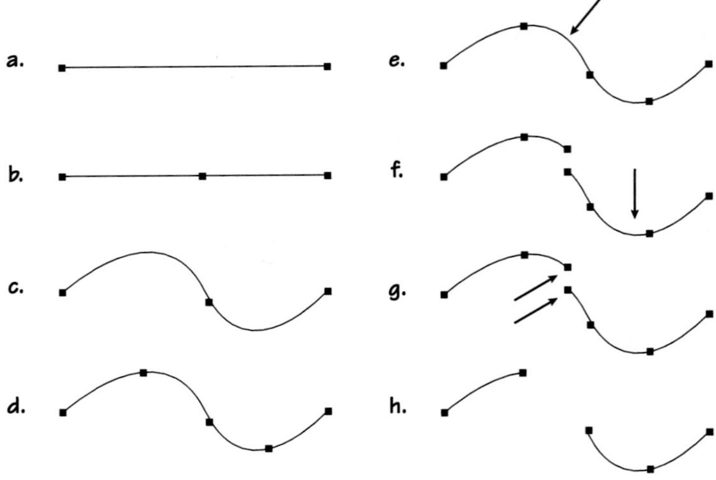

3. With the Convert-direction tool, drag on the added point to convert it to a Smooth Point (c.).

4. In the middle of each curve segment, add a new anchor point (d.).

5. With the Scissors tool, cut the second segment in the middle (e.).

6. Select the right side path and move it slightly downwards to show the split.

7. Use the Delete-anchor point tool to delete the endpoints of the two paths created by the Scissors tool (g.).

8. Observe how the original straight path has gone through a metamorphosis to produce two separate, curving paths (h.). Select the endpoint of each between the two segments, and **Object->Path->Join** them. Convert the join to a smooth path.

9. **Close** the document without saving.

Knowing when you need to change an anchor point from a corner to a smooth, or vice versa, is a skill that will come with experience. The more complex your work, the more likely you'll need to use this method.

Editing Anchor Points

1. **Open** the document **Convert Curves.AI.**

2. The paths of the objects have too many anchor points. Delete the unnecessary anchor points and adjust or convert the curves to make the path fit the guides in the background.

3. **File->Save** the file. **Close** the document.

Guides are sometimes the backbone of achieving accuracy in a design. Being without guides is like taking a roadtrip without a map. You might end up with unexpected results.

Fitting Paths to a Guide

1. **Open** the document **Baggy Outline.AI.**

2. The supplied closed path needs to be fitted to match the guide in the background.

3. Use the Selection tool and the Direct Selection tool as well as the editing tools to match the guide. It is important that it should be done with the least number of anchor points.

4. **Close** the document without saving.

Project C: Banana Boat Logo

Notes:

CHAPTER 8

MODIFYING PATHS

CHAPTER OBJECTIVE:

To practice techniques that modify and combine paths and shapes using specialized tools and options; to introduce you to the Pathfinder shape modification controls built into Adobe Illustrator. As you work through Chapter 8, you will:

- Know how to average and join selected points. This is a critical skill and necessary for productive development of your illustrations and designs.
- Learn more about the Path functions.
- Learn how to use the outline and offset commands, tools that allow automatic generation of common shapes and borders.
- Understand the use and importance of the Cleanup option — critical to efficient and accurate output of your work.
- Practice using the Pathfinder tools, Illustrator's most important subset of shape modification functions. Pathfinders allow you to use one shape to modify another, through joins, unites, intersections of common surfaces, outlines, trims, copies, and lighting effects.

PROJECTS TO BE COMPLETED:

- HoneyDo Hair Salon Logo
- HoneyDo Free Hairstyle Ad
- Banana Boat Logo
- Fleet's In! T-Shirt Design
- Tropical Suites Logo
- Heart Notes
- Banana Border
- Champagne Brunch Table Tent
- Tropical Postcard
- Last Mango Menu Cover
- Full Page Grocery Ad
- Perspective Graph
- Java Jungle Goodies Ad

Modifying Paths

The ability to join points, average the location of various objects, and create composite objects that start out as individual elements (such as joining a circle to a square to form an arch), is very important in the development of your drawing skills. Not only do these sorts of joining and compositing functions save you lots of time, there are instances where they can result in the creation of objects that you simply couldn't create any other way — or at least within any rational time constraints. There are two ways to modify or combine paths: the **Path** and the **Pathfinder** options in the **Object** menu.

We often use the word "developing" when talking about complex drawings. That's because it's rare that you sit down, start Illustrator, and complete a drawing in a linear manner. You develop a drawing or design, you don't just execute it.

Path

Path is another path modifying menu selection with these altering features:

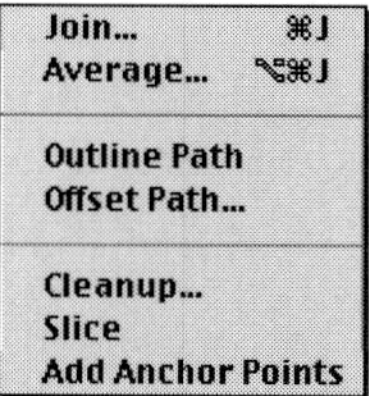

- **Join** — connects two selected anchor points (must be selected with the Direct Selection tool) with a segment.

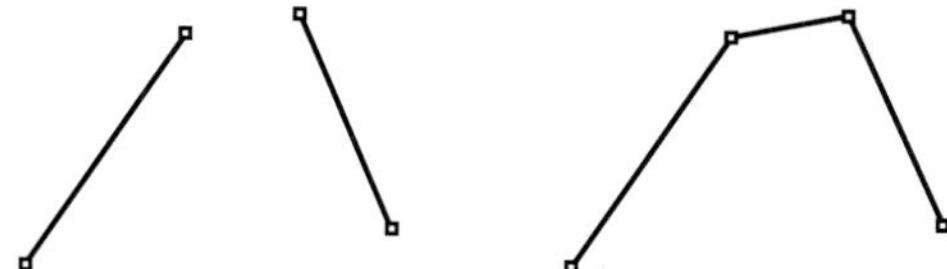

You can Average and Join two anchor points, simultaneously, by holding Command-Option-Shift-J (Macintosh) or Ctrl-Alt-Shift-J (Windows). Very handy.

- **Average** — averages the distance between two anchor points, and closes the gap at the average point between the two points. Don't be fooled. The averaged intersection which seems to be only one point is actually the two selected anchor points overlapped on one another. The two anchor points must be selected and **Joined**, if a closure is desired.

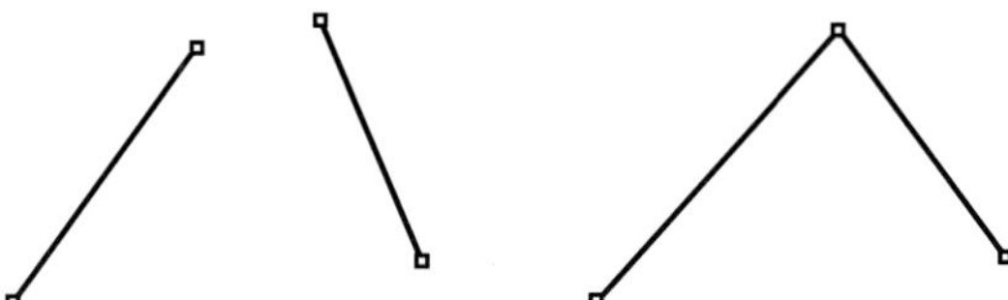

- **Outline Path** — outlines a path based upon how it is painted. It creates a new path outline from the original. This is discussed in detail later in this chapter.

- **Offset Path** — creates a new path that is a duplicate of the shape of the original, only smaller or larger, depending on the size you specify in the dialog box. This is also discussed later in this chapter.

Cleanup is a command that you should use whenever you're done with a drawing. There are always things left around; empty text items, stray points, and junk that you don't need anymore. It does not affect paths to simplify them.

- **Cleanup** — deletes objects you might have accidentally created or left unattended. The size of an Illustrator document is defined by a rectangle that includes all points. If you have one lying around somewhere far off the visible page, the final file size might be incorrectly calculated. The function allows you to delete Stray Points, Unpainted Objects, and Empty Text Paths.

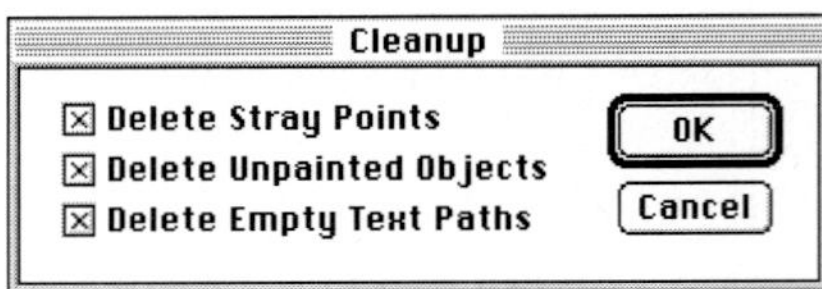

- **Slice** — is like a cookie cutter. The cutting path is placed on top of the target path, then selected. The shape of the cutting path is cut into the target path.

- **Add Anchor Points** — adds anchor points in between existing anchor points. The more you perform the operation, the more anchor points you end up with. This is a handy feature to use before you select a filter such as **Punk & Bloat**, that operates on the anchor points of a path.

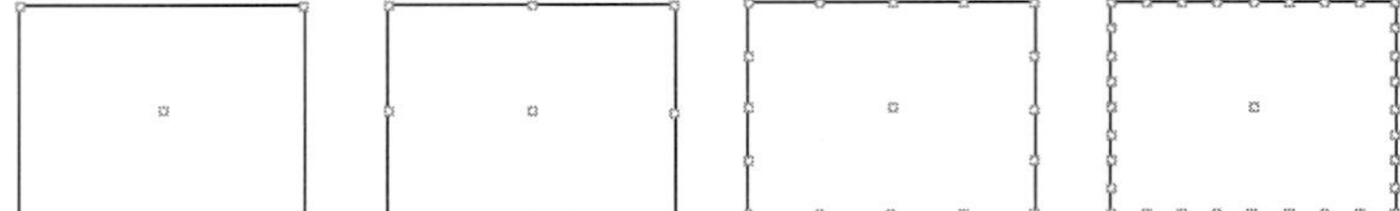

The essential asset of **Outline Path** is that it outlines the thickness of the Stroke you apply. This allows you to control the outlining by visual methods. If you get the Stroke looking the way you like, you then use **Outline Path** to achieve an exact offset duplicate path.

Compounding is the graphic feature that takes two paths overlapping each other, and creates a "see-thru" hole through them. It is an illusion to the eye to see a compounded object, such as the oval in this exercise, and think that it possesses a thick Stroke. Not so. Try it and see.

Using Outline Path

1. Create a **New** document.
2. Draw an oval with the Ellipse tool.
3. Paint it: **Fill** = None, **Stroke**= 15 pt. Black.

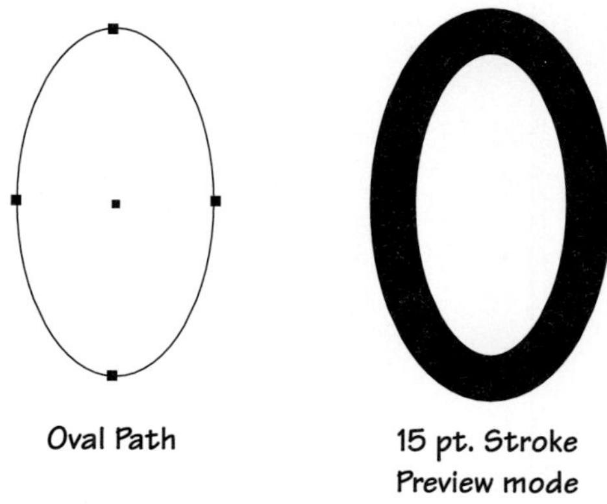

4. Select the path. Go to **Object–>Path–>Outline Path.**
5. **View** the result in **Artwork** mode, then in **Preview** mode. Keep in mind that the operation automatically compounds the two paths. In order to paint one path differently, you must release the compound.

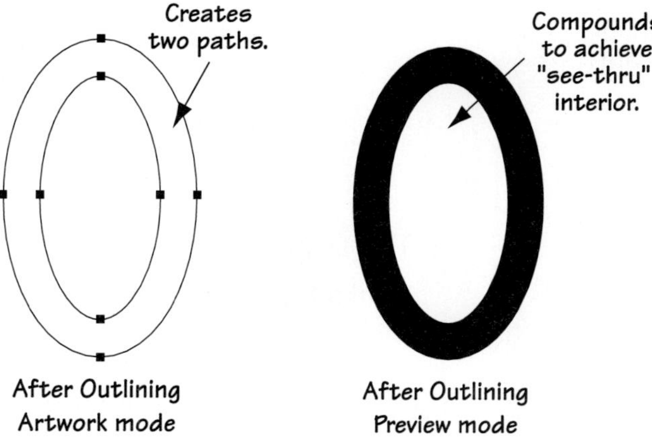

6. **Close** the document without saving.

Offset Path

When you use the **Copy** feature in the **Scale** dialog box to duplicate an object at the same time that you're Scaling it, you can't set the distance between the original and the duplicate objects to be the same. Rectangle 1 was Scaled with **Copy** clicked. The distances between the paths (a. and b.) are not the same.

If it is desired to duplicate a path and retain a consistent distance on all sides between the two objects (c.), this effect can be achieved with **Offset Path**.

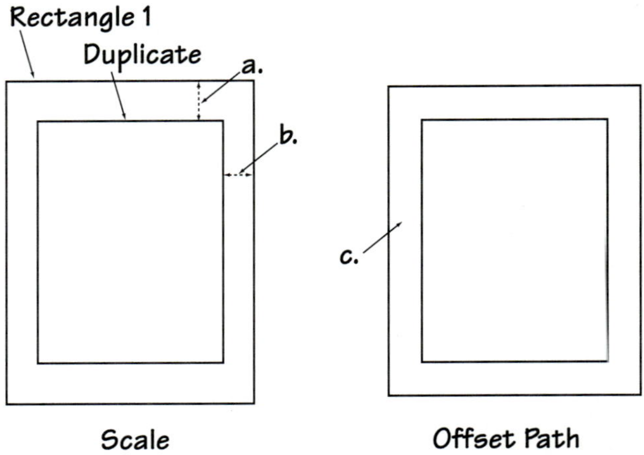

This feature makes a duplicate of the selected object. The distance between the path of the original and the duplicate is set in the dialog box.

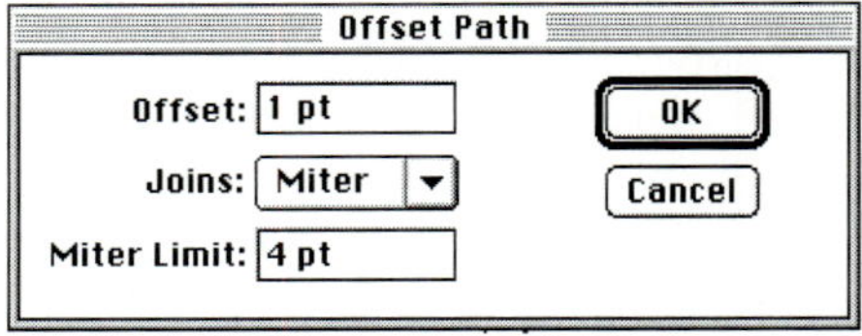

This feature is very handy for enhancing objects by **Offsetting** the path and **Stroking** the original with a thin, white rule.

Typing positive numbers for the **Offset** in **Offset Path** creates a duplicate outside of the original. If you want to offset the duplicate to the inside of the original, enter a negative number, such as "-45."

Using Offset Path

1. Create a **New** document. Go to **Artwork** mode.

2. Select the Rounded Rectangle tool and draw a rectangle.

Illustrator's built-in operations, such as **Outline Path**, are indispensable when trying to create certain objects, while facing a ticking clock and a deadline.

3. With the rectangle selected, go to **Object->Path->Offset Path.** In the **Offset Path** dialog box, set the **Offset** for "0.067" inches and press **OK.**

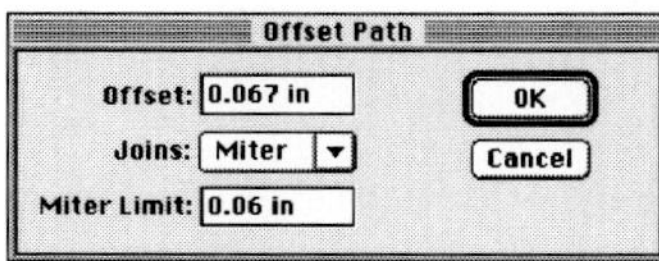

4. Go to **Artwork** mode. The result should look something like this, with two paths.

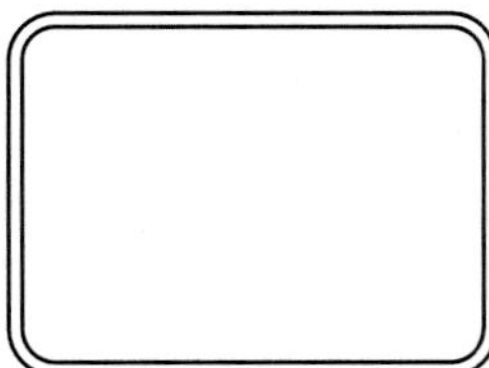

5. Paint the offset path (outside path): **Fill** = Black, **Stroke** = None.
   Paint the original (inside path): **Fill** = None, **Stroke** = 2 pt. White.

6. Go to **View->Preview** mode. The new image should look like this.

7. **Close** the document without saving.

Pathfinder

Pathfinder features perform many different operations in seconds that would take considerable time if done manually. We suggest, however, that you experiment with these operations to see which option gives you the effect you are looking for.

Here are some examples of how **Pathfinder** affects overlapping objects. In some cases, the operation shows no immediate visual effect. You will have to **Ungroup** the resulting object or use the Direct Selection arrow to move the paths apart in order to see the actual effect.

Some of the paths shown have been disassembled to show you how the operation affected the object.

When two objects are painted differently, then combined or extracted in the operation, some filters default to the color of the object in front. Look at samples **Intersect** and **Exclude** to see this. In the case of **Crop**, the gray color of the square (in back) is the default color. In the case of **Trap**, the objects must be painted with two different colors. The **Trap** filter creates a third path that overlaps the two objects. Refer to the chapter Printing & Separations for an in-depth study of trapping.

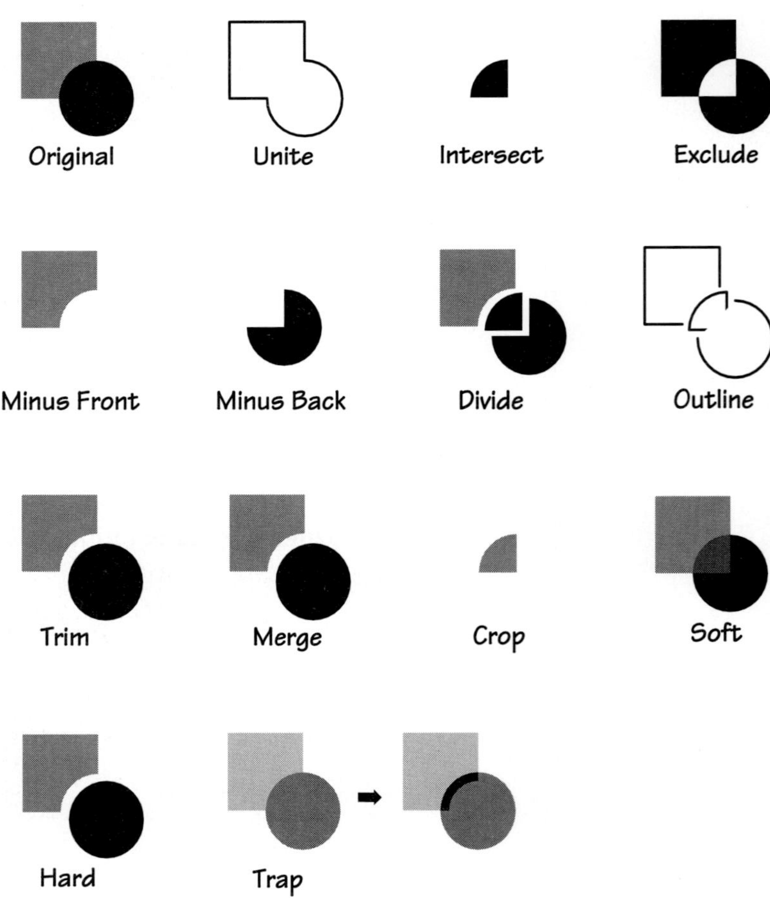

Pathfinder Features

1. Create a **New** document.

2. Draw two 1" squares and paint them with **Fill:** 100% Black**; Stroke** = None. Draw an oval that slightly overlaps the two squares. Paint the oval with: **Fill** = 50% Black, **Stroke** = None. Select them all.

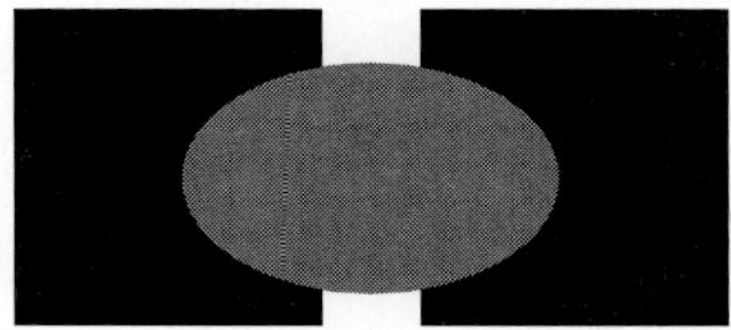

3. Go to **Object->Pathfinder->Unite.** This will be your result, seen in **Preview** mode (left) and **Artwork** mode (right). **Edit->Undo** to go back to the original.

The Pathfinder functions are probably the most important and least understood of the many tools available to the designer. We strongly suggest that you experiment with Pathfinder until you're familiar with the many options it provides.

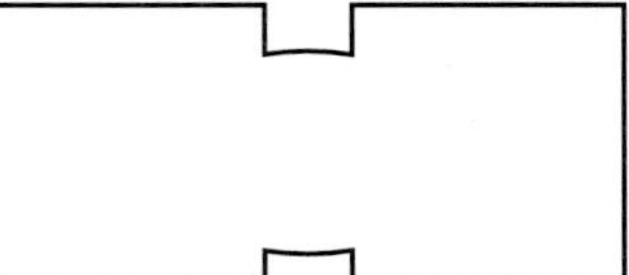

4. Go to **Object->Pathfinder->Crop.** This will be your result, seen in **Preview** mode. **Edit->Undo** to go back to the original.

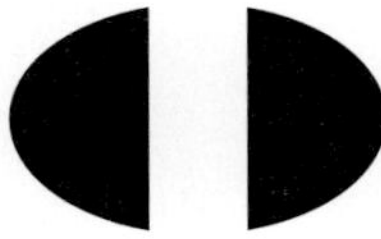

5. Select the original. Go to **Object->Pathfinder->Exclude.** This will be your result, seen in **Preview** mode. **Edit->Undo** to go back to the original.

6. Select the two squares and paint them with: **Fill** : C=100; M=100; **Stroke** = None. Paint the oval with: **Fill:** C=20; M=0; Y=100; K=0; **Stroke** = None.

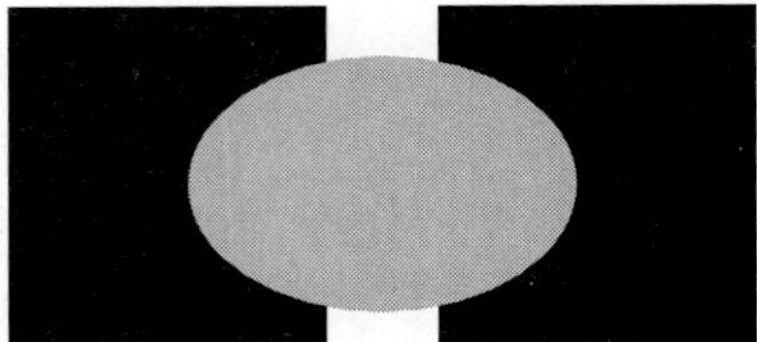

7. Go to **Object->Pathfinder->Soft**. In the **Soft** dialog box, leave the settings as they are. Click **OK**.

   Soft makes the oval seem transparent.

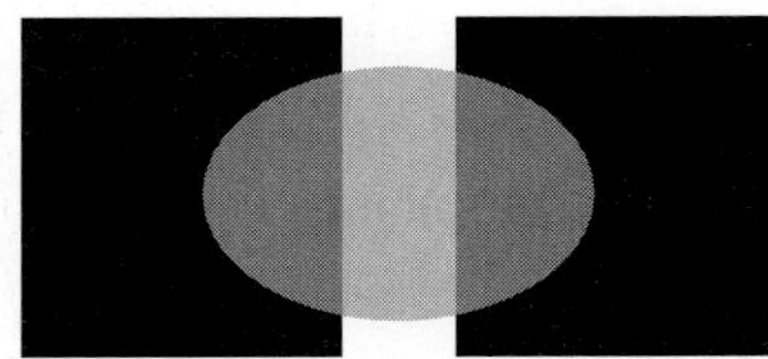

The transparent look is created by the feature dividing the various objects and painting them with screen values of the original color.

The separate paths that make up this transparent appearance are shown here to give you a better idea of how the **Soft** operation works. You can move the objects yourself by clicking on them with the Direct Selection tool.

8. **Close** the document without saving.

A good example of transparency is when you're drawing glass that partially obscures specific objects. The color of an object seen through the glass is softer than those parts not seen through the glass. A windshield on a convertible car comes to mind.

CHAPTER 9

WORKING WITH FILTERS

CHAPTER OBJECTIVE:

To introduce you to the concept of filters and how they work on different types of art elements; to allow you to practice working with several popular filters to gain an understanding of how they can be used to modify or enhance your designs. In Chapter 9 you will:

- Learn how different filters are used for vector and bitmapped images, and how and when to select the right filter for the job.
- Learn how filters affect lines and shapes.
- Become familiar with artistic filters, such as the Ink Pen, which offers an almost unlimited number of hatch and fill patterns.
- Understand how most filters require a number of settings which affect the intensity or application of the effect.
- Learn to use Free Distort to achieve perspective when developing objects with three dimensions.
- Practice working with distortion filters to create starbursts and other common design elements important to commercial illustrators.
- Learn to work with bitmap filters borrowed from Adobe Photoshop, which allow you to modify imported scans and continuous tone images.

PROJECTS TO BE COMPLETED:

- HoneyDo Hair Salon Logo
- HoneyDo Free Hairstyle Ad
- Banana Boat Logo
- **Fleet's In! T-Shirt Design**
- Tropical Suites Logo
- Heart Notes
- Banana Border
- Champagne Brunch Table Tent
- Tropical Postcard
- Last Mango Menu Cover
- Full Page Grocery Ad
- Perspective Graph
- Java Jungle Goodies Ad

Working with Filters

Filters are preprogrammed operations, styles, and features that modify elements of a drawing. In many cases these modifications would prove very complicated if done using regular Illustrator tools and commands. They're located under the **Filter** menu. The **Filter** menu provides a selection of tools that can be used on both Vector paths and Raster objects.

Some filters only work on vector (line) art, and others work on imported (or rasterized) bitmap elements. They're segregated in the **Filter** menu, with the Vector filters on top, and the Raster filters on the bottom.

The **Filter** menu itself is visually divided into these two categories. If you have a line-based (Vector) element selected, the top portion of the menu is active; if you have a Raster image (such as an imported scan), the bottom portion applies. To use a filter, select the object or path to which you want to apply an effect, and choose a filter from the **Filter** menu. After setting the parameters of the filter from a dialog box (not all filters have dialog boxes), the effect will be applied.

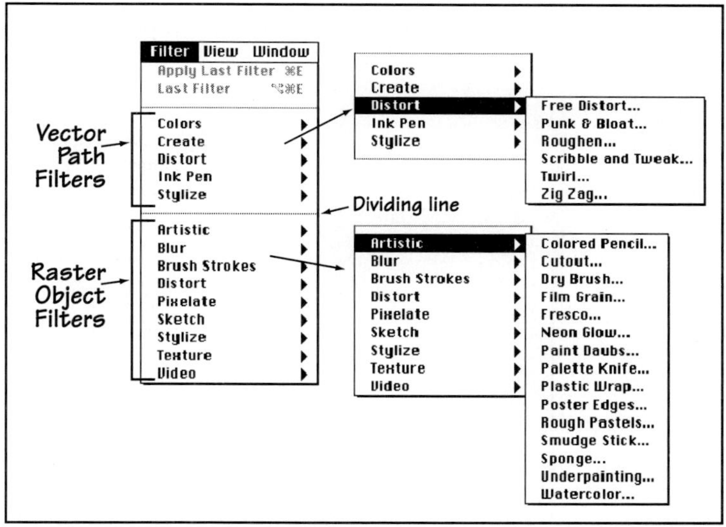

- Vector Path Filters — will work only on paths drawn in Illustrator, not Placed or Rasterized objects.
- Raster Object Filters — are available only on selected Raster objects, such as TIFF, PICT, BMAP, etc. These can be either Raster objects that were Placed in the document, or paths drawn in the document that were Rasterized by the **Rasterize** feature under the **Object** menu.

Filters for Vector Paths

Filters for vector paths can be applied to objects drawn within Illustrator, as well as on objects imported from other drawing programs — as long as they come into the Illustrator environment with their objects intact.

There are over 24 different filters that affect Vector objects. Here are a few of the more important ones:

Vector filters (ones that work on line art) can't really do anything that you couldn't do with the standard pen and/or transformation tools. For example, you could draw a "bloated" star without the filter; it would just take a lot longer.

Zig Zag

Found in **Filter->Distort->Zig Zag**, this filter adds an effect to illustrations that has become a very popular trend of artwork in the '90s. Before, it was necessary to draw these zig zags by hand, which was very time-consuming.

The zig zags are drawn automatically. You can designate the settings in the dialog box to customize the aspects of the effects by determining the total width of the zig zag, the number of times the zig zags occur, and whether you want sharp or rounded points.

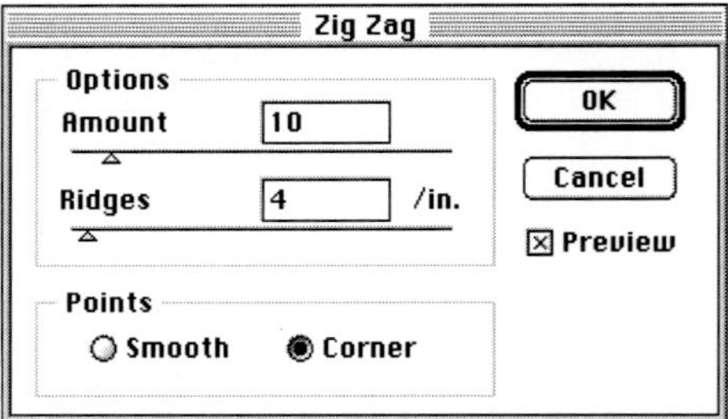

- **Amount** is the total width between the zig zag peaks. **Ridges** is the number of zig zags that will take place. **Smooth** is a rounded point.

- **Corner** is a sharp point of the zig zag. **Preview** allows you to view the results before clicking **OK**.

Here are some samples of the **Zig Zag** filter.

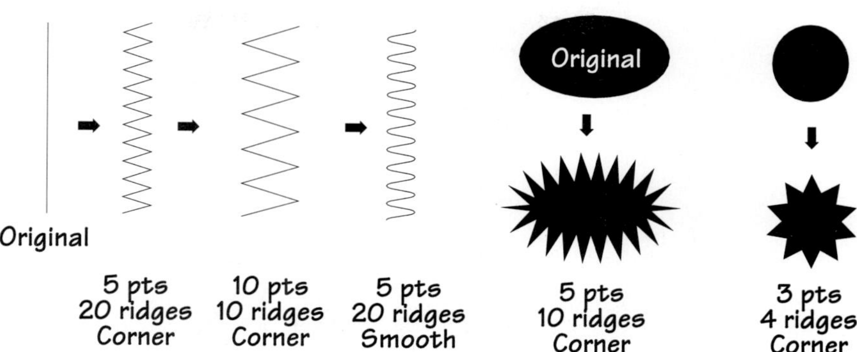

Creative Designs with the Zig Zag Filter

1. Create a **New** document, and draw a 45° line segment. Remember, clicking the second anchor point while holding the Shift key constrains the angle to 45° increments.

2. Paint the line segment with: **Fill** = Yellow & Purple Radial Gradient, **Stroke** = None.

3. Go to **Filter->Distort->Zig Zag.**

4. Type these settings in the **Zig Zag** window: **Amount** = 40, **Ridges** = 20, **Points** = Corner, **Preview** = Clicked. Click **OK.**

5. The result should look similar to this.

6. **Close** the file without saving.

When you're applying filters, it's usually a good idea to try a variety or range of settings until you get exactly what you're looking for. If you need a starburst, try the filter with four or five different values before you decide which one best suits your design.

Ink Pen

There are many styles of images that Illustrator can create with its tools, such as Pen tool, Pencil tool, Paintbrush, etc. There is no tool, though, that can give the rough, dry brush look that can be achieved by the **Ink Pen** filter.

Some of the effects from this filter are quite inventive and creative.

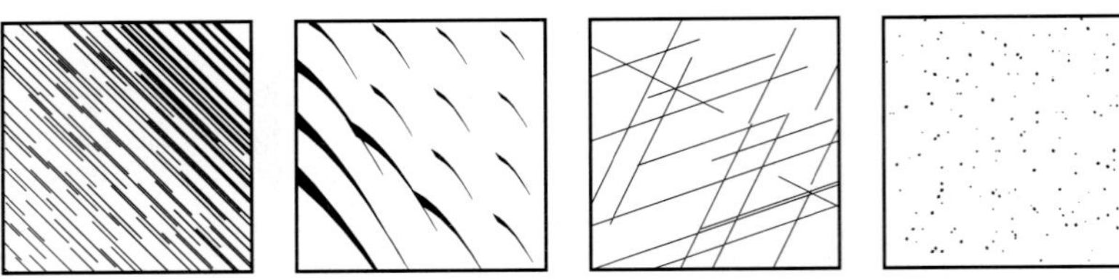

The **Ink Pen** filters are capable of creating very complex patterns, and, just like normal patterns, can result in files that are difficult to output. If you have a drawing that contains pen-filtered objects and won't print, try reducing the complexity, or using the **Object->Rasterize** function to turn the object into a bitmap.

The **Ink Pen** filter is found in the **Filter** menu.

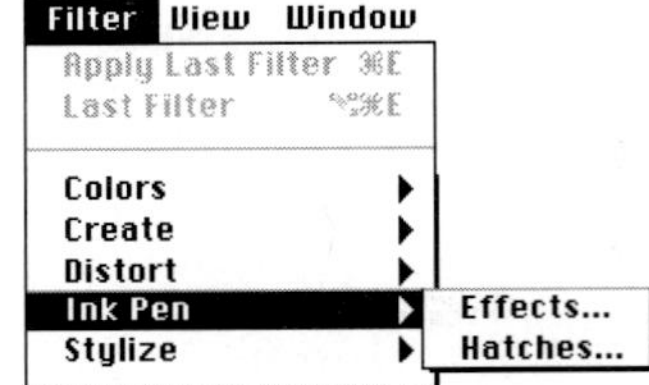

The **Ink Pen Effects** dialog box applies the selected **Ink Pen** designs to an object. The settings allow you to make many changes and modifications.

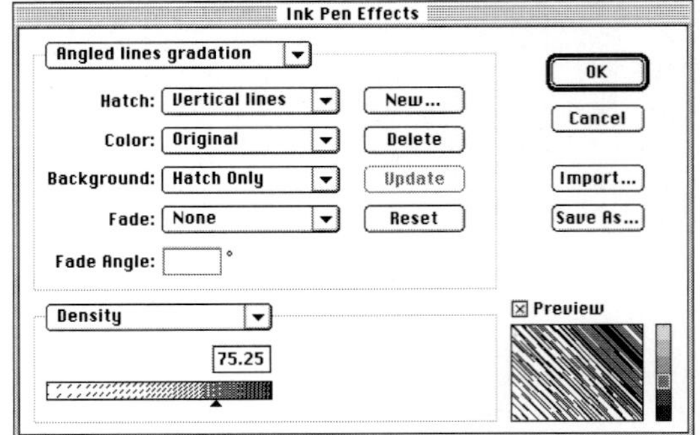

The top pop-up menu, showing **Angled lines gradation**, allows you to select the various hatches from the many settings supplied.

In many cases, hatches and pen strokes are used to add texture to individual objects, or to provide backgrounds for entire pages. Consider Placing a scanned image for backgrounds; this construction method often results in files that are easier to output.

The **Hatch** menu does not apply any effects to objects. You can choose an Ink Pen style in the **Hatch** pop-up menu. This can then be pasted into the document for modification. You can also create a new hatch or delete an existing one.

Applying an Ink Pen Filter

1. Create a **New** document. With the Rectangle tool, draw a 3" square.
2. With this object selected, access the **Filter->Ink Pen->Ink Pen Effects** window.
3. Click/hold the mouse on the first pop-up menu, at the top left.
4. Highlight and select **Swash texture gradation**. Click **OK**.

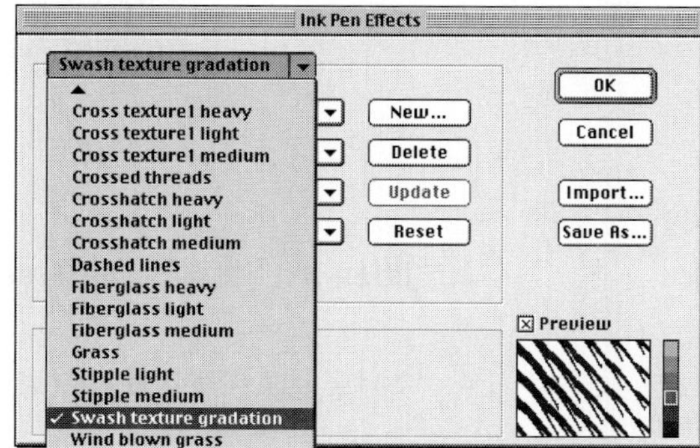

5. **View** the square in both **Artwork** and **Preview** mode to see how the effect is created.

6. **Edit->Undo** this effect.

7. With the square still selected, access the **Ink Pen Effects** window again.

8. Select **Wind blown grass** effect. Click **OK**.

Wind blown grass
Wood grain heavy
Wood grain light
Wood grain medium
Wood grain swirl

9. **View** the results in **Artwork** and **Preview** modes to see how the **Ink Pen** filter uses a Mask to see the **Ink Pen** hatch only inside the original path.

10. **Close** the file without saving.

You could spend a lot of time – probably a week or more – going through every possible Ink Pen filter. You have to balance experimentation for its own sake, and experimentation as a component of the design process.

Free Distort

The **Filter->Distort->Free Distort** filter will shear and skew an object or group of objects, allowing you to shape objects in the design to satisfy many different requirements — such as perspective or distortion. Once you've completed the stretching and pulling, press **OK** to apply it to the selected object.

Using Free Distort

The objective is to fit the Tropical Suites logo on the angled side of a cube.

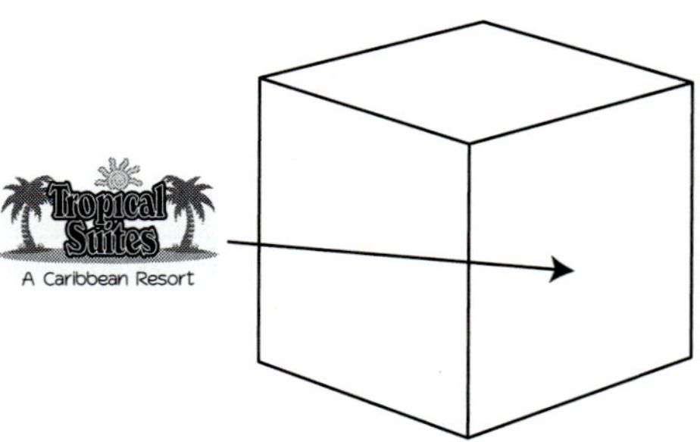

It will be your choice whether to use the **Free Distort** filter, or the Shear tool. The choice depends on the actual result desired, as well as your own personal style.

1. **Open** the Student File **Free Distort.AI.**

2. Select the **Tropical Suites** logo. Go to **Filter->Distort->Free Distort**.

3. The **Free Distort** window shows the outlines of the logo. Each of the four corners of this object are the working points to be moved.

Features like **Free Distort** or **Shear** provide a down-and-dirty way to achieve three-dimensional effects. For more realistic three-d objects, you might consider using Adobe Dimensions, a companion program that "extrudes" objects created in Illustrator.

4. Move the corners to achieve the angle and perspective that will make the logo fit the cube.

5. When the distorting is finished and you are satisfied with the shearing, press **OK** to apply these changes to the selected logo.

6. Moved the distorted logo to fit on the cube. All shearing was performed in **Free Distort** and not with the Shear tool.

7. **Close** the document without saving.

Filters for the Rough-drawn Look

There are two options in the **Filter->Distort** menu. **Roughen** and **Scribble and Tweak** lend themselves to distorting the path of an object to give it a coarse, jagged contour.

Roughen

The **Roughen** filter can give some very wild and explosive qualities to an object. It is advised to have the **Preview** button clicked in its dialog box so you can see the effects before you click **OK**.

When controlled, though, roughen gives some very attractive contours to an object.

The **Roughen** filter, like many of the filter dialog boxes, comes with a **Preview** button. This is handy for seeing how your settings will look when applied to a path.

Roughen

Roughen Filter

1. **Open** the file **UTA Caribe Island logo.AI.**

2. In **Artwork** mode, use the Pencil tool to draw a closed border around the logo. With the border selected, go to **Object->Arrange->Send To Back.**

3. With the border still selected, go to **Filter—>Distort—>Roughen.** Make these settings. **Size** = 2, **Detail** = 3, **Points** = **Smooth**. Press **OK**.

4. Paint the Roughened border: **Fill** = Aqua, **Stroke** = None. Go to **Preview** mode to see your design in color.

5. **File->Save** the file. **Close** the document.

Punk & Bloat

Filter->Distort->Punk & Bloat will move the anchor points in or out from the line of the selected path. In the **Punk & Bloat** dialog box, you indicate how much effect you desire. **Bloat** requires moving the slider to the right (positive numbers), and if you want to **Punk** an object, move the slider to the left, into negative numbers. Keeping **Preview** checked lets you see the effect before you click **OK** — something that seems pretty important to us!

Punk

This rounded corner rectangle was Punked -20%.

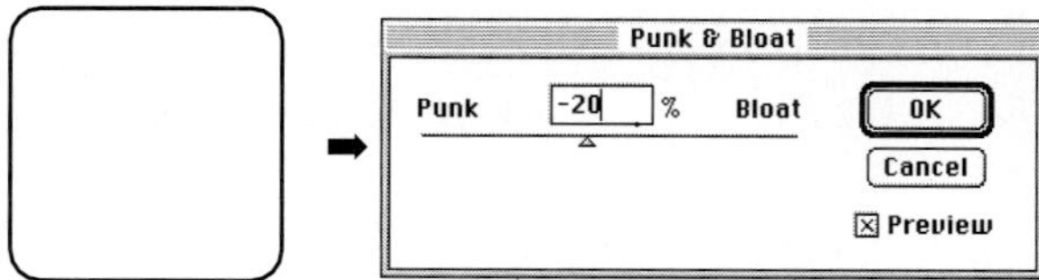

Observe how the anchor points of the rounded corner were thrown from the path. Also, notice how the straight lines of the original became curved.

Bloat

Bloat rounds the segments connected to the anchor points of the selected path. It is best to experiment with the filter on various objects to see how it looks. Here are some samples.

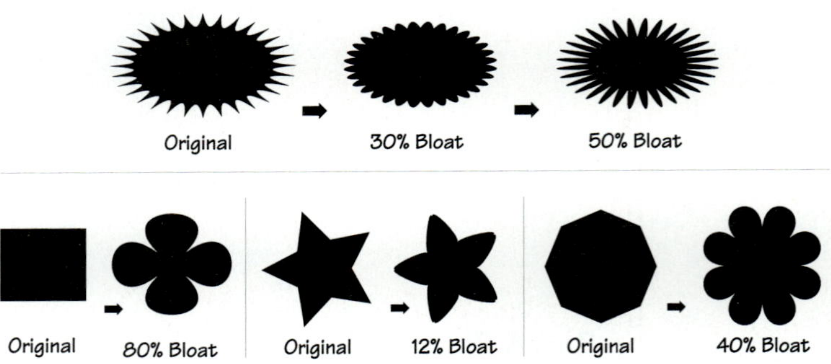

Creating a Starburst with Punk

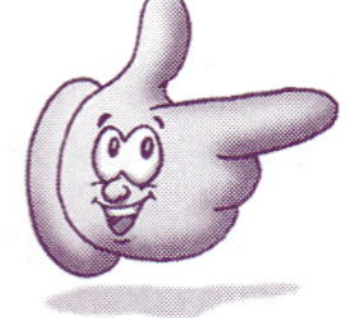

Starbursts are a very common design element, especially in retail work. While there are extensions that do this within page layout programs, it's usually a better idea to develop this type of graphic as an imported illustration.

1. Create a **New** document.
2. With the Ellipse tool, draw an oval (a.). Keep the oval selected.
3. Go to **Object->Path->Add Anchor Points** (b.). Add anchor points three more times to add enough points for this example.
4. Go to **Filter->Distort->Punk & Bloat.**
   Move the slider or type in -20%. Click **Preview** to see how it will look. Press **OK**. You have now made a starburst to use for an attention-getting balloon that will hold reversed type making an announcement (c.).

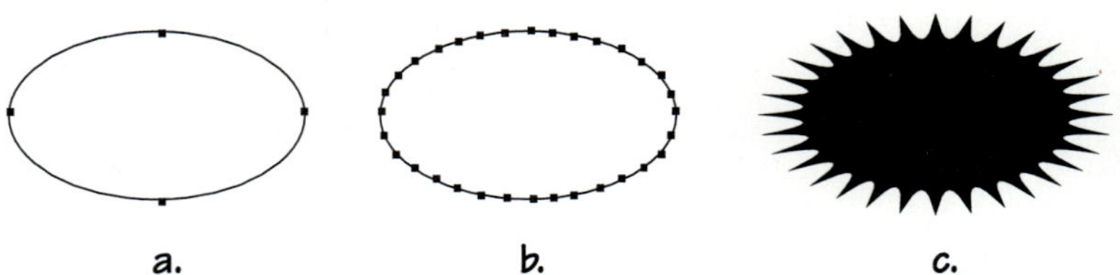

5. **Close** the document without saving.

Twirl

The **Filter->Distort->Twirl** filter makes very attractive and (to a designer) very handy curves to objects, saving much time in drawing and adjusting curves.

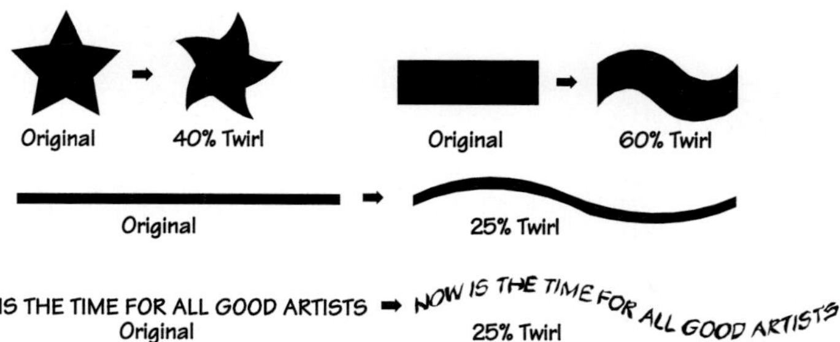

Scribble and Tweak

Filter->Distort->Scribble and Tweak adds some rough contours to a path that could resemble the scribbling of a child, or the artistic strokes of a chalk or pastel pencil. **Scribble** randomly moves anchor points away from the original object, while **Tweak** moves anchor points on the selected object by a specified amount.

Trim Marks

Filter->Create->Trim Marks show the printer where to trim the job with the paper cutting device. Here is a business card with appropriate Trim Marks.

When you use filters and the results aren't what you expected, it could be because there was a stray point somewhere in the illustration that was figured into the calculation. Press Command-Z (Macintosh) or Control-Z (Windows) to Undo the filter, then try using the **Cleanup->Stray Points** on the drawing and then reapply the filter.

When using the **Trim Marks** filter, it is best to search for stray anchor points. If they are selected along with your artwork, the trimmed area will be more than you bargained for.

Get rid of any stray points before selecting all. Trim Marks are used for cutting something from a piece of paper or film. Crop Marks are another thing altogether; if you have a dozen different things on a single page and put crop marks around them, saving the file as an EPS will result in only the cropped element being saved. Crop Marks define the bounding box, or outside dimensions, of the EPS file.

A surrounding rectangle does not have to be drawn. One has only to select the object or group of objects, then access the **Trim Marks** filter.

The filter will determine the extreme bounding dimensions, then apply **Trim Marks**. If extra margin is desired, a rectangle can be drawn around the objects, then **Trim Marks** applied to it. The rectangle can then be deleted.

In this example, all the objects in the design were selected (a.). **Filter->Create->Trim Marks** was then chosen (b.).

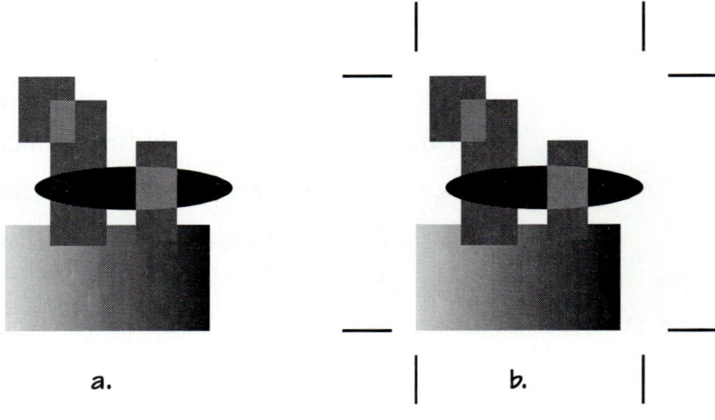

Creating Trim Marks

1. **Open** the Student File **Coffee Cup Trim Marks.AI.**

2. **Edit->Select All** the objects.

3. Go to **Filter->Create->Trim Marks.** This will set Trim Marks for the extreme bounding box of all the art. Trim Marks inform the commercial printer where to trim the final job.

4. **Close** the document without saving.

Raster (Bitmapped) Filters

The Raster filters work on Raster images only. There are two ways to get a raster image into your document: by using the **Object->Rasterize** function to turn an object that you've already drawn into a Raster object; or, by **Placing** external Raster images, such as scans or images from a CD-ROM.

The Raster filters can be used to alter Raster images with photographic and other special effects. These range from blurs (artistic strokes such as an artist uses on a painting canvas) and rippling effects, to filters that make the image look as if it were reproduced on a copier. They are all very unique, and can sometimes allow you to achieve an effect that can't be done any other way.

If you have selected a Raster object, the Raster filters become available under the **Filter** menu:

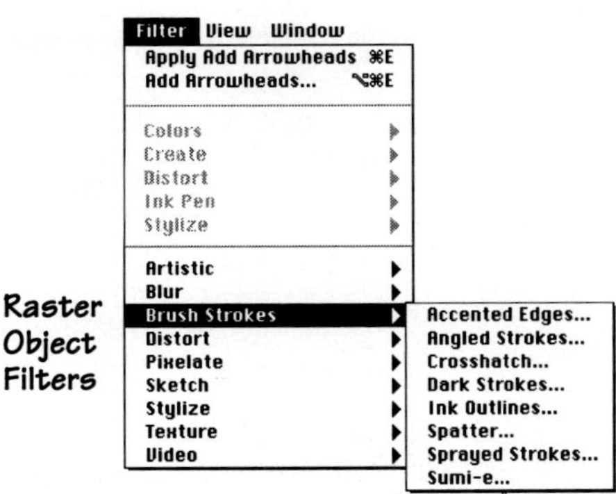

Each filter has its own dialog box. The exact specifications for each filter will be different, but there are some consistent aspects to each dialog box.

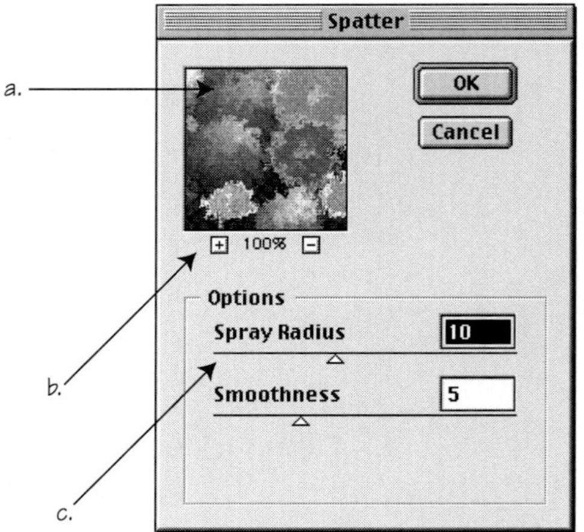

Raster effects are actually filters developed for another very popular Adobe program called Adobe Photoshop. Photoshop is an image editing and painting program that's in use in many commercial graphic environments.

a. Shows how the effect will look.

b. Plus/Minus buttons allow enlarging or reducing the image size in this dialog box.

c. The settings for each filter appear in the lower portion of the box.

Samples of Raster Filter Effects

The original photo below is a normal, untouched picture. It was then filtered with **Filter->Brush Strokes->Spatter** (right).

Original photo

Photo filtered

Here are some more examples of Raster filter effects.

Original

Accented Edges

Fresco

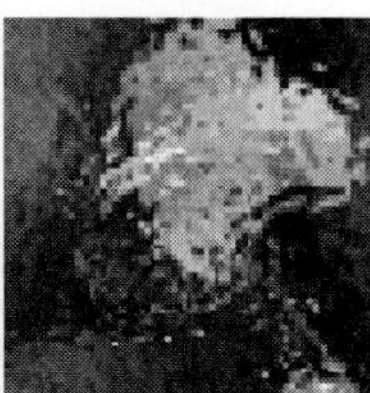
Glass

Grain

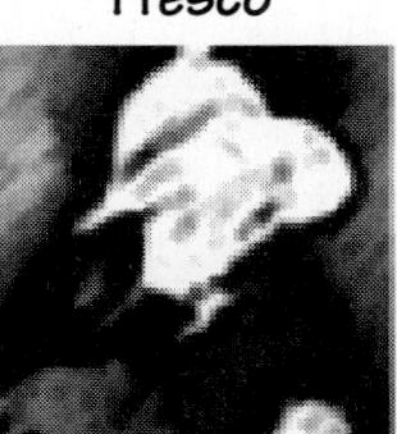
Sumi-e

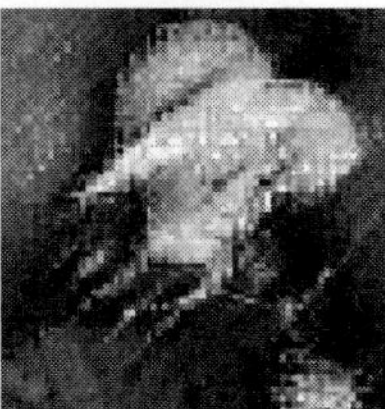
Rough Pastels

Using a Filter

1. Create a **New** Illustrator document.

2. **File->Place** the photograph **Conch Shell.TIF.**

3. Select the photo. Go to **Filter->Artistic->Rough Pastels.** Press **OK.**

4. Observe how the photo looks with the filtered effects.

5. **Close** the document without saving.

Using the Mosaic Filter

1. **Open** the file **UTA Island Mosaic.AI.**

2. **Edit->Select All.**

3. Go to **Object->Rasterize** and **Rasterize** the selection as: **Color Model** = RGB, **Resolution** = Medium, **Anti-alias** = On, **Create Mask** = Off (a.)

4. Select this image and go to **Filter->Texture->Mosaic Tiles.** Click **OK** (b.).

a.

b.

5. **File->Save** the file. **Close** the document.

Using Filters on Rasterized Paths

1. **Open** the Student File **Flower Lineart.AI.**

2. Use the Pencil tool to draw paths that can be Filled for the flower petals and leaves. Paint them any way you please. Gradients are great for this exercise. Once these paths are drawn and painted, select them all and go to **Object->Arrange->Send To Back.**

3. Keep these paths selected, then go to the **Object** menu and choose **Rasterize**. Make the settings: **Color Model** = RGB, **Resolution** = Medium, **Anti-alias** = On, **Create Mask** = Off. Click **OK**.

4. Select the rasterized object. Go to **Filter->Artistic->Rough Pastels.**

5. Make no setting changes in the dialog box. Click **OK.**

6. **File->Save** these changes. **Close** the document.

Project D: Fleet's In! T-Shirt Design

Notes:

REVIEW #1

CHAPTERS 1 THROUGH 9:

In the first nine chapters of *Adobe Illustrator: Advanced Digital Illustration*, you have reviewed important tools and functions, and have begun to explore some of the program's more complex and advanced features. At this point in the course, you should be familiar with:

- ✓ Controlling the many options you have relative to defaults, preferences, page and document setup attributes, and other controls. You should also have a solid understanding of the tool set — both the default tools as well as their many options. You should also know how to modify the Startup document to customize your specific working environment.
- ✓ All aspects of layers within an Illustrator document and how specific objects are assigned or reassigned within those layers.
- ✓ Creating high-quality type elements within the Illustrator page; how to control vertical and horizontal spacing, and how to manually or automatically track and kern words and individual letter pairs.
- ✓ Developing special effects using type elements. You should also know how to place type on a broad range of shapes and paths; within and on circles, and within and on irregular shapes created with the program's drawing tools. You should also know how to import copy created in other applications, and how to link text blocks and control text columns.
- ✓ Working with paths, anchor points, and segments. By this point in your development you should be able to add and remove anchor points as part of an editing process; you should be able to rough in a shape and refine it using path editing and management tools and functions.
- ✓ Using the Pathfinder tools to build complex shapes from simple components. You should understand the importance of the Cleanup function and be able to apply it to your drawings and layouts.
- ✓ The use of filters to achieve a wide variety of special effects. You should know the difference between Vector and Raster filters, and how their application is limited to specific types of design elements or imported images.

CHAPTER 10

THE TRANSFORMATION TOOLS

CHAPTER OBJECTIVE:

To expand your understanding of transformation tools; how they act, and how they can be applied to the development of symmetrical and asymmetrical objects. In completing the hands-on activities and exercises in Chapter 10, you will:

- Fully understand the concept of the Origin Point, or Point of Transformation; the spot from which a transformation takes place.
- Work more with the rotation functions, applying them both visually and mathematically.
- Work with the Shear tool in several different exercises that demonstrate their use and actions.
- Work with each tool's dialog box, which provides precision and accuracy when you apply them.
- Learn to apply shearing and other transform functions in order to fit images to other sheared objects.
- Work extensively with the mirror, or Reflect transformation tools.
- Gain more experience with the reflection tools.

PROJECTS TO BE COMPLETED:

- HoneyDo Hair Salon Logo
- HoneyDo Free Hairstyle Ad
- Banana Boat Logo
- Fleet's In! T-Shirt Design
- **Tropical Suites Logo**
- **Heart Notes**
- Banana Border
- Champagne Brunch Table Tent
- Tropical Postcard
- Last Mango Menu Cover
- Full Page Grocery Ad
- Perspective Graph
- Java Jungle Goodies Ad

The Transformation Tools

Developing a drawing efficiently requires more than just being able to draw shapes — you also have to know how to transform shapes for a variety of needs. This section covers Transformation methods — powerful tools that let you stretch, grow, shrink, rotate, and reflect the shapes you create with the geometric and pen tools.

Origin of Transformation

You should first understand the concept of *Origin of Transformation*, sometimes called The *Origin Point*. This is the point, or axis, about which the transformation performs its operation. It is like the center hole of a metal gear. The gear revolves around this center hole. The concentric hole (in the direct middle) would be the gear's Origin of Transformation, or axis.

An origin point is the point from which an object is modified. It's the point it spins around, enlarges from, shrinks to, or slides around. Once you go through the exercises in this chapter, these powerful methods will become a regular part of your arsenal.

In this example, the orginal square was selected and the Rotate tool clicked in the Toolbox. The tool's crosshair cursor was single-clicked to the right, setting the Origin of Transformation. The selected object was then rotated around the Origin Point by dragging on the object.

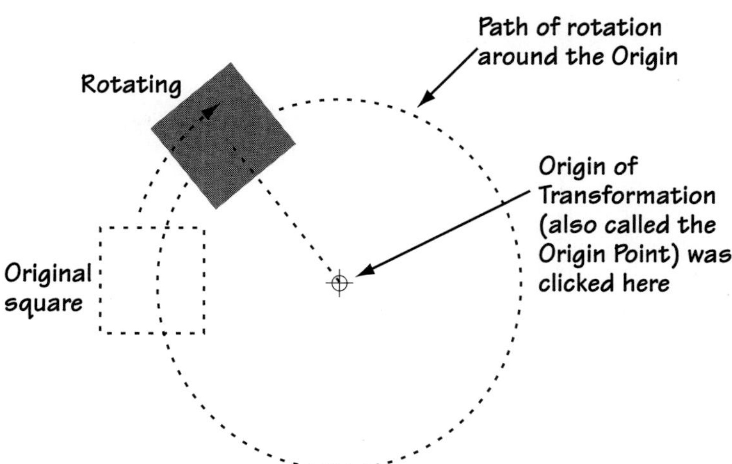

The default Origin of Transformation is the exact center of the object. If a group of objects is being transformed, the center of the combined objects becomes the Origin Point, unless you change it (which we'll get to later).

The Rotate Tool

The Rotate tool is used to rotate objects. It works two ways:

- Manually — after the tool is clicked in the Toolbox, the crosshair cursor is single-clicked (without holding any keys) on the page to set the Origin of Transformation, or the axis around which the object will rotate (a.). The cursor then becomes an arrow tip that is used to manually drag the object and rotate it (b.).

You can rotate lines (or blocks) of type just as easily as you can anything else. This is very useful when developing technical drawings or instructions.

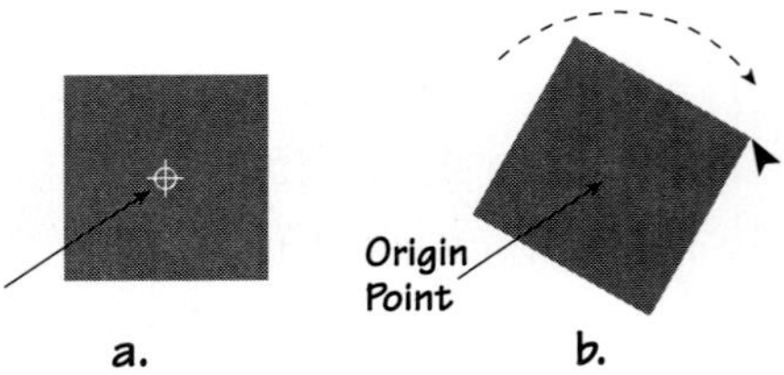

- Dialog Box — To rotate an object using the dialog box, double-click on the Rotation tool. The center of the object becomes the Origin Point. If you want to set your own Origin Point, single-click on the Rotation tool in the Toolbox, then hold the Option (Macintosh) or Alt (Windows) key as you click on the object to set an Origin Point. The dialog box will appear. You type in the rotation angle, then click **OK**. If you want to make copies and rotate them at the same time, click **Copy**.

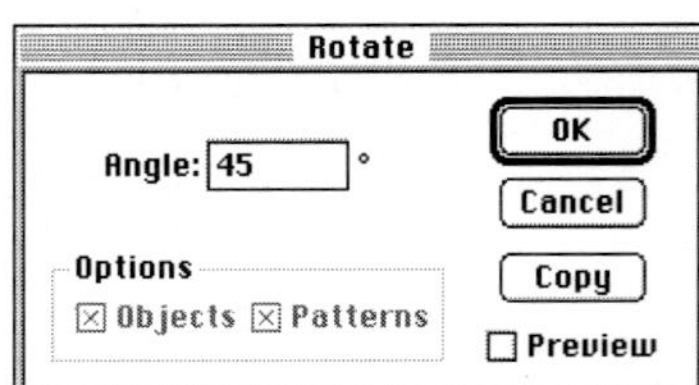

The Origin Point does not have to be set on the object rotated. There are times that an object (or group of objects) need to be rotated based on a center point at a different part of the page.

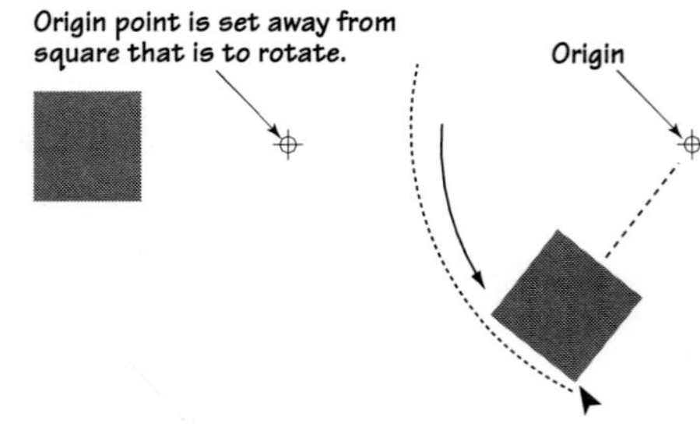

Manually Rotating Objects

1. Create a **New** document.
2. Draw a spiral with the Spiral tool.

Select the object drawn.

3. Click on the Rotate tool in the Toolbox. Click the crosshair cursor on the center of the spiral to set the Origin Point.
4. Drag on the spiral's end to rotate it. As long as the mouse button is held down, the object will freely rotate. When satisfied with the rotation, let go of the mouse button.
5. Select the spiral object.
6. Click on the Rotate tool in the Toolbox.
7. Hold the Option (Macintosh) or Alt (Windows) key and click the crosshair cursor an inch to the right of the spiral to set the Origin Point.

   The **Rotate** dialog box will appear.

8. Type "45" in the **Angle** box. Click **OK**.

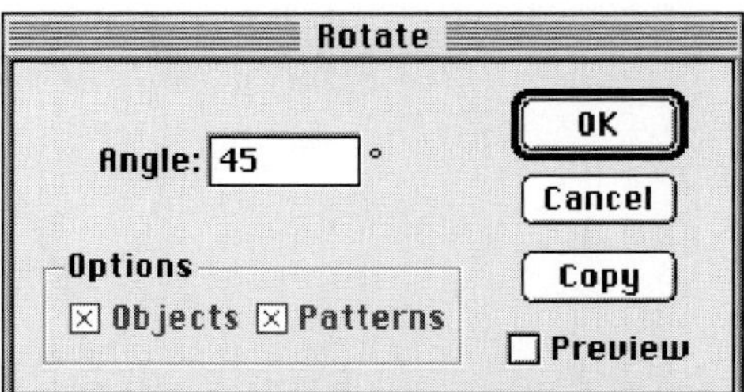

9. Observe how the spiral was rotated.
10. **Close** the document without saving.

During our discussion of the Document Setup dialog, we mentioned that one of the things controlled from there was the ability to automatically apply transformations to objects containing patterns. If you use a pattern and make multiple transformations, it will create a very complex document that you might have trouble printing.

The Shear Tool

The Shear tool is used for "skewing" your artwork. Skewing is the angular stretching or slanting of objects. It can add dimensional depth to your art.

Shearing can be performed two ways:

- Manually
- Dialog Box

Page layout programs provide a method of shearing artwork after it's been imported, but if you want to shear something, do it here in Illustrator. Shearing in a page layout program leads to inefficient output.

Manual Shearing

To Shear manually, the object is selected, then the Shear tool clicked in the Toolbox. Without holding a key on the keyboard, the crosshair cursor is clicked near the object to set the origin point. The mouse is then used to drag the object to skew the object.

Manual shearing can be quite difficult if the Origin of Transformation is clicked in an area that does not lend itself to the shearing angle desired. The best places to click are near the four corners of the invisible Bounding Box of an object. In this example, the Origin of Transformation was clicked near the upper right corner of the object.

The Shearing tool is very sensitive, and when you pull on an object with the selection tool active, you can easily stretch it to the ends of the known universe. If you do, simply Undo the stretch and start again. It doesn't take a lot of mouse movement.

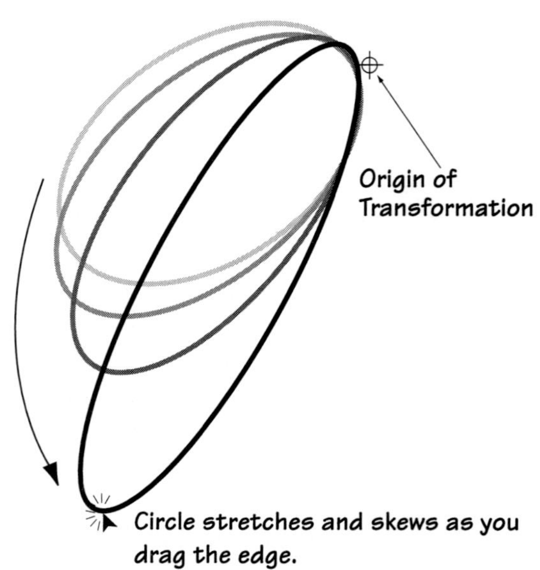

Using the Shear Dialog Box

The **Shear** dialog box allows precise angles to be applied to an object, either horizontally or vertically.

After selecting the object, the dialog box can be accessed two ways:

- Selecting the Shear tool, then clicking an Origin of Transformation point while holding the Option (Macintosh) or Alt (Windows) key.
- By double-clicking the Shear tool in the Toolbox.

Slanted type isn't normally as balanced as regular italics, but it can create an unusual look for special-use type, like headlines, sales announcements, and similar projects.

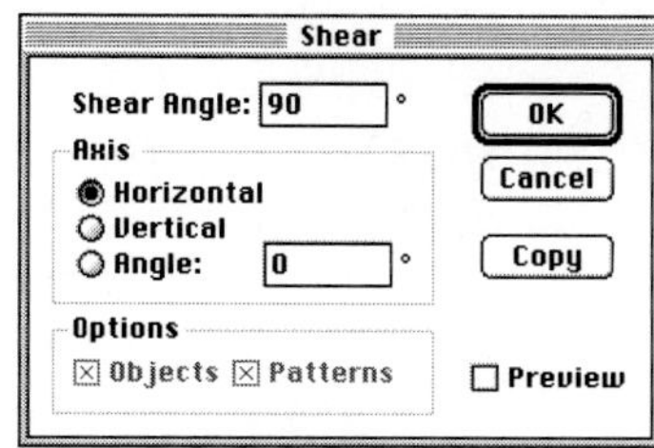

Here are some examples of Shearing with the dialog box.

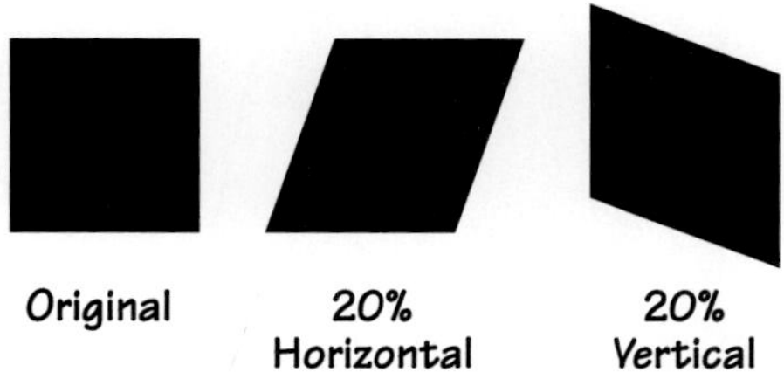

Text also can be modified using the **Shear** dialog box.

Photos can be Sheared for creative uses.

Fitting Objects with Shearing

1. **Open** the document **Banana Boat Shear.AI** that contains a table tent and the Banana Boat logo.

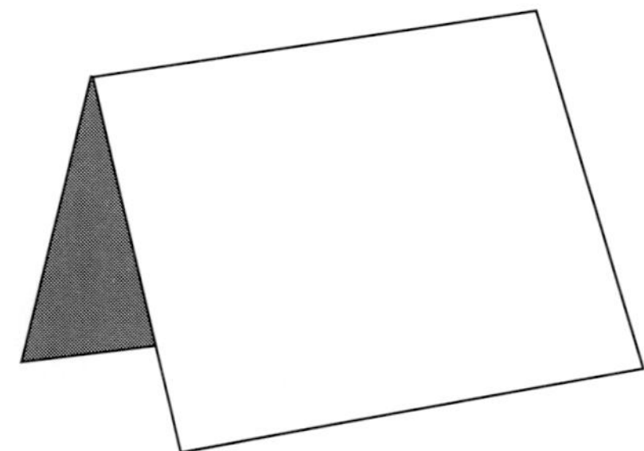

2. Manually Shear the logo to fit the angled face of the table tent.

3. Move the logo onto the table tent. Click the Origin Point on the left side of the logo, then drag on the right side to fit.

   You may need to Rotate the logo as well for more precise alignment.

4. **Close** the document without saving.

You might look into the **Free-Distort** option to see another way to accomplish the correct placement of the logo onto the table card.

The Reflect Tool

The Reflect tool flip-flops a selected object either up and down, sideways, or at a specified angle. To access the **Reflect** dialog box, you can either double-click on the Reflect tool in the Toolbox, or, after selecting the Reflect tool, click on the page while holding down the Option (Macintosh) or Alt (Windows) key.

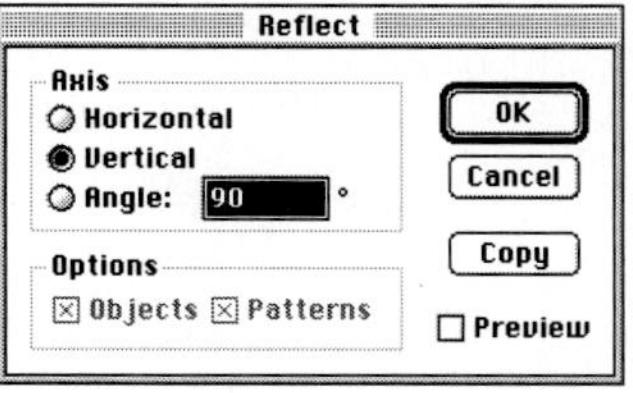

A great many designs utilize reflecting. As is the case with the wine glass we use here, any object that's symmetrical is a candidate for this technique, because you can draw one-half of the item and mirror it to complete the design. Shadows are another example of reflections.

Setting the Origin of Transformation

When you hold the Option (Macintosh) or Alt (Windows) key, then click the cursor on the page, you are setting the Origin of Transformation that determines the axis across which the object will reflect. The rule is to click the cursor where you want the axis to be. You designate vertical, horizontal, or angled reflection in the dialog box.

Here are some examples of vertical and horizontal reflecting.

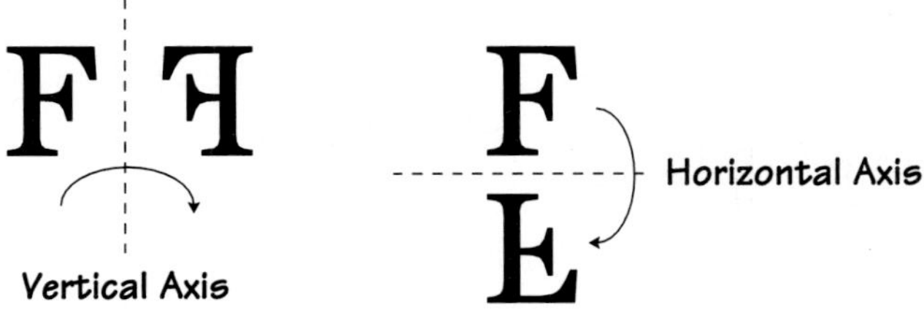

A practical use of reflecting is to create a wine glass. Half of the glass is drawn, reflected vertically with **Copy**, and finally **Joined**.

Using the Reflecting Dialog Box

1. Create a **New** document. Draw a 1" square (a.).
2. Use the Delete-anchor point tool to delete the lower right anchor point to make a triangle. Select the triangle.
3. Select the Reflect tool, then, while holding down the Option (Macintosh) or Alt (Windows) key, click the crosshair cursor off to the right of the triangle.
4. In the dialog box, choose **Vertical** axis, then click **Copy** (b.).

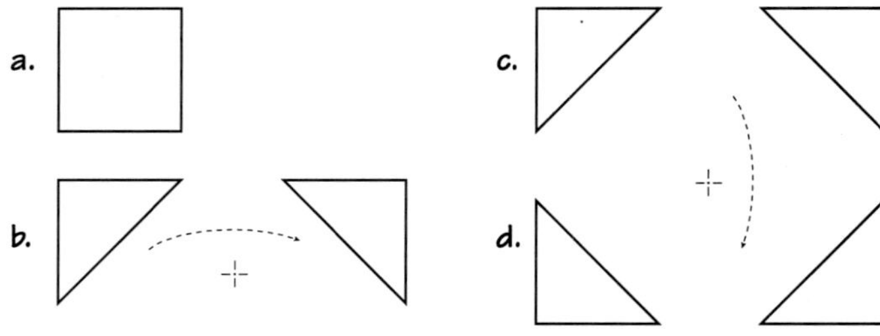

If you want to know the percentage an object has been manually transformed, after it is done, double-click on the tool in the Toolbox. The percentages of the last operation will be displayed in the dialog box.

5. Select the two triangles.
6. Click the Reflect tool, then, while holding down the Option (Macintosh) or Alt (Windows) key, click the crosshair cursor below the two triangles (c.).
7. In the dialog box, choose **Horizontal** axis, then click **Copy** (d.). You've now successfully reflected the object both vertically and horizontally.

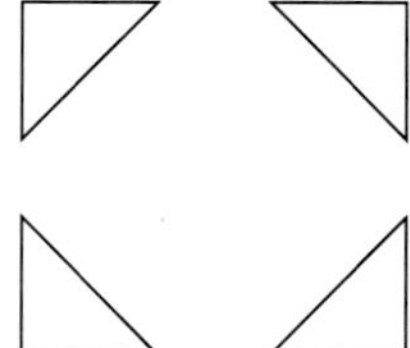

8. **Close** the document without saving.

The Scale Tool

You may need to enlarge or reduce objects to a desired size or proportion. Illustrator's Scale tool achieves this, but there's more to this feature than just making an object larger or smaller.

There are two ways to use the Scale tool:

- Manually — This allows you to size the object "by eye" according to how it looks as you scale with the cursor. Although very intuitive, the manual approach is not as precise as the dialog box method.

Remember that you can apply a series of transformations to achieve your end goal. Whenever you have to develop a drawing, it's a good idea to think about what you have to do, and in what order, before you start clicking the mouse.

- Dialog Box — To access the **Scale** dialog box, you can either double-click on the Scale tool in the Toolbox, or, after selecting the Scale tool, click on the page while holding down the Option (Macintosh) or Alt (Windows) key. The **Scale** dialog box appears.

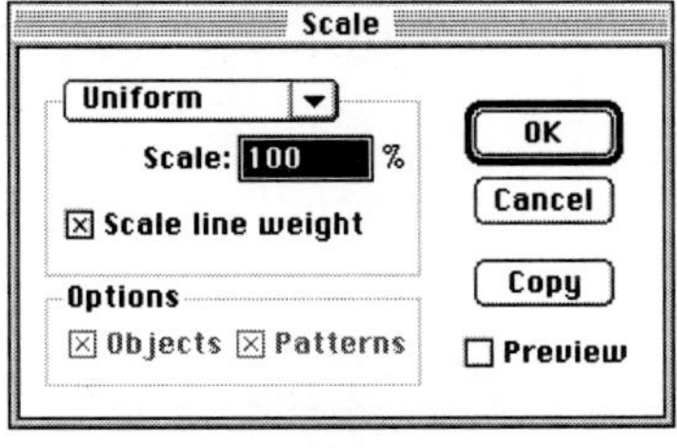

Scaling Basics

When the dialog box method is used, the object is sized based on just one of two styles: **Uniform** or **Non-uniform**. **Uniform** keeps vertical and horizontal dimensions proportional. **Non-uniform** separates horizontal from vertical and allows each to be sized individually.

Manual Scaling

When scaling by hand, the Scale tool cursor turns into a crosshair which is used to click the Origin Point for the scaling (a.).

Once the Origin Point is clicked, the cursor turns into an arrow. Use the arrowhead to drag the object (b.). If the Shift key is held down while dragging, the object will scale proportionally, constrained horizontally/vertically.

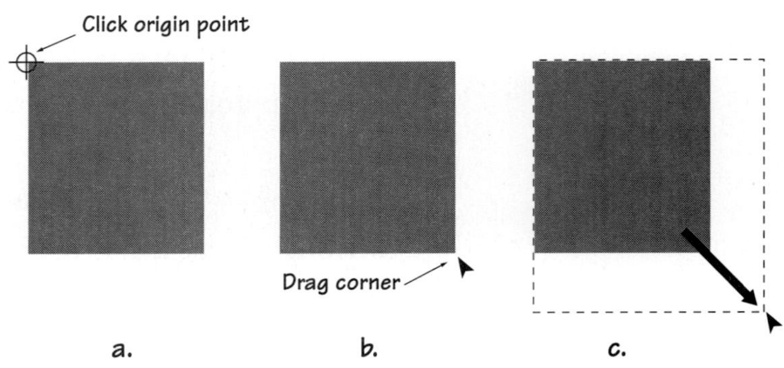

Manually Fitting Type to an Object

1. **Open** the document **Scale Type.AI** from the Student Files folder.

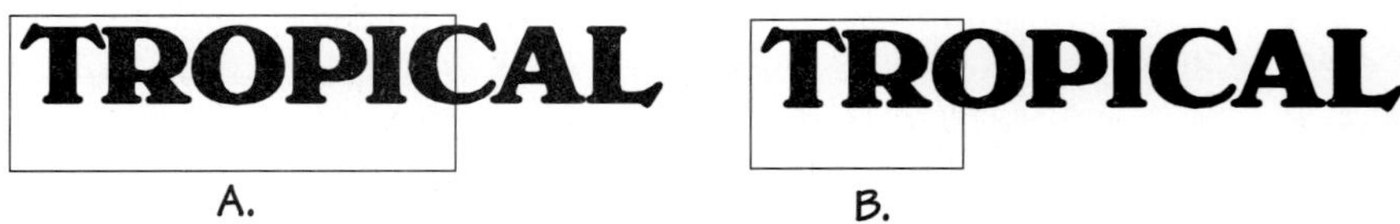

2. Select the type outlines in A. Click on the Scale tool in the Toolbox.

3. Click an Origin Point at the upper left corner of the "T." Click the cursor on the lower right part of the "L" to drag the type to fit the rectangle.

4. Do the same with the type in B. The results should look like this.

A. B.

5. **Close** the document without saving.

Scaling Objects into a Horizon

1. **Open** the document **Scaling Tree.AI.** Select the tree, then click on the Scale tool. Holding down the Option (Macintosh) or Alt (Windows) key, click the crosshair cursor on the point designated in the file, as shown here.

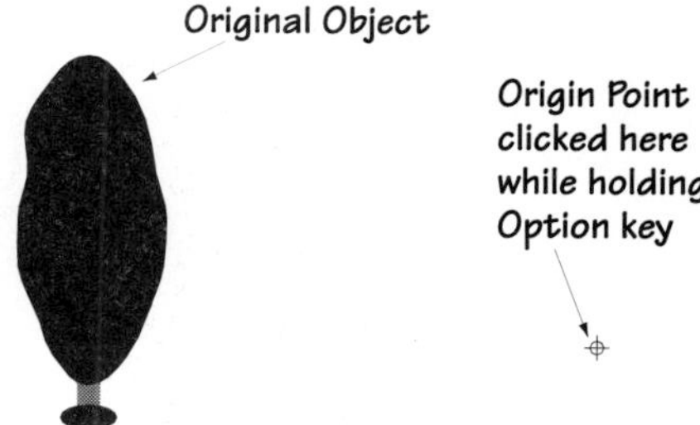

2. In the **Scale** dialog box, type "70" for **Uniform**. Click **Copy**.

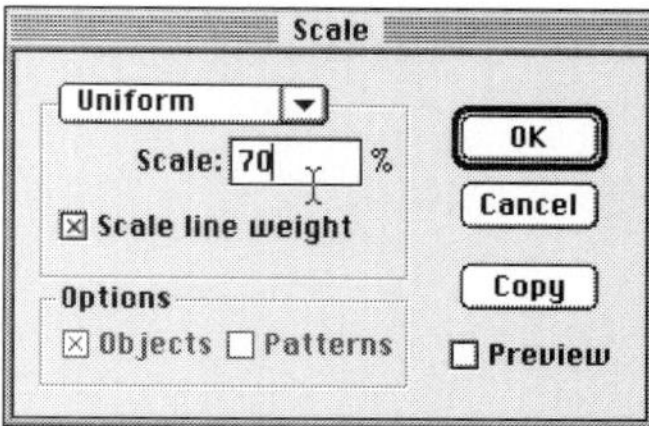

3. Press Command-D or Control-D (Windows) to Transform Again, five times. Observe how the duplicates move toward the Origin Point as they scale.

4. **Close** the file without saving.

Scaling objects to or from a "horizon" can be used to illustrate a vanishing point. Sequence perspectives include railroad tracks, the line in the middle of the road vanishing into the distance, telephone poles, or trees.

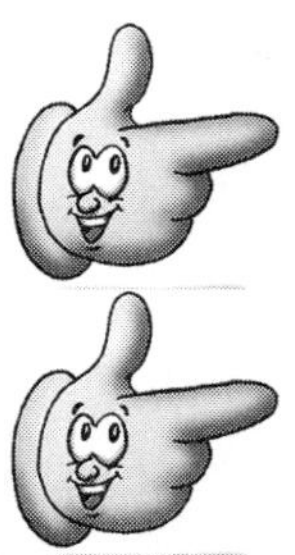

Project E: Tropical Suites Logo

Project F: Heart Notes

Notes:

CHAPTER 11

TRANSFORMATION TECHNIQUES

CHAPTER OBJECTIVE:

To build on the advanced concepts discussed in Chapter 10, and to teach methods of applying multiple transformations in single workflows, allowing the construction of common and complex design elements. In Chapter 11, you will:

- Learn to use Command-D (on the Macintosh) and Control-D (on Windows systems) to repeat transformations; a powerful and important method of creating commonly required design components.
- Understand how to use dialog boxes and manual entry before applying multiple transformations.
- Learn to create designs using transform again.
- Learn to apply multiple transformations to groups of objects, either randomly or in a structured manner.
- Understand how to avoid common problems that can result from the application of multiple transformations.

PROJECTS TO BE COMPLETED:

- HoneyDo Hair Salon Logo
- HoneyDo Free Hairstyle Ad
- Banana Boat Logo
- Fleet's In! T-Shirt Design
- Tropical Suites Logo
- Heart Notes
- **Banana Border**
- Champagne Brunch Table Tent
- Tropical Postcard
- Last Mango Menu Cover
- Full Page Grocery Ad
- Perspective Graph
- Java Jungle Goodies Ad

Transformation Techniques

Design often requires the symmetrical repetition of objects, or the placement of objects in a specific pattern relative to each other. A clockface is a perfect example: the numbers must be positioned at specific points on the circle of the face. They might all face the same direction, or their baselines might be aligned to the center of the watch, but they're all in the same place on the circle. Another example of repeating elements — this time with a reduction in size occurring at the same time — is a railroad track. There are many examples in nature, architecture, and all aspects of art and design.

The Transform Again function can be used for only one action at a time. You can't repeat a series of actions. Example: If you resize an object, rotate it, then duplicate it, Transform Again would repeat the last action performed, in this case, the duplication.

With the new feature, Transform Each, you can perform Scaling, Move, and Rotating all at one time, then use Transform Again to repeat the transformations.

Working with Transform Again

Often, the designs you create have objects that duplicate themselves horizontally, vertically, or at an angle. It would be tedious to repeat the process of accessing menus and dialog boxes to repeat the same action over and over. **Transform Again** repeats the last transformation.

The decorative border below (c.) was created by repeating a diamond shape. The first diamond was drawn by creating a square and rotating it 45° (a.).

It was then duplicated by Option (Macintosh) or Alt (Windows) dragging (b.).

Transform Again, Command-D (Macintosh) or Control-D(Windows), was then pressed 10 times to create the border (c.).

Using Dialog Boxes Before Transforming Again

When any dialog boxes or palettes are used to create an action that will be repeated, it is important to know how the repeating affects the objects.

The increments typed in the dialog box will be repeated on the duplicates each time **Transform Again** is accessed. This is important to keep in mind when planning special effects with transformation tools.

This is where you can begin to see how multiple transformations can reduce the time it takes you to execute a drawing.

The square was scaled using the **Scale** dialog box. The following values were given: **Horizontal** 110%, **Vertical** 90%, then **Copy.** The second square was the result. **Transform Again** was then selected. The next generation was resized according to the dialog box. Each generation of the object had 110% Horizontal, 90% Vertical values applied to it, resulting in a thinner and wider rectangle with each repeated transformation.

Manually Repeating Transformations

Transformations done manually on an object can also yield special effects.

Example: Here's a tree shown in various stages of transformation. It was sheared manually, then the **Transform Again** command was executed five times. The tree becomes more distorted with each transformation.

Duplicating Objects with Transform Again

If the Option (Macintosh) or Alt (Windows) key is pressed while doing the action, the object will duplicate with the transformation. **Transform Again** will continue to duplicate the object and apply the same transformation.

Using **Transform Again,** with this duplication addition, creates designs that would otherwise be time-consuming when working out distances and positions.

Creating a Design with Transform Again

1. Create a **New** document.
2. Draw a 2-1/2" diameter circle. Press Command-5 (Macintosh) or Control-5 (Windows) to turn the circle into a guide.
3. Draw a 0.25" smaller circle and position it at the top of the circle guide. Paint the circle **Fill** = 100% Black, **Stroke** = None.
4. With the small circle selected, access the Rotate tool. Hold the Option (Macintosh) or Alt (Windows) key and click the crosshair cursor on the exact center of the circle guide (a.).
5. In the dialog box, type "22.5," which is 1/15th of 360°. Click **Copy**. The circle will duplicate 22.5° to the left (b.).
6. Press Command-D (Macintosh) or Control-D (Windows) to **Transform Again** 14 times to complete the circumference of the circle guide (c.).

A little geometry is helpful here. Whenever you have to distribute objects around the 360° of a circle, simply divide 360 by the number of objects you require. For 36 objects, you would copy each at 10°. Can you think of how you would draw 60 evenly distributed tic marks — for example, the second-marks on a watch face?

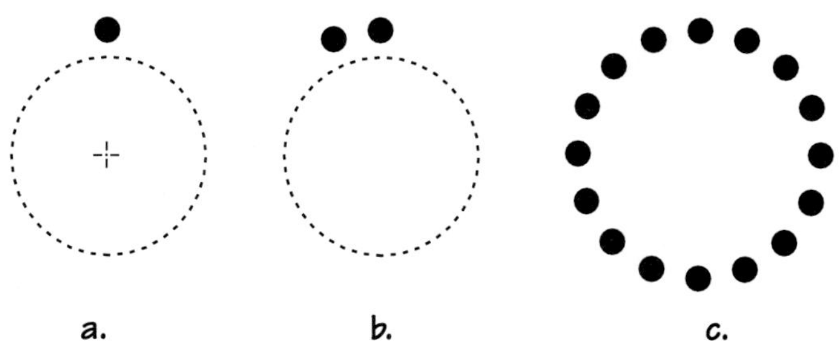

7. **Close** the document without Saving.

Working with Transform Each

The use of transformations as a development technique is a very powerful skill. However, it often requires a little preplanning. We find it helps to draw your concept on a piece of paper and mentally calculate approximate mutations, such as reductions, rotations, skews, etc. If you do this, your transformations will usually be right the very first time.

Transform Each is a composite function that allows you to **Scale**, **Move,** and **Rotate** objects — all from one dialog box.

This is very handy and convenient to use because it performs all these transformations at one time on either a single object or several.

Also, it contains a **Random** option that will perform random effects of Scaling, Moving, and Rotating on selected objects.

The **Transform Each** selection is found in the **Object->Transform** menu.

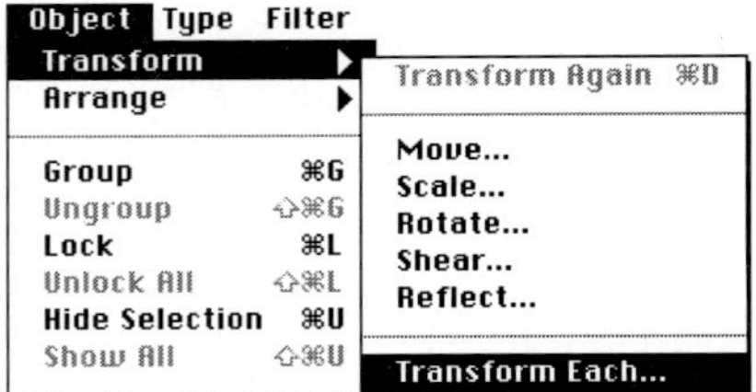

When you select it, you will see this dialog box.

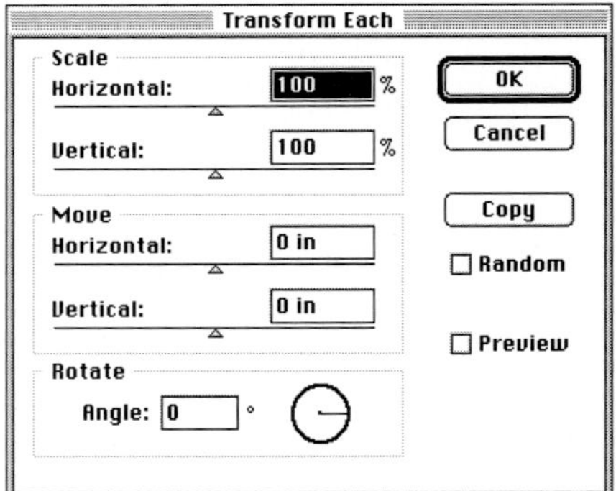

The creativity is in using all three functions on objects at one time. On the next page are some examples of how **Transform Each** can be used on single objects and multiple objects.

The **Random** transformations are designed to work with multiple objects. It's not often that you need to randomly change one object.

Transform Each Examples

A. This is an example of how **Transform Each** can be used on a single object. Then, using **Transform Again**, a unique design can be made.

B. This is a group of four objects that were are all selected, then **Transform Each** applied.

C. The **Random** effect was used on this same group of squares. The **Random** function applies miscellaneous numbers to the **Scale**, **Move,** and **Rotate** items in the dialog box.

D. The **Random** effect was again used on this group of circles.

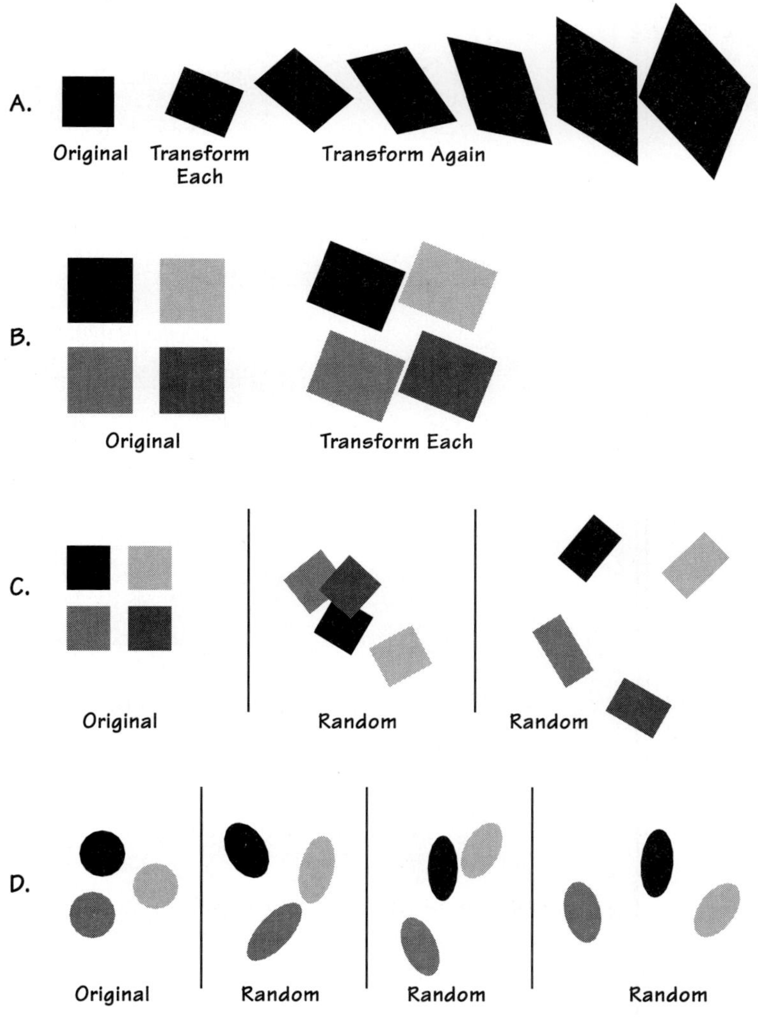

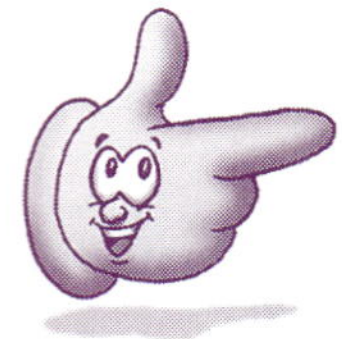

Using Transform Each

1. Create a **New** document. Draw four squares in offset order. **Edit->Select All.**

Transform Each is a very good feature for creating random backgrounds and patterns.

2. Go to the **Object->Transform->Transform Each** dialog box. Type in these settings.

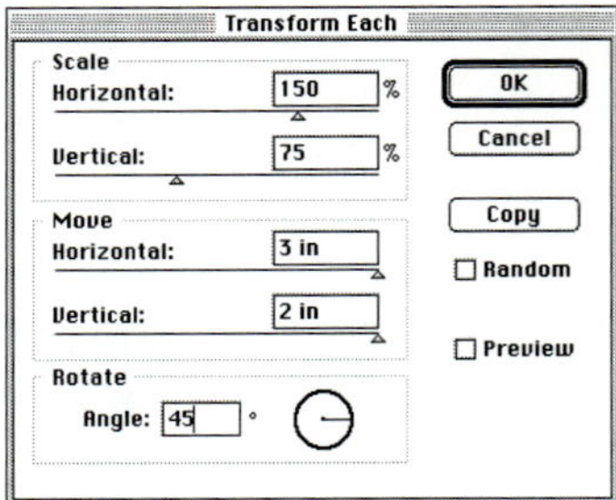

3. Click **Preview** in this palette to see the effect on the objects. Now, type in these settings.

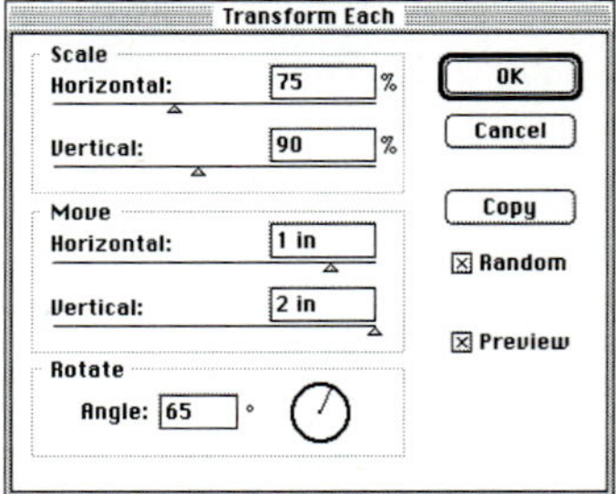

4. Click the **Random** and **Preview** buttons to see the random effects. Click the **Preview** button on/off each time for the random effect to change.

5. Click **OK** to apply the settings to the objects.

6. **Close** the file without saving.

Problem Transformations

Since in most cases you're looking at your artwork either in **Fit To Window** or zoomed into some detail, there are times when transformation methods can create stray, unwanted objects that, unfortunately, are not visible. There are other times when clicking the Pen tool too quickly will create stray points.

Common Problem Items

Stray points

Paths and objects, if you don't keep track of them, are prone to get moved out of view to the edges of the Artboard. If they are not deleted, they become a part of an Illustrator EPS file, making it larger than it should be. When this EPS file is placed into other programs, the edges of the file are determined by all the objects — both on the Artboard as well as in the "live" area.

Single points can be left behind when you create paths. Single-clicking the Pen tool will also create stray points. These points are invisible to the eye in both Artwork and Preview modes, yet their presence in the document will make the file size much larger.

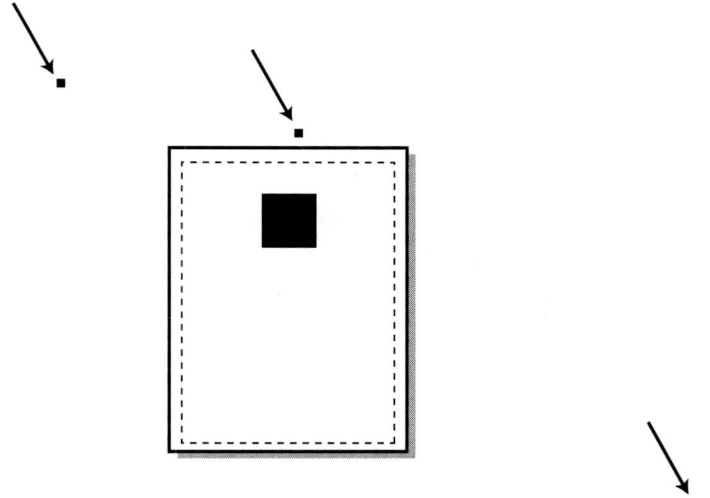

In the above sample, when the document with the square was **Saved As** an **Illustrator EPS**, with no stray points, it had a file size of 136K. When the stray points were added and saved along with the square, the file size zoomed up to 247K.

And that's not the worst problem: if you placed this object into a page layout program, you would wind up with your artwork, which you created to fit the space you needed perfectly, in only a small region of the space. The file size is determined by a rectangle containing *all* the objects on the page, not just the ones you drew on purpose.

Released Ruler Guides

Released Ruler Guides are caused by accidentally (or intentionally) releasing guides to become paths again. When released, they become paths with two endpoints. This can cause unseen problems.

These Released Ruler Guides are invisible to the eye, unless selected. They are easiest to locate using Command-A (Macintosh) or Ctrl-A (Windows) to **Select All**. The released guides will be selected along with all other objects on the drawing.

Stray points and released guides fall into the troubleshooting category. They are opportunities to introduce problems into your drawings that will cause workflow delays later down the line — as when the file is placed into a page layout program or an attempt is made to print the file. By being aware of these problems you can attempt to avoid them completely. At the very least, you should carefully check all artwork when it's done and ready to be used elsewhere or output.

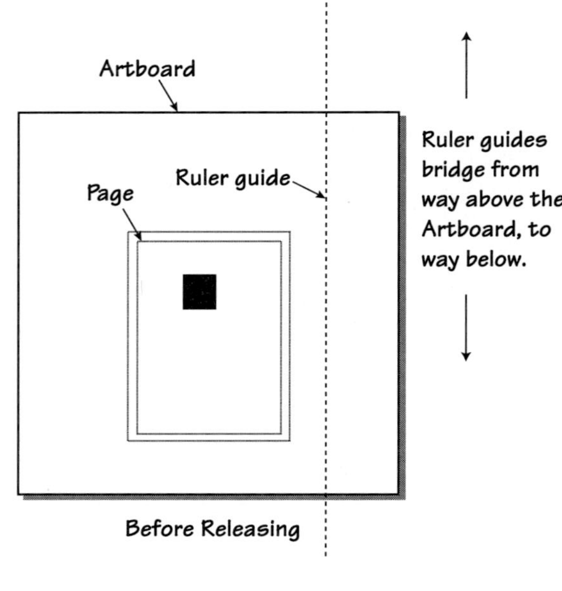

Before Releasing

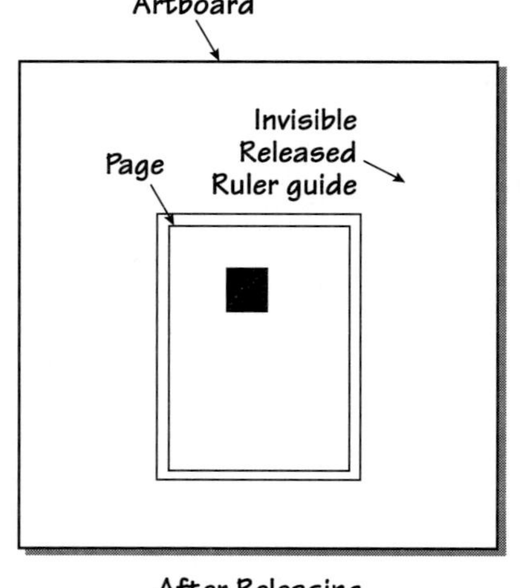

After Releasing

It's usually better to lock guides most of the time to avoid accidentally moving them. Since guides themselves are non-printing, releasing them creates a stroke with no color or width.

The following method will delete both the Stray Points and Released Guides.

Locating and Deleting Stray Objects

1. Create a **New** document.
2. Draw a 2" square and move it to the center of the page.
3. With the Pen tool, click once. Click on the Selection tool in the Toolbox to deselect. Continue to use the Pen tool to single-click stray points, then deselect. Create five stray anchor points.
4. Select the 2" square and **Object->Lock** it.
5. **Edit-Select All** to select the stray elements on the page.
6. Press Delete to remove the selected stray points or released guides.
7. **Object->Unlock** to unlock the square.
8. **Close** the file without saving.

Project G: Banana Border

Notes:

CHAPTER 12

MASKING AND COMPOUNDING PATHS

CHAPTER OBJECTIVE:

To teach you about the behavior of Masks and Compound paths, two very important and advanced functions of Illustrator; to teach the role of masking and compounding in the development of complex illustrations. Through the exercises and projects supplied in Chapter 12, you will:

- Learn what a mask is, and how it affects underlying graphic elements.
- Learn to create simple and stroked masks from elements that you create or import into your drawings.
- Learn to create masks using type elements that have been converted into outlines — a very common practice in commercial art and design.
- Learn to use masks as cookie cutters — isolating photographic images and placing them into containers of any imaginable shape.
- Learn how to create and manage compounded elements — elements that essentially have holes cut into their surface.
- Practice using several Pen tool options to modify existing masks and compounds without the need to rebuild them from scratch.

PROJECTS TO BE COMPLETED:

- HoneyDo Hair Salon Logo
- HoneyDo Free Hairstyle Ad
- Banana Boat Logo
- Fleet's In! T-Shirt Design
- Tropical Suites Logo
- Heart Notes
- Banana Border
- **Champagne Brunch Table Tent**
- Tropical Postcard
- Last Mango Menu Cover
- Full Page Grocery Ad
- Perspective Graph
- Java Jungle Goodies Ad

Masking & Compounding Paths

It won't be long before a job requirement causes you to need to isolate or silhouette a specific portion of an image. In Illustrator, it's done with something called *masks*. Masks allow you to use a shape to cover areas of an object while leaving others visible. Compounding refers to a method whereby you can actually cut a hole in an object, allowing whatever is positioned behind it to show through. A perfect example of this is the "counter" or white circle inside the letter "O." If you drew a black circle and simply put a white circle on top, you wouldn't be able to see through the letter — to the background, for example.

Masking

It is highly advised that all the objects belonging to a Mask be selected, then Grouped. These individual objects, without Grouping, can be accidentally selected and transformed, ruining the desired effects of the Mask.

The term "mask" refers to an object resting on top of other objects, allowing parts of the objects underneath to show through the contours of the masking shape. This example shows the sequence of creating a Mask.

a. The stripes and the circle are drawn separately.

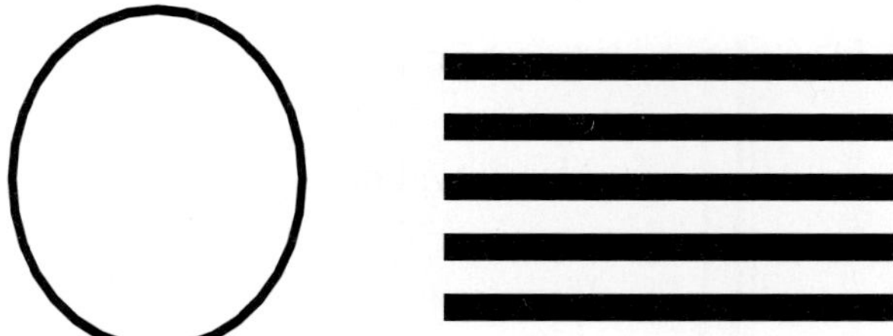

b. The circle, which will be the Masking object, is positioned in front of the stripes. The circle and the stripes are then selected.

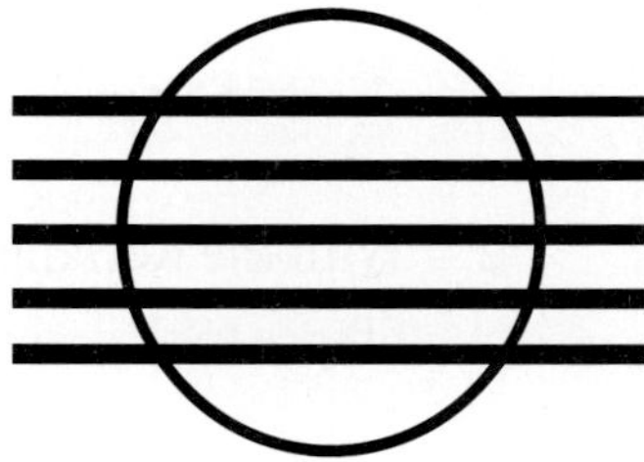

c. **Object->Masks->Make** is then chosen. The circle, which is the frontmost object, is then converted into a Mask so that the stripes show through its interior. Notice how the black Stroke of the circle was removed by the Masking process.

The parts of each stripe that extend beyond the edge of the circle are still present, but they disappear from view and won't print. The only way to see the stripes is in **Artwork** mode.

Remember, the Masking object must be in front of all objects that are part of the Mask operation. Check this if a Mask is attempted, but fails.

Stroking a Masking Object

If, for example, the Masking object is a square with a 2 pt. Black stroke, after **Object->Masks–>Make** is applied, the square will be stripped of any paint style it possessed before the Masking.

Also, it will not hold any paint style applied to it after the fact.

If you want to apply a stroke to a Masking object, you must copy it, then **Paste In Front** the duplicate, applying the stroke to it.

Making a Mask

1. Create a **New** document.

2. With the Rectangle tool, draw an approximate 2" square. Also, with the Ellipse tool, draw some small circles, as shown here.

   Paint the square: **Fill** = None, **Stroke** = 2 pt. Black.
   Paint the circles: **Fill** = 50% Black; **Stroke** = None.

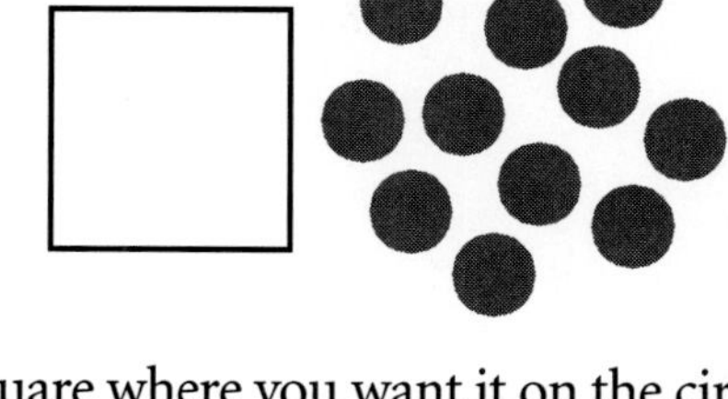

3. Position the square where you want it on the circles. With the square selected, go to **Object->Arrange->Bring To Front.** This is to ensure that the masking square is in front of all the circles.

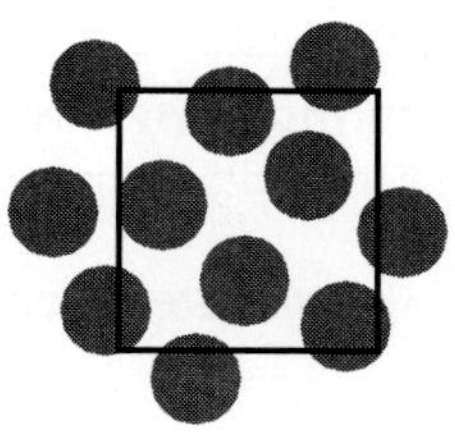

Using masks can result in difficult-to-print files. If you're having a problem outputting a file, you might have to redesign the element to remove the mask. This doesn't happen much, but complex masks have been known to cause problems at times.

4. Select the square and all the circles.

5. Go to the **Object->Masks->Make**.

6. The circles will show only through the square, which is the Mask.

Observe that Masking eliminates any paint attributes of the Masking object.

Now, you will learn to apply a stroke to the square.

7. Click on the masking square with the Selection tool.

8. Choose **Copy** from the **Edit** menu. With the square still selected, choose **Edit->Paste In Front.**

9. Paint the pasted object: **Fill** = None, **Stroke** = 2 pt. Black.

10. **Close** the document without saving.

Masking Images with Type

1. Create a **New** document.

2. Type the letters "UTA."

3. Highlight the type and access the **Type->Character** palette. Apply these settings: **Font** = ATC Cozumel, **Size** = 125 pt., **Leading** = Auto, **Tracking** = -40, **Horizontal scale** =100%.

4. Go to the **Type** menu and choose **Create Outlines.** Go to **Object->Group** to group the outlines. With the group selected, choose **Object->Compound Paths->Make.** The compounding will allow the letters to be Masked later.

When Masking one item such as the photo here into several objects such as these letters, the Masking objects must be Compounded. Experiment with this, on your own.

5. From **File->Place,** go to the **SF-ADV Illustrator** folder and Place **Sailboat Scene.TIF.** Go to **Object->Arrange->Send to Back.**

6. With the photo selected, **Edit->Copy**, then go to **Edit->Paste In Back.** Go to **Object->Hide** to hide the duplicate. It will be used later.

7. Move the "UTA" outlines into position, centered on the top half of the photo. Go to **Edit->Copy**, then **Edit->Paste in Back**. This will later be the black shadow. **Object->Hide** this duplicate.

8. With the Type tool, click on the image and type the words "CARIBBEAN ISLAND." Highlight the text. Access the **Type->Character** palette and apply these settings: **Font** = ATC Margarita Bold, **Size** = 36 pt., **Leading** = Auto, **Tracking** = -20, **Horizontal scale** = 90%.

CARIBBEAN ISLAND

Paint this text with: **Fill** = White, **Stroke** = None.

9. Select this text object with the Selection tool. **Edit->Copy** the text block, then **Edit->Paste In Back** the copy behind this original. Press the Right arrow key two times; the Down arrow key two times. Paint the selected duplicate: **Fill** = Black, **Stroke** = 1 pt. Black.

   Select both the CARIBBEAN ISLAND original and its duplicate. Go to **Object->Group.** Move the group into position, centered at the bottom of the photo.

Masking is particularly useful when you're working with scanned images and other photographic elements. This exercise is a good example of what we mean. This is another technique that you might try finding in contemporary design and reproducing for practice.

10. Select the photo and the compounded UTA outlines. Go to the **Object->Masks->Make.** Then, **Object->Group** the two Masked objects.

11. Go to **Object->Show All.** The photo duplicate and the UTA type shadow will appear.

    Select the photo duplicate and choose **Object->Arrange->Send To Back.**

12. Select the UTA black shadow; then **Edit->Cut** it.

13. Click on the Masked UTA object, then go to **Edit->Paste In Back.** Press the Right Arrow key two times and the Down Arrow key two times to offset the shadow behind the letters.

    The finished image should look like this.

14. **Close** the document without saving.

Compounding Objects

Compounding can be used to cut a shape out of an object, allowing you to see through to the background or to other objects that lie behind the original.

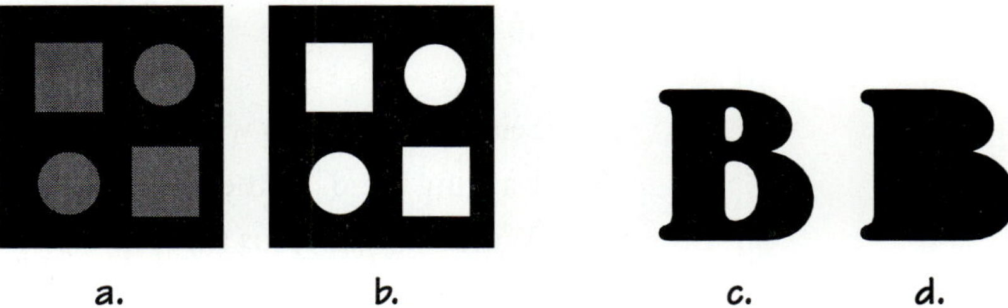

a. The small squares and circles are part of the interior of the large square.

b. When compounded, all interior pieces become "see-thru" (b.). If this were laid on top of another object, the underneath object would be seen through the compounded circles and squares.

c. Type turned into outlines is a good example of compounding, such as the letter "B", with two internal objects.

d. If the compounding is released, the interior objects default to the color of the enclosing object; in this example, Black.

A good example of a compound happens whenever you convert a type object into outlines. Do this with a large capital "O" or an "A" – any character with a "hole" in it (called a *counter* in typographic terms) is converted as a compound.

The "see-thru" effect of compounding is shown in this example:

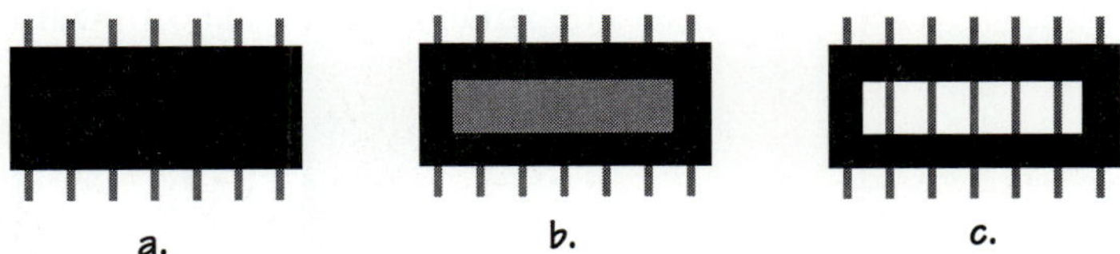

a. A black rectangle is positioned over ruled lines.

b. A smaller rectangle is drawn on top of the black rectangle.

c. The two rectangles are selected, then Compounded, turning the interior object into a hole through which you can see the bars.

Creating a Compound

1. Create a **New** document. Go to **View->Show Rulers** for measuring.

2. With the Pen tool, draw a single segment, 2" in height. Paint the segment: **Fill** = None, **Stroke** = 3 pt., 40% Black (a.)

   Select the segment with the Selection tool. Duplicate the segment by dragging it 1/8" to the right, holding the Option (Macintosh) or Alt (Windows) key, plus the Shift key to constrain the move (b.).

   Once the duplicating drag is done, press Command-D (Macintosh) or Ctrl-D (Windows) four times, to repeat the duplication (c.)

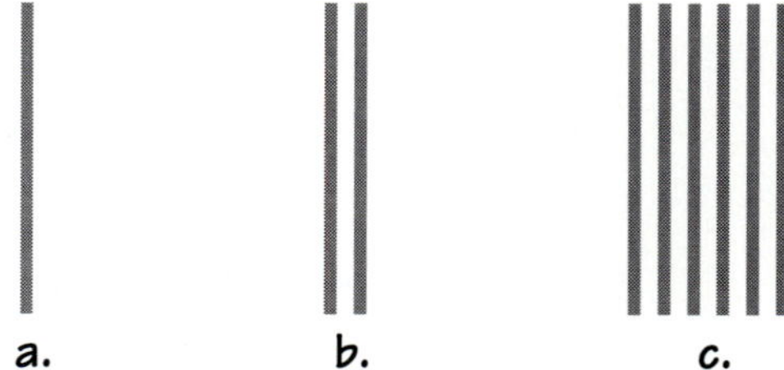

3. With the Rectangle tool, draw a black square and position it on top of the ruled lines (d.). **Object->Lock** the ruled lines.

4. With the Ellipse tool, draw three small circles on top of the square (e.).

5. Select the square and circles. Go to **Object->Compound Paths->Make.** The small circles will compound, and become "see-thru"(f.).

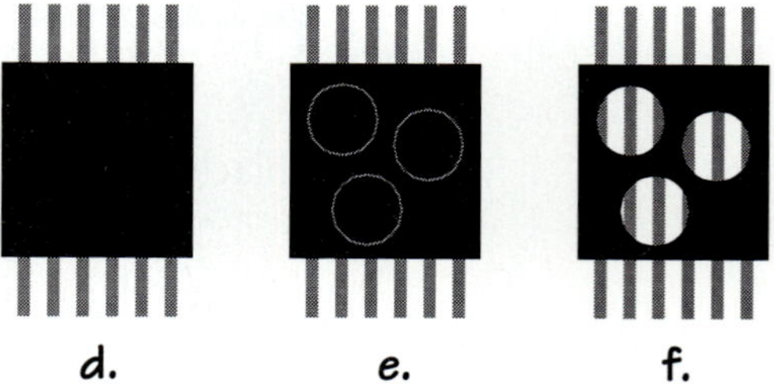

6. **Close** the document without saving.

There are several reasons that compounds don't work the way you expect them to. The first is because the stacking order of the objects was incorrect before you applied the compound. The second is because there are objects in the selection that you didn't see or count on. The third is because there are too many objects selected.

Troubleshooting the Compounding Mishaps

Sometimes compounding multiple objects does not create the "see-thru" effect on all the internal objects. To correct this, you will want to use the Direct Selection tool to select the object that is in question. Then, access the **Attributes** window found in the **Window** menu.

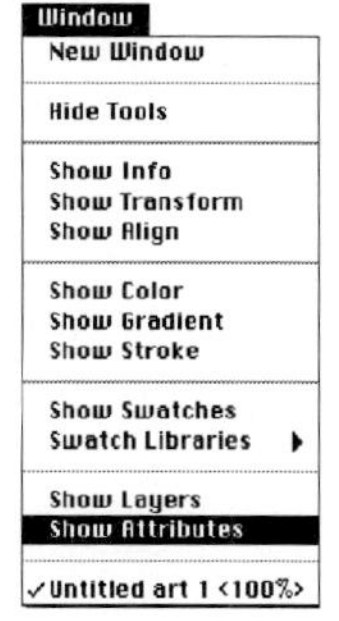

Reverse Path Direction

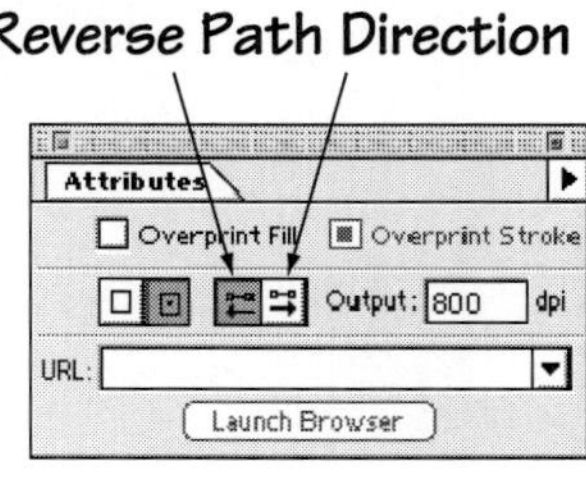

Reverse Path Direction are the two direction boxes (shown above) to be clicked. If one is already selected, select the other. It will reverse the path direction and make the internal object "see-thru."

Fixing a Compounded Path Flaw

1. From the **SF-ADV Illustrator** folder, **File->Open** the Student File **Compounding Fix-it.AI.**

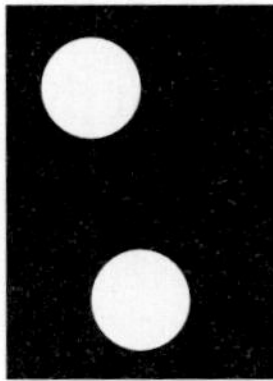

The objects were compounded, but one circle failed to compound.

2. Click the middle circle with the Direct Selection tool to isolate it.

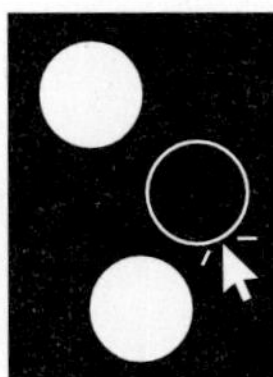

Try modifying a compounded object using the Direct Selection tool. It's a cool thing to see if there are objects behind the compound. It's also useful if you want to expose more (or hide more) of an object that's showing through a compound.

3. Go to **Window->Show Attributes**. Of the two Reverse Path Direction boxes, click the box that is not selected.

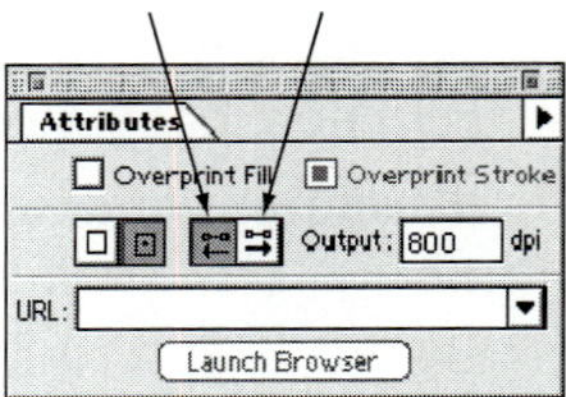

4. The circle will then be visible and "see-thru."

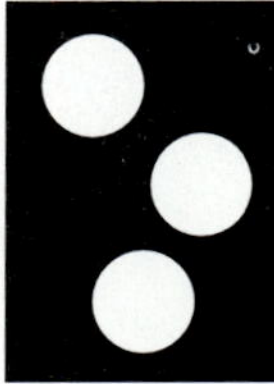

5. **Close** the file without saving.

Using Compounding as a Mask

1. Create a **New** document. From the **SF-ADV Illustrator** folder, **File->Place** the photo **Girl in Hat.TIF.**

2. Draw a 4" square and a 2" circle. Center the circle on top of the square. Paint them both: **Fill** = White, **Stroke** = None.
   Select both objects and **Compound** them.

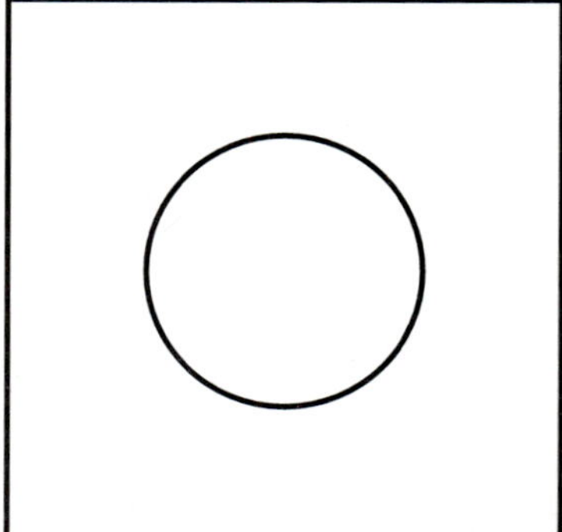

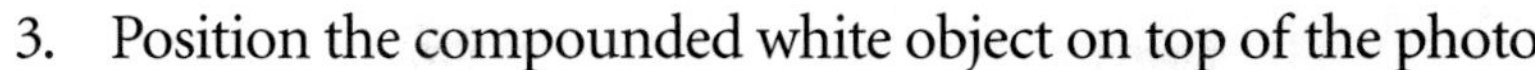

3. Position the compounded white object on top of the photo.

4. The photo will show only through the compounded, "see-thru" interior. This another way of masking objects you want to isolate.

5. **Close** the file without saving.

Project H: Champagne Brunch Table Tent

Notes:

Chapter 13

Working with Images

Chapter Objective:

To build on your knowledge of working with imported vector and bitmapped images; to teach you how to better manage high-resolution, continuous-tone images within your designs and layouts. As you work through the exercises and projects contained in Chapter 13, you will:

- Work more with EPS images, and learn the differences between importing vector artwork (like that drawn with Illustrator or other drawing applications) and scanned, or continuous tone (contone) images.
- Learn more about how Illustrator establishes links to images that you've imported into your drawing.
- Learn to embed imported artwork or scanned images into your drawings and layouts; learn to manage linked graphics to avoid workflow-related problems.
- Understand how artwork and preview modes can be used to identify linked or embedded raster images.
- Learn about Illustrator's powerful Rasterize function, which can convert vector artwork into bitmaps, or change the attributes of existing images.
- Apply these functions in both exercises and project assignments.

Projects to be Completed:

- HoneyDo Hair Salon Logo
- HoneyDo Free Hairstyle Ad
- Banana Boat Logo
- Fleet's In! T-Shirt Design
- Tropical Suites Logo
- Heart Notes
- Banana Border
- Champagne Brunch Table Tent
- **Tropical Postcard**
- Last Mango Menu Cover
- Full Page Grocery Ad
- Perspective Graph
- Java Jungle Goodies Ad

Working with Images

There will be many occasions when you'll need to incorporate graphics that were created with other applications into your projects. Good examples of this are importing scanned images into your drawings. Scanned images are called Raster images, and they're comprised of many thousands of individual pixels. Each pixel contains specific information about its brightness, hue (or actual color), and strength, or saturation (pink vs. red, for instance, or sky blue compared with the deep blue of the ocean). With 8 bits for each color, an RGB image with dimensions of 400 x 600 pixels will have over 5 million bits of data.

At other times, you might purchase commercial "clip art" that was created by other artists, and provided in Illustrator format. There are two categories, or formats, that are important for you to understand: Vector images (like those created with Illustrator), and Raster images, such as scans or Photoshop files. You can place these images using the **Place** command.

Vector EPS Images

Be careful when specifying EPS to be Placed. EPS images can be either Vector EPS (created by Illustrator) or Raster EPS (created by PhotoShop.) Both vector-based (line art) and bitmap (scans or photographic elements) can be saved as EPS files.

Some drawing programs can create a type of Vector file called a Vector EPS. These files work like any vector file insofar as they can be resized without degradation; however, they might not respond to certain filters, and you won't be able to take them apart.

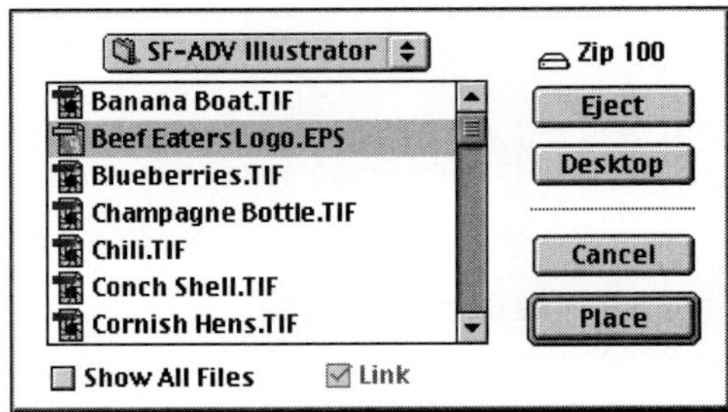

The **Place** dialog box, shown above, has a Link button that is dimmed and inaccessible if an EPS image is clicked on in the files shown. This is because Illustrator automatically links Vector EPS files without giving you the option to choose. Also, placed EPS images cannot be Rasterized. If an EPS file is Placed in the document, do not delete or move the original.

Raster (Bitmapped) Images

The other file format that you can Place into your projects is the bitmapped, or Raster image. You have the option to link Raster images by selecting the **Link** button in the **Place** dialog box. This option is not available when you select a Vector EPS image. Linking an image doesn't increase the file size of your document — Illustrator instead uses a small preview to display the image without actually importing it into your drawing. This is recommended for situations where you're working with large bitmaps and you want to keep the performance high and file sizes small.

If you choose to use this option, you must make sure that you send the placed image along with your drawing if you send it somewhere else for high-resolution output.

If you want to duplicate colors that are in raster photographs or art, the Eyedropper, when clicked on any part of the image, will put the color into the **Color** palette and list the CMYK colors that make up that color.

Linking for all File Formats

Raster images, when selected in the **Place** window, give you an option to **Link** the image when imported. Linking keeps track of the placed image, and gives you pertinent information about the image.

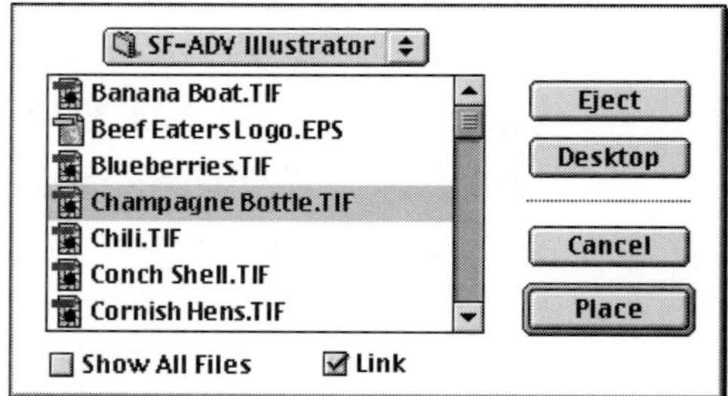

If the Raster image is not linked, Illustrator stores it inside the document. It will then be listed under **File->Document Info** as **Embedded Images**, as opposed to **Linked Images**.

Document Info/Selection Info

In the **File** menu, there is the option **Document Info**, which will be available as long as no object is selected.

If an object is selected, **Document Info** changes to **Selection Info** in the menu.

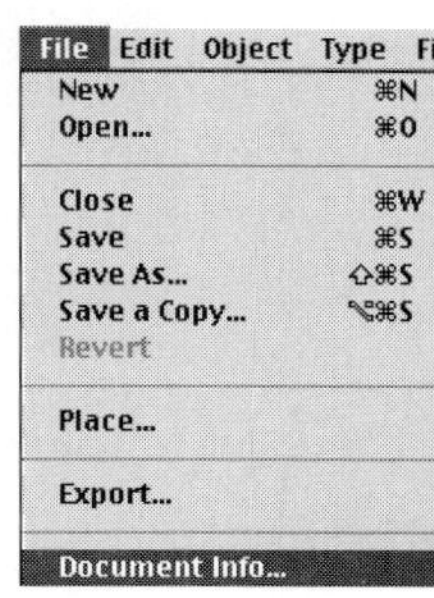

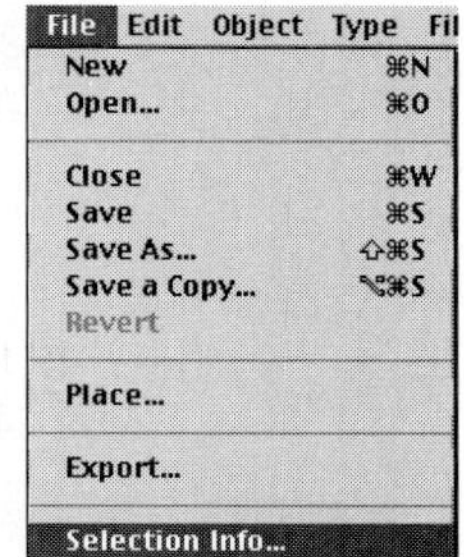

The only difference between the two is that **Document Info** gives information about the entire document. **Selection Info** only gives information about the selected object.

Raster images do not always require **Place** to bring them into a document.
Using **Open** to open the raster image will create a new document with the raster image resident in it. If you want more images, though, they will have to be **Placed**.

Whether **Document Info** or **Selection Info**, the Linked and Embedded images are detailed for their format Type, Bits per Pixel, Channels, Size, Dimensions, and Resolution.

The **Linked Images** window, when selected, also shows pertinent information about where the image was placed from, as well as the file name.

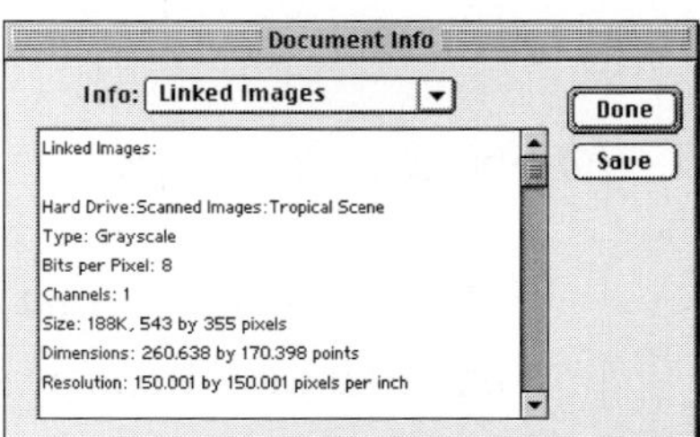

The **Embedded Images** window shows only the make-up of the embedded images, but not the name.

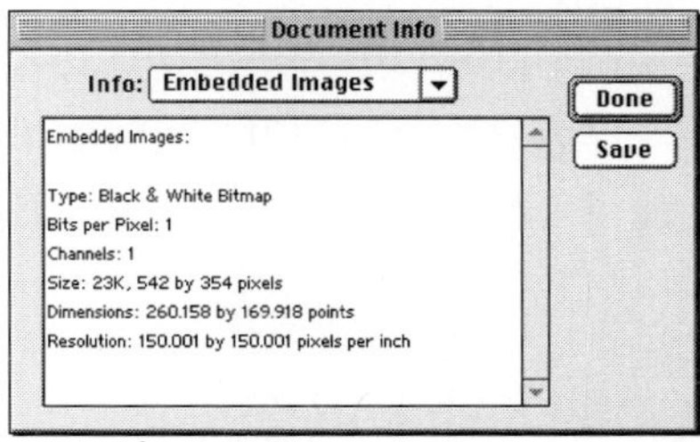

Recognizing Placed Raster Images

It is not easy to recognize a Raster image when viewed in **Artwork** mode. This placed TIFF is seen in **Preview** mode.

The same image, in **Artwork** mode, is seen as an empty box.

The only way to see a Raster image is to use the **Preview** mode.

The various Raster file formats (TIFF, PICT, JPEG, Photo CD, and IBM versions) are all treated the same way. It does not matter what Raster format they are in.

The 1-bit Bitmap Image

There is one file format that you must be careful with, the 1-bit (line art) bitmap image. Because it does not possess a color or grayscale background to work with, it cannot be used with Illustrator Raster filters (unless Rasterized).

But, this 1-bit line art image has one property that differentiates it from the other formats. That is, a 1-bit image (TIFF only) can have color applied to it from the **Swatches** palette and will appear in this color on the screen. If the applied color is a **Spot Color**, this will include the image in spot color separations. Only the 1-bit TIFF image will do this.

If you place a one-bit (black and white) image, Illustrator's filters don't have enough data to work with since there aren't any real color values in the file. If you want to apply a filter to a one-bit image, first convert it to grayscale by using **Object->Rasterize**. One-bit images can, however, be colorized by dragging a color swatch from the **Color** palette onto the image. This can only be done with a one-bit image.

Placing a Vector EPS Image

1. Create a **New** document.

2. Under the **File** menu, select **Place**.

3. From the **SF-Advanced Illustrator** folder, **Place** the file **Tropical Treasure Logo.EPS.**

5. **View** the file in both **Artwork** and **Preview** modes.

6. **Close** the document without saving.

Placing a Raster Image

1. Create a **New** document.

2. Go to **File->Place**. In the following window, select the file **Tropical Sunset.TIF**. Click **Open**.

Illustrator Raster filters cannot be used on images that are a bitmapped (one-bit) format. The image must be either RGB or Grayscale.

3. **View** this Placed image in **Artwork** mode, then in **Preview** mode.

4. **Close** the document without saving.

Rasterizing Images

Objects drawn in Illustrator are Vector objects, and can therefore be enlarged or reduced in another application without losing quality. Raster images, however, are very sensitive to resizing, and should be created at the size at which they're to be used. The **Rasterize** operation will turn Vector objects into Raster images. **Rasterize** is found in the **Object** menu.

A quick way to update a Placed image is to select it in the document. Then choose **Place** in the **File** menu. When the **Place** dialog box asks if you wish to **Replace** the old image, click **Replace**. The old version will be updated to the new.

Rasterizing Illustrator Vector Paths

The method is simple. The object is selected, then **Rasterize** is chosen from the **Object** menu. Once chosen, the **Rasterize** palette appears. The desired settings are then made. The result will be a bitmapped version of the image.

If you wish to retain the outlines of the paths, click **Create Mask** in the **Rasterize** dialog box. These are only Masking outlines, not the original paths. Always be ready to Undo, just in case the Rasterizing didn't give you what you wanted. The Rasterize operation will not work on Placed EPS images of the vector format.

You should make a duplicate of the Vector object you wish to Rasterize. This way, if any mishaps occur, you will not hurt your one-and-only original.

Rasterizing a Bitmap Image

Bitmap images do not need to be Rasterized since they are already in bitmap format. However, the Rasterize operation can modify these images to other Color Models as well as apply a different resolution or line screen.

For example, a Placed image may be an RGB Color Model but needs to be a Grayscale image. Rasterize can do this. The four Color Models of the **Rasterize** palette to choose from are: RGB, CMYK, Grayscale, and Bitmap.

Another instance to do this is when the Placed image is a 1-bit bitmap, and you want to apply a Raster filter (which works only on Grayscale, RGB, or CMYK) to it. You can select the 1-bit image, Rasterize it to a working format, and then apply a filter to it.

The Rasterize Palette

Here is the **Rasterize** palette.

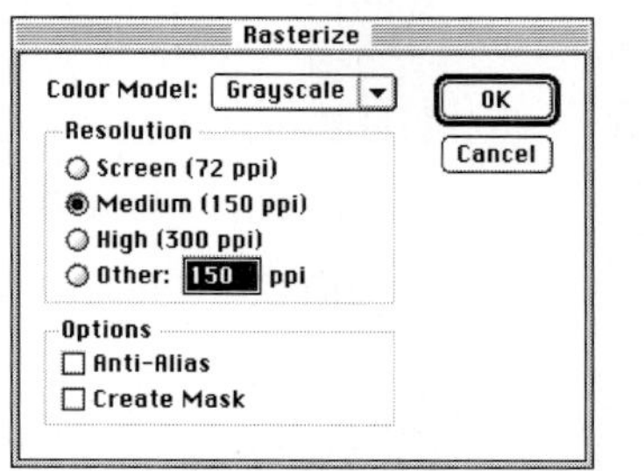

Being able to convert line art into bitmaps with the Rasterize command gives you the ability to create artwork that's outside the ability of the program's built-in tools. Filters dramatically expand your creative boundaries.

- **Color Model** — allows the choice of RGB, CMYK, Grayscale, or Bitmap (1-bit). This is useful for converting images to other formats.

- **Resolution** — lets you set the image's resolution.

- **Anti-Alias** — will add a soft anti-alias texture to the curves so that the image does not have jagged edges. You should click this option On.

- **Create Mask** — takes the paths of the Rasterized vector object and uses them to Mask the final Rasterized image. This option is particularly useful in the creation of images intended for on-screen viewing such as on the Internet and in multimedia presentations.

Using Rasterize on Illustrator Paths

1. **Open** the document **Rasterize Vector.AI.**

2. Press Command-A (Macintosh) or Control-A (Windows) to Select All paths.

3. Go to **Object->Rasterize**.

4. In the **Rasterize** palette, make these settings:

   Color Model = RGB, **Resolution** = Medium (150), **Anti-Alias** = Off, **Create Mask** = Off. Click **OK**.

5. Now click on the resulting image. You have Rasterized the paths into a single TIFF image. Go to **Edit->Undo.**

6. Now do the Rasterizing again with these settings: **Color Model** = RGB, **Resolution** = Medium (150), **Anti-Alias** = Off, **Create Mask** = On. Click **OK**.

7. Use the Selection tool to marquee a portion of the image. What do you see? **Create Mask** has taken the artwork paths and used them to mask out the opaque background.

8. **Close** the document without saving.

Using Rasterize to Convert a Photograph

1. Create a **New** document. **Place** the file **Tropical Palms Convert.TIF.**

One-bit TIFF images are totally black/white with no gray tones. The white portion is transparent, which becomes a useful design element. Anything placed behind the 1-bit image will show through the white sections.

2. Go to the **Object** menu and access **Rasterize.**

3. In the **Rasterize** dialog box, make these settings:

   Color Model = Bitmap, **Resolution** = Medium, **Create Mask** = Off.

4. Click **OK**. The graphic will be changed to a 1-bit TIFF image.

5. Draw several objects (squares, ovals, etc.) and color them as you wish. Bring this new 1-bit image to Front, and position it over the colored objects. You will see how the 1-bit is "see-thru" and this technique can be used for creative designs.

6. **Close** the document without saving.

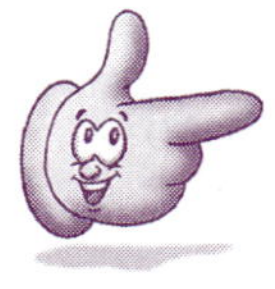

Project I: Tropical Postcard

CHAPTER 14

DESIGNING WITH PATTERNS

CHAPTER OBJECTIVE:

To provide you with more experience creating, applying, and managing patterns; to instruct you in the creation of seamless pattern tiles that ensure consistent coverage. In Chapter 14, you will:

- Learn more about the relationship between a fill element and the defining rectangle.
- Work with creating new patterns and managing them within the Swatch palette.
- Learn to create both simple and seamless pattern tiles, opening a broad range of design possibilities.
- Learn to transform fill patterns within an object without changing the object itself.
- Work with expanding pattern methods, which allow you to scale entire patterns or the elements within them.
- Create several custom patterns for use in project assignments.

PROJECTS TO BE COMPLETED:

- HoneyDo Hair Salon Logo
- HoneyDo Free Hairstyle Ad
- Banana Boat Logo
- Fleet's In! T-Shirt Design
- Tropical Suites Logo
- Heart Notes
- Banana Border
- Champagne Brunch Table Tent
- Tropical Postcard
- **Last Mango Menu Cover**
- Full Page Grocery Ad
- Perspective Graph
- Java Jungle Goodies Ad

Designing with Patterns

Patterns abound in many contemporary designs. You may think that the first thing that comes to mind when someone mentions patterns are those found on wallpaper or clothing fabrics. Not so. Look closely at magazines, ads, and packaging designs, and you will see the many uses of patterns. We show you how to use a pattern design to fill a menu cover in a Project in the back of this book.

To see and print your patterns, you must have Preview & Print Patterns clicked in the Document Setup option of the File menu.

We see patterns every day of our lives. The most obvious example is wallpaper — which often repeats a specific element in a pattern over short distances (and must be carefully matched when being applied). Other examples of patterns are floor tiles, which often contain patterns. Decorative fabric is another. We're sure you get the idea.

Illustrator treats patterns as special fills. Several attractive patterns are included with the program.

Stars

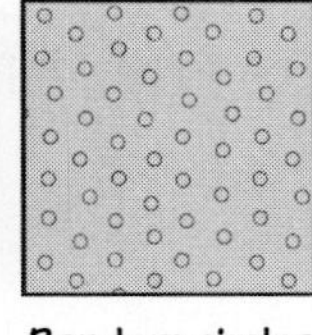

Random circles

Polka dots

Waves-scroll

You also have the ability in Illustrator to use your imagination to create objects that can be turned into patterns in more ways than you can think of.

Saving Time with Patterns

Fitting a duplicated object to a desired closed path can be tedious and time-consuming. For example, this single object could be manually duplicated repeatedly to fill a rectangle.

But, think of the time that would be wasted duplicating, measuring, Transforming Again, only to find out, after much work, that the duplications did not fit the rectangle as you desired. The solution is to create a pattern with the object.

Turned into a pattern

Rectangle filled with the pattern

How Patterns Work

Understanding the concept of patterns and how objects repeat in the pattern is essential when attempting to make one.

Picture a tiled floor. It is filled with repeating tile squares. Any object occupying each tile must be positioned with such accuracy that all repeating objects will be spaced evenly across the area they fill.

Patterns can accomplish effects that simply aren't possible through simple repetition. An example is the ability to fill an uneven shape with a pattern.

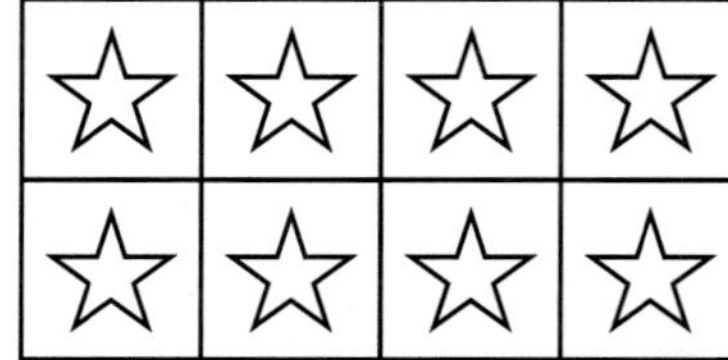

Objects equally spaced in tiles

Filling a rectangle as a pattern

Precision Alignment of Pattern Objects

To make attractive patterns, though, you should stagger the objects. There are strategic areas of the pattern-making square that, when used, ensure that you will have fewer and fewer patterns that go wrong. The five components of the square that you use to your advantage are the four anchor points and the center point. If you position objects by their center points on the anchor/center points of a square you will get an accurately spaced, staggered pattern.

Do not apply a pattern to the Stroke of an object. Illustrator will allow you to do this, but all you will get is a gray stroke image.

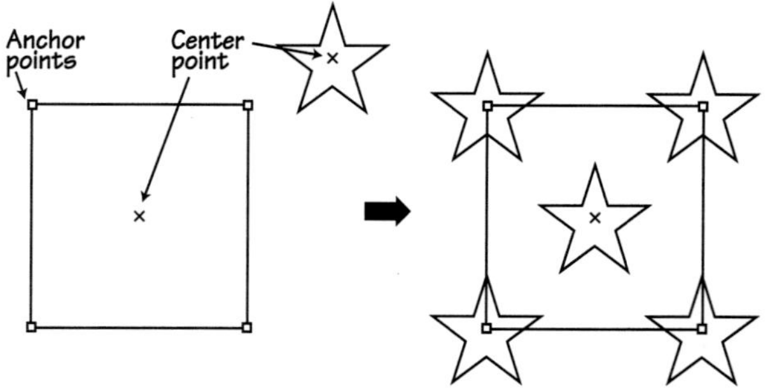

Viewed in Artwork mode

Not all objects show a center point. The Rectangle and Ellipse tool will show a center point for their drawn objects, but other tools, such as Polygon and Star, do not.

To see center points of objects is quite simple. Select the object, then go to **Window->Show Attributes**. In the **Attributes** palette, you will see the Show Center Point icon. Once clicked, selected objects will show their center points.

The pattern-making square should not be painted, unless you want it to be a part of the pattern. Also, this square should be in back of all the pattern objects. To be safe, after the objects are in place, use **Object->Arrange ->Send To Back** to make sure the square is behind the objects.

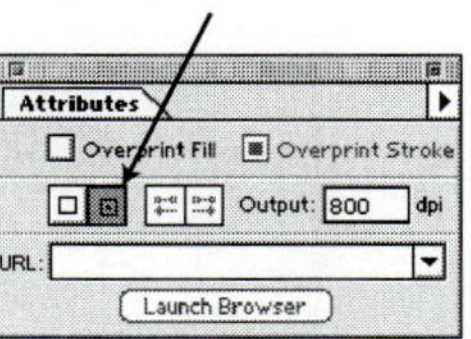

Defining the Pattern

When the objects are positioned in place on the square, they are ready to be turned into a pattern. All elements of the pattern are selected, then the **Define Pattern** option is chosen in the **Edit** menu.

The **New Swatch** window appears for you to name your pattern. The **Process/Spot Color** option is gray because you can't assign color status to a pattern here. When **OK** is clicked, the new pattern name appears in the **Swatches** palette.

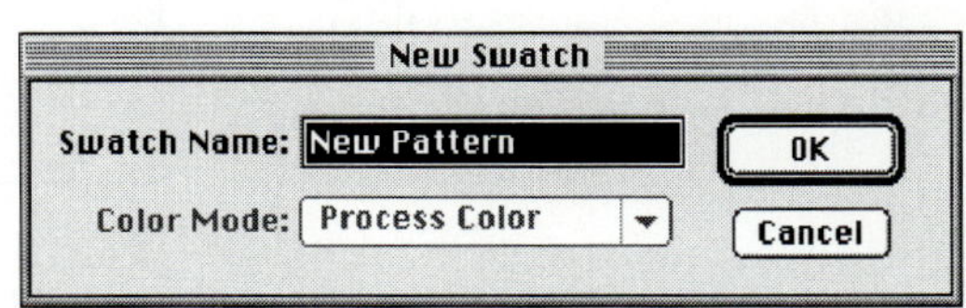

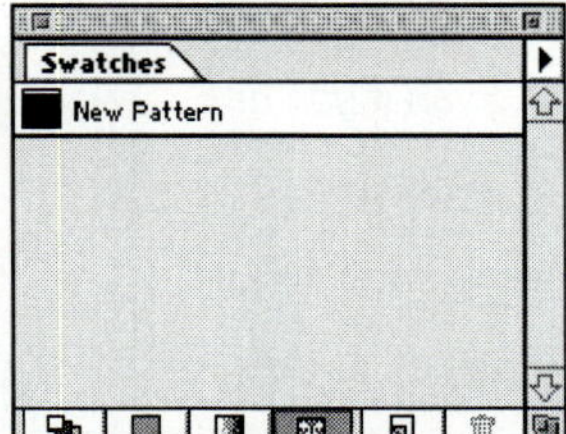

Try to find patterns that you can reproduce for purposes of learning more about how they work, how to construct them, how to color them, and how to manage them within your documents.

In this example, the stars and square were selected, **Define Pattern** chosen, and the new pattern applied to a rectangle.

Using the four anchor points and center of the square, we have observed how objects can be used to create staggered, attractive patterns. You are limited only by your imagination as to what shapes you create. You could use:

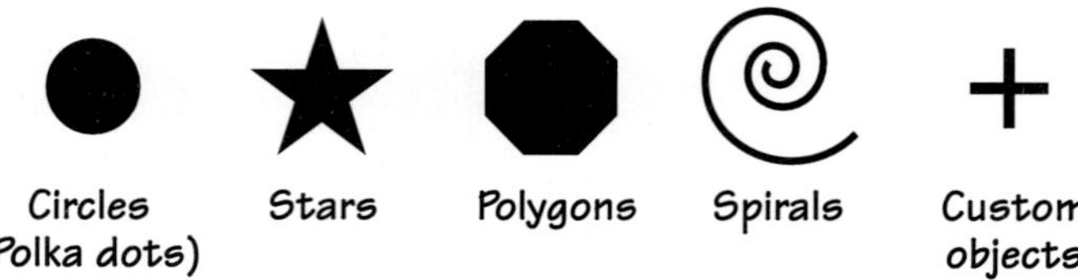

Creating a Pattern with a Polygon

1. Create a **New** document.

2. Select the Polygon tool and click the crosshair on the page. In the dialog box, enter **Radius** = 0.15 in., **Sides** = 8, then click **OK**.

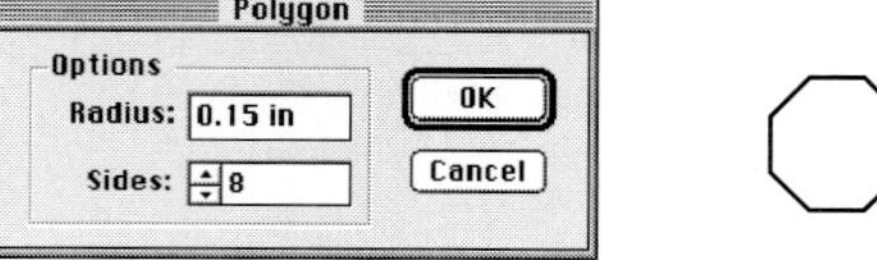

3. Select the Rectangle tool and click the crosshair on the page. In the dialog box, enter **Width** = 1 in., **Height** = 1 in., then click **OK**. You will have your polygon and pattern-defining square to work with.

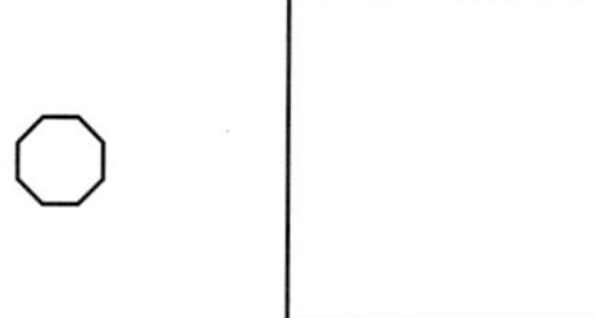

The unpainted object that defines the pattern should be a square. Even if you use a polygon or circle, the pattern-making feature will draw an unpainted square bounding box around all the objects to determine its own square. Any defining object other than a square gets unexpected results.

4. Select the polygon and paint it: **Fill** = None, **Stroke** = 6 pt. Black (a.). Go to **Edit->Copy**, then **Edit->Paste In Front**. Paint the duplicate: **Fill** = Black, **Stroke**= 1 pt. White (b.). Select the two polygons and **Object->Group** them.

Patterns can be stored in your Illustrator startup document so that they're available to you whenever you start a new drawing.

Patterns, especially transformed patterns, can cause problems when you go to output the file. This is particularly true if you create a pattern, use it in a design, and then export that design for use in a page layout program. Even when they work, they take an inordinate amount of time to print.

5. Go to **Artwork** mode to see the paths and their center points better. Select the polygon group you just made. Go to **Window->Show Attributes** and click on the Show Center Point icon.

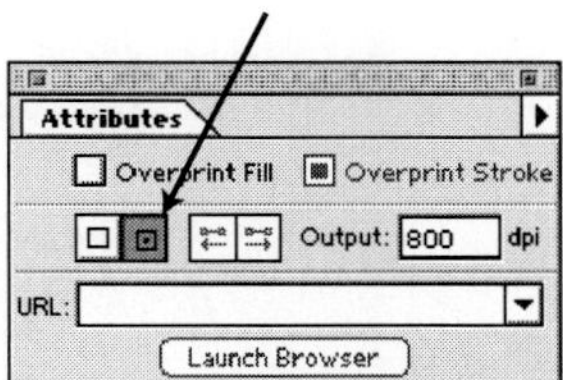

6. The center point of the polygon will appear (a.). Move the polygon so that its center point matches the center point of the square. Drag a copy of the polygon, holding the Option (Macintosh) or Alt (Windows) key, up to the upper left corner of the square. Position the polygon so that its center point is on top of the square's upper left anchor point.

   Holding the Option (Macintosh) or Alt (Windows) key, drag a copy of the polygon to the square's upper right anchor point, holding the Shift key to constrain the drag. Position this polygon's center point on the upper right anchor point of the square (b.).

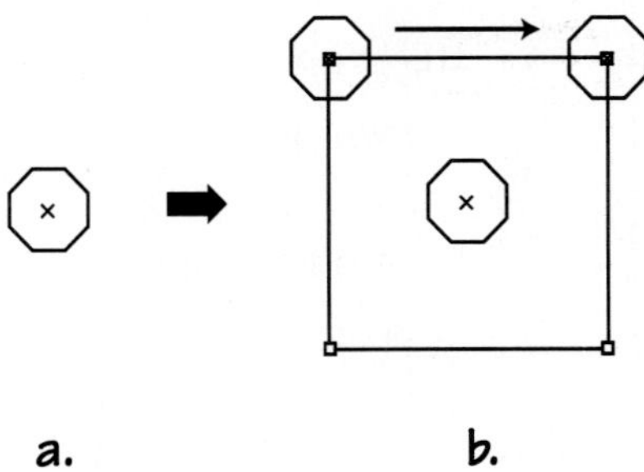

a. b.

7. With the Selection tool, select the two corner polygons, and drag copies down to the square's bottom anchor points. Hold the Shift key as you drag to constrain the drag. Position the copies so that their center points are on top of the corner anchor points.

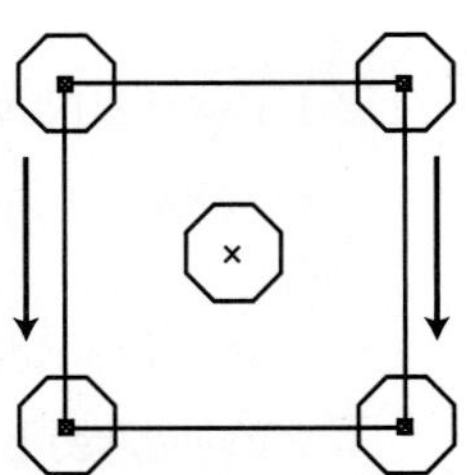

8. Go to **Preview** mode. Select the square and go to **Object->Arrange->Send To Back**, just to make sure that the square is behind all the polygons. Paint the square: **Fill** = None, **Stroke** = None. You should have a design that looks like this.

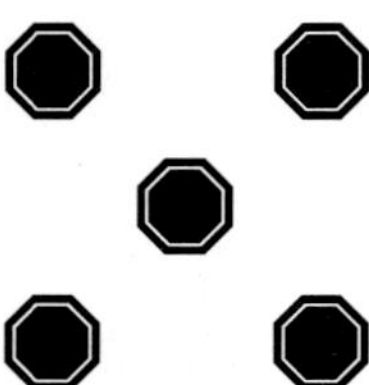

9. With the Selection tool, marquee around the entire group to make sure you are selecting all objects, including the unpainted square.

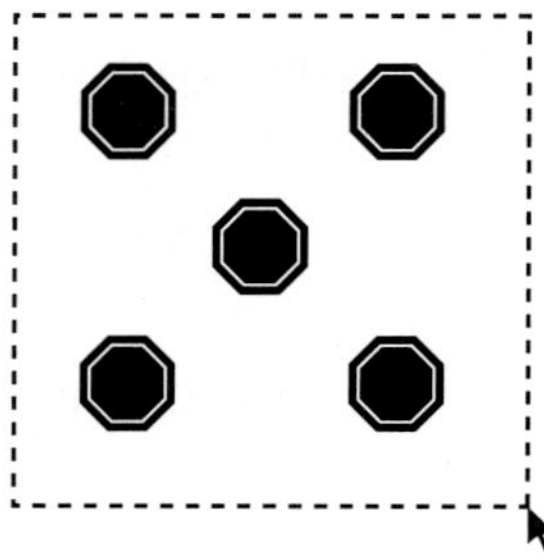

Expanding a fill pattern lets you take it apart, modify it, and send it back to the patterns palette.

10. With the objects selected, go to **Edit->Define Pattern**. The **New Pattern** window will appear. Click **OK**.

11. Go to **Window->Show Swatches**, and click on the Patterns icon of this palette. View the items by name, and scroll down to the New Pattern.

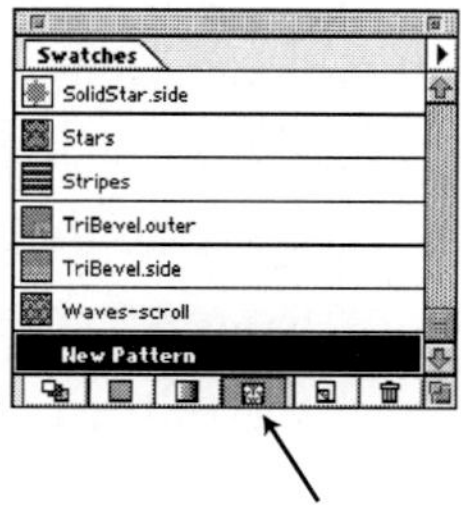

12. Drag the New Pattern swatch over to the Fill box of the Toolbox. Set the **Stroke** for None.

13. Select the Rectangle tool in the Toolbox, and draw a rectangle (of any size you desire) onto the page.

14. The rectangle will be filled with your new pattern.

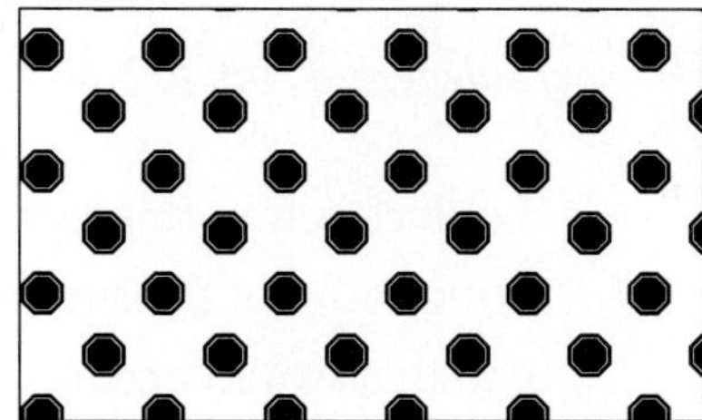

15. **Close** this document without saving.

Remember the Adobe Illustrator Startup document. Any objects painted with patterns or gradients that are assigned to the **Swatches** palette in this document, then saved, will be available in all future Illustrator documents after the application has restarted.

Creating Patterns with Random Objects

The patterns we've looked at so far have all been very structured, with exact measurements and placement of objects. Very pretty, but some backgrounds are made from erratic or random objects or shapes. Here are some examples of patterns of this nature that come with the Illustrator program.

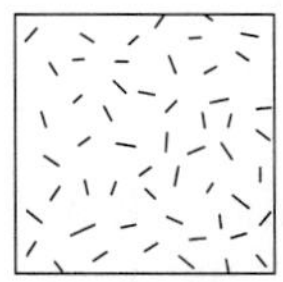

Confetti

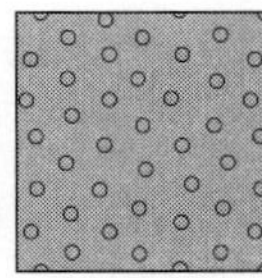

Random circles

Leaves-fall

Go back to the "tiled floor" concept. Patterns are repeating squares, and these squares butt up to each other. Any objects that extend outside of the square, must be in position to extend into an adjoining square.

It's sometimes easier to work on patterns if you expand the view and zoom in closer. Patterns are often made of small elements.

In this example, the two stars were positioned inside a pattern-making square, then staggered to add interest. But, part of the star got cut off by extending outside of the square. When this design was turned into a pattern, and applied to fill a rectangle — look what occurred!

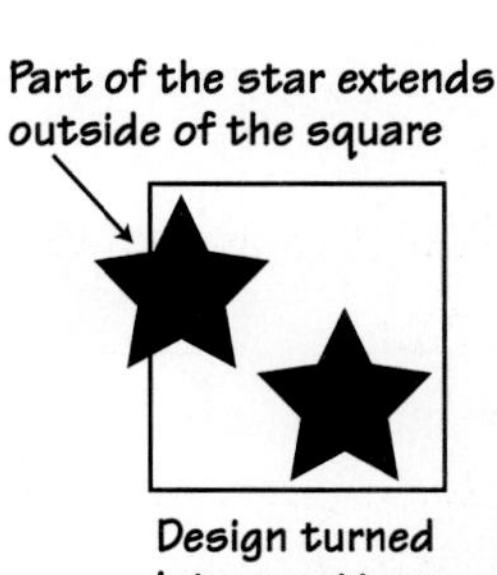

Design turned into a pattern ➡ Rectangle filled with this pattern

The pattern-making rule is:

What extends outside of a square must go back into the square from the other side. Side to side, top to bottom.

Look closely at this example. Observe how all objects that extend past the boundaries of the square have counterparts on the opposite side that fill in the gap that would occur.

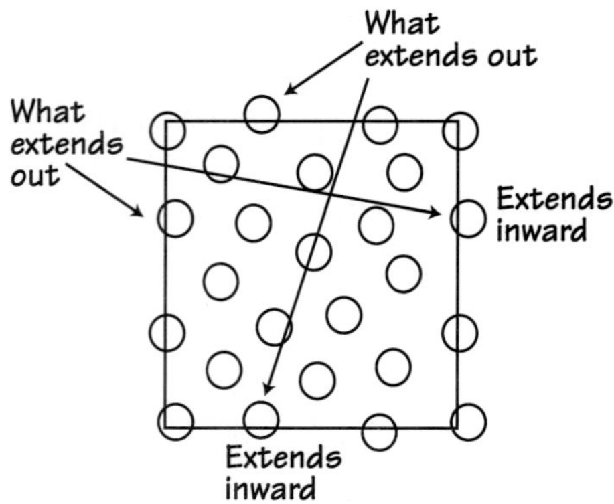

Filling the Gaps

A simple technique that allows you to obtain the needed portions to avoid cutting off an object is to duplicate the objects and the square to the side (or up and down), making sure that the squares butt up to each other. This is to ensure proper alignment of the objects.

In this example, the original design is almost finished, lacking only the counterparts of the objects that extend outside of the square. The square and objects are duplicated to the side, supplying the needed counterparts exactly in place on the right side of the original square. The unneeded objects are deleted, leaving the right/left sides complete.

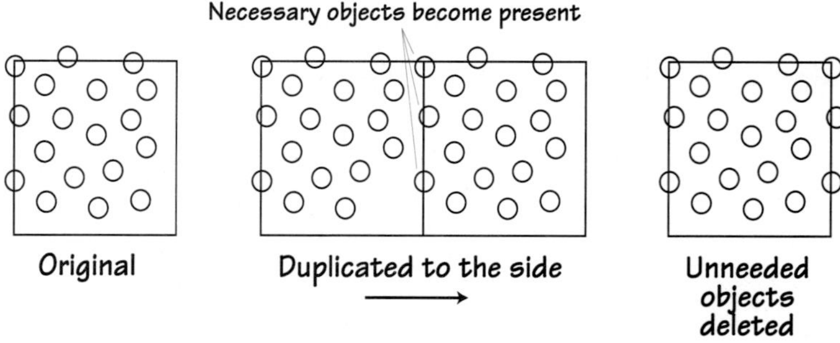

This partially completed design was then duplicated downward. The necessary objects, correctly aligned in place, became evident. All unneeded objects were deleted, leaving the square and objects that would create a working pattern.

You cannot make Patterns out of objects Filled with Gradients, other Patterns, or Masked objects.

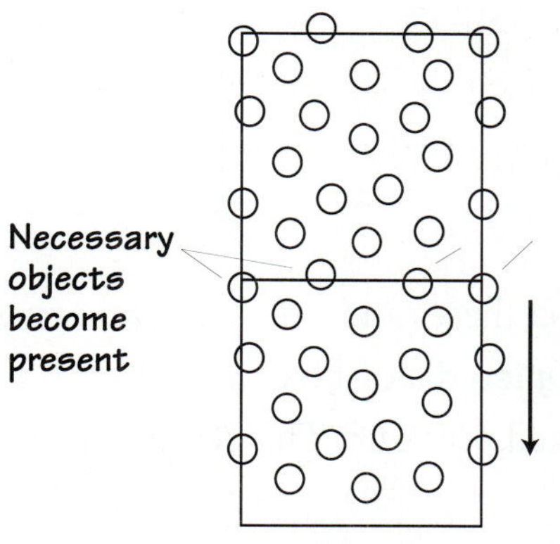

Unneeded objects deleted, leaving the objects that will make the pattern.

The final step was to paint the square with a Fill/Stroke of None, and to Fill the circles with black (a.). The objects were selected, Define Pattern chosen, and the pattern applied as a Fill to a rectangle (b.)

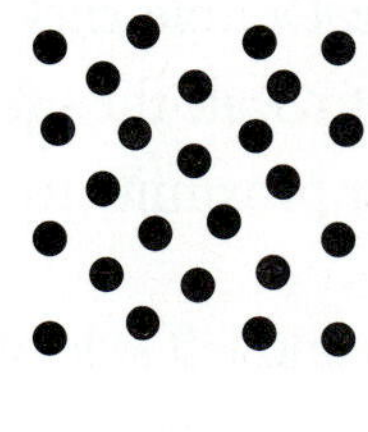

a.

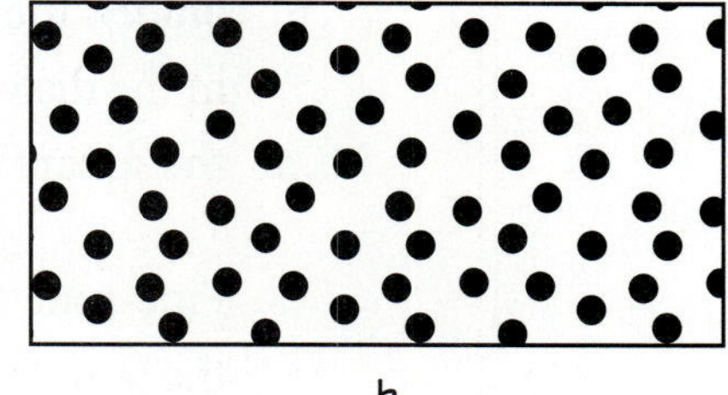

b.

Creating a Pattern from Random Objects

1. Create a **New** document. Go to **Artwork** mode.

2. With the Rectangle tool, draw a 1-inch square, and **Lock** it.

3. Select the Paintbrush tool and double-click on its icon in the Toolbox. In the **Paintbrush** dialog box, set the width for 5 pt.

4. Randomly click the Paintbrush tool on the 1-inch square, creating erratic objects.

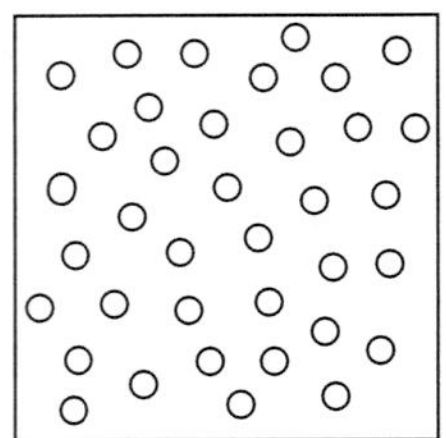

5. Select these random objects and go to **Filter->Distort->Roughen**. In the **Roughen** dialog box, make these settings: **Size** = 26, **Detail** = 31, **Corner** = clicked. Click **OK**. This will give rough, distorted shapes to the objects.

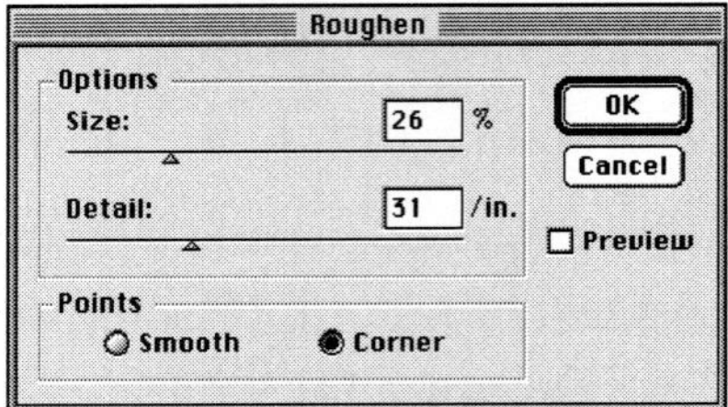

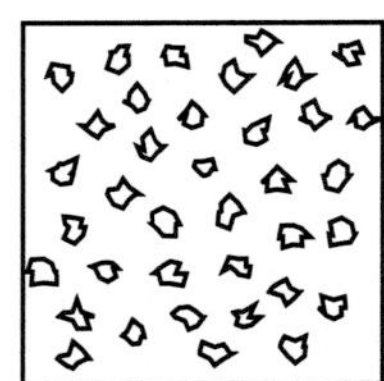

6. **Unlock** the square. Double-click on the Scale tool in the Toolbox. Enter 80 in the dialog box to Scale the square 80% Uniform. Click **OK**. This will give the square a closer proximity to the roughened objects(a.).

   Fine-tune the top and left side of the square to move the objects touching the segment so that they overlap it (b.).

   Fine-tune the right side and bottom of the square so that there are no overlapping objects touching the square (c.).

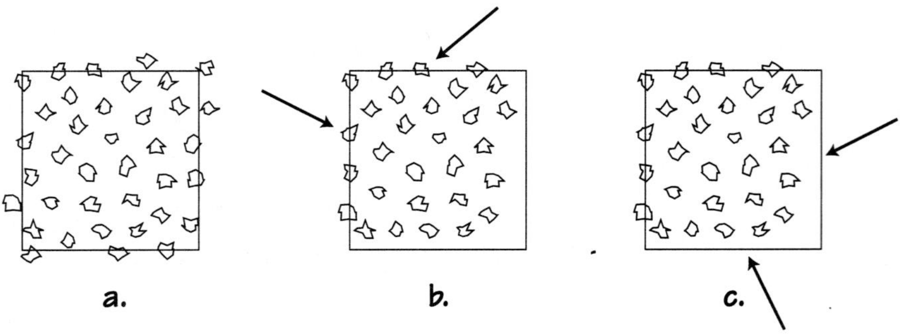

7. Select the square and all the objects. Drag-duplicate them to the side, holding the Option (Macintosh) or Alt (Windows) key. As you drag, hold the Shift key to constrain the movement (a.). Delete the duplicate square, then delete all the duplicate objects, save for those that are overlapping the original square's right side (b.).

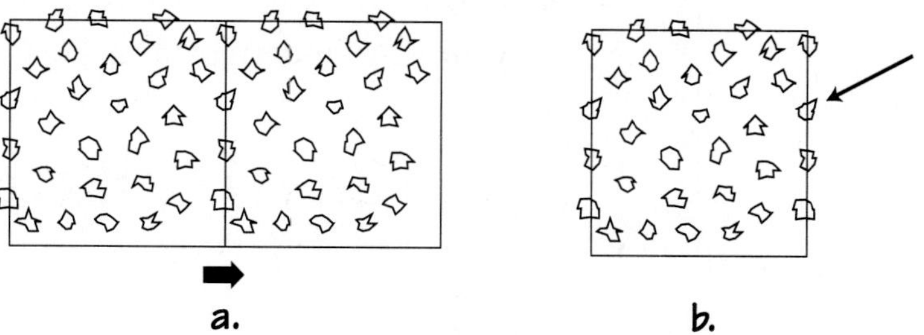

8. Select the square and all the objects again. Drag-duplicate them downward, holding the Option (Macintosh) or Alt (Windows) key. As you drag, hold the Shift key to constrain the movement (a.).

   Delete the duplicate square, then delete all the duplicate objects, save for those that are overlapping the original square's bottom segment (b.).

   Without moving any of the objects that overlap the square's segments, use your artistic taste to fine-tune the inside objects to be more evenly spaced throughout the square. Remember, do not touch any objects that overlap the square's segments (c.).

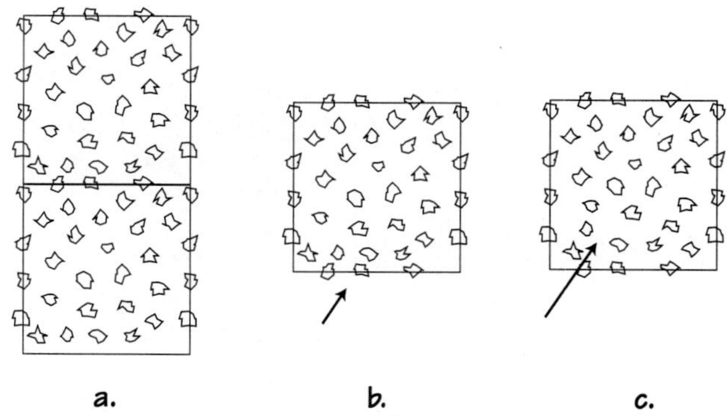

9. You now have the random objects in place. Lock the square, then select all the objects. Paint them: **Fill** = Black, **Stroke**= None. Unlock the square and paint it: **Fill** = None, **Stroke**= None. Use **Object->Arrange-> Send To Back** to send the square behind all the objects.

10. Marquee-select all the objects and the square. Go to **Edit->Define Pattern.** In the **New Pattern** window, name the pattern "Random Dots." Click **OK.**

11. Select the Rectangle tool in the tool box. Draw a 4" x 2" rectangle. Make sure the Fill box is selected in the Toolbox. Go to the **Swatches** palette, and view the patterns by name. Scroll down to Random Dots pattern, and drag its swatch over to touch the rectangle. This will fill the rectangle with your new random pattern. Do not delete the rectangle.

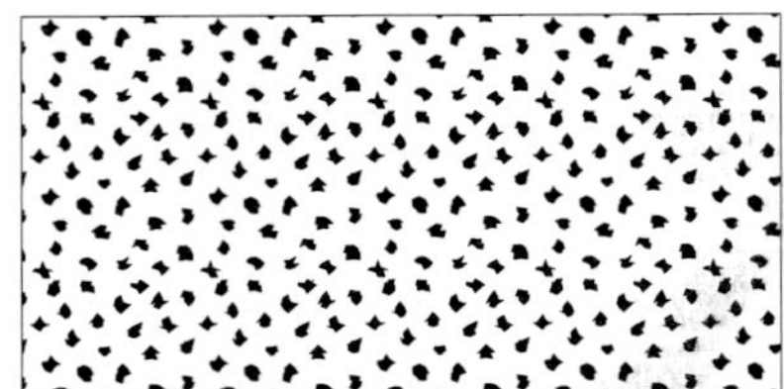

12. **Save As** the document in **Illustrator 7.0** format. Name the file "Random Dots Pattern.AI." Leave the document open for the next exercise.

Transforming Patterns

The transformation tools (Scale, Rotate, Reflect, Shear) have the ability to perform their operations on objects that are Filled with a pattern. The option to do this is located in the dialog boxes of these tools. You have to click on **Patterns** to transform the pattern in the selected object. Click the **Objects** button Off if you do not want the object to transform.

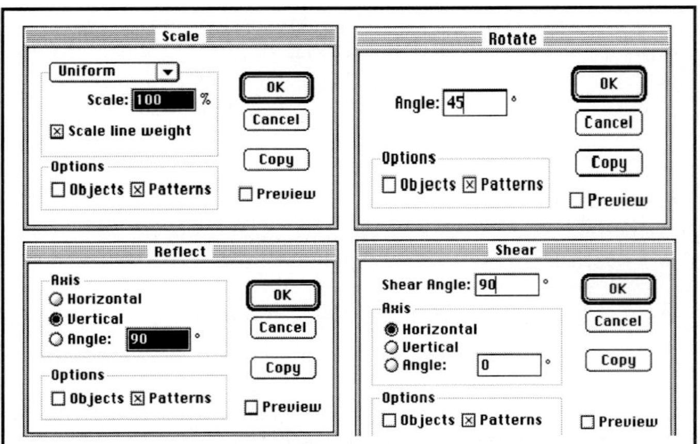

The transformation effects are the same as if performed on a path. Here are some samples of transforming patterns.

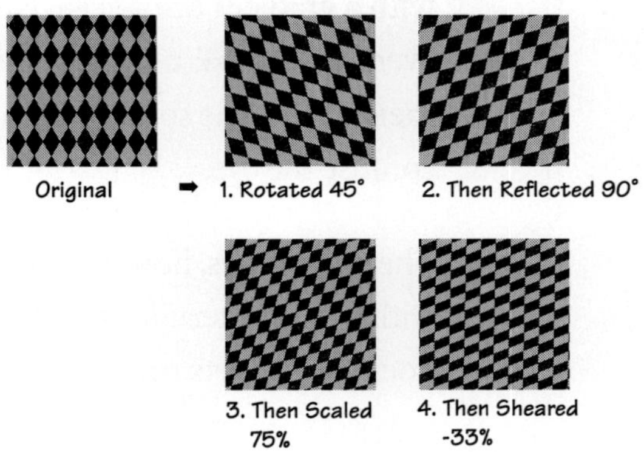

Using Transforming Tools on Patterns

1. Continue in the Random Dots document you left open.
2. Select the rectangle you drew earlier.
3. Double-click on the Rotate tool in the Toolbox. Make these settings in the dialog box. **Angle** = 45, **Objects** = Off, **Patterns** = On. Click **OK**.
4. Observe how the objects rotated in the pattern. Select **Edit->Undo**.
5. Double-click on the Scale tool. Make these settings in the dialog box. Uniform = On, **Scale** = 50, **Objects** = Off, **Patterns** = On. Click **OK**.
6. Note the difference in size of the objects in the pattern. Select **Edit->Undo**.
7. Double-click on the Reflect tool. Make these settings in the dialog box. **Vertical** = On, **Angle** = 90, **Objects** = Off, **Patterns** = On. Click **OK**.
8. Observe how the objects changed in the pattern. Select **Edit->Undo**.
9. Double-click on the Shear tool. Make these settings in the dialog box. **Shear Angle** = 20, **Axis** = Angle 20, **Objects** = Off, **Patterns** = On. Click **OK**.
10. Notice the objects are sheared at angles. **Close** the file without saving.

Working with Expand Fill

Expand Fill, found in the **Object** menu, operates on paths that have been Filled with a gradient or pattern. Normally, when a path has a gradient or pattern Fill, even in **Artwork** mode you do not actually see the gradient sections or paths of the pattern. The sometimes complicated nature of the pattern paths would confuse the eye.

There are times, however, when you might like to use specific paths from within the pattern for another element in the drawing. This is what **Expand Fill** does — converts paths from within a pattern into regular Vector objects.

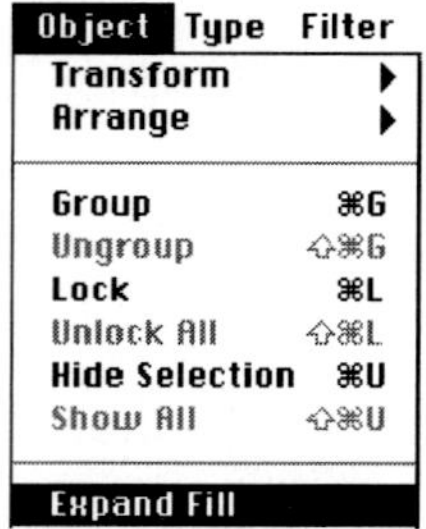

Here is a square filled with the Diamonds pattern.

It was selected, then **Expand Fill** chosen from the **Object** menu.

Expand Fill will expand the paths of the pattern into objects occupying a pattern-making square. It will also tile the squares (or rectangles), butting them up against each other.

The object that was filled with the pattern will act as a Mask, so the extending paths, outside of the object, will not be seen. This is evident only in **Preview** mode. Only in **Artwork** mode can you see all the paths that have been expanded.

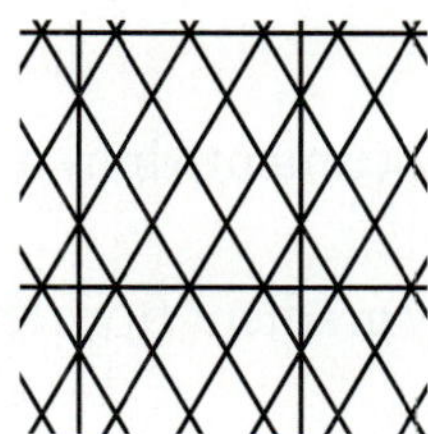

Viewed in Preview mode. Masking is still On.

Viewed in Artwork mode.

If you want to work on these paths in both **Preview** and **Artwork** modes, you must release the Masking through the **Object->Masks** menu.

Expand Fill also works on Gradients. It will expand all the paths making up the gradient. Use this only if you are experienced in working with gradients. Otherwise, it can become quite confusing, with too many objects to work with.

Using Expand Fill on a Pattern

1. Create a **New** document. Draw an object (a square or circle).
2. **Fill** it with any pattern you desire from the **Swatches** palette.
3. Make sure you are in **Preview** mode. With this object still selected, go to **Object->Expand Fill**. What result do you see?
4. Go to **Artwork** mode. Now what do you see?

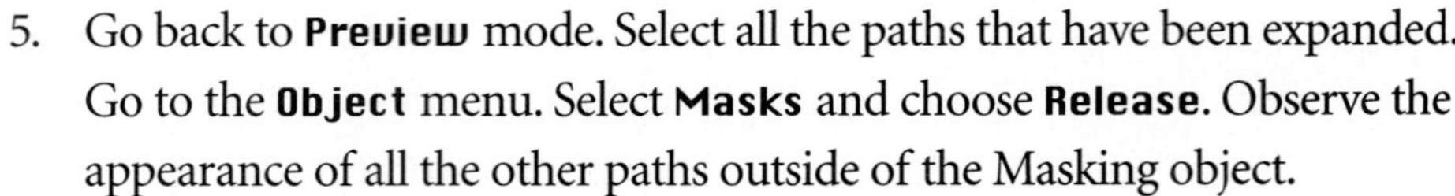

5. Go back to **Preview** mode. Select all the paths that have been expanded. Go to the **Object** menu. Select **Masks** and choose **Release.** Observe the appearance of all the other paths outside of the Masking object.

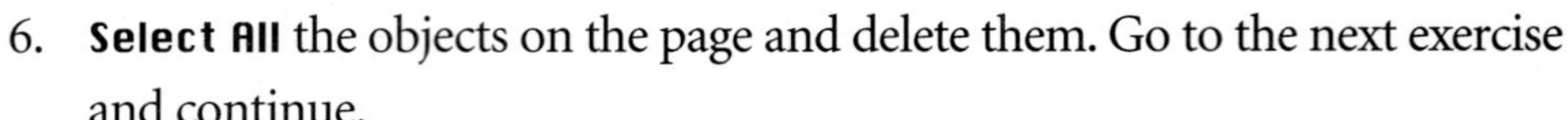

6. **Select All** the objects on the page and delete them. Go to the next exercise and continue.

Using Expand Fill on Gradients

1. In the open document, draw a 3" square with the Rectangle tool.

2. **Fill** it with any gradient from the **Swatches** palette.

3. With the object selected, go to the **Object** menu and choose **Expand Fill.**

4. Type "30" for steps. Click **OK.**

5. Go to **Artwork** mode to see the 30 paths making the gradient. Go to **Preview** mode to see the gradient in color.

6. With the Direct Selection tool, click on different paths in the gradient to see how their color and screen tint values change.

7. **Close** the file without saving.

Creating and Using a Pattern.

1. From the **SF-Advanced Illustrator** folder, Open the file **Shell for Pattern.AI.**

2. Select the shell, then go to **Window->Show Attributes.** Click on the Show Center Point icon.

This will show the center point in the shell object.

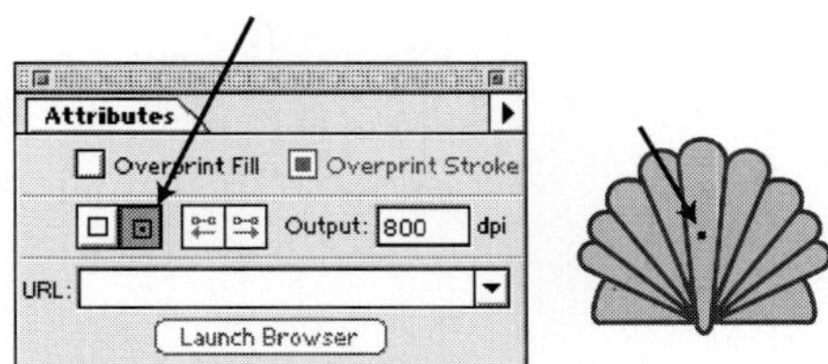

3. Draw a 1" square next to the shell. With the square selected, go to **Object ->Arrange->Send To Back**. Go to **Artwork** mode so you can see the anchor points and center points better.

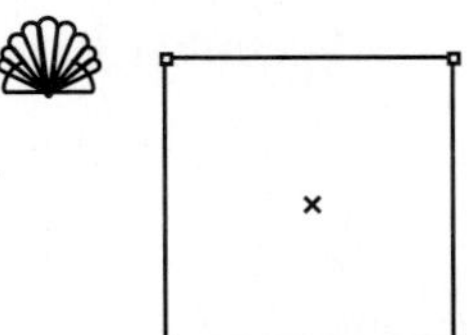

4. Move the shell so that its center point matches the center point of the square (a.).

   Drag-duplicate the shell so that the center point of the copy is on top of the upper left anchor point of the square. Then, holding the Shift key for constraining, drag-duplicate a copy of the shell so that it matches the upper right anchor point of the square (b.).

   Select the two corner shells and drag-duplicate them downward, so that their center points are on top of the lower anchor points of the square (c.).

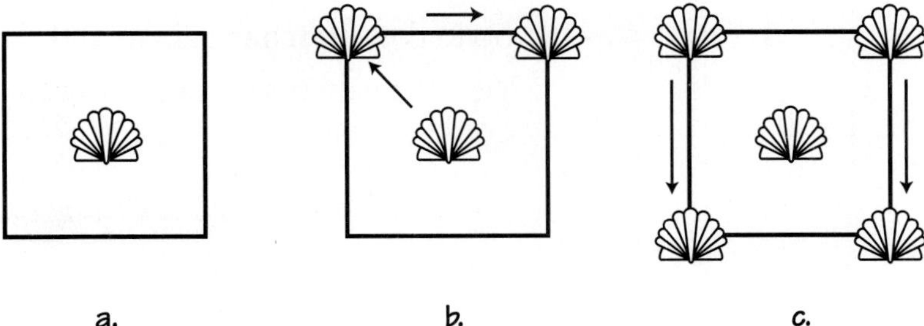

a. b. c.

5. Select the square. Paint it: **Fill** = Blue, **Stroke**= None. Go to **Preview** mode to see the design in color.

6. You will now turn this design into a pattern, but watch out. If you were to select all these objects and go to **Define Pattern**, you would get a rather peculiar looking pattern.

   Why is this? Because you have painted the square that defines the pattern. The defining square must be unpainted, and in back of all objects that will be part of the pattern. But, this is quite simple to fix.

7. Select the painted square and **Edit->Copy** it. Then go to **Edit->Paste In Back**. Paint this copy: **Fill** = None, **Stroke** = None.

8. Now, marquee-select all objects, then go to **Edit->Define Pattern.**

9. In the **New Swatch** window, name the pattern "Shell Pattern." Click **OK**.

10. Go to the **Swatches** palette, and click on the Patterns icon at the bottom. View the patterns by name, and scroll down to see your Shell Pattern.

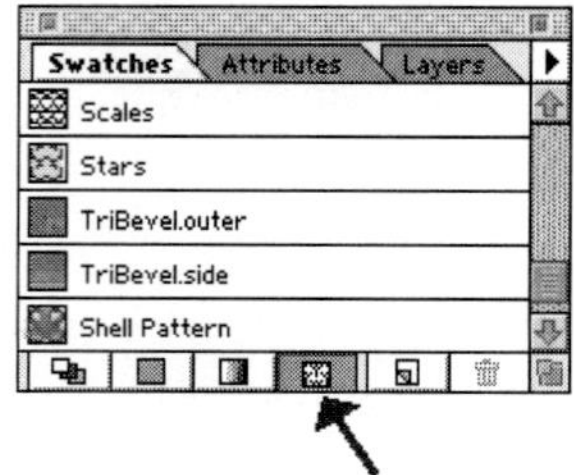

11. To see the pattern, draw a 4" x 2" rectangle on the page and Fill it with the Shell Pattern.

12. **Save As** the document in **Illustrator 7.0** format, naming it "Shell Pattern.AI."

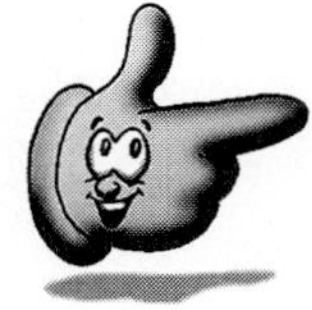

Project J: Last Mango Menu Cover

Notes:

Chapter 15

Illustrator as a Page Layout Tool

Chapter Objective:

To teach you to look at Adobe Illustrator as a stand-alone page layout tool for specific types of applications; to teach you how to set up an Illustrator document for the design and layout of single-page layouts. In Chapter 15 you will:

- Look at document setup and how it affects the trim and bleed sizes of the finished layout.
- Learn more about the Artboard and the live tile area, and how they affect your output and should be considered before beginning a page.
- Learn how to use non-printing guides as a component of a page layout, as opposed to a tool used only to develop a drawing.
- Learn to develop standard guides required by commercial printers.
- Develop a grid and layout that you will use to build a highly complex, full-page grocery ad as a project assignment.
- Execute four sophisticated page designs using supplied components and elements you have created in other exercises.

Projects to be Completed:

- HoneyDo Hair Salon Logo
- HoneyDo Free Hairstyle Ad
- Banana Boat Logo
- Fleet's In! T-Shirt Design
- Tropical Suites Logo
- Heart Notes
- Banana Border
- Champagne Brunch Table Tent
- Tropical Postcard
- Last Mango Menu Cover
- **Full Page Grocery Ad**
- Perspective Graph
- Java Jungle Goodies Ad

Illustrator as a Page Layout Tool

Most people identify Illustrator simply as a drawing tool. We've seen plenty of cases where every element on a page was drawn in Illustrator, and then imported into a page layout program to create the final design. This is a perfect example of duplication of effort, and using too many programs to achieve the desired effect.

With the sole exception of long, multi-page documents (like this course, for example), many different types of projects can be executed totally within Illustrator, without the need even to open a page layout application.

Since Illustrator provides fully functional type handling, color controls, highly accurate placement, the ability to import scanned images, and the ability to work in a variety of different color models, it makes a lot of sense to consider using the program to fully execute page designs for a wide variety of work. This includes ads, package designs, even small booklets.

There are people we've talked to that find it incredible that we would use Illustrator instead of a page layout program. We feel that in many cases – specifically single-sheet or page projects like advertisements, packages, signs, etc. – there's no need to use a second program. It only slows things down – it takes more time to use two programs than it does to use one.

Document Setup

Setting up the document is very important. Your working area must be uncluttered and simple to use. The working area is called the **Artboard**, which holds the page.

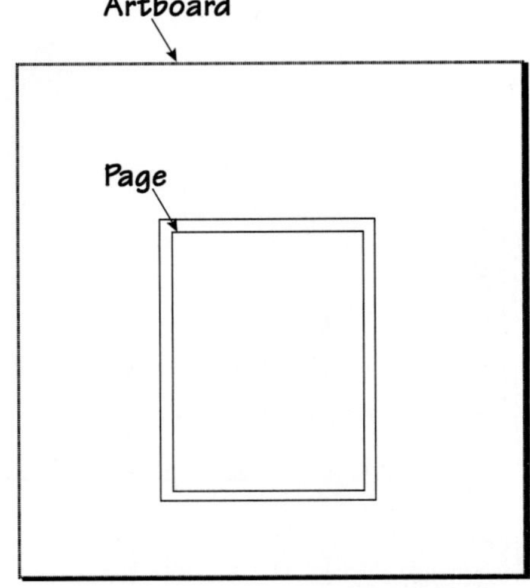

As you can see from this discussion, you're really not limited as to page size. We know a lot of people that use Illustrator to design packages and boxes.

Adjusting the size of the **Artboard** is done in the **Document Setup** option in the **File** menu. A standard size to use is 20" x 20", which allows plenty of room for the working page, plus extra artboard area to keep objects and type. This window offers three choices for how your page layout will look:

- **Single full page**
- **Tile full pages**
- **Tile imageable areas**

Depending on how you like your ruler units (some like inches, some prefer picas), you can change the measurement system of units here.

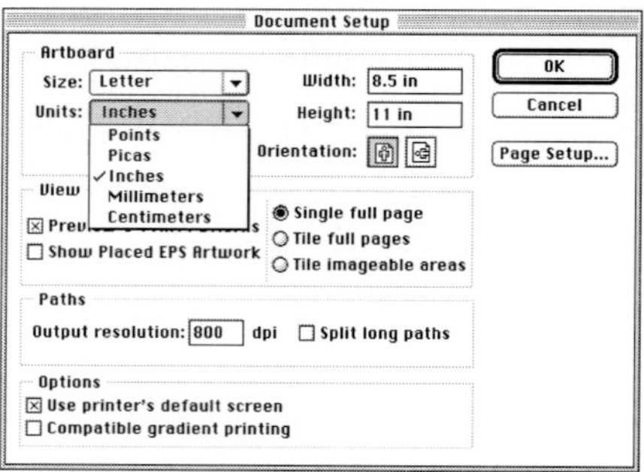

Macintosh

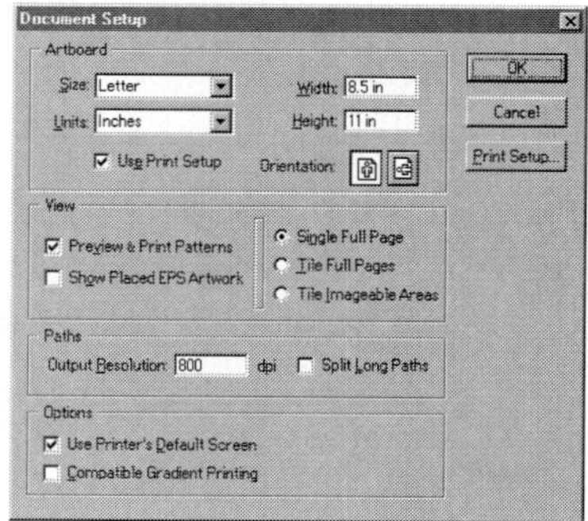

Windows

The page size is set in the **Page Setup** (Macintosh) or **Print Setup** (Windows) option in the **File->Document Setup** dialog box. It is here that you designate whether the page size is **Letter, Legal,** or **Tabloid.**

The actual Artboard size should be much larger than the known size of the artwork. This is to give the artwork extra breathing room, especially if crop marks are going to be used.

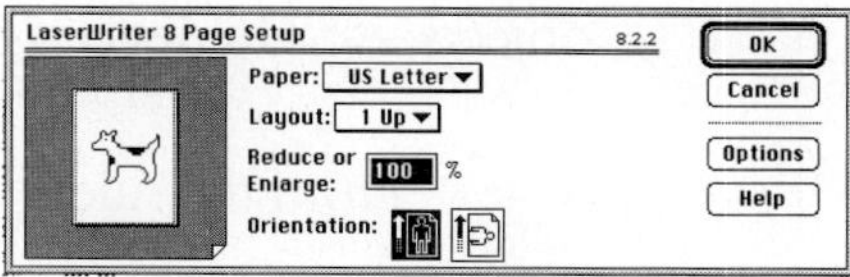

Macintosh

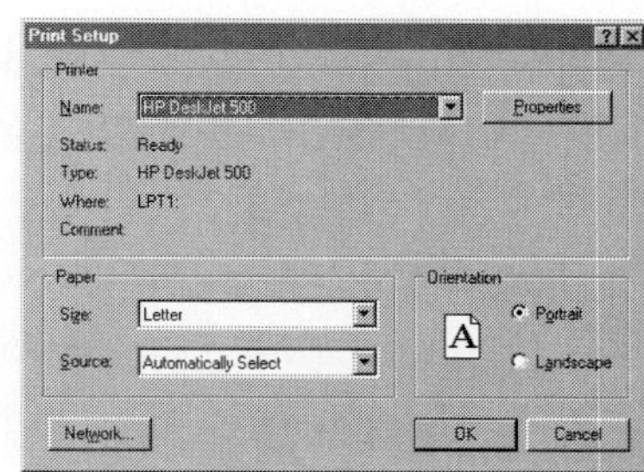

Windows

If you watch an experienced operator work, you'll see that they make extensive use of guides. On the other hand, if you check out the finished work of these same people, you'll find that they've deleted all the guides before they sent out the file for output. This is a good idea, since left-over guides can sometimes cause output problems on certain systems.

The only time you should be concerned whether your artwork is on the page is when printing. Illustrator will print only what is on the page, not any other objects that are on the Artboard.

If you want to change the location of the page to fit objects on it better, use the Page tool, in the Toolbox.

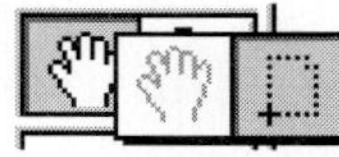

Select this tool, then drag the crosshair on the artboard. The page will move with the cursor.

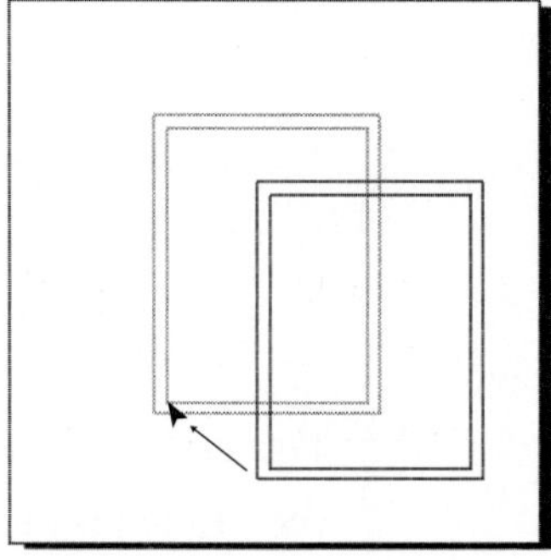

Using Guides

Grab a magazine, randomly select about a dozen or so different ads. Analyze them and see if you can visualize what sort of guides were used in the layout. You might consider laying a piece of tissue over the ads and drawing in guides.

Guides are the heart of a good layout. They show the centers of image areas, ruler measurements, dimensions of objects, positioning markers for Placing objects, etc. Guides can be made in two different ways:

- From the rulers
- From paths

The simple way to make vertical or horizontal guides is to click-hold the mouse on the ruler and drag the guide to where you want it.

The other method is converting paths to guides. By choosing **View->Make Guides**, any path can be turned into a guide. By default, guides are **Locked.**

Setting Guides for an Ad

The ad specifications are: Size = 4.25" x 5.5", margins = 0.5", bleed = 0.125".

1. Create a **New** document. Go to **View->Show Rulers** to see the rulers.

2. Drag a vertical guide to the 4.25" mark of the horizontal ruler.
   Drag a horizontal guide to the 5.5" mark of the ruler on the vertical ruler.
   This will show the center of the page.

If you don't get the guides pulled accurately the first time, you must **Unlock Guides** to reposition them.

3. Select the Rectangle tool. Option-click (Macintosh) or Alt-click (Windows) the crosshair on the center point of the page where the guides meet. Make these settings: **Width** = 4.25 in., **Height** = 5.5 in., **Corner radius** = 0. Click **OK**.

4. Press Command-5 (Macintosh) or Ctrl-5 (Windows) to convert the rectangle to a guide. Drag the Zero Point of the ruler to the upper left corner of the rectangle (a.).

5. Drag horizontal and vertical guides to 1/2" inch inside the rectangle guide (b.).

6. Drag vertical and horizontal guides to 1/8" outside of the rectangle border, to show the bleed (c.).

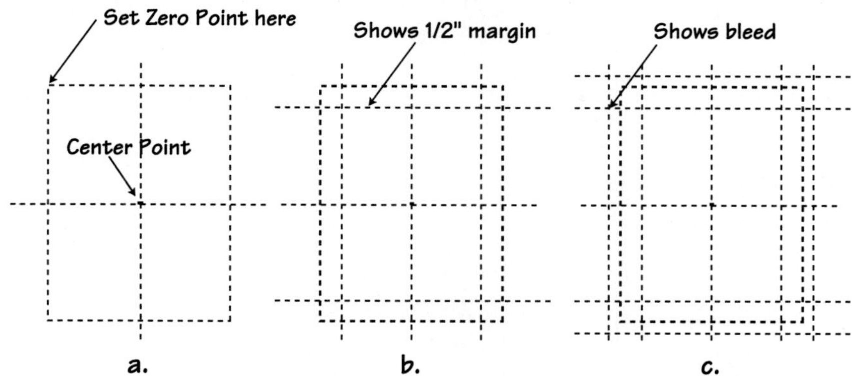

7. **Close** the file without saving.

Laying Out a Three-Panel Brochure

1. Create a **New** document. Go to **View->Show Rulers** for measuring.

2. Go to **File->Document Setup** to set up the Artboard for 11" x 17".

3. Click on **Page Setup** (Macintosh) or **Print Setup** (Windows) in **Document Setup**. Make the orientation Horizontal. Close **Document Setup**.

4. With the Page tool, drag the page to the center of the Artboard.

Drag the Zero Point to the upper left corner of the Page Tiling.

Drag a horizontal guide to the 4.5" mark of the vertical ruler. Drag a vertical guide to the 5.5" mark of the horizontal ruler. This will show the page center.

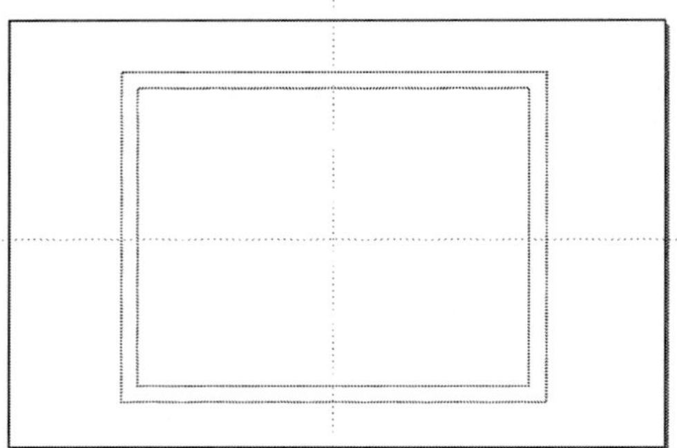

The Trim Marks in this exercise will obviously not show up on a letter-sized page printed on a laser printer. This method is for a commercial printer to do high-resolution output to an 11" x 17" page which will show the marks.

5. Select the Rectangle tool in the Toolbox. Option-click (Macintosh) or Alt-click (Windows) on the center point of the page marked by the guides. Make these settings: **Width** = 11 in., **Height** = 8.5 in., **Corner radius** = 0 in. Click **OK**. The brochure-sized rectangle will be centered on the page. Drag the Zero Point to the upper left corner of this new rectangle.
6. Drag a vertical guide to the 3 11/16" mark of the horizontal ruler. Drag a vertical guide to the 7 3/8" mark of the horizontal ruler. They will designate the panels.
7. **View->Unlock Guides**, then **View->Release Guides**. Delete the two guides showing the center. Then, go to **View->Lock Guides**.
8. Select the working rectangle. Go to **Filter->Create**. Choose **Trim Marks**.

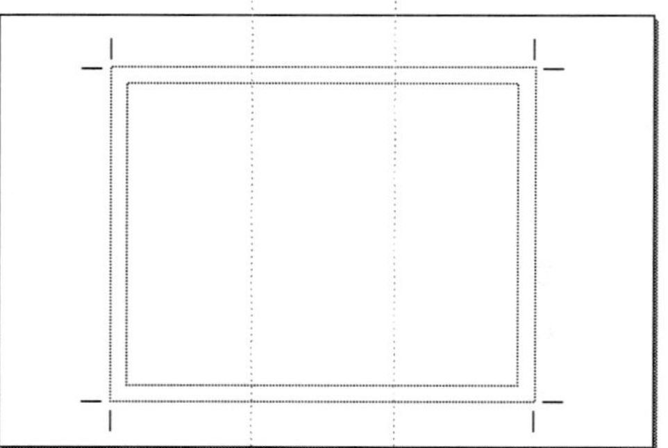

9. **Close** the document without saving.

Laying Out a Full Page Ad

1. Create a **File->New** document. Go to **View->Show Rulers**. Move the Zero Point to the upper left corner of the page.

2. Drag a vertical guide to the 4.25" mark of the horizontal ruler. Drag a horizontal guide to the 5.5" mark of the vertical ruler on the left side. This will show the center of the page.

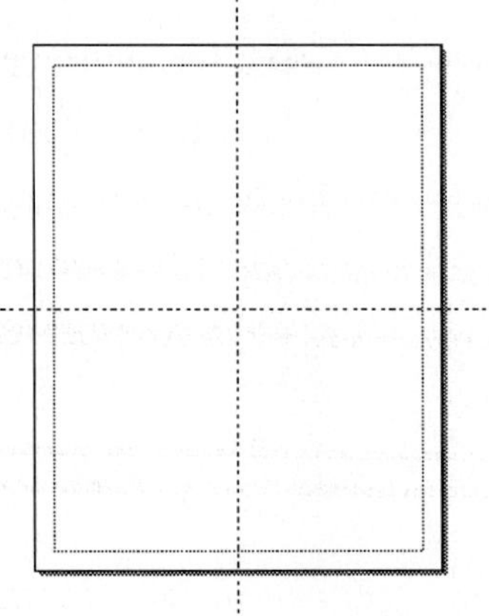

3. Drag vertical guides to the 2.25" and 6.25" marks of the horizontal ruler across the top of the document window.

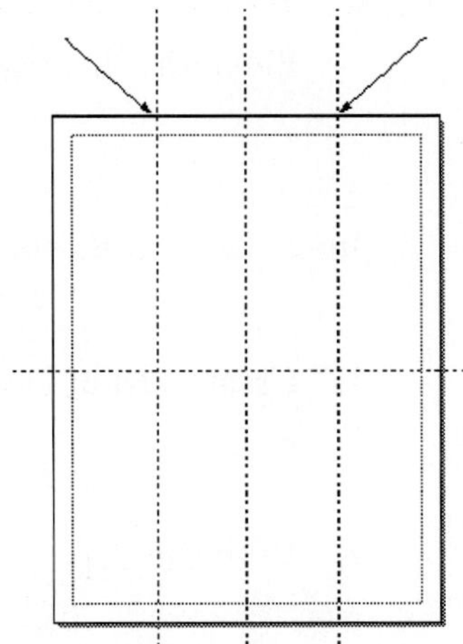

4. Now drag horizontal guides down to the 1.75", 3", 4.25", 6.75", 8", and 9.25" marks of the vertical ruler on the left side of the document window.

People who are involved in printing packages will often supply you with something called a "die" that's used to define the various cuts, panels, and "live areas" of a specific project. If you're designing a package, be sure to check with them before you start clicking and dragging. Dies are critical and shouldn't be re-built if possible. Some packagers can supply you with dies in Illustrator format – and the guides are already in place!

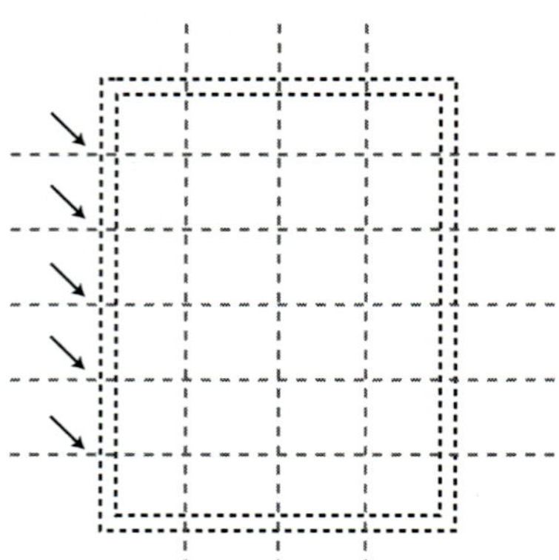

5. You have now created a full-page grid that can be used for many layouts. This grid will be used later for the Grocery Ad Project.

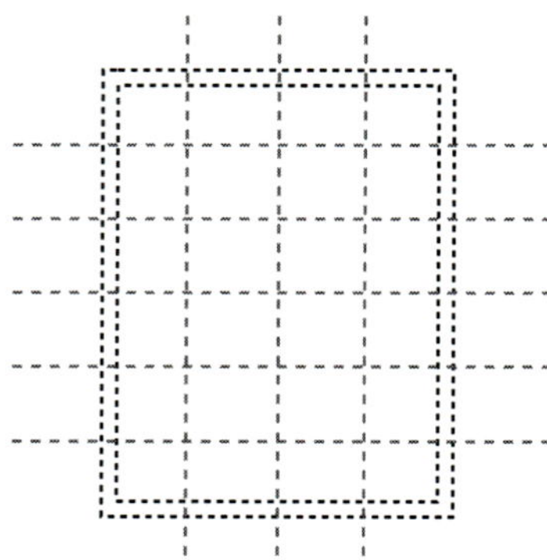

6. **Save As** the file in **Illustrator 7.0** format; name it "Full Page Ad Grid.AI." **Close** the document.

A Quick Three-Column Page Layout

1. Create a **New** Document. Use Guides to show a 1/2 in. margin inside the page.

2. With the Type tool, draw a text block the exact size of the margin.

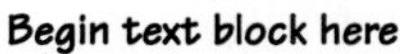

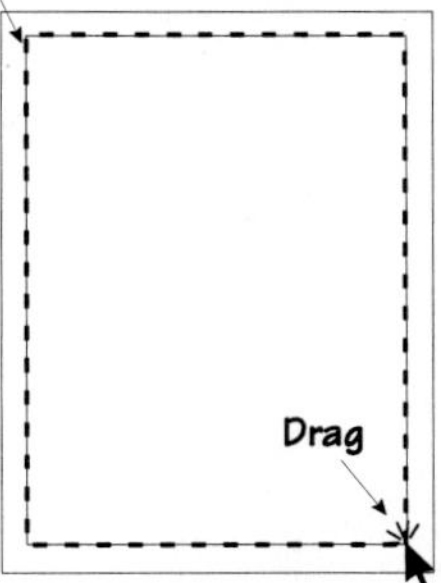

3. Select the text block with the Selection tool. Go to **Type—>Rows & Columns**. Set the columns for 3. Leave the rest as-is. Click **OK**. Three text columns will appear. Use these to position guides to show the columns.

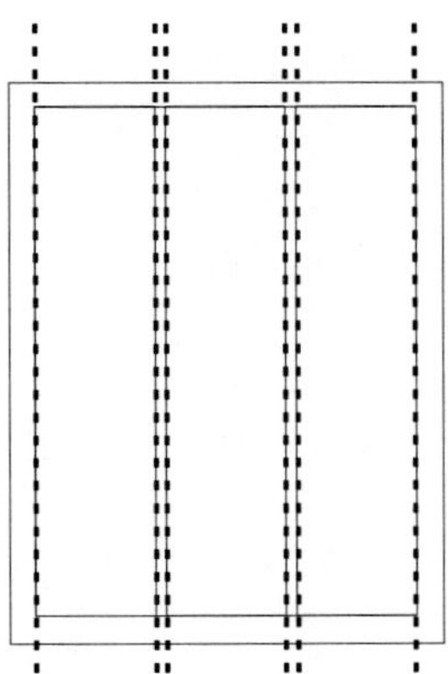

4. **Close** the document without saving.

Project K: Full Page Grocery Ad

Notes:

CHAPTER 16

PERSPECTIVE GRIDS

CHAPTER OBJECTIVE:

To teach you how to develop perspective grids, such as those used by traditional illustrators and designers to add depth and realism to certain types of drawings and designs. In Chapter 16 you will:

- See several different perspective grids that you can create using nonprinting guides and anchor-point copying techniques.
- Create a perspective grid that will be used in the development of a project assignment.
- Complete a project using a perspective grid that you develop in a hands-on exercise.

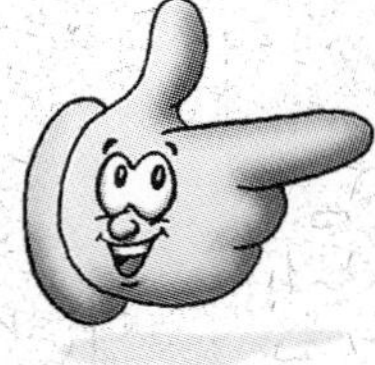

PROJECTS TO BE COMPLETED:

- HoneyDo Hair Salon Logo
- HoneyDo Free Hairstyle Ad
- Banana Boat Logo
- Fleet's In! T-Shirt Design
- Tropical Suites Logo
- Heart Notes
- Banana Border
- Champagne Brunch Table Tent
- Tropical Postcard
- Last Mango Menu Cover
- Full Page Grocery Ad
- Perspective Graph
- Java Jungle Goodies Ad

Perspective Grids

Although Illustrator isn't technically a three-dimensional drawing program, you can certainly draw upon techniques that have been used successfully by artists the world over for hundreds of years: perspective grids. This chapter will explore how to create such grids, and how to apply several different types to your drawing efforts.

There are many examples of artwork – especially from classical periods – that didn't make use of perspective. Check out artwork from the early middle-ages. Also look at ancient work from the Egyptians and others. Wonderful, beautiful artwork that didn't accommodate a vanishing point.

Creating perspective grids is a combination of drawing paths and then turning them into guides. The Horizon and the Vanishing Point are the two basics for adhering to perspective drawing.

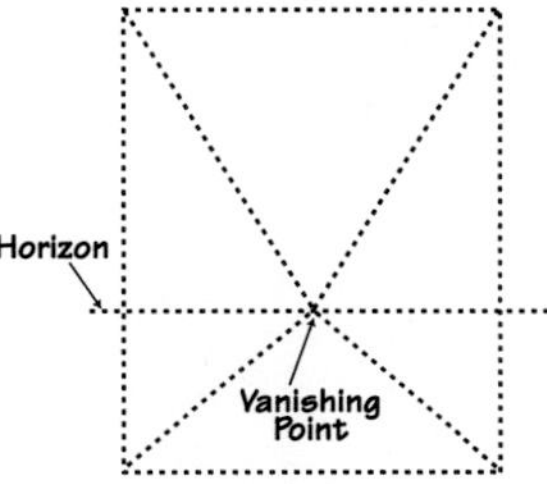

As long as the lines descend into the horizon aiming at the vanishing point, the perspective is correct. Depending on the complexity of the drawing, the perspective grid can be as simple or as detailed as you wish to make it. Here are two examples of how perspective grids can be drawn:

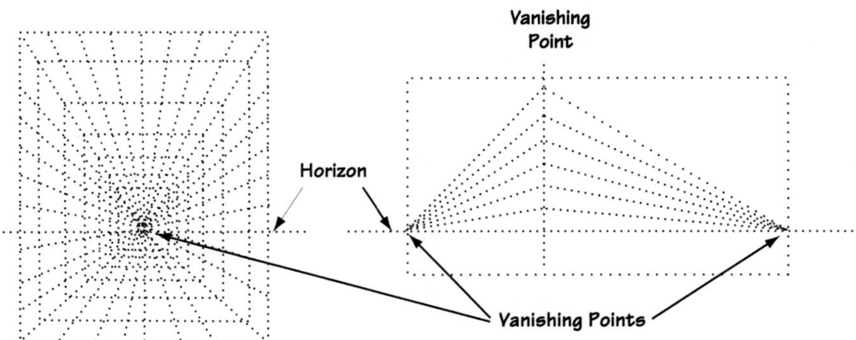

Scaling and Transform Again are your most useful tools for making an object descend in size towards a vanishing point.

Descending an Object into a Vanishing Point

1. **Open** the Student File, **Arch into Vanishing Point.AI.**

2. Click on the arching brick object to select it. Access the Scale tool in the Toolbox. Hold the Option (Macintosh) or Alt (Windows) key and click the crosshair on the vanishing point.

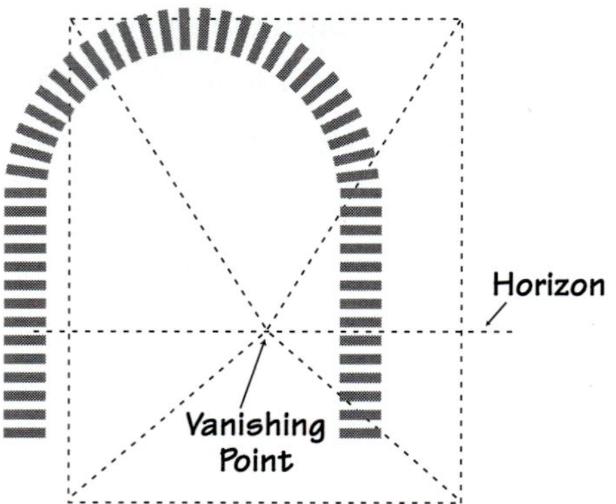

3. In the **Scale** dialog box, set **Uniform** for 75%. Press **Copy.**

4. Press Command-D (Macintosh) or Control-D (Windows) four times to **Transform Again** .

5. Observe the perspective descent of the archway as it scales into the vanishing point.

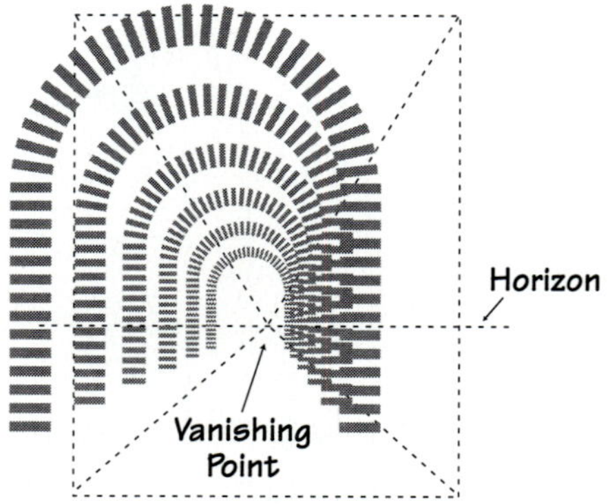

6. **Close** the document without saving.

It helps to use the Blend tool in modifying objects to match the angles of the perspective. In this example, two rectangles were drawn to angle into the vanishing point (a.).

The two rectangles were chosen for blending, and in the **Blend** dialog box, five steps were typed. Five intermediate rectangles were created (b.).

All the squares were grouped. Then, the **Scale/Transform Again** process was used to size them into the vanishing point (c.).

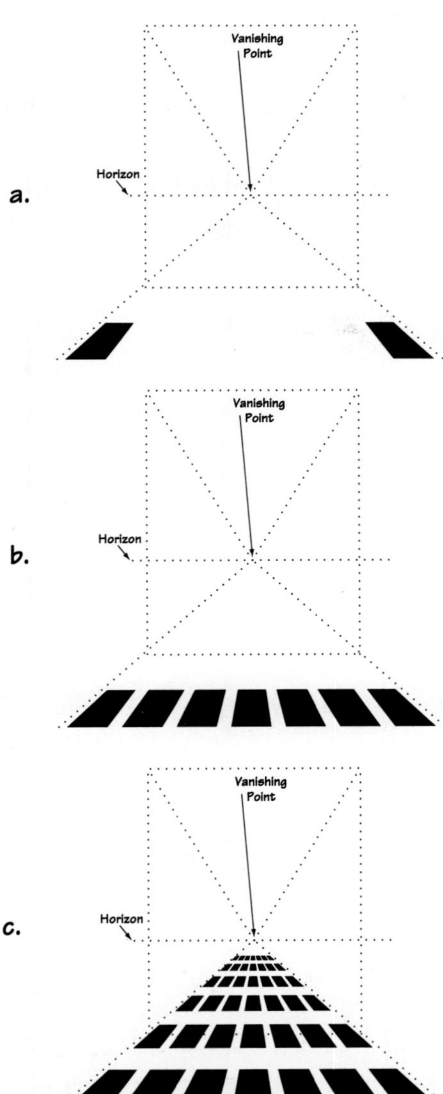

Creating a Perspective Grid

1. Create a **New** document. Go to **View->Show Rulers** for your rulers.

2. Draw a rectangle that is 4" x 2".

3. Drag guides to show the center point of the rectangle.

4. Use the Add-anchor point tool to add points where the guides touch the rectangle.

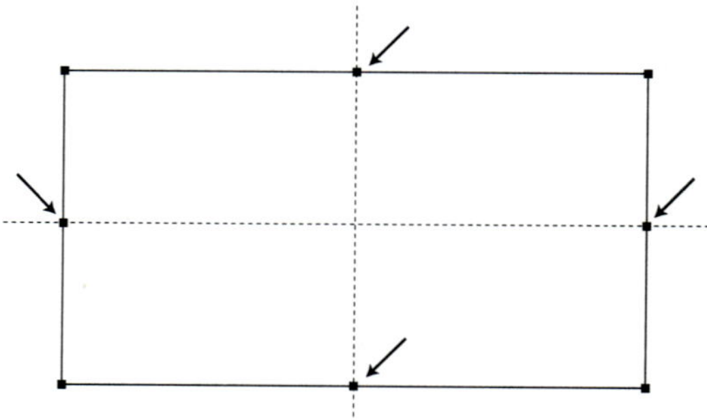

5. Pull the upper left and right anchor points down to the halfway guide.

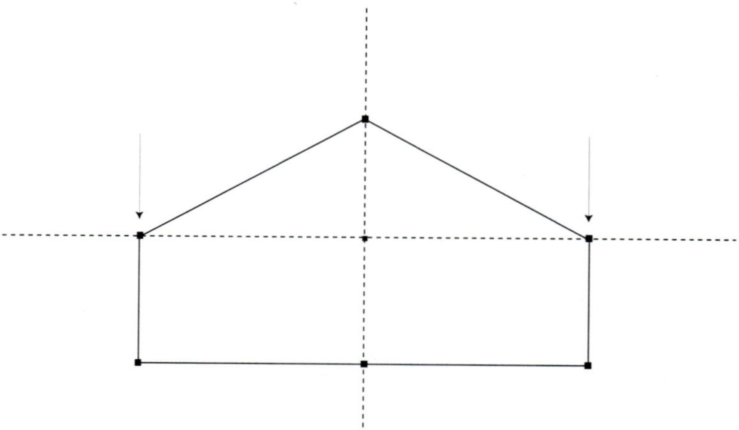

6. Move both far right anchor points to the right 1 inch.

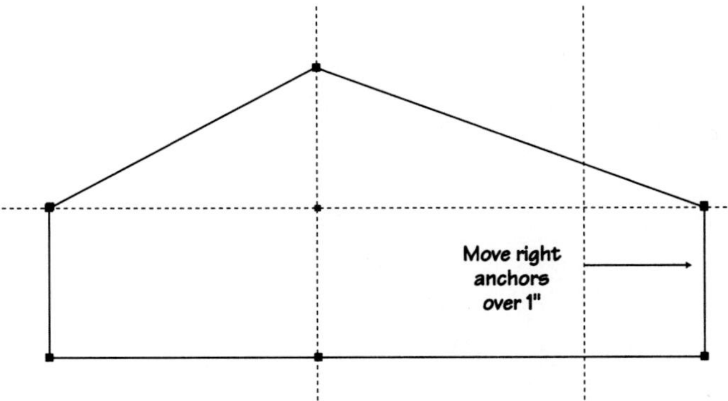

We discussed the importance of using objects to generate guides – as opposed to using only ruler guides in the development of your drawings. Here's an excellent example of that technique in practice.

7. Select the path. Press Command-5 (Macintosh) or Control-5 (Windows) to convert it to a guide. Delete the center horizontal guide.

   The result is a perspective grid that can be used for creative graphs, and designs of any kind.

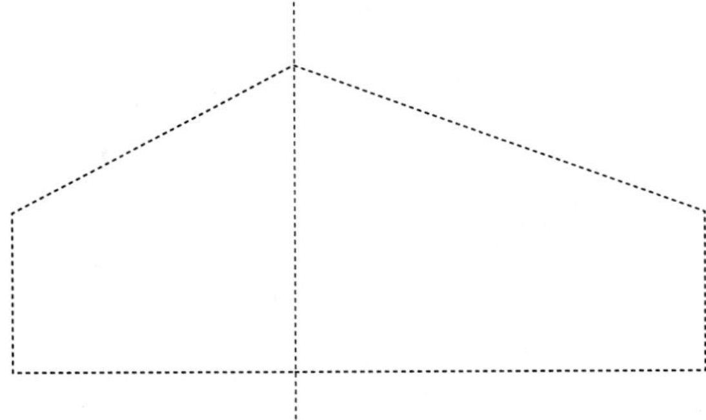

8. This perspective grid will be used for a Project you will do later, so save the file for this purpose.

9. **Save As** the file in **Illustrator 7.0** format. Name it, "Student Perspective Grid.AI." **Close** the document.

Notes:

CHAPTER 17

WORKING WITH GRAPHS

CHAPTER OBJECTIVE:

To teach you how to use Adobe Illustrator's graphing functions; to learn how to visually display statistical data using both traditional and custom business graphic formats. In Chapter 17 you will:

- Learn about the different graph types built into Illustrator's graphic dialog boxes.
- Learn about the Graph Data spreadsheet, where you can assign numeric values to build your graphs.
- Create a simple pie chart and learn to modify the visual attributes of the graph itself.
- Learn to import and manage text elements in your graphics.
- Use the techniques you worked with in the last chapter to develop a three-dimensional, custom chart.

PROJECTS TO BE COMPLETED:

- HoneyDo Hair Salon Logo
- HoneyDo Free Hairstyle Ad
- Banana Boat Logo
- Fleet's In! T-Shirt Design
- Tropical Suites Logo
- Heart Notes
- Banana Border
- Champagne Brunch Table Tent
- Tropical Postcard
- Last Mango Menu Cover
- Full Page Grocery Ad
- **Perspective Graph**
- Java Jungle Goodies Ad

Working with Graphs

Informational graphics are an important part of professional communications — finding their way into corporate reports, proposals, briefings, newspapers, television programs, web sites, and any place else that someone needs to talk about numbers. Charts are a heck of a lot more interesting to look at than columns of mind-numbing numbers. Not only that, but people can understand relatively complex data sets if they can see a picture of them instead of the underlying numbers.

There are tons of examples of business graphics in contemporary design. All you have to do is look at Newsweek, Time, USA Today, annual reports, business analysis – they're almost everywhere. Normally dull and boring numbers can be made more understandable and even fun when filtered through the eyes of a designer.

Illustrator has nine resident graph styles for you to choose from. There are also custom utilities that allow you to create your own symbols depicting the information shown in the graphs.

Selecting a Graph Type

In order to choose a graph type, either click-hold on the Graph tool to see the types, or double-click the Graph tool to see more options available.

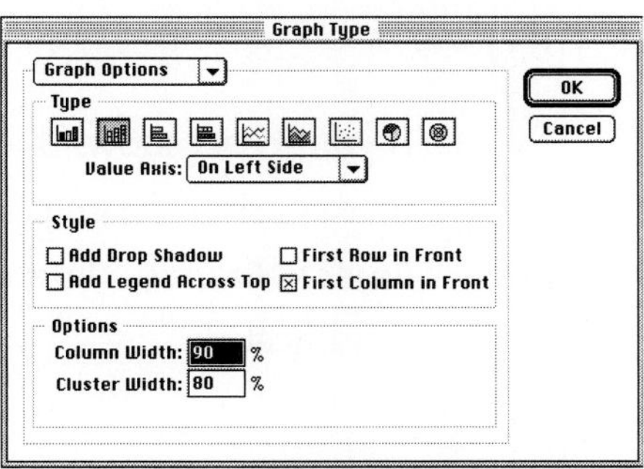

Once the **Graph Type** is selected and **OK** is clicked, the cursor turns into a crosshair. If you click the crosshair on the page, you will be given a graph dimensions window, allowing you to specify exact dimensions of the chart. The manual method is to drag the crosshair on the page, drawing the box to the size you prefer, visually, for the chart.

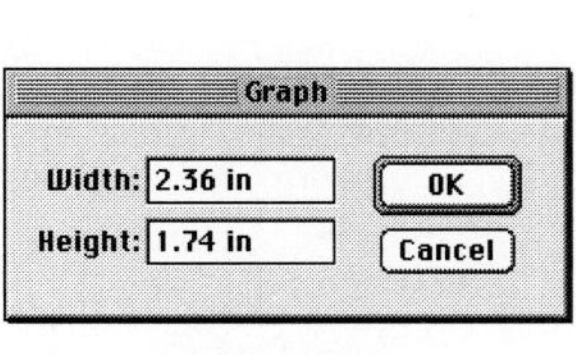

Dialog Box

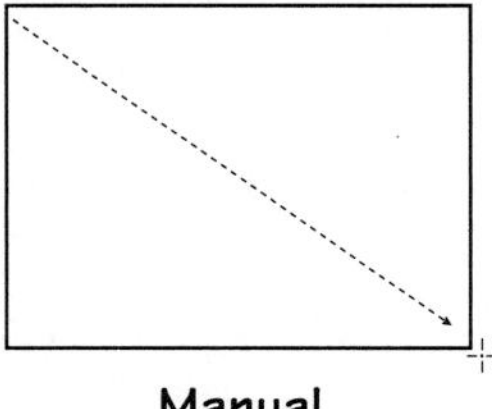
Manual

You can import data from almost any popular spreadsheet or database program. This often makes the job a lot easier. Typing a lot of numbers into a grid isn't something most designers relish.

Sometimes warnings can get tedious, and even aggravating. They can be turned off in the **Preferences-> General** window. It is listed as "Disable Warnings" in the **Options** section of this window.

The **Graph Data** spreadsheet appears. Here the necessary information to be shown in the graph is typed. A default number of "1.00" is present in the first cell. You click the cursor in each cell in which you wish to enter numbers, or use the Tab key to go from cell to cell.

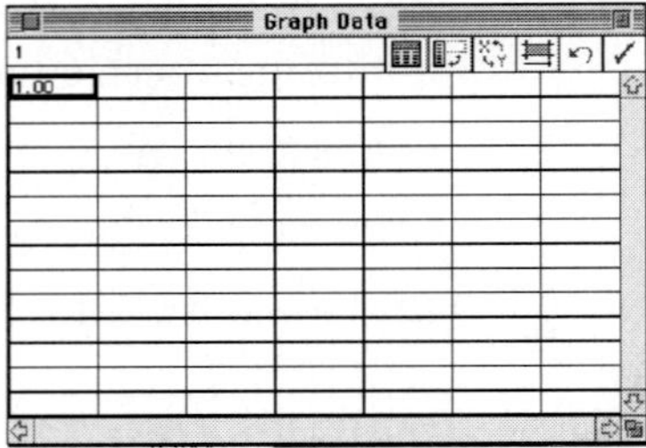

After the information is typed in, the window should then be closed. A warning appears, asking if you want to save this new data in the chart. Save should be clicked, then you will see a graph representing your typed information.

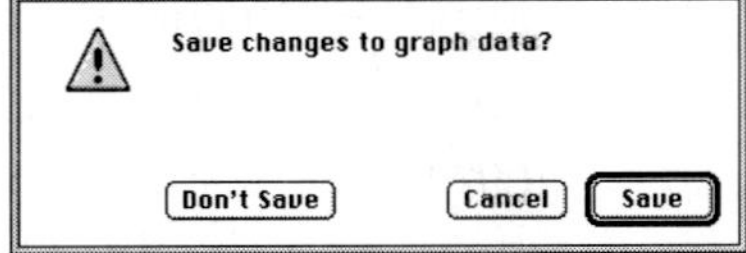

If your chart shows that you made a mistake typing in the information, you merely select the graph with the Selection tool, then go to **Object->Graphs->Data** and you will be back in the **Graph Data** window for modification.

Keep in mind, these graphs are all paths with changeable type that can be modified in the same manner as other Illustrator art/type objects.

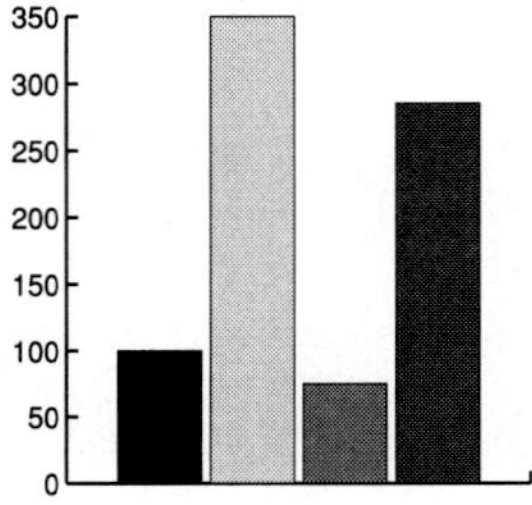

Creating a Graph

1. Create a **New** document. Double-click on the Graph tool.

2. In the **Graph Type** dialog box, select the Pie graph style. Click **OK**.

3. Single-click the crosshair on the page. Enter in the data boxes: **Width** = 2", **Height** = 2". Click **OK**.

4. In the appearing **Graph Data** dialog box, type this data. Close the window.

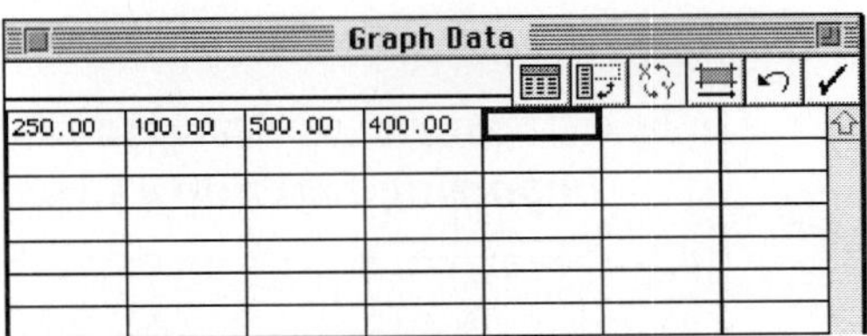

5. You will be asked if you want to save this data to the graph. Without your data, the graph will be empty, which is its default state. You do want your new information saved to the graph, so click **Save**.

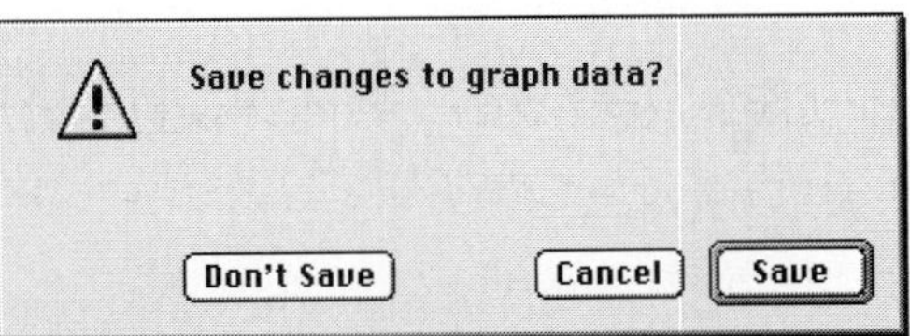

You can use the Tab key to move around the Graph Data grid. Tab moves you forward (to the right), Shift-Tab moves you backwards (to the left). You can also use the Arrow keys to navigate around the sheet.

6. The Pie chart, representing this data, will appear.

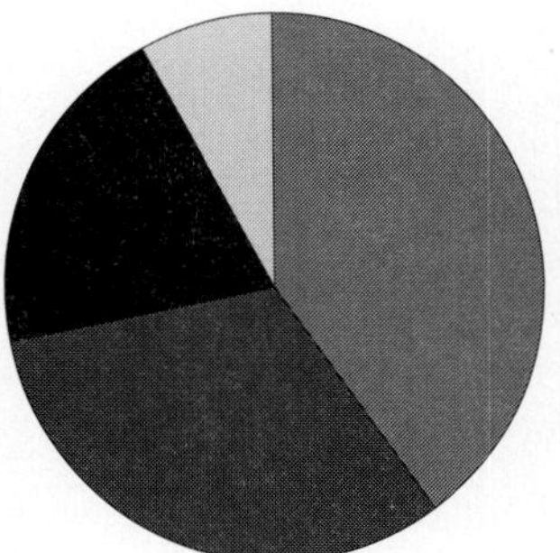

7. Create four separate text blocks that depict the chart information.

250 100 500 400

Apply a White **Fill** to the text. Apply a Black **Fill** to the "100". Move these text blocks into position on the appropriate slice.

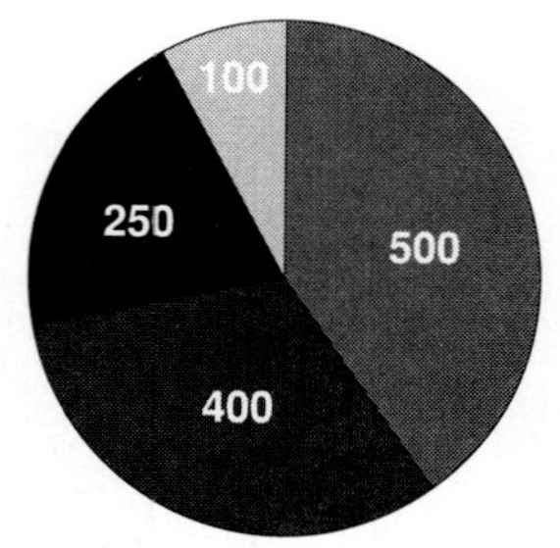

8. **Close** the file without saving.

Importing Text into a Graph

1. Create a **New** document. Double-click on the Graph tool.

2. In the **Graph Type** dialog box, select the Stacked Column graph style.

Click **OK**.

3. Single-click the crosshair on the page. Enter in the dialog box: **Width** = 5", **Height** = 3." Click **OK**.

4. In the appearing **Graph Data** dialog box, select the Import option.

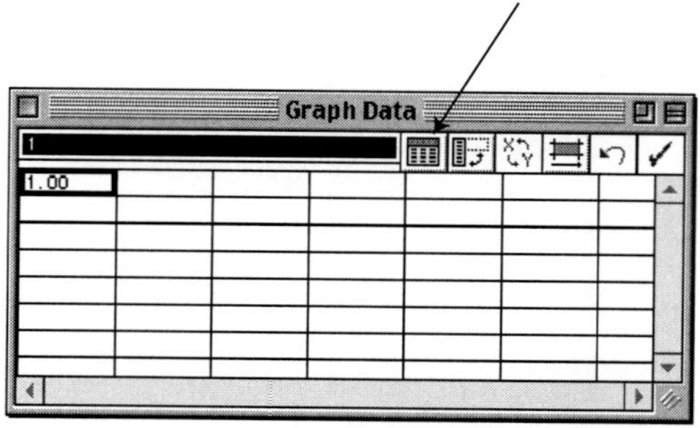

5. In the appearing window, go to the **SF-Advanced Illustrator** folder and choose **Graph Import.TXT.** The data will appear in the cells. Close the **Graph Data** window.

6. The graph representing this information will appear.

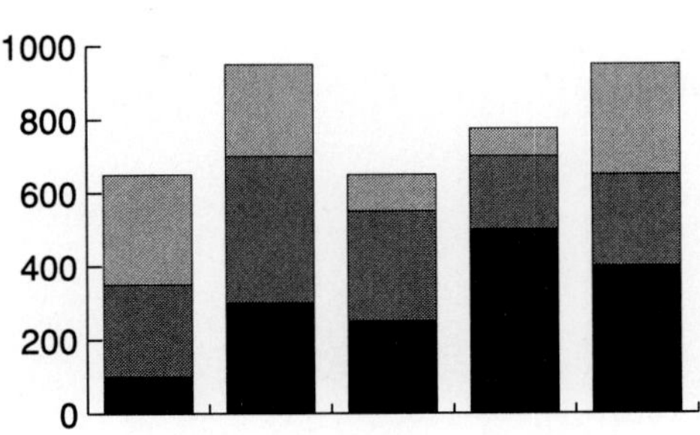

7. **Close** the file without saving.

Project L: Perspective Graph

Notes:

CHAPTER 18

PRINTING AND SEPARATIONS

CHAPTER OBJECTIVE:

To expose you to the many complex issues surrounding accurate and effective output of color-separated Illustrator files; to teach you how to prepare and output Illustrator files that meet the demands of commercial color printers. In Chapter 18 you will:

- Learn the differences between process and spot (or custom) colors and how they affect output of color separations.
- Learn the basics of trapping — purposeful distortions built into artwork to accommodate vibration and slippage on a printing press. You will learn both manual trapping and the use of the Pathfinder trapping filter.
- Learn the difference between overprint and knockout, attributes that determine how certain inks are applied on the press.
- Work with Separation Setup, a set of preferences that control how images separate when output.
- Learn to create spot color separations, a common requirement in the commercial design environment.
- Complete a project that requires accurate color separations.

PROJECTS TO BE COMPLETED:

- HoneyDo Hair Salon Logo
- HoneyDo Free Hairstyle Ad
- Banana Boat Logo
- Fleet's In! T-Shirt Design
- Tropical Suites Logo
- Heart Notes
- Banana Border
- Champagne Brunch Table Tent
- Tropical Postcard
- Last Mango Menu Cover
- Full Page Grocery Ad
- Perspective Graph
- **Java Jungle Goodies Ad**

Separations Setup

The ability to properly output files — particularly for professional mass production such as commercial printing — is a critically important issue facing today's artist. Once upon a time, illustrators didn't particularly worry about the magic behind color separation; they simply turned their artwork over to a separation house or professional prepress organization, and let them take care of scanning an image and doing whatever they had to do to get it on press (without radically changing its appearance).

Most color printing is done with four pieces of film – one for each of the primary (cyan, magenta, yellow, and black) inks. Each object's components are placed on these films at output, according to their color values. Spot colors, when used in a drawing, can result in extra pieces of film – ones that no one expected and no one budgeted for. If you're printing a four-color job, be sure to select any spot colors and convert them to process colors before you send the file out.

This isn't the case anymore. You have to have at least a general knowledge of printing conditions, and how your artwork is going to be reproduced somewhere down the line in the project's lifespan.

Color Issues

There are two ways that colors are reproduced on a printing press:

- Process color, comprised of four primary colors (cyan, magenta, yellow, and black), which when combined on press as halftone dots simulate a wide range of colors, or

- Spot Colors, which are actually colored ink. A good example of this is when you add red ink to a regular black and white flyer. The second ink is known as a spot color. Process colors cannot reproduce every color there is, so sometimes you'll find yourself using specific ink colors in your drawings to achieve the desired effect.

Process Colors

This is known as "Four-color Process" or sometimes referred to as just four-color printing. In Process printing, the printer takes the four process colors and makes a printing plate for each:

- C - Cyan
- M - Magenta
- Y - Process Yellow
- K - Process Black

Spot Colors

Spot Colors are very important for making Spot Color separations, since they can be printed on laser printers for silk-screen printers.

To generate separations, you can use Illustrator, which has a built-in separations function, or you could save the Illustrator document as an Illustrator EPS and Place this into a publishing program such as PageMaker or QuarkXPress.

If the publishing program method is used, **Paint** the design with **Spot Colors** and **Save As** an Illustrator EPS. This EPS is Placed into a publishing program. In the program's color palette, these Spot Color names will appear. The publishing program uses its own separation method to do Spot Color separations based on separating by color names.

The issue of Spot Colors isn't limited solely to the elements in the drawing. If you've imported an EPS element from another program, it might contain spot colors that you didn't create.
Combining spot colors and process colors in one document is not advised. Final verdict: only use Spot Colors when you know the document is ultimately designated to be Spot Color separated, say for screenprinting purposes.

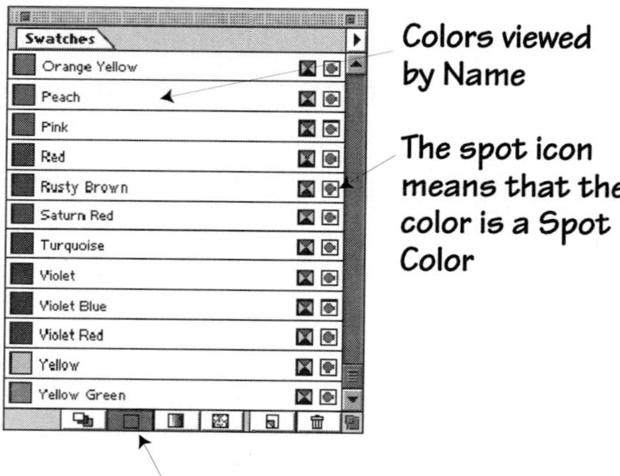

Colors viewed by Name

The spot icon means that the color is a Spot Color

Spot Colors are selected and named in the **New Swatch** window. This window can be accessed by double-clicking on the color name in the **Swatches** palette. It is in this window that the choice to make a color either Process or Spot is determined.

What Is Trapping?

Trapping is the art of compensating for misregistration of plates during the printing process. Misregistration sometimes occurs due to plates shifting or paper stretching on the press.

No trapping applied. White blemishes between touching colors.

With trapping applied.

Trapping is a difficult technique whose requirements differ from printer to printer. Although we discuss it here, so that you'll understand the concept a little better, it's our opinion that trapping should not be done by the artist, but applied by the printer or imaging company that you work with. It's not a design function, it's a manufacturing issue.

It is very important, before applying trapping, that you speak to the printing manager of the company who will print the job. In most cases, the printers or service bureaus prefer that the artist does not apply the trapping. They prefer that their own art department set trapping where needed.

If you elect to trap your job, do so by clicking the **Overprint** button of either Fill or Stroke in the **Attributes** palette.

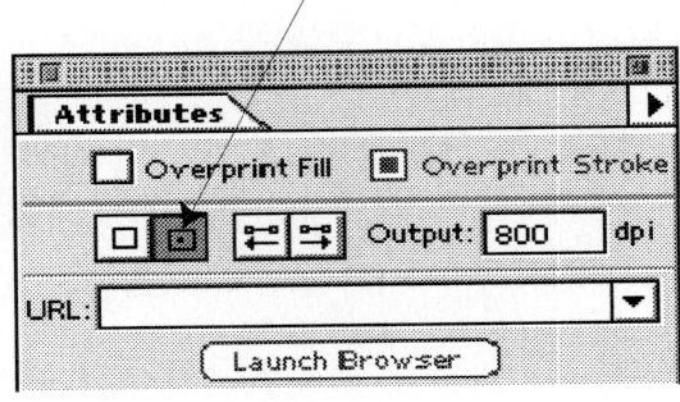

How Trapping Works

It is very important to understand what Overprint actually does and what elements it affects. To put it simply, any object set with Overprint will not knock out the object(s) underneath it. Rather, it will "Print Over" the underneath object(s).

In this example the yellow square is underneath the black oval. In the "With Trapping" sample, the **Overprint Fill** box was clicked in the **Attributes** palette. There is no physical way to see trapping on the objects themselves.

The Illustrator must know from experience how the trapping, when applied, will affect the objects in question.

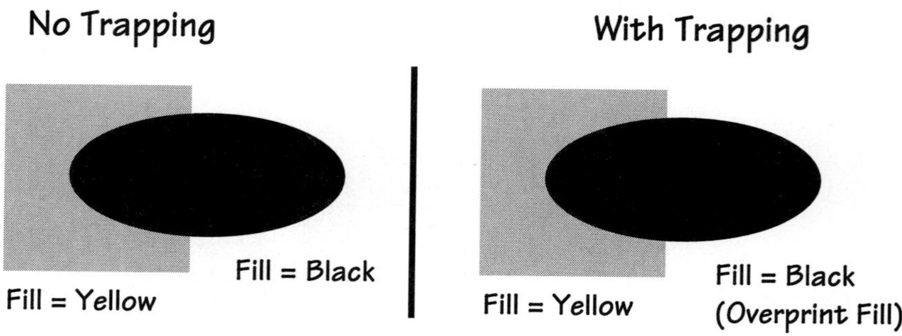

If you do intend to build traps (for some unknown reason), be sure to check with your printer, and have them carefully double-check your work before they put it on press. They know more about what they need than any designer could.

When separated, the above plates would look like this (below). The yellow square in the "No Trapping" sample was knocked out by the oval. The "With Trapping" yellow square was untouched. This means the black oval will print over the yellow.

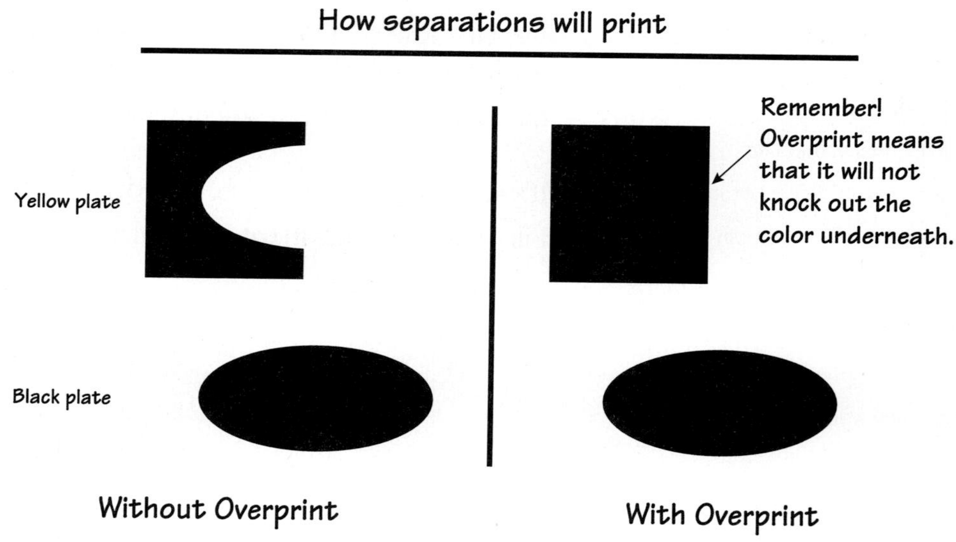

Applying Trapping to Strokes

In many cases, one does not want the Fills of the colors to Overprint the other colors. When colors touch, it is only necessary to Overprint the Strokes so that there are minute trapping overlaps.

It is important to know how a Stroke works, so that you know how much of an overlap will be achieved. The Stroke weight is divided in half by the path.

In this example, the oval was painted with a 10 pt. rule (a.). The thickness does not extend 10 pts. outward from the path; 5 pts. extend outward, 5 pts. go inward (b.).

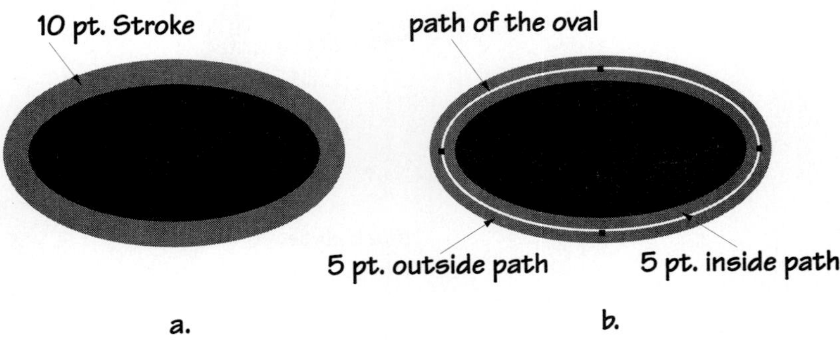

Trapping is press, paper, and ink-specific. Traps tha work fine in a magazine will not work properly if the same element is reproduced for a newspaper ad. The different paper stocke and different presses eacl have their own specific trapping requirements.

This means that if you want to have a 2-pt. overlap extending outward to the touching color, you must paint the **Stroke** weight as 4 pt.

In this example, the oval "With Trapping" was painted with a 4-pt. **Stroke** that was set to **Overprint**.

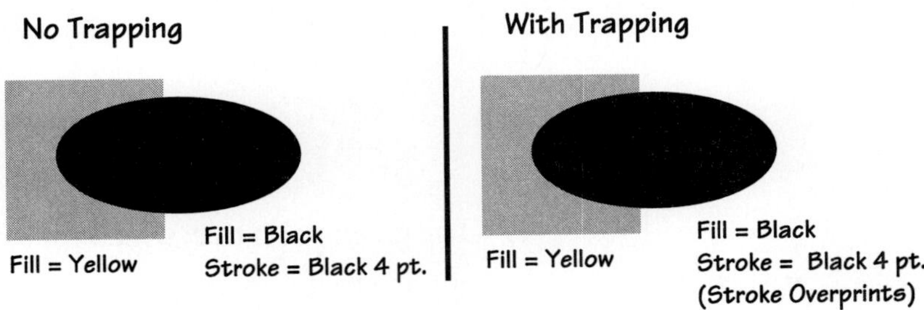

Here we see the plates after they have been separated. The side with "No Trapping" has a yellow square that the oval knocked out right up to the oval path (A.).

The "With Trapping" oval was set with a 4 pt. **Stroke** to Overprint. The 4-pt. **Stroke** extended 2 pts. into the yellow square area, which the oval could Print Over. The 2-pt. trapping is shown here by a screened rule (B.).

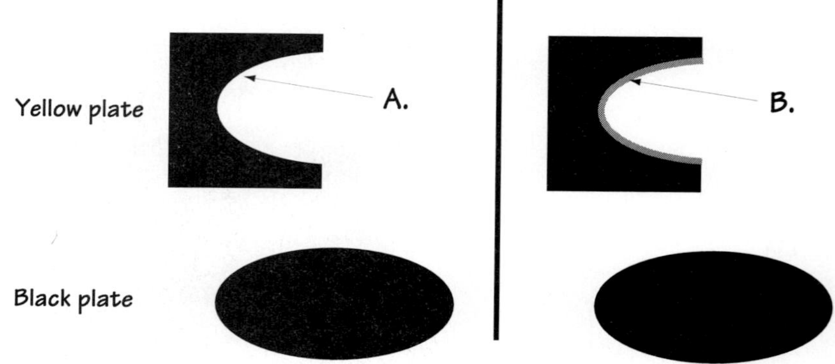

Applying Trapping to Artwork

1. **Open** the Student File **Trapping Palm.AI.**

2. The green palm tree, which rests on the yellow sun, needs to have trapping applied to it.

3. Click on the palm, which is filled with ATC Green.
   Add a **Stroke** of the same color with a weight of 2 pts.
   In the **Window->Attributes** palette, click on **Overprint Stroke.**

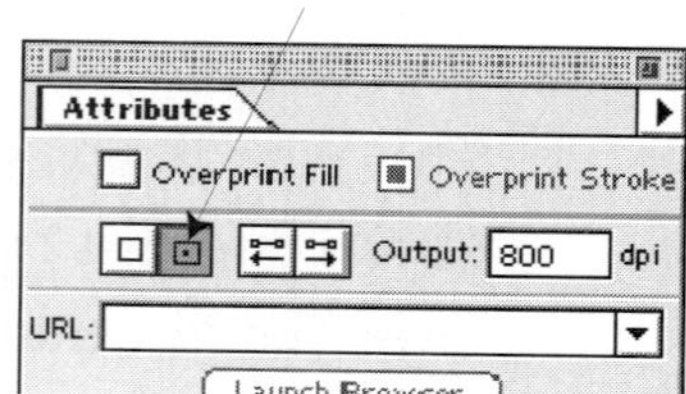

This will add a trapping Stroke of 1 pt. (half of 2 pt.) that will overlap into the yellow plate. In the next illustration, the gray in the yellow plate shows the 1-pt. overlap that will trap on the green plate.

Yellow Plate
(trapping shown in gray)

Green Plate

4. **File-Save** the file. **Close** the document.

The Trapping Filter

Trapping is one of the most overlooked and misunderstood aspects of printing, especially when utilizing desktop solutions.

Illustrator has a Trapping filter that creates a trap (an overlap of color) between two touching colors.

Using the Trapping Filter

1. Create a **New** document.
2. Draw a rectangle, then draw a circle. Position the circle so that it overlaps the rectangle halfway.

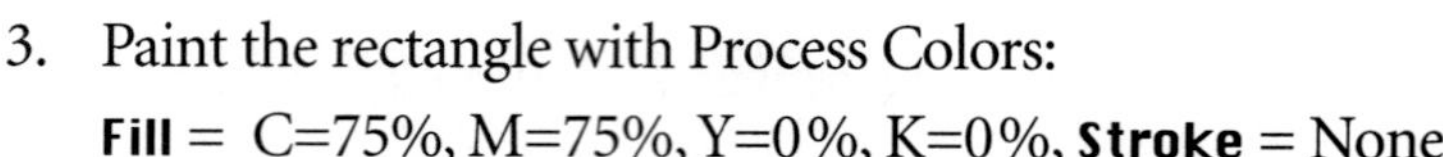

3. Paint the rectangle with Process Colors:
   Fill = C=75%, M=75%, Y=0%, K=0%, **Stroke** = None.

   Paint the circle: **Fill** : Yellow=100%, **Stroke** = None.

4. Select the two objects and go to the **Object->Pathfinder** menu to find the **Trap** option.

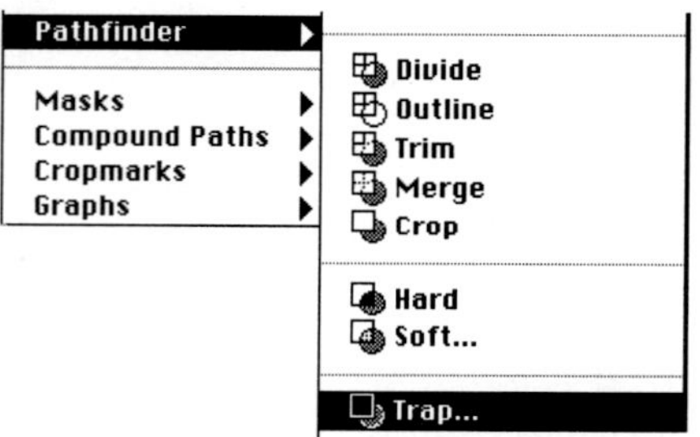

5. In the **Pathfinder Trap** dialog box, type in the **Thickness** of the trapping path, the **Height/Width** of the trap, and the **Tint Reduction,** which softens the trap color so that there won't be harsh colors showing as the colors overlap.

The trapping filter does a decent job of trapping specific Illustrator elements. If you're going to use it, you might consider running a few tests with your printer to make sure you have the settings correct for their specific manufacturing conditions.

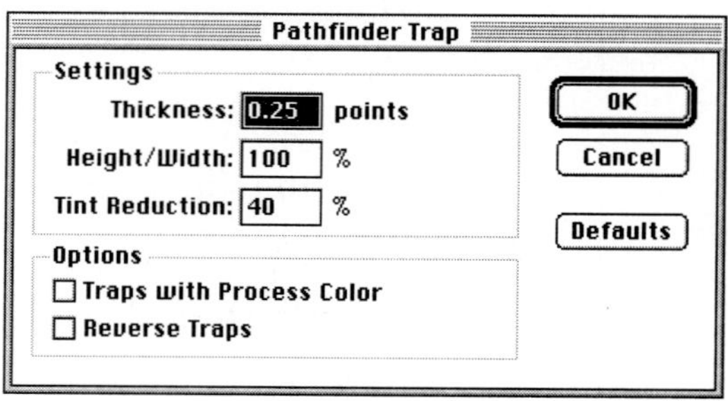

You can determine if the trapping is done with Process color. There's also an option to Reverse Traps — the darker color gets the tint reduction rather than the lighter color.

Click **OK.** The filter goes to work and creates a separate path between the paths of the two objects.

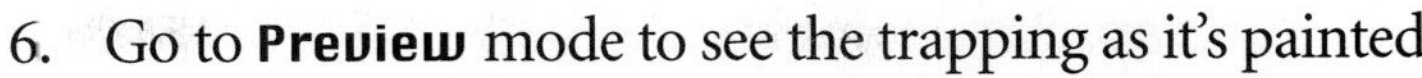

6. Go to **Preview** mode to see the trapping as it's painted.

Some popular output devices – in particular, color printers – don't support separations from a desktop system. They're meant to print *composites*, which is the entire job, with all the colors in proper place. That's because they're normally used for interim proofs, not for generating films.

7. Go to **View->Artwork.** The filter created a new path where the circle and rectangle paths touch. This separate path will be painted by the filter to blend with the two.

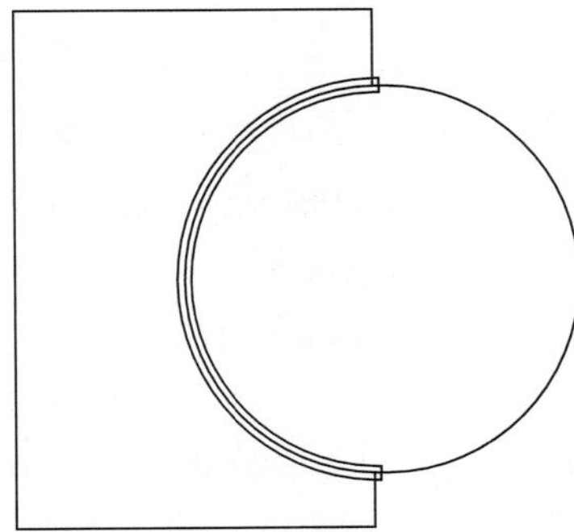

8. Move the circle to the side so you'll see the trapping path more clearly.

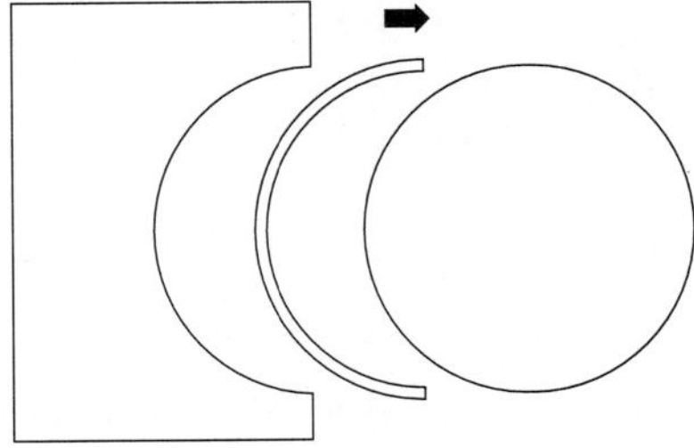

9. **Close** the dsocument without saving.

Separation Setup

Illustrator can actually print its own color separations, however, they must be configured using the **Separation Setup** option. This can be accessed two ways:

- In the **File** menu, near the bottom. You may use the **Separation Setup** this way, but it will not give you the option to print.

- For most printers, the **Print** window, after selecting **Print** from the **File** menu, shows a **Separation Setup** button to click. If you wish to set up your settings, then print the separation, it is handier to use this method.

Printing separations is another thing that might be outside your job as an illustrator. In many environments, the people who design pages and the people who output them (and are responsible for manufacturing tasks) are two completely different groups. Often, they're not in the same building, or working for the same company.

This separation function can send color separations to the printer in one of two ways:

- Process Colors
- Spot Colors

To use this separation facility, you must have some knowledge of color, separations, and the commercial printing process that ultimately will use the separations.

Let's look at how **Separation Setup** approaches an Illustrator document. If you have not utilized the **Separation Setup** in your Illustrator application, this feature must know what printer you want to use for separation purposes. You do this by clicking on **Open PPD** and going to the PPD folder to select your printer. After you have done this, the full features of **Separation Setup** will be available.

Here is a sample design (**Three Suns.EPS** available in the Student File folder).

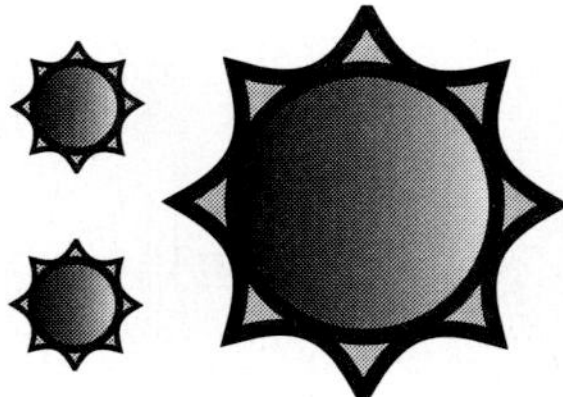

Notice that the large sun is on the right. This is important when you initially see the main separation window.

The first thing you'll notice when you see the separation window is that the sun design has flip-flopped so that the large sun is now on the left.

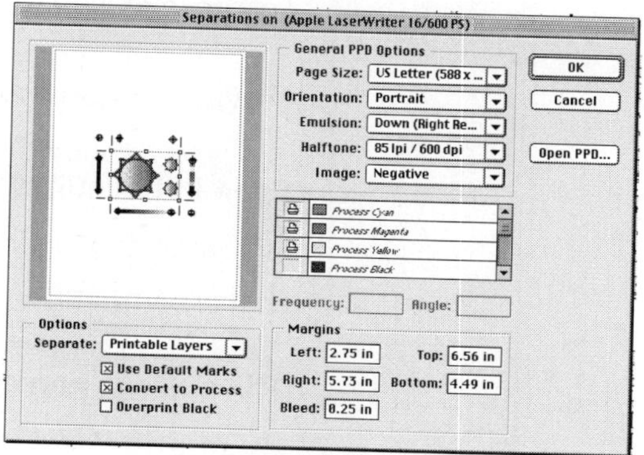

Don't be alarmed. The reversal is based on the way the Emulsion chooser is set as a default. The choices are Right Reading Up and Right Reading Down. The default is set to **Down (Right Reading)** so that the film will be able to create a printing plate with minimum distortion. If you print to film, this should be your choice. For a laser proof choose **Up (Right Reading)**.

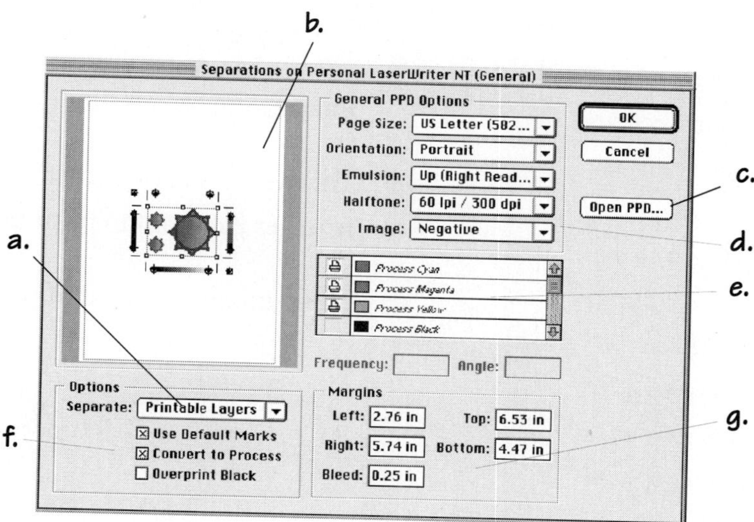

Here are descriptions of the marked sections of the window.

a. **Printable Layer** selector. This lets you choose what is to be printed.

   Separate Printable Layers refers to any objects that have been put on Layers in the **Layer** window. In the **Layers Option** submenu of the **Layer** window, you can assign whether or not an object on that layer will be printed.

Separate Visible separates only what's visible. Anything Hidden will not separate.

Separate All will separate anything you have in the document.

b. Preview Window allows you to see the image you are separating.

c. **Open PPD** requires that you choose a Postscript Printer Description (PPD) from the PPDs that came with Adobe Illustrator. Select the one that is compatible with the printer you are printing to.

d. The **General PPD Options** selectors refer to the settings of the page you are printing.

Page Size is the size of the page you wish the image printed to.

Orientation is either Portrait (vertical) or Landscape (horizontal).

Emulsion refers to printing to negatives and whether or not the emulsion is Right Reading Up or Right Reading Down.

Halftone lets you pick the halftone resolution of the separations.

Image controls output to be positive or negative images.

e. This window allows you to choose the colors you wish to print, and whether you want to print certain Spot colors as process.

The symbols at the left of each color name are very important to know.

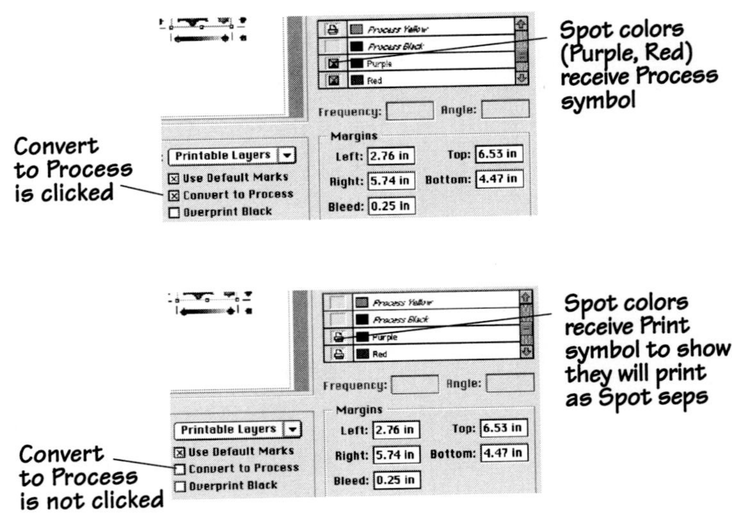

Solid inks can reproduce colors that are outside the scope of four-color printing. While four-color work seems to reproduce every color of the rainbow, that's not true – it's actually very limited. When you create a spot color and change it to a four-color process color, the hue or shade can change – sometimes a lot. This is called "color shift," and is something you need to be careful of.

If you click on the space at the left of each color name, you will see a Printer icon, which means that the color it is next to will print.

If you have **Convert to Process** clicked, the Spot colors will receive a Process icon, which means they will be included in the separations as Process.

You can click Off all the normal Process colors (C-M-Y-K), and still separate the Spot colors as Process, if **Convert to Process** is On.

Underneath the color printing selector window are four more choices:

Most of these settings cannot be selected randomly – they're extremely site- and press-specific. This is another area where consultation with your printer is clearly in order.

Options:

f. **Use Default Marks.** If you wish to have crop and register marks on the separation, then click this button.

Convert to Process. A Spot color is actually a spot color that can be separated individually by name. If a design using Spot color has to be separated as Process, then click this button.

Overprint Black. Sometimes the printer requires that the black elements in the design overprint any underlying images. This helps with trapping.

Margins:

g. **Left, Right, Top, Bottom.** These choices refer to the actual size of the image you are separating. If you need more room around the image on the separation, enlarge these numbers appropriately.

Bleed. Click this button if your image is going to bleed past the crop marks shown in the viewing window.

Making a Spot Color Separation

1. **Open** the Student File **Three Suns.EPS**.

2. Access the **Separation Setup** option in the **File** menu. If a PPD (PostScript Printer Description) has not been set, you will be asked to choose a PPD. Click **Open PPD**. Go to the Printer Descriptions folder that is in the Illustrator application folder, and select your laser printer.

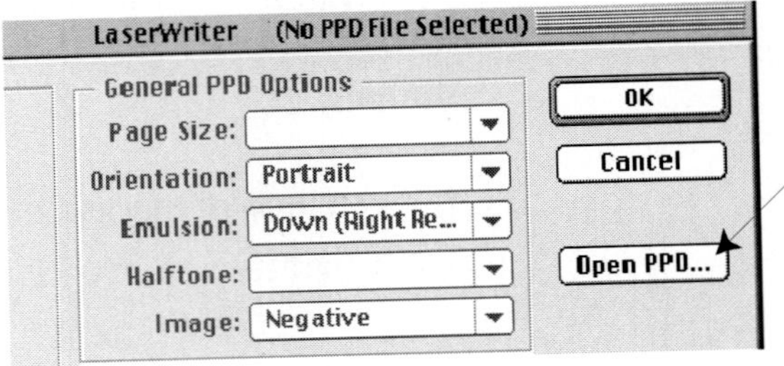

3. You will then be shown all the options of the **Separations Setup** window. In the **Separations** window, make these settings:

   - In the Options (lower left corner) click-hold on **Printable Layers** and choose **Separate All**.

   - In the upper right section, make these settings:

     Set **Orientation** to **Portrait**.

     Set **Emulsion** to **Up** (**Right Reading**).

     Leave **Halftone** set as is for now.

     Set **Image** for Positive to see positive images on the printout.

     Make sure **Convert to Process** is not clicked.

- In the color selecting section, click the Print square next to each Spot color, Purple, Red, Yellow, so the Printer icon shows.

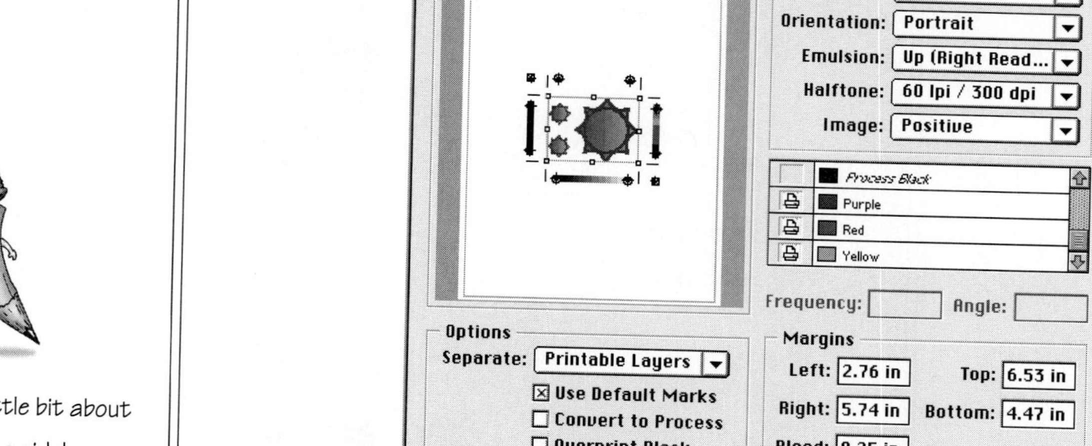

We talked a little bit about crop marks in a sidebar earlier in the course. This exercise should make that discussion perfectly clear – it was about the difference between trim marks (used for cutting) and crop marks (which define the portion of an image that will be saved when you save a file in EPS format).

Make sure no Process colors are clicked to print.
Leave all other settings as-is.

4. Click **OK.** Go to **File->Print** and click **Print** in the dialog box. Observe the results on the printed paper. **Close** the document without saving.

Crop Marks

Crop Marks is a standard printing term that refers to an image, such as a photograph, and how only certain portions of the image will be printed. It is the same principle as Trim Marks, in which the bounding box is determined by the marks.

In Illustrator, the Crop Marks represent the new bounding box, useful only in doing separations in the Illustrator program. Do not set Crop Marks on an image; in this case, even though the image will have Crop Marks which are visible in Illustrator, these marks will not show in the publishing program, rather, **Save** the file as an Illustrator EPS that is then Placed in a publishing program.

Creating Crop Marks

1. **Open** the Student File **Three Suns.EPS**

2. Draw a rectangle, painted with None, around the big sun. Select the rectangle.

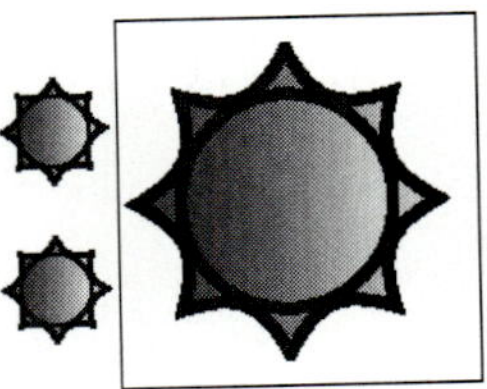

3. Go to **Object->Crop Marks->Make.**

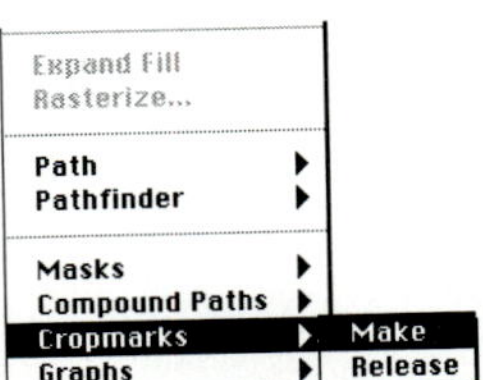

The rectangle will be replaced by the Crop Marks.

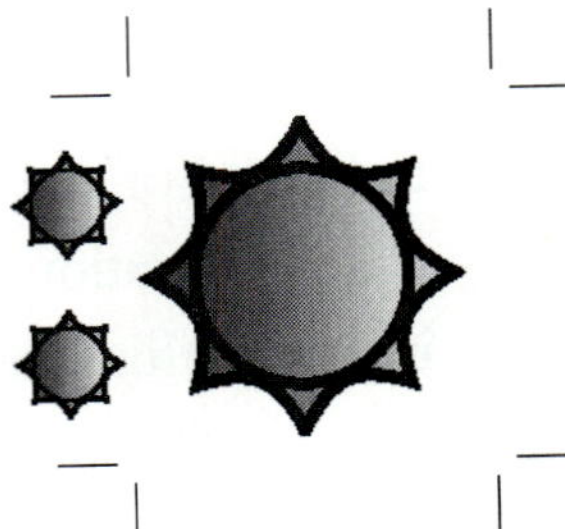

4. Go to **File–>Separation Setup.**

5. In the **Separation** window, select **Open PPD** if no printer has been selected. Select an appropriate printer.

6. Next to the **Emulsion** option, set the box to **Up (right reading).**

7. In the Preview box of the **Separation** window, observe how the object with Crop Marks has been singled out by a bounding box.

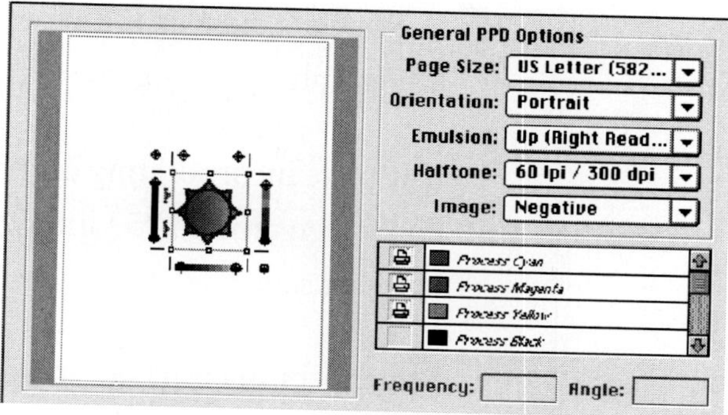

8. **Close** the document without saving.

Separations for Screenprinting

Preparing separations for screenprinting requires no special devices or distortions to accommodate the printing process. There are, however, certain restrictions that screenprinting puts on the artwork when you are designing it. The process of screenprinting is the pressing of inks through a nylon mesh screen. The screens come in many degrees of tightness of mesh. A tight mesh can handle more detail than a coarse mesh.

Though the mesh can handle photographic halftones, it cannot handle tight line screens, such as 133 Lines Per Inch, that are used with the metal plates of lithographic printing presses.

If you are incorporating bitmapped artwork into a screenprint design, keep the line screen around 75 Lines Per Inch. It is always important, though, to check with the screen print manager as to what line screen is preferred.

Screenprinting is based on Spot Color separations. When preparing designs with several colors, it is mandatory that **Spot Colors** are used. With screenprinting, do not expect the precision of lithographic printing for colors that touch.

Trapping, a slight overlapping of colors that touch, is sometimes needed, but only for those screenprinters who require it. Not all screenprinters want trapping. They prefer that their own production staff do the trapping.

Again, check with the screenprinter doing the job to get information on how the art needs to be prepared.

Another consideration is printing one ink on top of another. The most common need for this is when black shirts are printed on. Since the outlines of most art are black to define the shapes of the images, this poses problems when printed on a black shirt.

The standard procedure most screenprinters use is first to print a white background that encompasses the design, then to Flash Dry it. This dried white background then makes the artwork look normal when printed.

Creating a White Background for a Black Shirt

If art that has black outlines or detail is printed on a black shirt, the effect is lost. To give the design a neutral background for the black ink to contrast with, a separate white ink background must be printed first.

1. **Open** the Student File **Fleet's In! Design.AI.**

If you ever find yourself involved in silkscreening projects, this technique should come in handy. It lets you print on dark objects by creating a white area in which to work.

2. **Edit->Select All** paths. Go to **Object->Pathfinder->Unite.**

3. **Edit->Select All** remaining paths. Paint them: **Fill** = Black, **Stroke** = 16 pt. Black. This will give the design an extra 8 pt. of white around the perimeter. Be sure to set the **Joins** for rounded. This will smooth out the edges.

4. This black art will be the screen for a white ink background.

5. **Save As** the file in **Illustrator 7.0** format. Name it "Fleet's In.Flash Dry.AI." **Close** the document.

Project M: Java Jungle Goodies Ad

Notes:

Final Review

Chapters 10 through 18:

In the final chapters of *Adobe Illustrator: Advanced Digital Illustration*, you have continued to work with the program's advanced features, and have come to the point where you can not only develop complex and professional illustrations and layouts, but are comfortable getting them to print correctly when it's time for commercial reproduction. In the last half of the course, you have learned:

- ✓ To be fully familiar with all aspects of Transformation tools and applications; how the Origin Point affects the application of the scale, shear, rotate, and reflection tools; how to apply multiple transformations both manually and through the use of dialog box attributes.
- ✓ Understand the concept of a mask, and know when to use it to achieve effects that aren't possible to create any other way. You should also be familiar with the concept of compounds, and how compounded objects act and how they can be modified to suit your design needs.
- ✓ How to import elements created in Illustrator or in other applications, such as scanned images or so-called continuous-tone images. You should be familiar with both linking and embedding imported art elements into your drawings, and the implications of each method.
- ✓ How to create, manage, and modify patterns and pattern tiles. You should also know how to apply transformation tools and methods to both elements containing patterns and the patterns within those elements.
- ✓ How to look at Adobe Illustrator as a stand-alone page layout tool. At this point you should be able to develop single-page layouts without ever leaving the Illustrator working environment.
- ✓ How to create and apply traditional perspective grids, in use for centuries as a method of adding depth and realism to illustrations and designs.
- ✓ To create a wide variety of statistical charts and graphs, such as pie charts and bar charts. You should know how to modify both the numeric values of your charts as well as the elements themselves.
- ✓ How to manage your elements and drawings when you need to output high-quality separations from your designs. You should be familiar with both four-color process separations, as well as how to generate separations for custom, or spot colors. You should also have a basic knowledge of trapping.

Project A: HoneyDo Hair Salon Logo

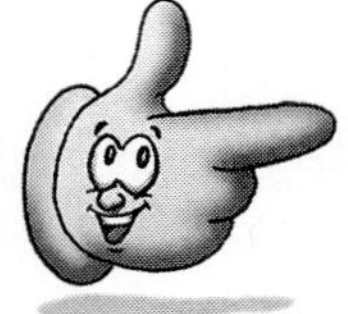

Editing a Streamlined Image

1. From the **SF-Adv Illustrator** folder, **Open** the document **HoneyDo Girl.AI.**

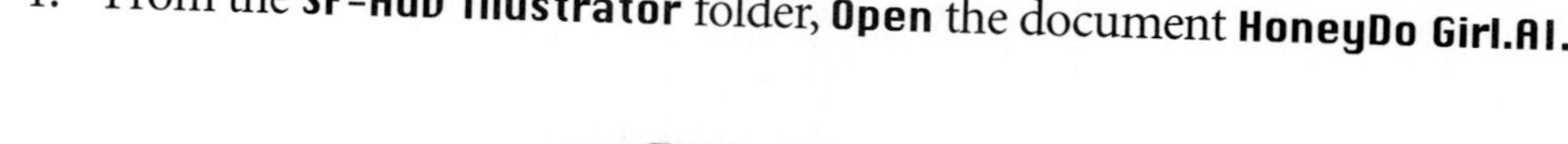

2. This image was traced by Adobe Streamline, which sometimes puts in more anchor points than are necessary. Therefore in **Artwork** viewing mode, use the editing tools to add, delete, or convert the anchor points so as to have as few points as possible, while staying true to the original image. When finished, select all the paths and **Object->Group.**

3. **File->Save** these changes. **Close** the document.

Using Path Modification to Create Objects

4. Create a **New** document, and **View->Show Rulers.**

5. With the Pen tool, draw a horizontal line 3.5" wide.

6. Paint the path: **Fill** = None, **Stroke** = 60 pt. Black, rounded caps.

7. Select the segment. Go to **Object->Path->Outline Path.** This will create a closed path.

8. Go to **Object->Path->Offset Path**. Set the **Offset** for 3 pt. Leave the other settings as-is. Click **OK.**

9. **Offset Path** draws a duplicate path at 3 pt. distance outside of the original.

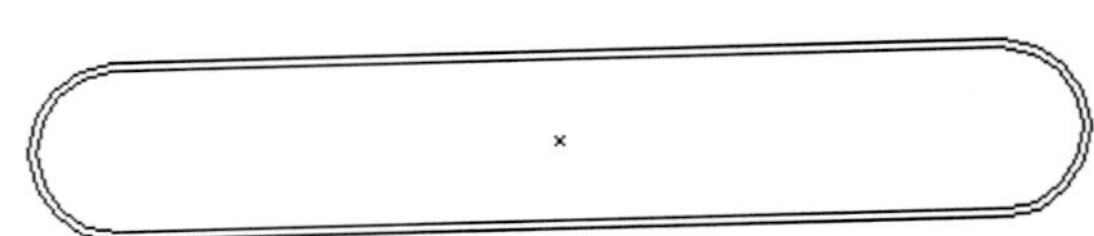

10. Paint the outside path: **Fill** = Black, **Stroke** = None.
    Paint the inside path: **Fill** = None, **Stroke** = 1 pt. White.
    Select both paths and **Object->Group** them.

11. Leave this document open. You will come back to it.

Fitting Type on a Curved Path

12. Create a **New** document. **File->Place** the Student File **HoneyDo Logo.TIF.** Make the image a template on its own layer, using **Dim Images** in **Layer Options.**

    Go to **Preview** mode. Remember, the template will be visible only in **Preview** mode. Be sure to keep the rulers on screen for measuring.

13. With the Ellipse tool, draw a circle with a **Width** and **Height** of 3 inches. Click **OK.**

14. Paint the circle: **Fill** = None, **Stroke** = 1 pt. Black. In **Preview** mode, position the circle so that its upper curve fits the middle of the HoneyDo letters.

15. Pull a horizontal guide to show the extreme ends of the HONEYDO curving word in the template (a., b.). Make a vertical guide that shows the circle's center point (c.)

16. With the Scissors tool, cut the circle where the guide touches it (a., b.). Select the bottom half of the cut circle. Delete it.

17. Select the remaining path and Option-drag (Macintosh) or Alt-drag (Windows) a duplicate off to the right, out of the way, for later use.

18. Select the Path-type tool. Click the cursor I-beam on the path.

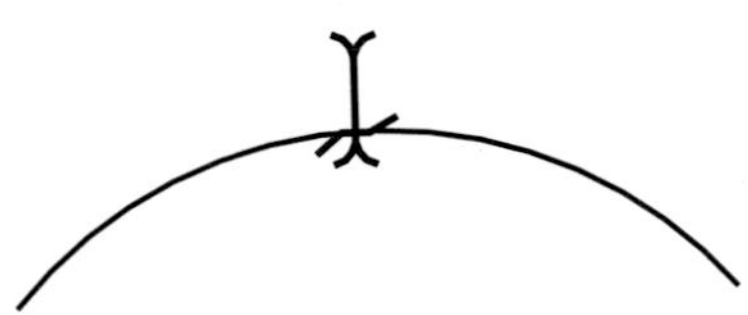

19. Type the word "HONEYDO." Highlight the text, and access the **Type ->Character** palette, and apply these settings: **Font** = ATC Kiwi, **Size** = 24 pt., **Leading** = Auto, **Tracking** = 0, **Horizontal scale** = 70%.

    Set the **Alignment** for this text to **Center.**

20. Some of the letters may need the spaces between them tightened. This is called "kerning," which adjusts the Tracking or spacing between letters. To do this, click the I-beam between the two letters that need kerning. You hold the Option (Macintosh) or Alt (Windows) key and press the Left Arrow key for tighter kerning, and the Right Arrow key for wider kerning.

    After the kerning is done, the HONEYDO letters should look like this.

21. The letters need to fit inside the surrounding border of the template. Then use Baseline shift to adjust the letters up and down. Click on this text block with the Selection tool to select it. Holding the Shift-Option (Macintosh) or Shift-Alt (Windows) keys, press the Down Arrow key three times.

    Select the text with the Selection tool and fine-tune to fit the template. Then go to **Type->Create Outlines**. Press Command-G (Macintosh) or Control-G (Windows) to **Group** the letters.

Fitting Type to an Object

22. Access the Type tool and click the cursor on the page and type the words:

    HAIR & NAIL SALON

    Highlight the text and make these settings. **Font** = ATC Kiwi, **Size** = 26 pt., **Leading** = Auto, **Tracking** = 0, **Horizontal scale** = 70%.

    Highlight all the text and kern by holding Option (Macintosh) or Alt (Windows) key and pressing either Left Arrow or Right Arrow keys to tighten the tracking or expand it. The finished text should look like this.

    HAIR & NAIL SALON

    Click on the Selection tool in the Toolbox. Go to **Type->Create Outlines.** Press Command-G (Macintosh) or Control-G (Windows) to Group the outlines. Paint the group: **Fill** = White, **Stroke** = None.

23. Use the **Window** menu to switch over to the Untitled document in which you created the border.

    Click on the object to select it. Press Command-C (Macintosh) or Control-C (Windows)to Copy the border. **Close** this document without saving

24. You will be back in the working document. Press Command-V (Macintosh) or Control-V (Windows) to Paste the border. Use **Object ->Arrange->Send To Back.** Move the HAIR & NAIL SALON text block to fit the border. Select the text and the border, then **Object->Group** them.

    HAIR & NAIL SALON

25. Go to the rounded path (from the cut circle) that was duplicated off to the right earlier. Paint the path: **Fill** = None, **Stroke** = 30 pt. Black, rounded caps.

26. Select the path and go to **Object->Path->Outline Path.** With this new closed path still selected, go to the **Object->Path->Offset Path** menu. Set the **Offset** for 3 pt. Click **OK**.

27. Go to the **Artwork** mode to see the two paths better for selecting.
    Paint the outside path: **Fill** = Black, **Stroke** = None.
    Paint the inside path: **Fill** = None, **Stroke** = 1 pt. White.

    Go to **Preview** mode. Select the inside and outside paths, then **Object ->Group** them. Go to **Object->Arrange->Send To back.**

28. Move the HONEYDO type outline so that it fits inside the border. Paint the type outline: **Fill** = White, **Stroke** = None. Select the type outline and the border, then press Command-G (Macintosh) or Control-G (Windows) to **Group** them.

29. Select this group and position it on the template.

30. Move the HAIR & NAIL SALON object under the HONEYDO object.

31. Fine-tune the positions of the objects and their distance from each other. The HAIR & NAIL SALON object should touch the HONEYDO object. Keep the document open.

Fitting Objects to a Layout

32. **Open** the document **HoneyDo Girl.AI**. Select the grouped object. Press Command-C (Macintosh) or Control-C (Windows) to **Copy** the object. **Close** the document without saving.

33. Back in the working document, press Command-V (Macintosh) or Control-V (Windows) to **Paste** the girl.

34. Keep this grouped object selected. Go to **Edit->Copy**, then to **Edit->Paste In Back**. This will paste a duplicate behind the original. Keep the duplicate selected. Apply a White **Stroke** of 2 pt. to the entire duplicate.

35. Select the duplicate and original, then **Object->Group** them.

36. Move this group into position on the logo, to match the template. Make sure she fits the area without obscuring any letters of the text.

37. When the fine-tuning is done, the HoneyDo logo is finished.

    The completed logo should look like this:

38. **Save As** the file in **Illustrator 7.0** format, naming it "HoneyDo Logo.AI." **Close** the document.

Notes:

Project B: HoneyDo Free Hairstyle Ad

Flowing Text Around an Object

1. Create a **New** document. **Show Rulers** for measuring. Move the Zero Point to the upper left corner of the page.

2. Locate the center of the page, and mark this with guides.

3. Access the Rectangle tool and click the crosshair once on the page center. In the dialog box, make the settings for a rectangle 4" x 6". Click **OK.**

4. Paint the rectangle: **Fill** = None, **Stroke** = 6 pt. Black. **Edit->Copy** the rectangle. Press Command-F (Macintosh) or Control-F (Windows) to **Paste In Front** of the selected rectangle. Paint the duplicate: **Fill** = None, **Stroke** = 1 pt. White.

5. Select both rectangles and press Command-G (Macintosh) or Control-G (Windows) to **Group** them, then **Object->Lock** the group.

6. Drag the Type tool on the page to draw a type container that is 3.25" x 4.25". Click the cursor inside this container. Now go to **File->Place.** From the Student Folder, **Place** the text file **HoneyDo Wrap.TXT.**

   Highlight the text. Access the **Type->Character** palette. Make these settings: **Font** = ATC Colada, **Size** = 14 pt., **Leading** = 24 pt., **Tracking** = 0, **Horizontal scale** = 90%.

The HoneyDo staff welcomes you to receive a FREE hairstyle on your birthday. Please bring your driver's license when you come to take advantage of this offer. We want you to look your best on your natal day. Enjoy!

7. **Open** the document **HoneyDo Girl.AI.** Select the grouped artwork, **Edit ->Copy** the art. **Close** the document without saving.

8. Back at the working document, press Command-V (Macintosh) or Control-V (Windows) to Paste the HoneyDo Girl group into the document.

9. With HoneyDo Girl selected, double-click on the Scale tool in the Toolbox. Set the **Uniform** scaling for 250%. Press **OK**. Move the scaled HoneyDo Girl into position in the ad.

10. Select the text block with the Selection tool. Press Command-U (Macintosh) or Control-U (Windows) to Hide the text block. Use the Pencil tool to draw an outline around the HoneyDo Girl. This outline will be used to wrap the body text.

Paint this outline: **Fill** = None, **Stroke** = None. Go to **Artwork** view so that you can see the unpainted outline.

11. **Object->Show All**, bringing the hidden text back to view. Select both the text container and unpainted outline. Go to the **Type** menu and choose **Wrap->Make.** The reason for the outline is that it gives a little extra space away from the artwork.

12. With the Type tool, drag a new text container for the headline that fits inside the width of the border, above the wrapped body text. Type the words "FREE HAIRSTYLE." Highlight the text. In the **Type->Character** palette, make these settings. **Font** = ATC Bahama, **Size** = 18 pt., **Leading** = 24, **Tracking** = 400, **Horizontal scale** = 100%. In the **Type->Paragraph** palette, set the alignment for **Center**.

FREE
HAIRSTYLE

13. Position the headline to fit the top of the ad.

FREE
HAIRSTYLE
The HoneyDo staff welcomes you to
receive a FREE hairstyle on your
birthday. Please bring your driver's

14. Go to the Student Folder and **Open** the logo file you made previously, **HoneyDo Logo.AI.** Select all the paths and **Group** them. **File->Copy** the group to the Clipboard and **Close** the document without saving. In the working document, **Paste** the group, then use the **Scale** dialog box to reduce the logo 50% **Uniform**. Position it in the lower center of the ad. The ad is finished.

15. **Save As** the file in **Illustrator 7.0** format, naming it "HoneyDo Ad.AI." **Close** the document.

Project C: Banana Boat Logo

Editing a Hand-Drawn Object

1. In the Student Folder, **File->Open** the document **Banana.AI.**

2. Use the Pencil tool to trace the guide supplied. Do not try to be exact as you draw. Merely rough in the necessary paths. After the rough sketch is drawn, use the path-editing and selection tools to adjust the anchor points and curves to fit the drawing to the guide.

   Paint the banana: **Fill** = 100% Yellow, **Stroke** = 1 pt. Black.
   The small endpiece of the banana: **Fill** = Black, **Stroke** = None.
   The single segment: **Fill** = None, **Stroke** = 1 pt. Black.
   Edit->Select All, then **Object->Group.**

3. **File->Save** the file. **Close** the document.

Editing Geometric Shapes

4. **Open** the document **Banana Sails.AI.** You will see the guides to work from.

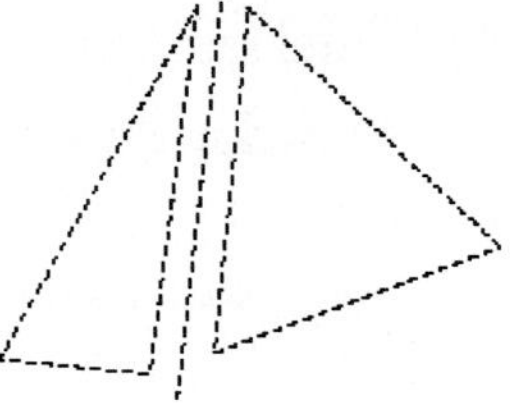

5. Draw two rectangles and a single segment that can be edited to fit the guides. The idea is to make these objects close to the size of the guides, then you will use the various path editing tools to fit the paths to the guides. Paint the rectangles: **Fill** = White, **Stroke** = 1 pt. Black. Paint the segment: **Fill** = None, **Stroke** = 3 pt. Black, rounded caps.

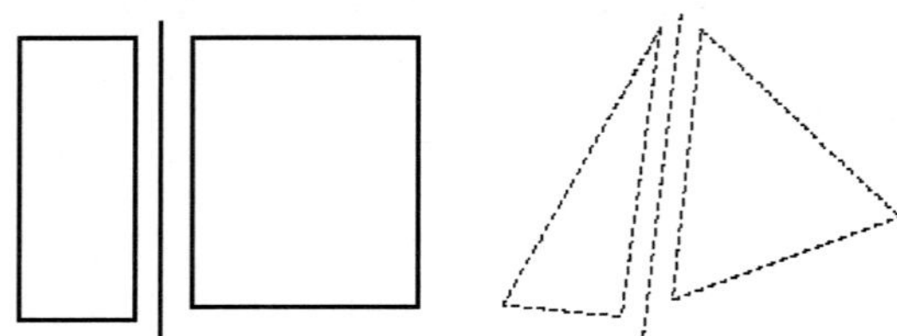

6. Edit the drawn objects to fit the guides. Select and **Group** all paths.

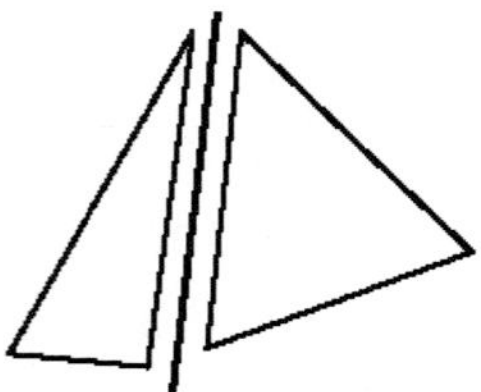

7. **File->Save** the file. **Close** the document.

Using Filters to Create Objects

8. Create a **New** document. **File->Place** the Student File **Banana Boat.TIF** as a template on its own layer, using **Dim Images** in **Layer Options.**

9. **Show Rulers** for measuring, then access the Pen tool and draw a horizontal segment, anywhere on the page, 3-5/8" long. Hold the Shift key while clicking the second anchor point to constrain the path.

10. Paint the segment: **Fill** = None, **Stroke** = 60 pt. Black, with rounded caps.

11. Go to **Object->Path->Outline Path.** With the outlined path selected, go to the **Window->Show Attributes** palette, click the Show Center Point icon.

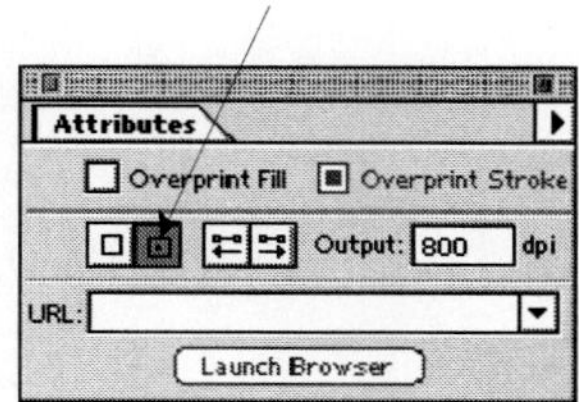

12. Go to **Artwork** mode to see the closed path and the center point.

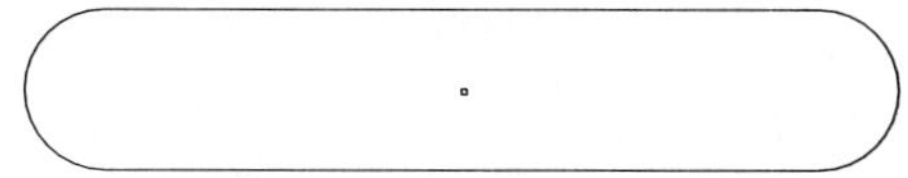

13. Access the Ellipse tool in the Toolbox. Holding the Option (Macintosh) or Alt (Windows) key, click the crosshair on the center point (a.) of the border. Make the settings: **Width** = 2.5 in., **Height** = 2.5 in. to create a circle.

    Stay in **Artwork** mode. With the Direct Selection tool, marquee the bottom anchor point of the circle (b.).

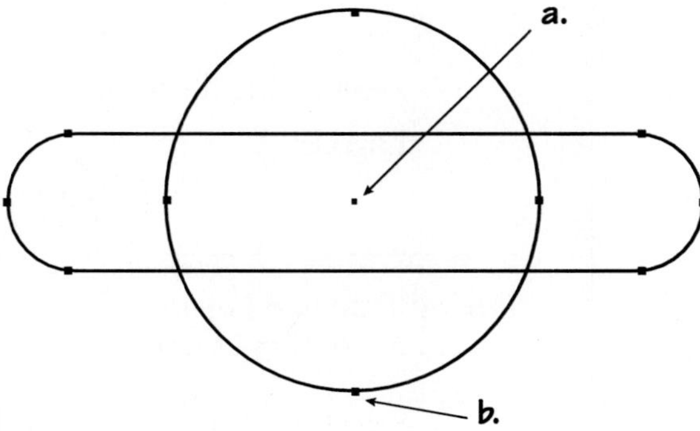

14. Press the Delete key to delete the bottom anchor point. Select both paths.

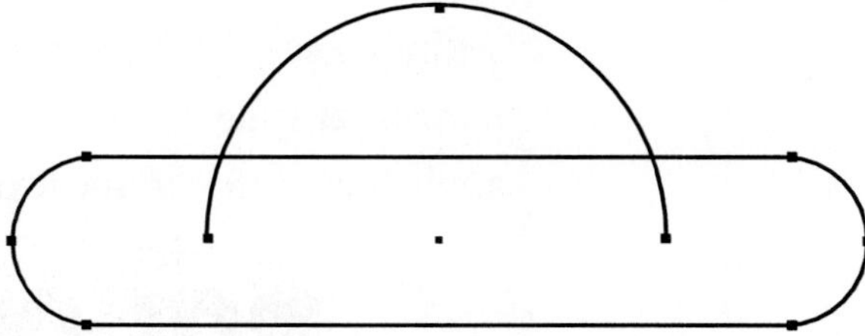

15. Go to the **Object->Pathfinder** menu and choose **Unite.** This will eliminate the internal paths and create one closed path. Keep this object selected.

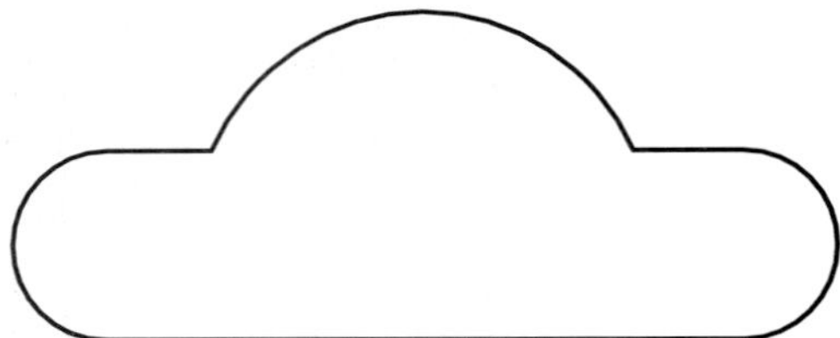

16. Go to the **Object->Path** menu and choose **Offset Path.**
    Set the offset to be 4 pts. Click **OK**. Paint the outside path: **Fill** = Black, **Stroke** = None. Send this path to the back.

    Paint the inside path: **Fill** = None, **Stroke** = 1 pt. White. Select the two paths and **Group** them. Position the group to fit the template.

17. **Save As** the file in **Illustrator EPS** format, naming it "Banana Boat Logo.EPS."

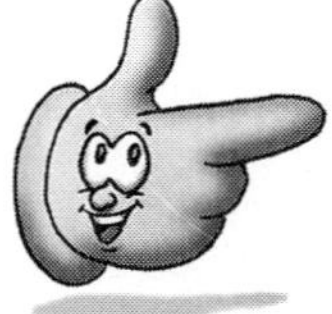

Fitting Type to a Layout

18. Select the Type tool in the Toolbox. Click the cursor on the template and type the words "BANANA BOAT."

    Highlight the text. Go to the **Type->Character** palette, and make these settings: **Font** = ATC Jamaica, **Size** = 55 pt., **Leading** = Auto, **Tracking** = 0, **Horizontal scale** = 70%. Press Return (Macintosh) or Enter (Windows) to apply the settings to the text.

BANANA BOAT

19. Click on the Selection tool in the Toolbox. Go to the **Type** menu and choose **Create Outlines**; then **Object->Group** the outlines. Paint the group: **Fill** = 100% Yellow, **Stroke** = None.

20. Access the Type tool, click the cursor on the template and type the phrase "A DRINKING ESTABLISHMENT." Highlight the text and, in the **Type Character** palette, apply these settings: **Font** = ATC Margarita Bold, **Size** = 21 pt., **Leading** = Auto, **Tracking** = 0, **Horizontal scale** = 110%. Press Return (Macintosh) or Enter (Windows) to apply the settings to the text.

A DRINKING ESTABLISHMENT

21. Click on the Selection tool in the Toolbox. Go to the **Type** menu and choose **Create Outlines**; then **Object->Group** the outlines. Paint the outlines: **Fill** = Black, **Stroke** = None.

22. Select the BANANA BOAT outline group. Move it into position on the border.

23. Select the A DRINKING ESTABLISHMENT group. Move the text outlines into position, centered below the border.

24. **Open** the document **Banana.AI**. Select the banana, then **Edit->Copy** it. **Close** this document without saving.

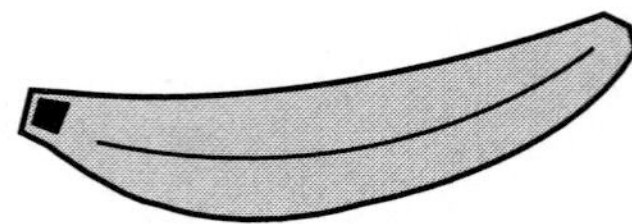

25. In the working document, **Edit->Paste** the banana, keeping it selected. Go to **Object->Arrange->Bring to Front**. Move the banana into position above the Banana Boat outlines.

26. **Open** the document **Banana Sails.AI**. Click on the sail group to select it, then **Edit->Copy** the group. **Close** this document without saving.

27. In the working document, **Edit->Paste** the group, keeping it selected. Go to **Object->Arrange->Bring to Front**. Move the sails into position on the banana. Fine-tune the banana and the sails to match the template.

28. The Banana Boat logo is complete. **File->Save** the file. **Close** the document.

Project D: Fleet's In! T-Shirt Design

Making Waves with Twirl

1. Create a **New** document in which the page is legal size with a horizontal orientation.

   Move the Zero Point to the upper left page corner, then drag a vertical guide to the 7" mark of the horizontal ruler. This will show the page center.

2. To create the waves behind the banana boats, draw a single path that is 1-5/8" long (a.). Select the path and go to **Filter->Distort->Twirl**. Set the twirl for 60°. Press **OK** (b.).

   Option-drag (Macintosh) or Alt-drag (Windows) the twirled path to the right (pressing the Shift key after the drag has begun). This duplicates the path so that the two endpoints meet (c.).

   Press Command-D (Macintosh) or Control-D (Windows) three times to Transform Again.

a. 

b.

c. 

3. Select all the twirled paths and paint them: **Fill** = None, **Stroke** = 10 pt. Black, rounded caps .

With paths still selected, go to **Object->Path->Outline Path.**

Select these paths and go to **Object->Pathfinder->Unite.**

Seen in Artwork mode

Paint the path: **Fill** = 100% Cyan, **Stroke** = 2 pt. 100% Cyan.
Go to **Filter->Stylize->Drop Shadow**. Change no settings. Click **OK**. Drop Shadow makes a shadow of the original and groups them together.

Click on the drop shadow with the Direct Selection tool to select it.
Paint the shadow: **Fill** = 100% Black, **Stroke** = None.

4. With the Selection tool, click on the wave. Both objects will be selected because they are grouped. Hold down the Option (Macintosh) or Alt (Windows) key, then the Shift key, and drag the wave and shadow down to make a copy of it. Press Command-D (Macintosh) or Ctrl-D (Windows) two times to Transform Again.

5. Select all the wave objects and **Object->Group.**

6. Go to the Student Files folder and **Open** the **Banana Boat Logo.EPS** file. Delete the black background. Marquee the banana and its sails to select them, then **Object->Group. Edit->Copy** the group. **Close** this file without saving.

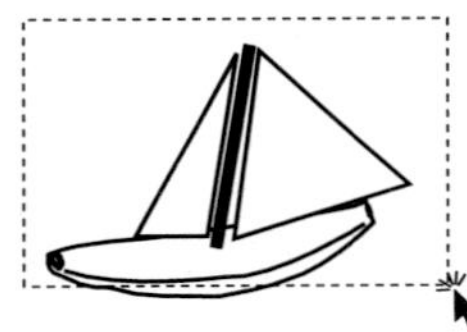

7. Back at the working document, **Edit->Paste** the group. Double-click the Scale tool, type 180% **Uniform, Scale Line Weight.**

8. Option-drag (Macintosh) or Alt-drag (Windows) the banana boat to the right, holding the Shift key, to duplicate it (a.). Select the duplicate and go to **Object->Pathfinder->Unite** (b.). Paint the United path: **Fill** = Black, **Stroke** = None. Position the duplicate so that it is a shadow offset from the original. When in position, **Cut** it, select the original boat, and choose **Paste In Back** (c.).

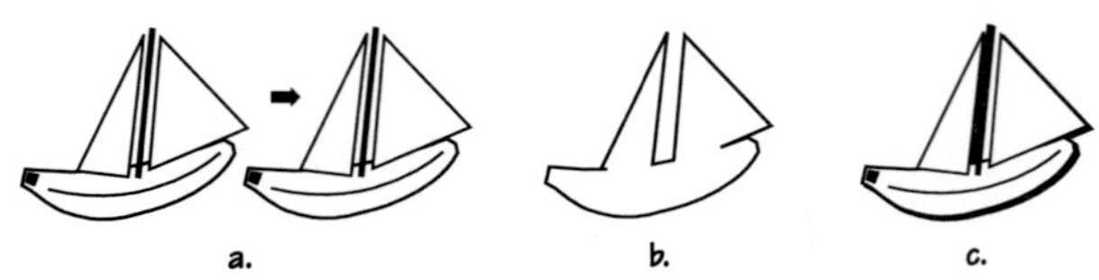

9. Select the banana boat, sails, and shadow, then **Object->Group.**

10. Option-drag (Macintosh) or Alt-drag (Windows) the group to the left to duplicate it. Press the Shift key after the drag has begun to constrain. Press Command-D (Macintosh) or Ctrl-D (Windows) two times to Transform Again. Select all four banana boats, then **Object->Group** them.

    Scale all four banana boats at 50% **Uniform.**

11. Position the banana boats on the waves. Bring them to the front. Center them on the waves.

12. Go to the Student Files folder and **Open** the file **Banana Boat Logo.EPS.** Select the background border behind the banana boat. **Edit->Copy** it. **Close** this document without saving.

13. In the working document, **Edit->Paste** the object, then **Object->Group** it.

14. Position the background above the boats/waves in the upper left.

    Access the Scale tool. Click the crosshair in the upper left corner of the background's bounding box. Drag on the lower right corner of the background to enlarge it. Hold the Shift key so the enlargement will be uniform. Make the background almost as wide as the waves. Position the background so that it is centered in the design. Send it to the back, behind the waves.

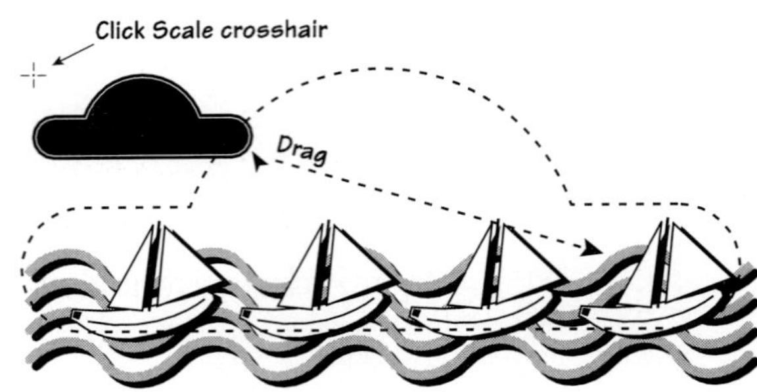

15. The border of the background is composed of two paths, painted differently.

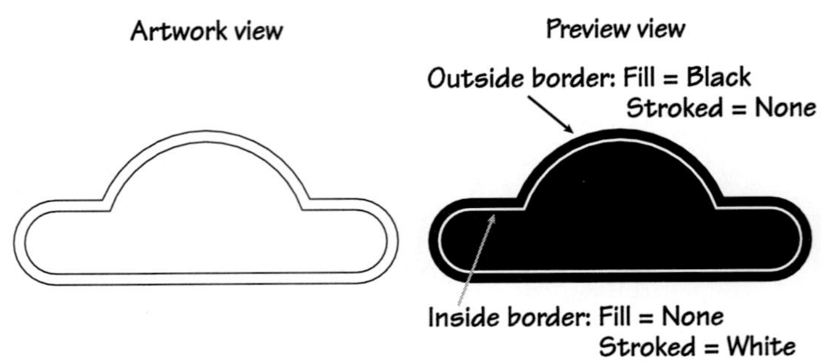

16. With the Direct Selection tool, click the outer border to select it. Paint it: **Fill** = Blue, **Stroke** = None.

17. **Edit->Copy** this outer border. Use **Paste In Back** to create a drop shadow behind the border. Paint the Shadow: **Fill**=50% Blue, **Stroke**=None. Select all borders and position them accurately centered in the design.

18. Click the Type tool on the page. Type the words "FLEET'S IN!." Highlight the text and apply these settings. **Font** = ATC Plantation, **Size** = 72 pt., **Leading** = Auto, **Tracking** = -15, **Horizontal scale** = 100%.

FLEET'S IN!

19. Select the text with the Selection tool. Go to the **Type** menu and choose **Create Outlines. Object->Group** the outlines.

20. Paint the outlines: **Fill** = 100% Yellow, **Stroke** = None (a.). Go to **Edit ->Copy**. Press Command-B (Macintosh) or Ctrl-B (Windows) to **Paste In Back** of the selected outlines. Paint the duplicate: **Fill** = None, **Stroke** = 10 pt. Black, rounded joints (b.).

21. Marquee-select the apostrophe (both outlines, yellow and black) with the Direct Selection tool, while holding the Option (Macintosh) or Alt (Windows) key. Press the Up Arrow key 6 times (c.).

a. FLEET'S IN!

b. FLEET'S IN!

marquee

c. FLEET'S IN!

22. Select the two outline groups of "FLEET'S IN!," then **Object->Group** them. Move this group into position in the upper left of the border.

23. Access the Scale tool. Click the crosshair on the upper left of the "F" in FLEET.

Drag on the lower right of the exclamation point. Do not press the Shift key, so as to allow free arrangement for fitting the text to the area.

When enlarged to your satisfaction, position the object to fit the area with balance and equal spacing between the object and the background.

24. Select the "FLEET'S IN!" object. **Edit->Cut** it, then select the background border. Press Command-F (Macintosh) or Control-F (Windows) to **Paste In Front** of the border. Now, selecting the "FLEET'S IN!" object and the background border, go to **Object->Arrange->Send To Back**, to put the letters and border behind the boats and waves.

25. With the Direct Selection tool, select one of the Banana Boats (without the shadow) and **Copy->Paste** a duplicate.

26. Select the banana boat, then double-click on the Scale tool in the Toolbox. In the **Scale** dialog box, set **Uniform** for 215%. Click **OK**.

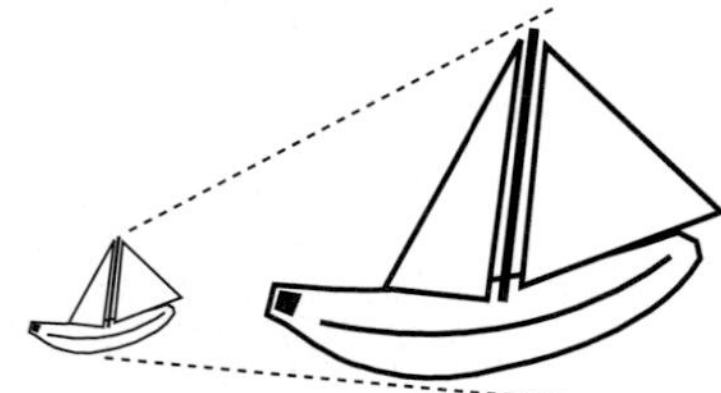

27. Move the enlarged banana boat into position above the FLEET'S IN!

28. Click the Type tool, then type the phrase:

AT BANANA BOAT LOUNGE

Highlight the text and apply these settings. **Font** = ATC Margarita Bold, **Size** = 36 pt., **Leading** = Auto, **Tracking** = 0, **Horizontal scale** = 100%. The type should look like this.

AT BANANA BOAT LOUNGE

29. With the text still selected, paint it: **Fill** = 100% Yellow, **Stroke** = None.

30. Select the text object with the Selection tool. Go to the **Type** menu and choose **Create Outlines.**

Object->Group the outlines. Go to **Filter->Stylize->Drop Shadow.** Make these settings.

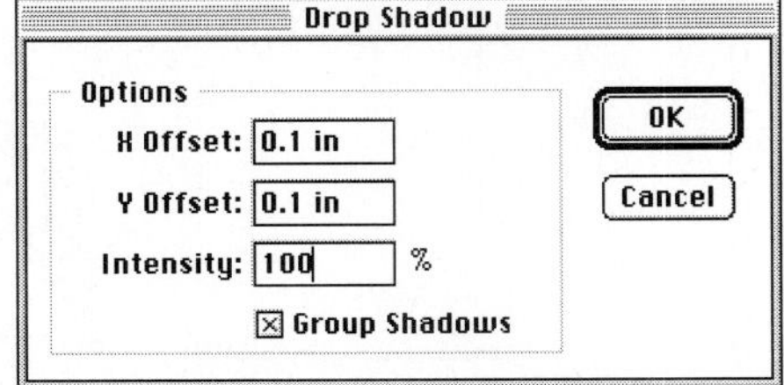

AT BANANA BOAT LOUNGE

31. Click on the Rectangle tool, then draw a rectangle that surrounds the text with sufficient space around the letters. Paint the rectangle: **Fill** = Blue, **Stroke** = None. Go to **Object->Arrange->Send to Back** so the rectangle will be behind the type.

32. Select the rectangle and go to **Filter->Stylize->Drop Shadow.** Make these settings:

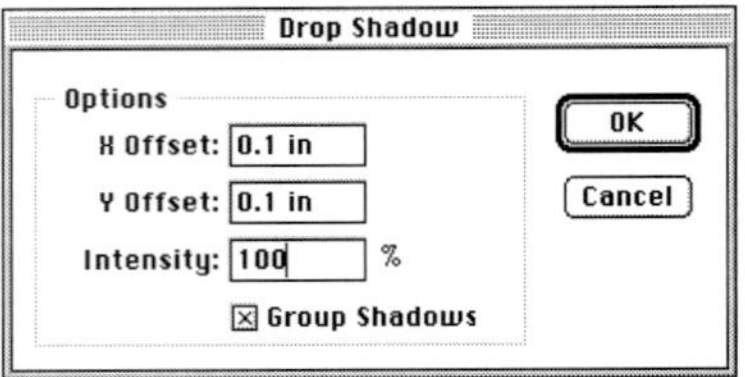

33. Select the text outlines and their shadows, also the rectangle and its shadow. Go to **Filter->Distort->Twirl** and **Twirl** the selected objects 30°. Click **OK**. Then, **Object->Group** these objects.

34. Move the twirled group into position on the design.

35. Access the Ellipse tool. Single-click the crosshair on the page. In the dialog box, make these settings.

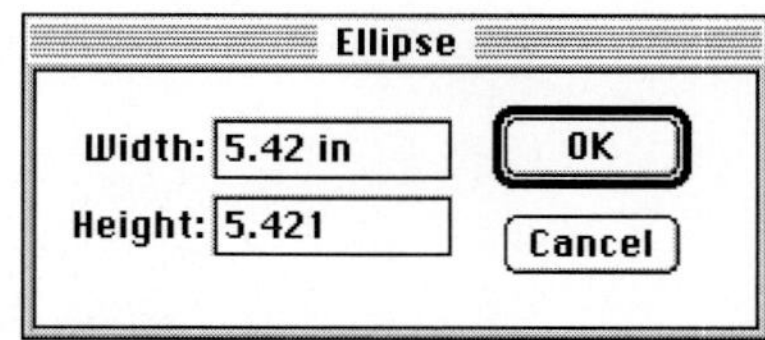

36. Access the Path-type tool. Click the cursor on the top anchor point of the circle. Type the phrase:

A DRINKING ESTABLISHMENT

Highlight the phrase and make these settings. **Font** = ATC Margarita Bold, **Size** = 16 pt., **Leading** = Auto, **Tracking** = 0, **Horizontal scale** = 100%.

37. Set the text alignment to **Center.** Use the Selection tool to drag on the I-beam to adjust the type so that it is balanced on the curve.

38. Move this curving text object into position under the twirled banner.

39. The design is now complete.

40. **File->Save** the file. **Close** the document.

Project E: Tropical Suites Logo

Reflecting Objects

1. **Open** the document **Reflect Palm.AI.**

2. Draw a 2" x 5" rectangle starting on the left side of the palm and dragging to the right. Press Command-5 (Macintosh) or Ctrl-5 (Windows) to turn it into a guide. Drag two ruler guides (vertical and horizontal) to show the center of the rectangle.

3. Select the palm and beach half. Select the Reflect tool in the Toolbox. Hold the Option (Macintosh) or Alt (Windows) key, and click the crosshair on the center of the rectangle guide.

4. In the **Reflect** dialog box, select **Vertical** and **Copy**. The palm will reflect across the vertical axis, duplicating itself. Use the Direct Selection tool to select the endpoints of the beach so that you can **Join** them.

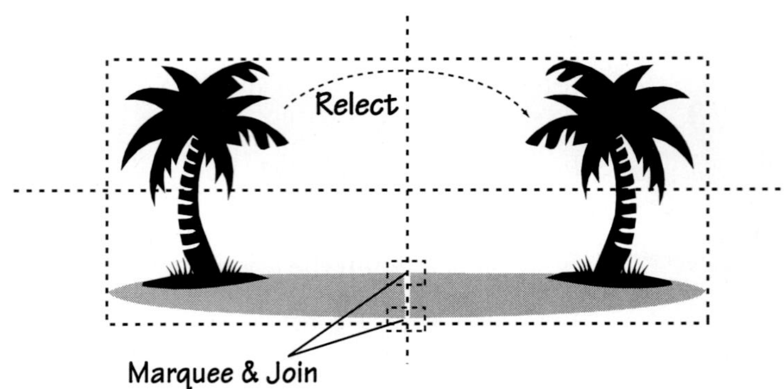

5. **File->Save** the file. **Close** the document.

Beginning the Tropical Suites Sun

6. **Open** the document **Tropical Suites Sun.AI.**

7. Use the Pencil tool to create the sun spiral and the one sun ray.

8. Once the paths are roughed in with the Pencil tool, use the various editing tools to match up the paths to the guides.

9. **File->Save** the file.

10. Keep the document open.

Finishing the Tropical Suites Sun

11. Continue in the open document.

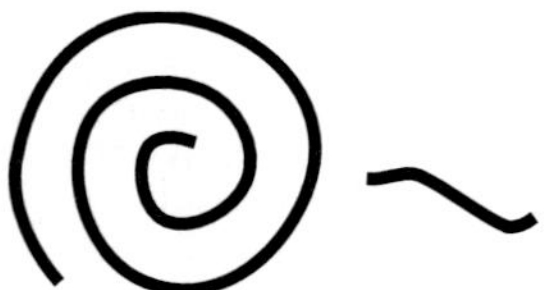

12. Select the sun spiral. Press Command-L (Macintosh) or Ctrl-L (Windows) to **Lock** the spiral. Select the sun ray.

13. Click on the Rotate tool. Click the crosshair on the center of the spiral sun to set an origin point. Hold down the Option (Macintosh) or Alt (Windows) key to duplicate and manually rotate the ray about 38°. If it's a little more or less, this is acceptable.

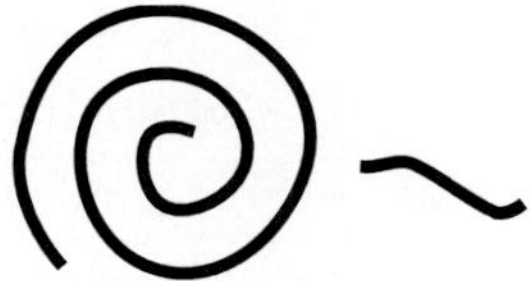

14. Press Command-D (Macintosh) or Ctrl-D (Windows) four times to repeat the rotation four more times.

15. **Object->Unlock All** the spiral sun. **Edit->Select All** the paths. **Object->Group** the paths.

16. Paint the group of paths: **Fill** = None, **Stroke** = 100% Yellow 6 pt. Set the endpoints for **Rounded Caps**.

17. Select the spiral sun group.

    Go to **Object->Path->Outline Paths**. This will create closed paths that are Filled with the **Stroke** color. **Object->Group** these closed paths.

18. **Edit->Copy** the group to the clipboard. With the group still selected, press Command-B (Macintosh) or Ctrl-B (Windows) to **Paste in Back** a duplicate of the paths.

19. Paint the duplicate: **Fill** = None, **Stroke** = 15 pt. Orange.

20. The individual sun rays can be moved slightly after selecting them with the Direct Selection tool. If needed, select the sun rays this way to adjust them to look better with the spiral sun. **Select All** paths, then **Object ->Group** them.

21. Your finished sun and its rays should look similar to this.

22. **File->Save** the file. **Close** the document.

Adding Outlined Type

23. Create a **New** document. **Place** the **Tropical Suites.TIF** file. In the **Layers** palette, create a new layer to be used as a template. Assign the Placed image to this layer. Double-click on the Layer 2 name. In the **Layer Options** window, name the layer "Template." Use **Dim Images** to gray the template. **Lock** it, as well. Click **Print** off, so the image won't print.

    Move the Template layer under Layer 1. Remember to always keep the Template layer at the bottom of the layer list.

    Click on Layer 1 to make it the active layer, and continue.

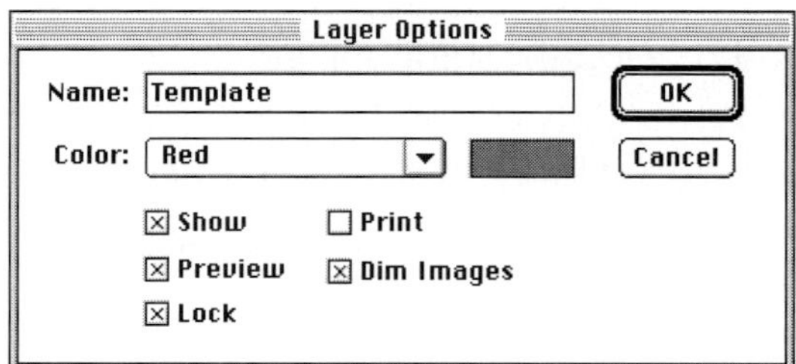

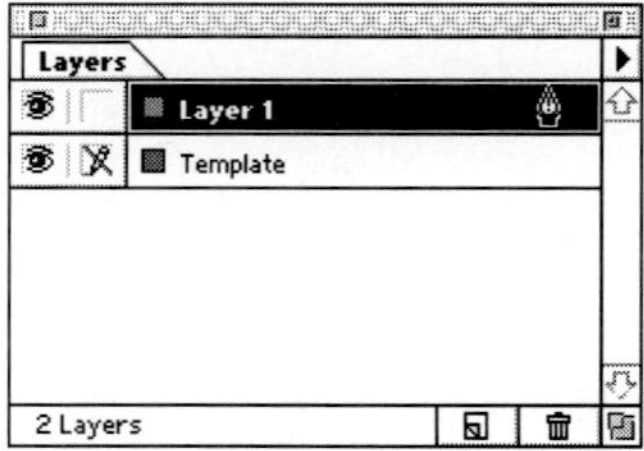

24. With the Type tool, click on the page and type the words "Tropical Suites."

25. Highlight the text and apply these settings. **Font** = ATC Sea Breeze, **Size** = 66 pt., **Leading** = Auto, **Tracking** = 0, **Horizontal scale** = 60%.

Tropical Suites

26. Select this text block with the Selection tool. In the **Type** menu, choose **Create Outlines**. Marquee the word "Tropical" and **Object->Group** it. Marquee the word "Suites" and **Object->Group** it.

27. Position the word "Suites" under "Tropical."

Tropical
Suites

28. Select the two objects, then **Object->Group** them.
Select this new group. Paint it: **Fill** =Black, **Stroke** = 12 pt. Black.
In the **Stroke** palette, choose **Round Joins**.

29. **Edit->Copy** the group. Press Command-F (Macintosh) or Ctrl-F (Windows) to **Paste In Front** a duplicate.
Paint the duplicate: **Fill** = None, **Stroke** = 1.5 pt. White.
Select both groups of outlines and **Object->Group** them.

Open the **Layers** palette. Rename Layer 1 "Type."

Create a new layer. Name it "Palms."

30. **Open** the document **Reflect Palm.AI.**

Select the two palms and the beach. **Edit->Copy** them. **Close** this document without saving.

31. Back in the working document, **Edit->Paste** the objects.

32. Position the palms and beach to match the template.
Position the Tropical Suites type into position, matching the template.

In the **Layers** palette, reassign the Palms/Beach to the Palms layer.
Drag the Palms layer to the level below the Type layer.

33. Click on the Type layer so the next type will be instantly assigned to it.
Click the Type cursor on the page and type the phrase:

A Caribbean Resort

Highlight the text and apply these settings. **Font** = ATC Sunset, **Size** = 28 pt., **Leading** = Auto, **Tracking** = 0, **Horizontal scale** = 100%.

34. Move the Caribbean phrase into position, matching the template.

35. **Open** the document **Tropical Suites Sun.Art.**

Select the sun group, then **Edit->Copy** it.
Close the document without saving.

36. Press Command-V (Macintosh) or Ctrl-V (Windows) to Paste the sun group.

Create a new layer and name it "Sun." Select the sun and assign it to this layer. In the **Layers** palette, move the Sun layer to be just under the Palms layer.

37. In the Tropical Suites type object, marquee the dot above the "i" with the Direct Selection tool, holding the Option (Macintosh) or Alt (Windows) key to select it. Delete the dot.

38. Move the sun group into position above the "i" so as to give the impression that the sun is dotting the "i."

39. **Scale** the sun to fit the template, then reposition.

40. Make sure the layer sequence is (starting at the top of the list) Type, Palms, Sun. Delete the Template layer.

41. The logo is now complete. **Save As** the file in **Illustrator EPS** format, naming it "Tropical Suites logo.EPS." **Close** the document.

Project F: Heart Notes

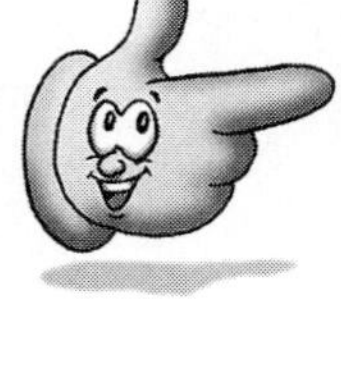

Using Transformational Tools

1. In the **SF-Adv Illustrator** folder, **Open** the document **Heart Notes.AI.**

2. Select the Rectangle tool. Click the cursor on the upper left corner of the rectangle guide. In the **Rectangle** dialog box, type these settings: **Width** = 0.5 in., **Height** = 0.625 in. Click **OK**.

3. Move the new rectangle so that its center point is on the upper left corner of the rectangle guide.

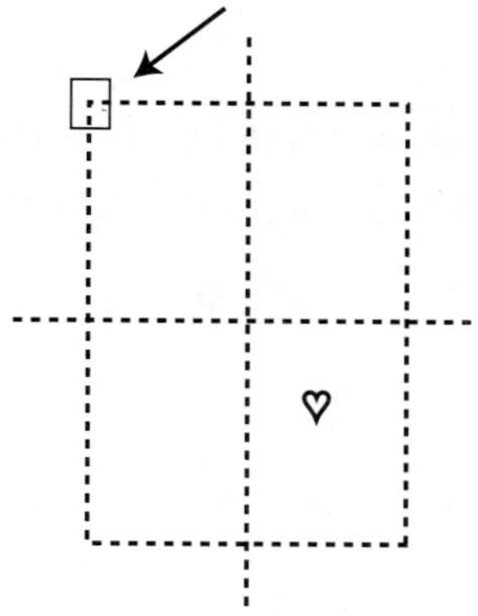

4. Holding the Option (Macintosh) or Alt (Windows) key, drag a duplicate of the heart outline. Position the duplicate so that its center point matches the center point of the small rectangle. Move the original heart outline off to the right, out of the way for now.

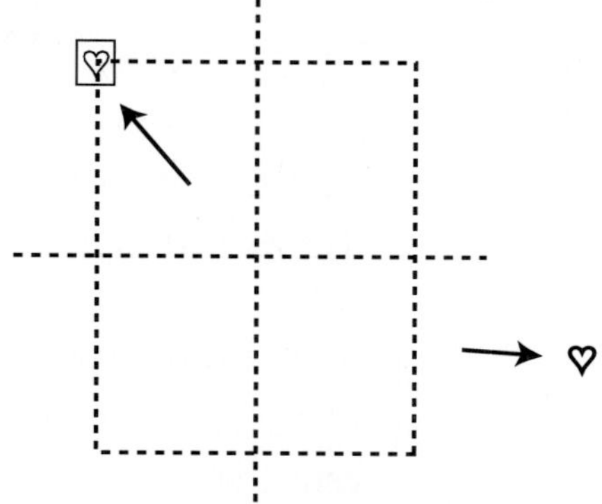

5. Go to **Preview** mode. With the duplicate selected, go to **Object->Arrange ->Bring To Front** to position the heart in front of the small rectangle.

6. Paint the small rectangle: **Fill** = 100% Black, **Stroke** = None. Paint the heart: **Fill** = 100% Magenta, 100% Yellow, **Stroke** = None. Select the two corner objects, then **Object->Group** them.

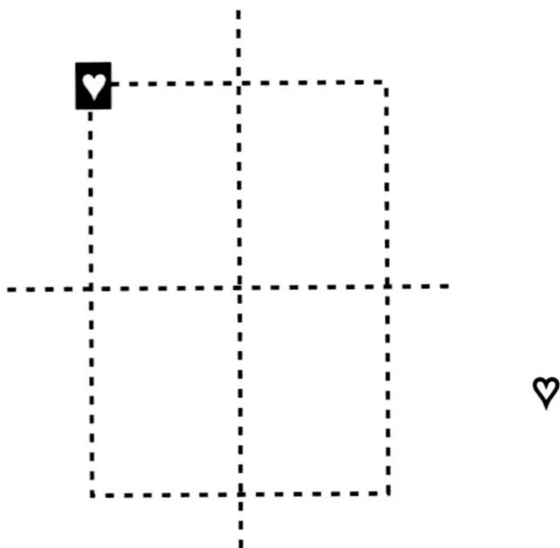

7. Select the Rotate tool in the Toolbox. Holding the Option (Macintosh) or Alt (Windows) key, click the crosshair on the horizontal guide.

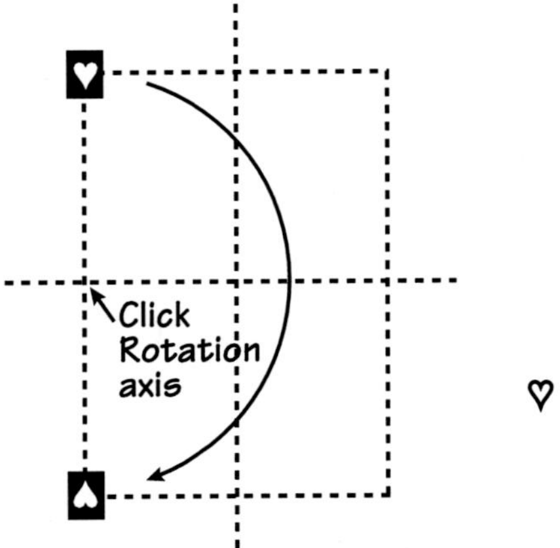

8. In the Rotate dialog box enter "180" for the **Angle**, then click **Copy**. The rotated copy will appear on the bottom left corner.

9. Select the two corner objects. Click on the Reflect tool. Holding the Option (Macintosh) or Alt (Windows) key, click the crosshair on the center point of the rectangle guide. In the **Reflect** dialog box, select **Vertical** for the axis and click **Copy**.

The two corners will reflect and duplicate to the other side.

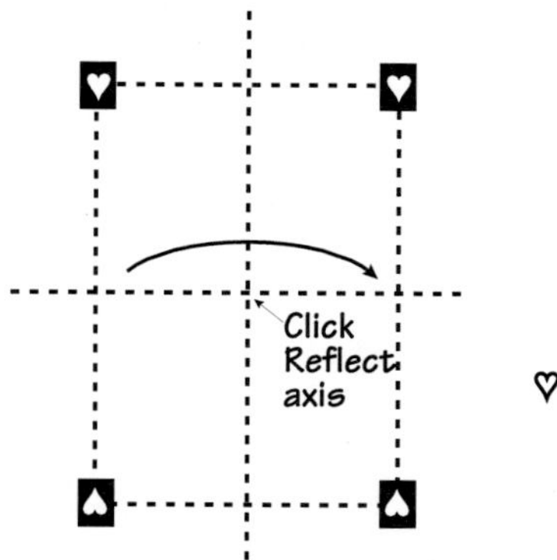

10. With the Selection tool, select the four corner objects, then **Object-> Group** them.

11. With the Rectangle tool, draw a rectangle to match the rectangle guide in the document. Paint the rectangle: **Fill** = None, **Stroke** = 10 pt. Black.

12. **Edit->Copy** the rectangle to the clipboard. With the rectangle still selected, **Edit->Paste In Front** of the original. Paint the duplicate: **Fill** = None, **Stroke** = 2 pt. White. Marquee-select these two rectangles and **Object ->Group** them.

When two objects are resting in perfect alignment on top of each other, it is necessary to use the Selection tool to draw a marquee that touches the objects. This selects the objects that are marqueed.

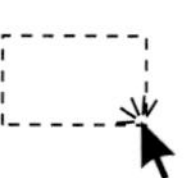

13. Access the **Layers** palette from the **Window** menu. Create two new layers: "Corners," and "Border." Assign the corner pieces to the Corners layer. Assign the border to the Border layer. Move the Border layer to be under the Corners layer in the **Layers** palette.

14. Select the original heart outline that came with the document. Move it back into the interior of the border. Paint the heart outline: **Fill** = 100% Magenta, 100% Yellow, **Stroke** = None.

15. Double-click on the Scale tool in the Toolbox. In the **Scale** dialog box, set the scaling for **Non-Uniform** and type these settings: **Horizontal** = 738, **Vertical** = 843. Click **OK**.

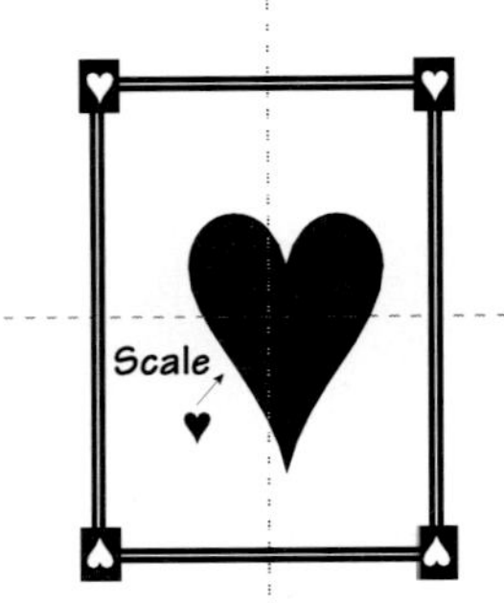

16. With the heart still selected, click on the Shear tool in the Toolbox. Click the crosshair cursor in the bottom left area near the outline. Drag on the upper right portion of the outline and pull slowly to the right. Shear the heart so that it looks as if it were falling over, as seen below.

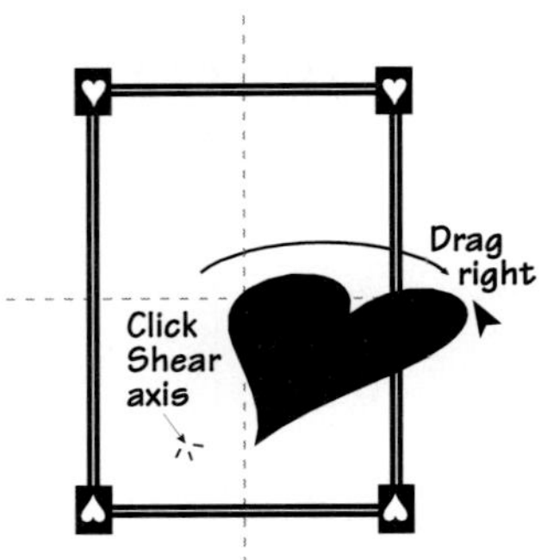

17. Double-click on the Scale tool in the Toolbox. In the **Scale** dialog box set **Uniform** to 50%. Click **OK**. Move the heart to the lower right corner of the design.

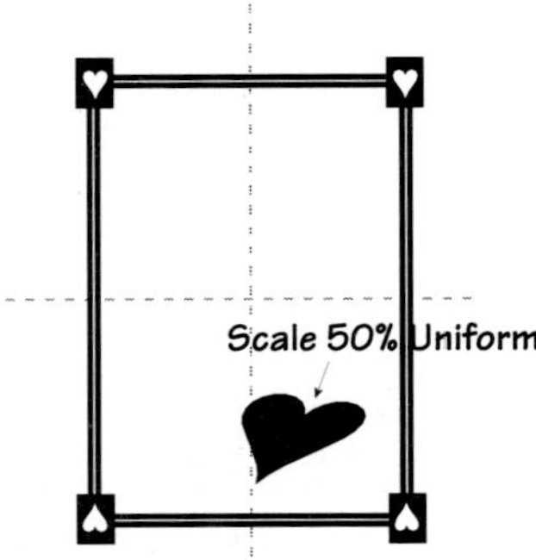

18. In the **Layers** palette, rename Layer 1 as "Heart." Assign the sheared heart to this layer.

    In the **Layers** palette, drag the Heart layer to the bottom of the list. Arrange the layers so that the objects are stacked as shown here:

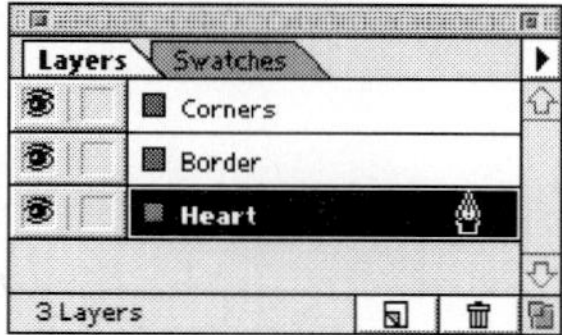

19. Keep the Heart layer active. Drag a duplicate of the heart off to the right of the border. Paint this heart: **Fill** = 40% Black, **Stroke** = None. Draw a rectangle around the duplicate heart. Paint the rectangle: **Fill** = None, **Stroke** = None.

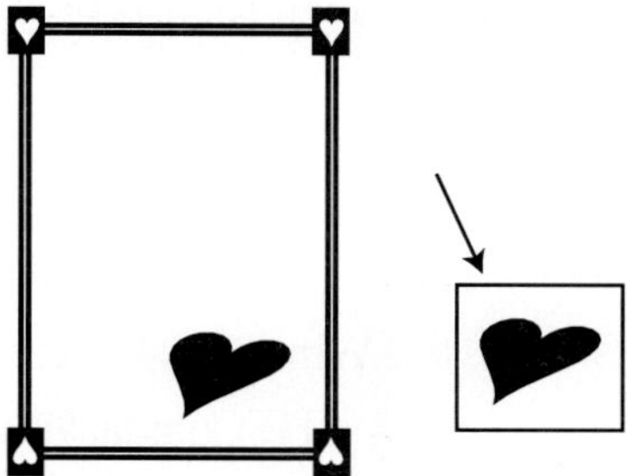

20. Select the duplicate heart and its rectangle. Go to **Object->Rasterize** and set: **Color Model** = Grayscale, **Resolution** = 300, **Anti-alias** = On, **Create Mask** = Off. Click **OK**. With the object still selected, go to **Filter->Brush Strokes->Spatter** and set: **Spray Radius** = 15, **Smoothness** = 1. Click **OK**.

21. Use **Object->Arrange->Send To Back**. In the Heart layer, this will allow the rasterized duplicate to be behind the original.

22. Move the rasterized duplicate over to the original heart, and it will appear as a shadow.

23. Deselect the rasterized heart. In the **Layers** palette, create a new layer, naming it "Type". Leave it at the top of the layer list, and keep it clicked as the active layer.

24. Select the Type tool in the Toolbox. Click the cursor on the page, inside the border. Type these words with returns as shown in step #26:

    Heartfelt notes from the desk of

25. Highlight this text and press Command-T (Macintosh) or Control-T (Windows) to access the **Type->Character** palette. Apply these settings: **Font** = ATC Colada, **Size** = 20 pt., **Leading** = Auto, **Tracking** = -25, **Horizontal Scale** = 90. In the **Paragraph** palette, set alignment for Align Left.

26. Position this text in the upper left corner of the border. The finished border should look similar to this.

27. **Save As** the file in **Illustrator 7.0** format, naming it "Heart Border.AI." **Close** the document.

Project G: Banana Border

Using Transform Again for Duplication

1. **Open** the **SF-Adv Illustrator** folder **Banana Border.AI.**

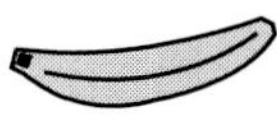

Happy Hour
at
BANANA BOAT
LOUNGE

Daquiri
Dee-lights
from
4:00 to 5:00 P.M.

You name the fruit,
we'll make the drink!

2. The Illustrator document shows the page with a margin, represented by a dotted line. The banana border you create in this task will use this margin as a guide. Turn Page Rulers on and drag the Zero Point to the upper left corner of the page. Drag vertical and horizontal guides to mark the center of the page.

3. To begin work on the single banana supplied to you, select the banana and use the Scale tool dialog box to scale the banana 50% **Uniform**. Hold the Option (Macintosh) or Alt (Windows) key and drag a duplicate for later use.

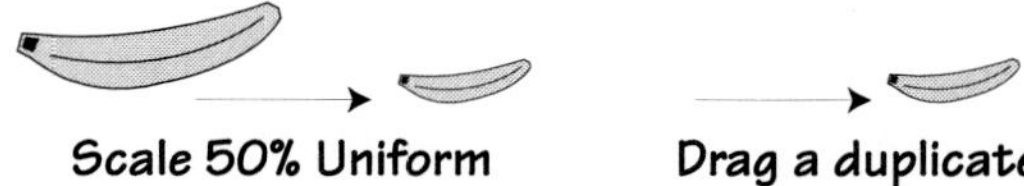

4. Select the reduced original and use the Rotate tool dialog box to rotate the banana 45 degrees.

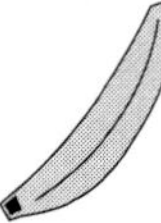

*Objects that are not Grouped will be affected individually by the **Align** or **Distribute Objects** from the **Align** palette. Grouped objects act as a single piece when aligned or distributed.*

5. Double-click on the Reflect tool in the Toolbox. This sets the default Origin of Transformation to the banana's center point. In the dialog box, select **Vertical** axis and click **Copy**. This will flip-flop a duplicate, criss-crossing the original. Select these two bananas and **Object->Group**.

6. Position this group into the upper left corner of the page, butting up against the margin corner.

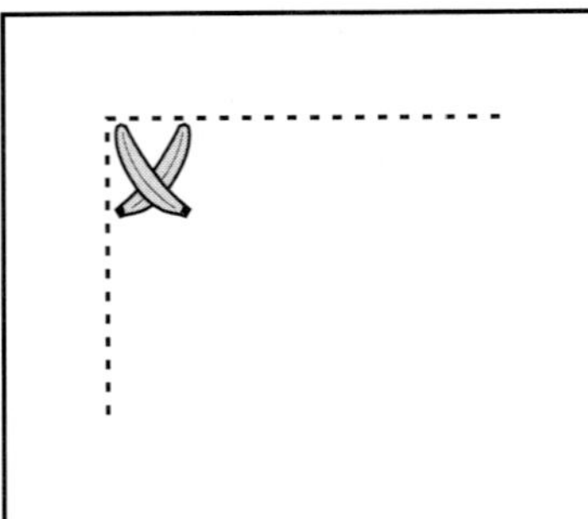

7. With the banana group selected, select the Reflect tool in the Toolbox, and, holding the Option (Macintosh) or Alt (Windows) key, click the crosshair cursor anywhere on the vertical guide. In the dialog box, click **Vertical** and **Copy.** A reflected duplicate will appear at the upper right margin corner.

8. Go to the banana you duplicated and moved off for later use. Select it and Scale the banana 75% **Uniform**. This is to add some contrast in size versus the banana group corners. Move the scaled banana to the upper left corner, close to the banana corner group.

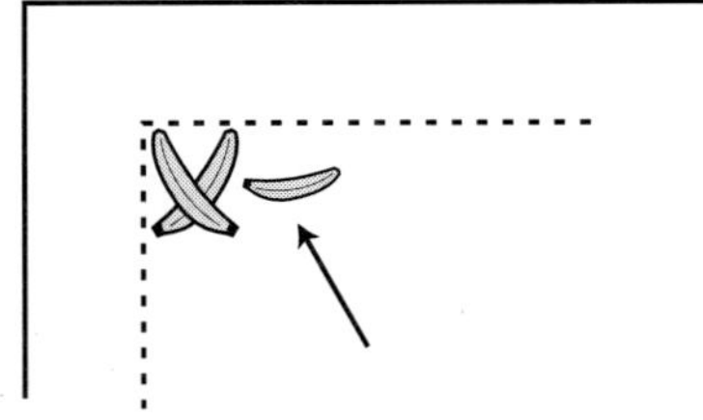

9. Holding the Option (Macintosh) or Alt (Windows) key, drag the single banana slightly to the right. Hold the Shift key after you begin the drag, so as to constrain any vertical movement. Once you've made this one duplicate, press Command-D (Macintosh) or Control-D (Windows) to **Transform Again**, 24 times.

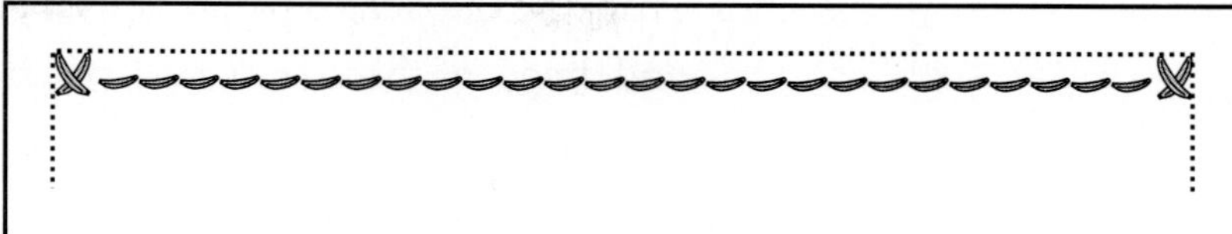

10. With the Selection tool, marquee-select the two top banana corners, and the bananas in between. You will need to fine-tune their spacing and alignment. Go to **Window->Show Align.**

11. Click first on the Align Objects Horizontally by Center Points option.

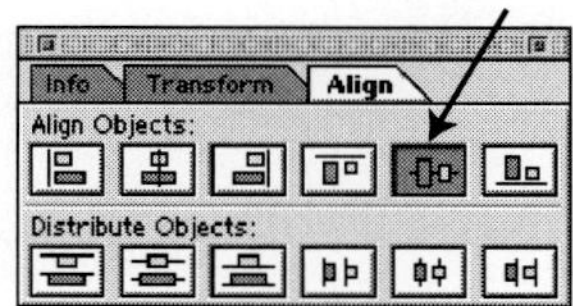

Then, click on the Distribute Objects Vertically by Center Points option.

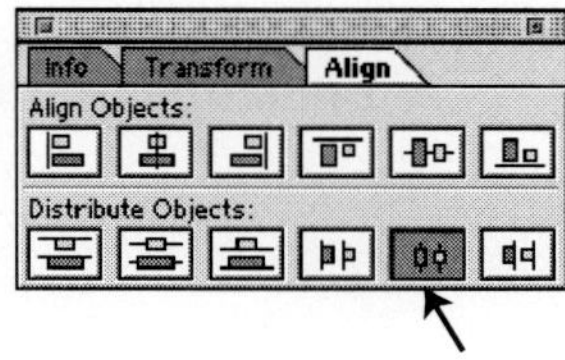

12. With these objects still selected, access the Reflect tool in the Toolbox. Holding the Option (Macintosh) or Alt (Windows) key, click the crosshair cursor anywhere on the horizontal center guide. In the dialog box click **Horizontal** and **Copy.**

13. From the duplicated bananas at the top section, select one of the bananas and drag it to the side margin, pressing the Option (Macintosh) or Alt (Windows) key to make a duplicate.

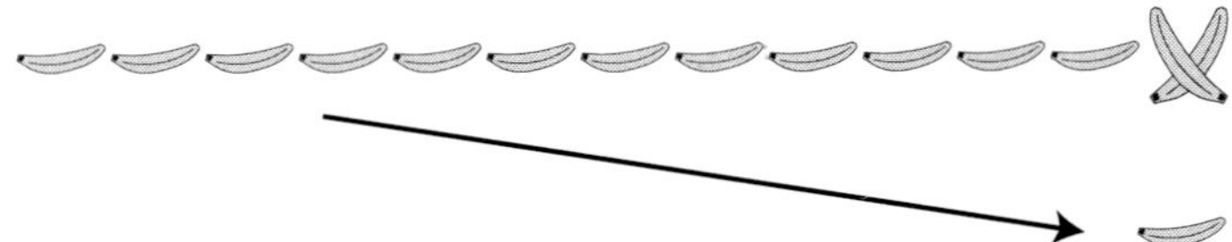

14. Select this banana and double-click on the Rotate tool in the Toolbox. In the dialog box, enter -90, and click **OK** to rotate it 90 degrees clockwise.

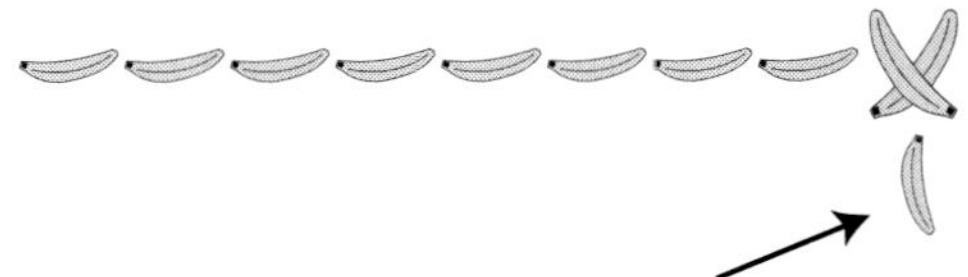

15. Position the banana under the corner group. Holding the Option (Macintosh) or Alt (Windows) key, drag the banana downward slightly, pressing the Shift key after the drag has begun to keep it constrained.

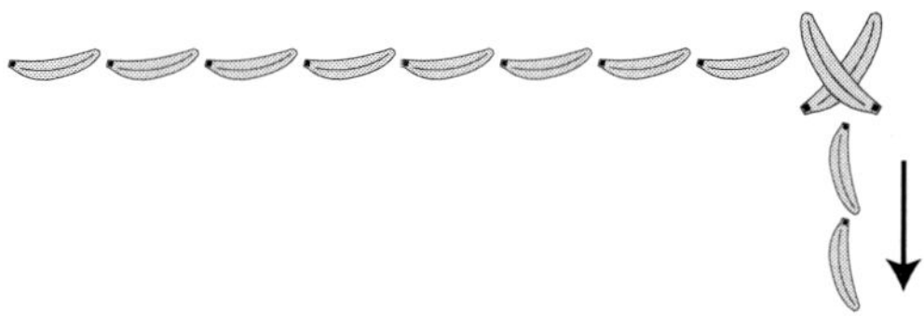

16. After duplicating the banana, press Command-D (Macintosh) or Ctrl-D (Windows) 33 times to **Transform Again** the bananas down to the lower right corner.

17. With the Selection tool, marquee-select the bananas starting with the top-right corner and extending down to the bottom right corner.

18. Go to **Window->Show Align**. Click first on the Align Objects Vertically by Center Points option.

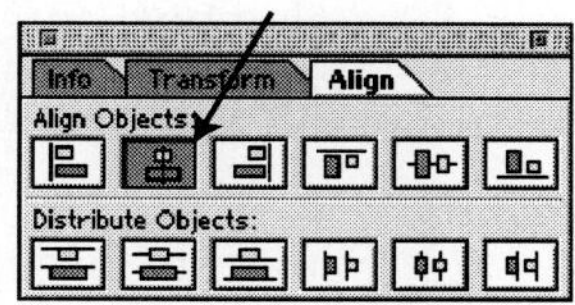

Then, click on the Distribute Objects Horizontally by Center Points option.

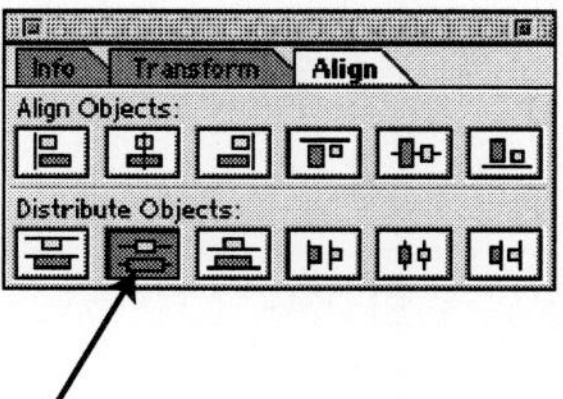

19. With the Selection tool, marquee-select only the bananas between the top right and bottom right corners. Do not include the corner bananas.

    Click the Reflect tool in the Toolbox, then click the crosshair on the center point of the page, while holding the Option (Macintosh) or Alt (Windows) key. In the dialog box, select **Vertical**, then click **Copy**.

20. All bananas are in place, aligned and distributed for correct alignment. You will now work on the borders that encompass the bananas.

21. For the border on the outside of the bananas, select the Rectangle tool in the Toolbox. Holding the Option (Macintosh) or Alt (Windows) key, click the crosshair on the center of the page as marked by the guides. In the dialog box, enter these dimensions: **Width** = 7.88 in., **Height** = 10,25 in. Click **OK**.

22. Paint the border: **Fill** = None, **Stroke** = 2 pt. Black.

23. Select the Rectangle tool in the Toolbox. Holding the Option (Macintosh) or Alt (Windows) key, click the crosshair on the center of the page as marked by the guides. In the dialog box, enter these dimensions: **Width** = 7.15 in., **Height** = 9.40 in. Click **OK**. The paint attributes were set on the previous rectangle, so it is not necessary to paint this rectangle.

24. The bananas and borders are created and in position. The final step is to add type to this design.

25. Select the Type tool in the Toolbox, then click the cursor on the page to create a text block. Press Command-Shift-C (Macintosh) or Control-Shift-C (Windows) to set the type alignment for Align Center.

26. In the text block, type the following:

    Happy Hour

    at

    BANANA BOAT

    LOUNGE

    Daquiri

    Dee-lights

    from

    4:00 to 5:00 P.M.

    You name the fruit,

    we'll make the drink!

27. Highlight all the text and apply the ATC Colada font, with **Leading** set for **Auto**.

28. Highlight "Happy Hour at" and change the size to 36 pt.

    Make "BANANA BOAT LOUNGE" 48 pt.

    "Daquiri Dee-lights from 4:00 to 5:00 P.M." is 38 pt.

    "You name the fruit, we'll make the drink" is 30 pt.

29. Insert appropriate line returns to make the type fit the layout as shown.

Happy Hour
at
BANANA BOAT
LOUNGE

Daquiri
Dee-lights
from
4:00 to 5:00 P.M.

You name the fruit,
we'll make the drink!

30. Center the text block with respect to the borders. The design is now finished. It should look similar to this.

31. **Save As** the file in **Illustrator 7.0** format. Name it "Banana Border.Art." **Close** the document.

Project H: Champagne Brunch Table Tent

Placing and Masking Images

1. Create a **New** document.

2. From the **SF-Adv Illustrator** folder, **File->Place** the image **Champagne Bottle.TIF.**

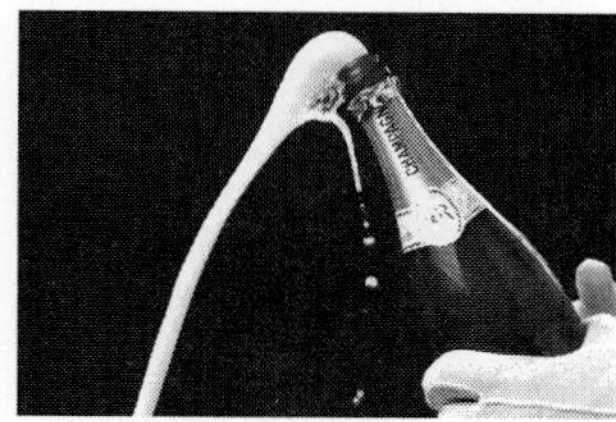

3. Using the Pen tool, trace the bottle and foam.

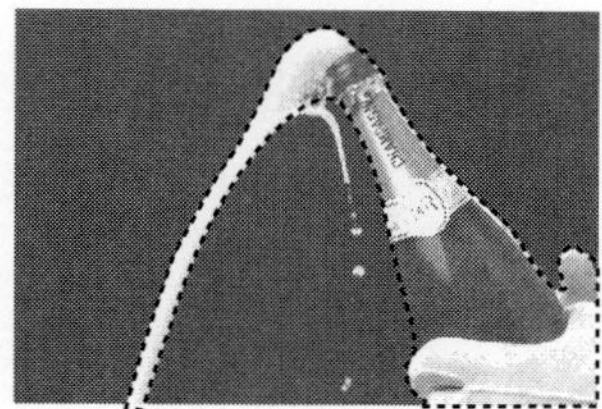

   Select both the photo and the traced path..

4. Go to **Object->Masks** and select **Make**. The champagne bottle becomes the only object visible, seen through the Mask.

   Use the Direct Selection tool to fine-tune your masking path. Select the photo and the mask, then **Object->Group** them.

5. **Save As** the file in **Illustrator EPS** format as "Champagne Bottle Mask.EPS." **Close** the document.

Creating Backgrounds, Adding Images

The Champagne Brunch Table Tent has two Masked elements: the champagne bottle and the lunch plate.

6. Create a **New** document. Use **Window->Swatch Libraries->Other Library** to open the Student File **ATC Custom Colors.AI**.

7. Draw a rectangle 4.25" x 5.5". Move it to the center of the page. Press Command-5 (Macintosh) or Control-5 (Windows) to make it a guide. Move the Zero Point to the upper left corner of the rectangle guide. Pull a vertical guide to the 2 5/8" ruler mark.

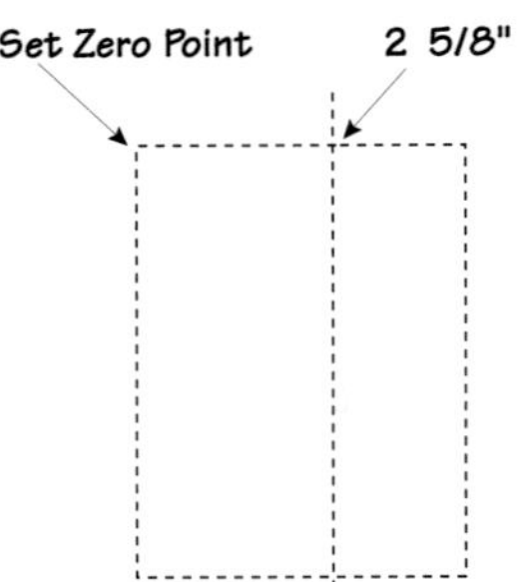

8. Draw a rectangle on the left side of the middle guide. Paint it: **Fill** = ATC Beige, **Stroke** = None.

9. Draw another rectangle on the right side of the middle guide. Paint this rectangle: **Fill** = ATC Dual Gradient, **Stroke** = None.

   With the Gradient tool, drag from the top of the rectangle, and end at the bottom.

10. **Place** the photo **Lunch Plate.TIF.** Draw an oval beginning from the center. The oval should almost fit the oval shape of the plate. Use the Direct Selection tool to adjust the anchor points and curves to fit the contours of the plate (a.).

a. b.

11. Select the masking oval and the photo. Go to the **Object->Masks** menu and choose **Make** (b). Press Command-G (Macintosh) or Control-G (Windows) to **Group** the two elements. Move the Masked plate into position in the table tent.

12. **Open** the document **Champagne Bottle Mask.EPS.**

Select the Masked champagne bottle, and **Edit->Copy** it. **Close** the document without saving.

13. You will be back in the table tent document. Press Command-V (Macintosh) or Ctrl-V (Windows) to Paste the Masked champagne bottle.

With the Masked image selected, double-click on the Scale tool in the Toolbox. Set the **Uniform** scaling for 85%. Press **OK**. Move the champagne bottle into place on the table tent, and go to **Object->Arrange->Bring to Front.**

14. **File->Place** the photo **Family Brunch.TIF.**

Draw a rectangle the exact size of the photo, positioning the rectangle on top of the photo. Press the Down Arrow key and the Right Arrow key three times each. Paint the rectangle: **Fill** = Black, **Stroke** = None. Go to

Object->Arrange->Send Backward to send the rectangle behind the photo, becoming its shadow.

Select the photo and the shadow, then **Object->Group** them. Position the group onto the table tent layout. When in position, go to **Object->Arrange->Send Backward** so the family will be behind the lunch plate.

15. Go to the Student Folder and **Open** the document **Last Mango Cafe Logo.EPS.** Select and **Scale** the logo 65% **Uniform.** Select all the objects and **Object->Group** them, then **Edit->Copy** the group. **Close** the file without saving.

16. In the working document, **Edit->Paste** the logo, and move it into position on the table tent, in the top-right corner.

17. Viewing the layout of the table tent below, fine-tune the positions of these elements on the page.

18. Keep the document open for the next exercise.

Setting Type for Champagne Brunch

19. Continue in the open document.

20. With the Type tool, type the capital letter "C". Highlight the letter and apply these settings. **Font** = ATC Rum Runner Script, **Size** = 282 pt., **Leading** = Auto, **Tracking** = 0, **Horizontal scale** = 60%.

21. Select the text block of the letter and **Rotate** it -5 degrees.

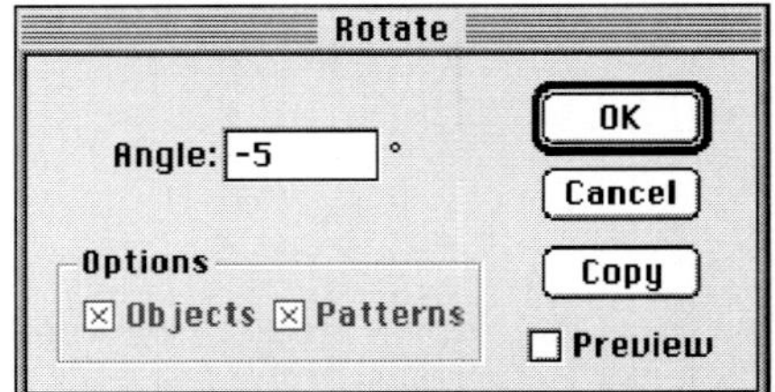

22. With the Type tool, create another text block. Type the word "hampagne." Create a new text block and type the word "brunch."

23. Select both text blocks with the Selection tool. Apply these settings. **Font** = ATC Rum Runner Script, **Size** = 72 pt., **Leading** = Auto, **Tracking** = 0, **Horizontal scale** = 100%.

hampagne brunch

24. Move the "hampagne" and "brunch" text blocks into position with the capital "C".

25. Select these three text objects and **Object->Group** them. Move them into position on the table tent layout.

26. With the Type tool, click a text block on the page and type:

EVERY

SATURDAY

Highlight the text and access the **Type->Character** palette. Make these settings: **Font** = ATC Sands, **Size** = 36 pt., **Leading** = Auto, **Tracking** = 0, **Horizontal scale** = 60%. Apply the settings. Paint the type: **Fill** = Black, **Stroke** = None.

Move the type into position on the table tent layout, as shown here.

27. The table tent design is complete. **Save As** the file in **Illustrator 7.0** format, naming it "Champagne Brunch Table Tent.AI." **Close** the document.

Project I: Tropical Postcard

Assigning Objects to Layers

Greetings From
UTA
Caribbean Island

1. Create a **New** document. Go to the **File->Place->SF Adv Illustrator** folder to import the Grayscale image **Tropical Palms Convert.TIF.**

2. Go to **Window->Show Layers.**

3. Rename Layer 1 "Palm Trees Layer." Create three new layers:

   Beach Layer   Sunset Layer   Sun Layer

4. Select the Placed Grayscale image and assign it to the Palm Trees Layer. In the **Layers** palette, click the Lock/Unlock square button to the left of the Palm Trees Layer. This will Lock the layer until it is needed.

5. Use the Pencil tool to draw the beach.

   Paint the beach path: **Fill** = 25% Magenta, 50% Yellow, **Stroke** = None. Assign the beach to the Beach Layer. **Hide** this layer by clicking the Eye icon to the left of the name.

6. Draw a rectangle the exact size of the Placed image.
   Paint the rectangle: **Fill** = Yellow & Orange Radial, **Stroke** = None.
   Assign the rectangle to the Sunset Layer. **Hide** this layer by clicking the Eye icon to the left of the name.

7. Draw a circle with a 0.383" diameter. In the design, move the circle to the lower left corner, just above the beach. Paint the circle: **Fill** = 50% Yellow, **Stroke** = None. Assign the circle to the Sun Layer.

8. **Show All** layers in the palette. **Unlock** the Palm Trees Layer. Arrange the layers this way:

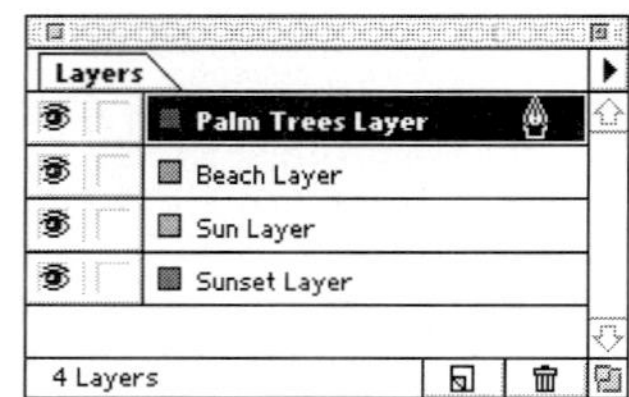

9. The Grayscale image of palms will be in front of all other objects.

   The **Placed** image is a Grayscale, which means it will block out all objects behind it. The secret to seeing the objects behind it is to **Rasterize** the Grayscale image and convert it to a Bitmap (1-bit) Color Model.

10. Click the Placed raster image to select it. Go to the **Object** menu and choose **Rasterize.** Make these settings.

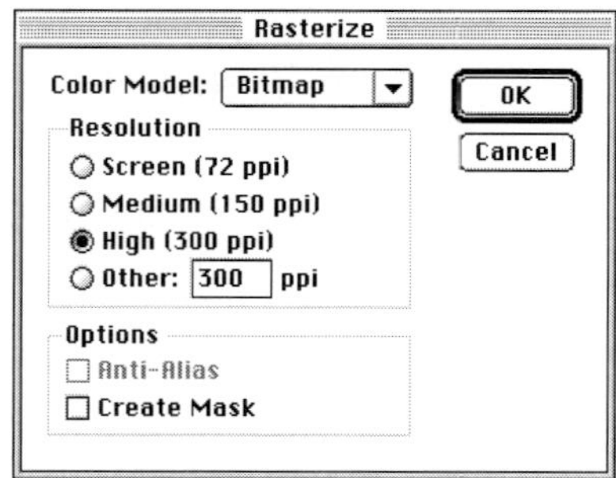

11. Click **OK**. Observe the design after the Grayscale image is converted to Bitmap. The sun, sunset, and beach will be seen; the design is complete.

12. **Save As** the file in **Illustrator EPS** format, naming it "Tropical Sunset Task.EPS." **Close** the document.

Creating the Postcard Layout Mechanical

13. Create a **New** document.

14. To create a 4" x 6" postcard outline, access the Rectangle tool, then click the crosshair on the page. In the **Rectangle** window, make these settings.

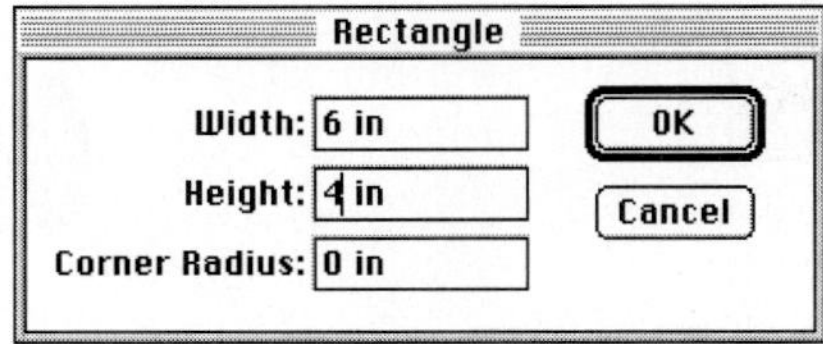

15. Move the postcard outline so it is located in the top half of the page.

Don't be alarmed if rotated images have a white shadow or outline. The screen image shown on the monitor is only a representation of what the printed document will look like. When you print the document, you will not see this shadow.

16. Paint the rectangle: **Fill** = 75% Cyan, 100% Yellow, **Stroke** = None.

17. Use **File->Place** to import the image made in the previous task, **Tropical Sunset Task.EPS.** Position it in the upper left area of the rectangle. **Rotate** the image 10°.

Fitting Type to a Layout

18. Access the Type tool, click the cursor on the page, and type:

Greetings From

19. Highlight the text and, with the **Type->Character** palette, apply these settings: **Font** = ATC Margarita Bold, **Size** = 36 pt., **Leading** = Auto, **Tracking** = 0, **Horizontal scale** = 100%.

Greetings From

20. Click on the Type tool in the Toolbox to deselect this text, then click the cursor on the page and type:

UTA

21. Highlight the text and, with the **Type->Character** palette, apply these settings: **Font** = ATC Margarita Bold, **Size** = 125 pt., **Leading** = Auto, **Tracking** = 0, **Horizontal scale** = 100%.

The type should look like this:

UTA

22. Click on the Type tool in the Toolbox, then click the cursor on the page to create a new text block, and type:

Caribbean Island

23. Highlight the text and, with the **Type->Character** palette, apply these settings: **Font** = ATC Margarita Bold, **Size** = 36 pt., **Leading** = Auto, **Tracking** = 0, **Horizontal scale** = 100%.

24. You should have three separate text blocks. Select them all with the Selection tool. Paint them: **Fill** = White, **Stroke** = None.

25. With the Selection tool, move each text block onto the postcard as shown here.

26. **Save As** the file in **Illustrator 7.0** format, naming it "Tropical Postcard.AI." **Close** the document.

Notes:

13. Go to **Object->Pathfinder->Unite.** This eliminates the internal segments of the two paths and combines them to make this one path (b.).

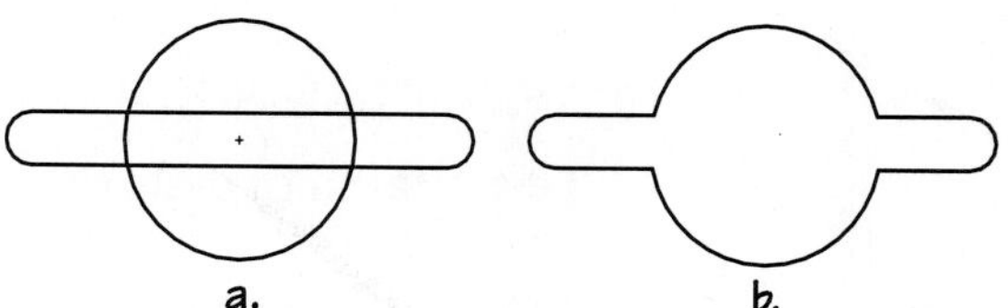

Adding Logo Background to Menu Cover

14. Go to **Preview** viewing mode.

15. Use **Window->Swatch Libraries->Other Library** to open the Student File **ATC Custom Colors.AI** to have the colors available to you.

16. Using the **ATC Custom Colors.AI** swatch palette, paint the path: **Fill** = None, **Stroke** = 15 pt., ATC Brown.
 Edit->Copy the path. **Edit->Paste In Front** the duplicate.
 Paint the duplicate: **Fill** = ATC Beige, **Stroke** = White, 2 pt.

17. From the **File** menu, use **Place** to go to back again to the Student Folder and Place the graphic file, **Last Mango Cafe Logo.EPS.** Scale the logo to fit the circular part of the border you are building.

18. **Edit->Select All** the objects in this document. Press Command-G (Macintosh) or Control-G (Windows) to **Group** them, then **Edit->Copy** the group. **Close** this document without saving.

19. You will be back in the working document, **Shell Pattern Menu.AI.** Go to **Edit->Paste** to paste the border/logo group into the document.

20. Center the pasted logo group into position on the menu cover. Scale the logo group, if needed, to fit the cover more aesthetically.

Embossing Type Outlines

21. You will now create type for the cover.

22. Draw a rectangle in the lower center section to cover the shells where the embossed text (to be created) "MENU" will go. Paint the rectangle: **Fill** = Blue, **Stroke** = None. **Object->Lock** this rectangle.

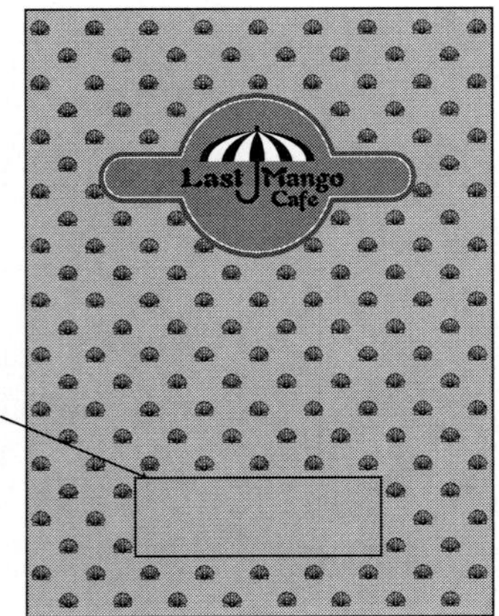

23. With the Type tool, type "MENU." Highlight this, and apply these settings: **Font** = ATC Mango, **Size** = 96 pt., **Leading** = Auto, **Tracking** = 0, **Horizontal scale** = 100%.

24. Select this text object with the Selection tool. Go to the **Type** menu and choose **Create Outlines**, then **Object->Group** the outlines. Paint the group: **Fill** = ATC Coral, **Stroke** = None.

25. **Edit->Copy** the MENU outline group. Press Command-B (Macintosh) or Control-B (Windows) to **Paste In Back** of the selected original. The Pasted copy will be the selected object. Press the keyboard Right Arrow key three times, then the Down Arrow three times. Paint this copy: **Fill** = Black, **Stroke** = None.

26. To add the embossing effect, you will create the white, light source type. But, in order to help see it, draw a temporary rectangle that surrounds the MENU type objects. **Object->Arrange->Send to Back** the rectangle. Paint it: **Fill** = ATC Blue, **Stroke** = None.

27. Select the original MENU outline. Press Command-C (Macintosh) or Control-C (Windows) to **Copy** it. Press Command-B (Macintosh) or Control-B (Windows) to **Paste In Back** of the selected original. Press the keyboard Left Arrow key two times, then the Up Arrow one time. Paint this copy: **Fill** = White, **Stroke** = None.

Select the three MENU outline groups, then **Object->Group** them.

Unlock All to unlock the temporary rectangle you drew. Select the rectangle and Delete it.

28. Move the embossed MENU group into position on the menu cover where the first rectangle that covered the shells was drawn.

29. The menu cover is complete. **File->Save** the file. **Close** the document.

Project K: Full Page Grocery Ad

Constructing the Mechanical

1. **Open** the document **Full Page Ad Grid.AI** that you previously created.This will be the grid for creating the ad. The ad size is: 8.5" x 11", margin: 0.5".

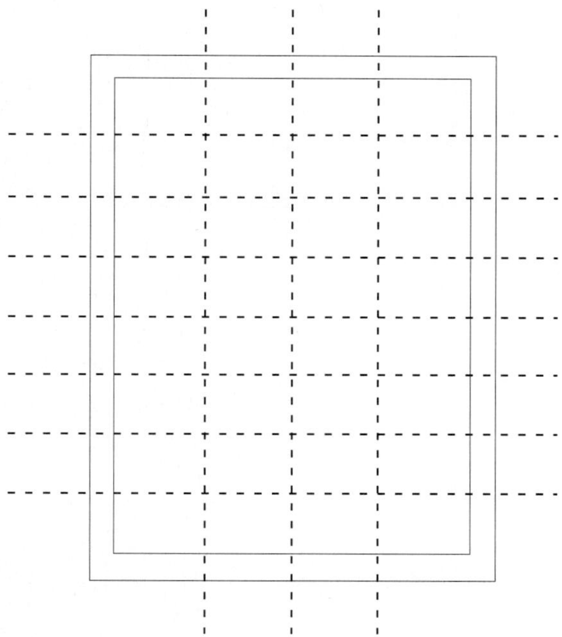

You will need to import special colors, so go to **Window->Swatch Libraries->Other Library** to open the **ATC Custom Colors.AI** from the Student Files folder.

2. The first element is the background at the top behind the Honeydo Market logo. The dimensions of this background are 7.5" x 2". Draw a rectangle this size using the **Rectangle** tool dialog box for exact measurements. Paint this background: **Fill** = ATC Dual Gradient, **Stroke** = None.

3. Go to the Student Files folder and **Open** the file **Honeydo Market Logo.EPS.** Select all paths, **Object->Group** them, then **Edit->Copy. Close** the file without saving. In the working document, **Paste** the image and center it on top of the rectangle just drawn.

4. Under the Honeydo Market logo, create a single text object with the Type tool and type these two lines:

   Prices effective Thursday May 30 thru June 20, 1998
   Credit Cards Accepted • Quantity Rights Reserved

   Highlight the first line of text and apply these settings: **Font** = ATC Plantation, **Size** =14 pt.
   Highlight the second line of text and make it: **Font** = ATC Plantation, **Size** = 12 pt.

   Select this text object with the Selection tool and set the alignment for Center. Move the center indicator of the text object to the center guide marking the page.

5. The next background rectangle is 7.5" x 4.25." Draw this rectangle and paint it: **Fill** = ATC Yellow 20%, **Stroke** = None. Position it underneath the background rectangle at top. Go to the Student Folder and **Open** the file **Beef Eaters Logo.EPS**. Select all paths, **Group** them, then **Edit->Copy**.

   Close the file without saving. In the working document, **Edit->Paste** the image. Then **Scale** it to fit the layout.

There will be times that Placed color images will be RGB in format. Only when saving your document as an Illustrator EPS will you be warned that the document contains RGB images. If you are preparing the document for Process color printing, the RGB images will cause problems. Illustrator's Rasterize feature will convert RGB to CMYK very quickly, rather than using external applications to do this.

File->Place the TIFF images: **Roast Beef.TIF, Cornish Hens.TIF, Turkey.TIF.**

Position and **Scale** them to fit the layout. Draw rectangles to fit the TIFF images. They will be the drop shadows. Paint them: **Fill** = Black, **Stroke** = None. Use **Paste in Back** to paste the shadows behind the TIFF images. Use the keyboard arrow keys to offset them.

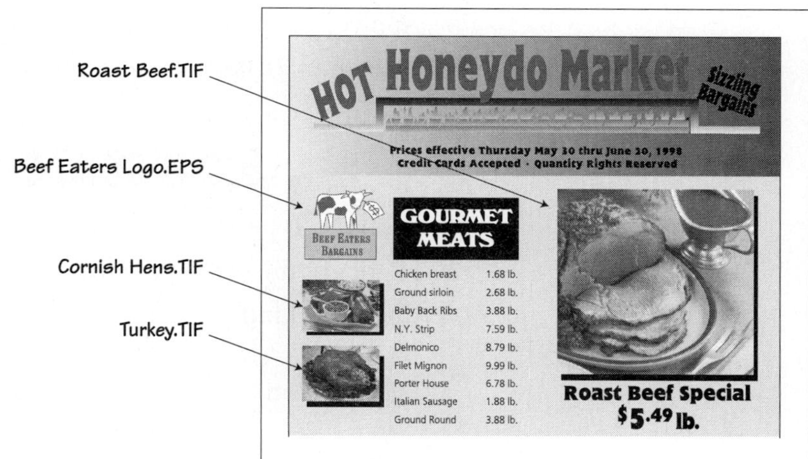

6. Create a new text object. Type the words "GOURMET" and "MEATS" on two lines, pressing Return (Macintosh) or Enter (Windows). Select the text and make the alignment Center. Apply these settings: **Font** = ATC Sea Breeze, **Size** = 24 pt., **Leading** = Auto, **Tracking** = 0. Paint the text: **Fill** = White, **Stroke** = None.

7. Draw a 2" x 1" rectangle. Paint it: **Fill** = ATC Navy Blue, **Stroke** = None. Position the "GOURMET MEATS" type so that it centers the rectangle, then **Object->Arrange->Bring To Front**. Select the text block and the rectangle, then **Object->Group** the two. Move this group into position on the layout.

8. With the Type tool, draw a new text object. Keep the type cursor clicked inside the object. Go to **File->Place** and, from the Student Files folder, import the text file **Grocery Text 1.RTF**.

   Highlight the text and apply these settings: **Font** = ATC Sands, **Size** = 13 pt., **Leading** = 21.5, **Tracking** = 0. Position the text object on the page under the "GOURMET MEATS."

9. With the Type tool, type the phrase: "Roast Beef Special."
   Apply these settings: **Font** = ATC Plantation, **Size** = 24, **Leading** = Auto, **Tracking** = 0, **Horizontal scale** = 100%.

Roast Beef Special

10. With the Type tool, create a new text object. Type "$549 lb.".
    Highlight the text. Apply these settings: **Font** = ATC Plantation, **Leading** = Auto, **Tracking** = -20.

    Highlight only the "$". Make the **Size** = 24 pt., Baseline shift = 14.

    Highlight only the "5". Make the **Size** = 48 pt., Baseline shift = 0.

    Highlight only the "49". Make the **Size** =24 pt., Baseline shift = 14.

    Highlight only the "lb.". Make the **Size** =24 pt., Baseline shift = 14.

$549 lb.

11. Move the "Roast Beef Special" and the "$5.49 lb." into position on the page under the Roast Beef photo.

12. Next, to prepare the PRODUCE section, draw a 3.5" square.
    Paint it: **Fill** = None, **Stroke** = 1.5 pt. Black.

Draw a 3.5" x 0.5" rectangle.
Paint it: **Fill** = ATC Dual Gradient, **Stroke** = None.
Position this rectangle at the top of the larger square, as shown here.

13. With the Type tool, click on the page and type the word "PRODUCE."
    Make these settings:
    Font = ATC Sea Breeze, **Size** = 26 pt., **Leading** = Auto, **Tracking** = 0.
    Paint the type: **Fill** = White, **Stroke** = None.

    Select this text object with the Selection tool, then **Edit->Copy** it. Go to **Edit->Paste In Back**. Once pasted, the duplicate will be selected. Press the Right Arrow key two times, then the Down Arrow two times to offset it.
    Paint the duplicate: **Fill** = Black, **Stroke** = None.

14. Select these two text objects, then **Object->Group** them. Move the group so that it centers the ATC Dual Gradient rectangle.

15. Go to **File->Place** and import the three TIFF images: **Salad.TIF, Chili.TIF, Oranges.TIF**. Draw rectangles the exact size of the photos. Paint each rectangle: **Fill** = Black, **Stroke** = None. Select the three rectangles. Press

the Right Arrow key three times, the Down Arrow 3 times. Now, **Edit->Cut** the rectangles, then select the three photos. Access **Edit->Paste in Back** to send each black rectangle to the back, behind each respective photo.

Select these three photos and their shadows and **Group** them. Move this group into position under the PRODUCE header.

16. With the Type tool, draw two text blocks that are one-half the width of the PRODUCE box. Leave the type cursor in the first block drawn. Go to **File ->Place** to import the file **Grocery Text 2.RTF** from the Student Files folder. With the Selection tool, select both text containers, then go to **Type->Blocks->Link**. The text will fill both blocks.

    Highlight all the text and apply these settings: **Font** = ATC Sands, **Size** = 13 pt., **Leading** = 19.5, **Tracking** = -20, **Horizontal scale** = 90%.

17. With the text and photos in position, the PRODUCE section is complete. Select all of its elements and move them into position on the layout.

18. To begin making the two coupons, draw a rectangle 3.5" x 1.75". Paint it: **Fill** = None, **Stroke** = Black 2 pt., Dashed Line 3 pt. dash, 3 pt. gap.

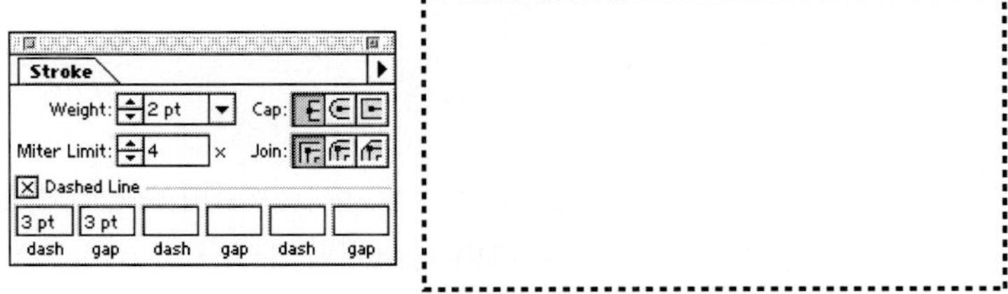

19. Draw another rectangle. Make the dimensions: 2" x 0.3125". Paint it: **Fill** = Black, **Stroke** = None.

20. With the Type tool, click on the page and type the word "COUPON." Highlight the text and apply these settings: **Font** = ATC Plantation, **Size** = 18 pt., **Leading** = Auto, **Tracking** = 0.

Paint the text: **Fill** = White, **Stroke** = None. Move the text object so that it centers the smaller rectangle.

COUPON

21. Select both the "COUPON" text and the smaller rectangle, then **Object->Group** them. Move the group into position on the dashed rule rectangle.

22. Select the COUPON rectangle group and the dashed-rule rectangle. Move them into position in the ad layout at the top of the remaining empty space.

23. With this group still selected, Option-drag (Macintosh) or Alt-drag (Windows) them downward (pressing the Shift key after the drag has begun) to make a duplicate coupon.

24. With the Type tool, type these words on separate lines:

Ocean

Spray

Juice

Create a new text object and type these words on separate lines:

Vlasic

Olives

Select both text objects and apply these settings: **Font** = ATC Plantation, **Size** = 30 pt., **Leading** = 30 pt., **Tracking** = 0, **Alignment** = Center.

Ocean
Spray
Juice

Vlasic
Olives

25. Create a new text object and type "$199". Highlight the text and apply these settings: **Font** = ATC Plantation,
Size = 42 pt., **Baseline shift** = 0, **Leading** = Auto, **Tracking** = -50.

26. Highlight only the "1". Apply these settings: **Size** = 80 pt., **Baseline shift** = -22.

27. Create a new text object and type "99¢". Highlight the "99" only and apply these settings: **Font** = ATC Plantation, **Size** = 80 pt., **Baseline shift** = 0, **Leading** = Auto, **Tracking** = -75.

Highlight the "¢" only and apply these settings: **Font** = ATC Plantation, **Size** = 42 pt., **Baseline shift** = 18, **Leading** = Auto, **Tracking** = -75.

$199 **99¢**

Highlight the text objects and kern them by holding the Option (Macintosh) or Alt (Windows) key and using Left or Right Arrow keys to make the spacing tighter or wider.

28. Select each text object separately and move into position in the coupon.

29. With the Type tool, create a new text object. Go to **File->Place**, and import the text file **Ocean Spray.TXT**. Apply these settings: **Font** = ATC Sands, **Size** = 13 pt., **Leading** = Auto, **Tracking** = -20, **Alignment** = Center. Move this text object so that it centers in the space under the $1.99.

30. With the Type tool, create a new text object. Go to **File->Place**, and import the text file **Vlasic Olive.TXT**. Apply these settings: **Font** = ATC Sands, **Size** = 13 pt., **Leading** = Auto, **Tracking** = -20, **Alignment** = Center.

31. From this imported text, highlight and **Edit->Cut** "Regularly $1.99." Create a new text block and **Edit->Paste** this text into it. Move the two text objects into position on the Vlasic Olives coupon.

32. With the coupons finished, the entire ad is now complete.

33. **Save As** the file, in **Illustrator 7.0** format, naming it "Honeydo Grocery Ad.AI." **Close** the document.

Notes:

Project L: Perspective Graph

Creating a Perspective Graph

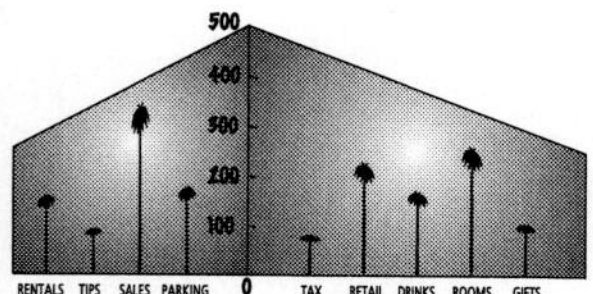

1. **Open** the document that you created earlier called **Student Perspective Grid.AI**. Use this as the guide for the graph of this task.

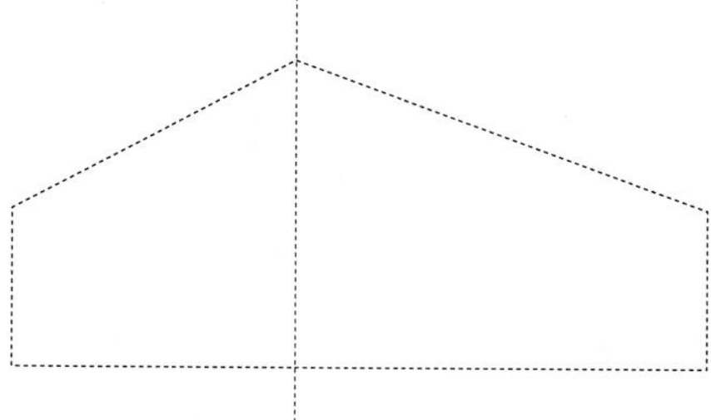

2. Double-click on the Graph tool in the Toolbox. In the **Graph Type** window, make sure it is set for Column Graph. Make no other changes. Click **OK**.

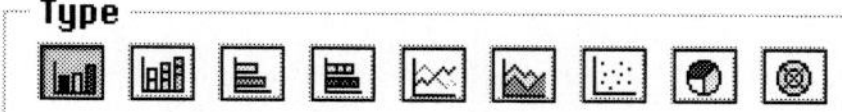

3. Using the right half of the guide to follow for your graph, use the crosshair to create the box that will hold the graph. Begin the box on the top center point of the perspective grid, and drag down to the lower right corner.

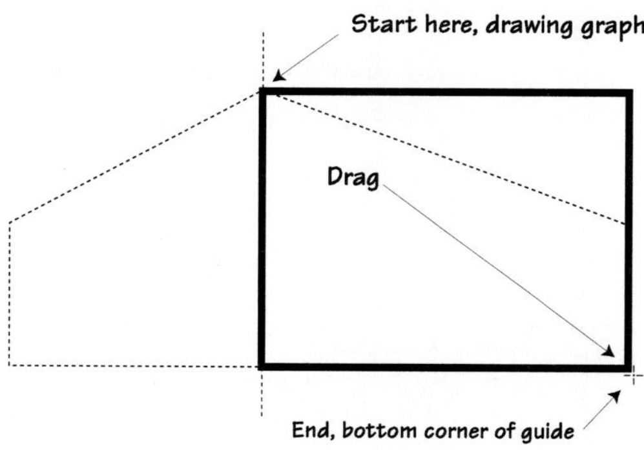

4. In the **Graph Data** dialog box, type this information.

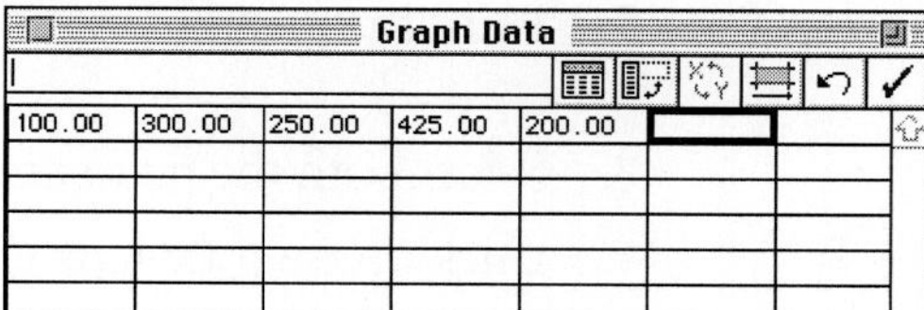

Once the information is typed into the cells, **Close** the window. You will be asked if you wish to save your changes to the graph data. Click **Save**. This will apply your new figures to the graph.

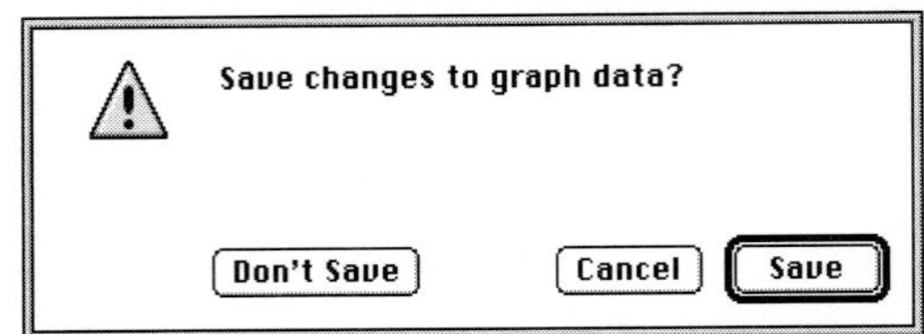

5. The result should look like this.

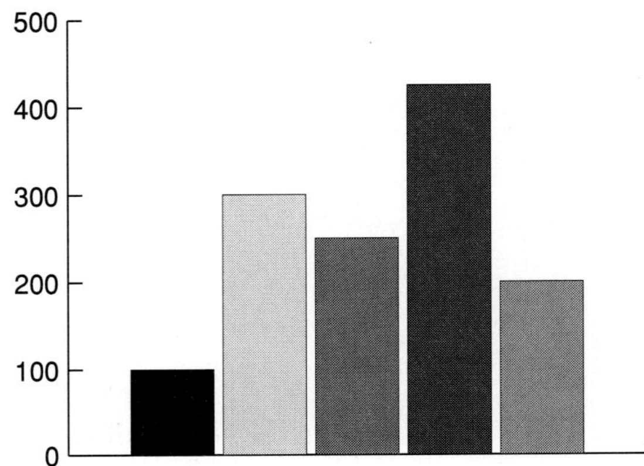

6. From the Student Folder, **Open** the file **Graph Custom Palm.AI**. Draw a rectangle that surrounds the palm. Select the rectangle and **Object->Arrange->Send to Back**. To create a custom pattern, the surrounding rectangle must be in back.

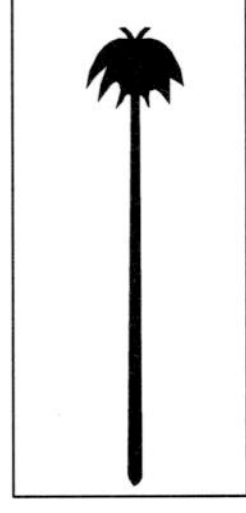

7. Paint the rectangle: **Fill** = None, **Stroke** = None.

8. Select both the palm and the rectangle. Go to **Object->Graphs->Design**. Click on **New Design.**

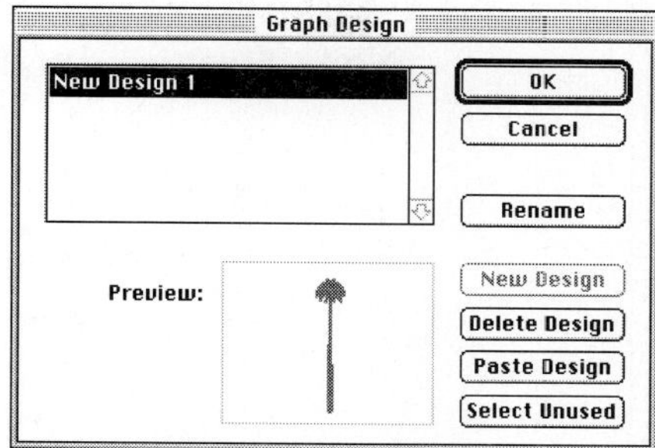

9. Click on **Rename** to name the **Pattern** "Palm Pattern." Click **OK**. Keep this file open.

10. Use the **Window** menu to go back to your working document, **Student Perspective Grid AI.**

11. Select the graph with the Selection tool. Go to **Object->Graphs->Column.**

12. In the **Graph Column** dialog box, the Palm Pattern will appear in the window. Select it and click **OK**.

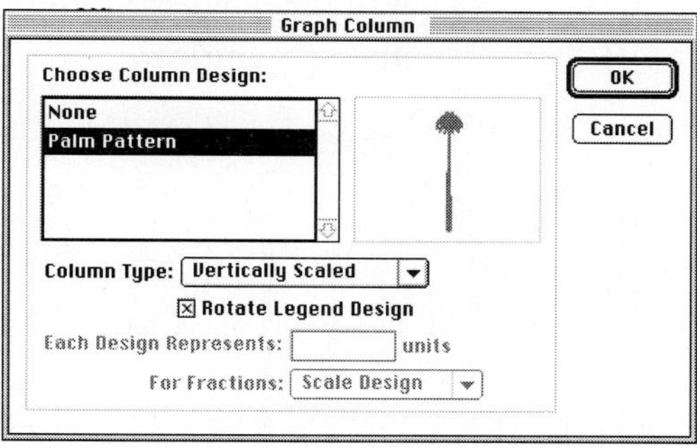

13. Observe the graph's columns after this modification.

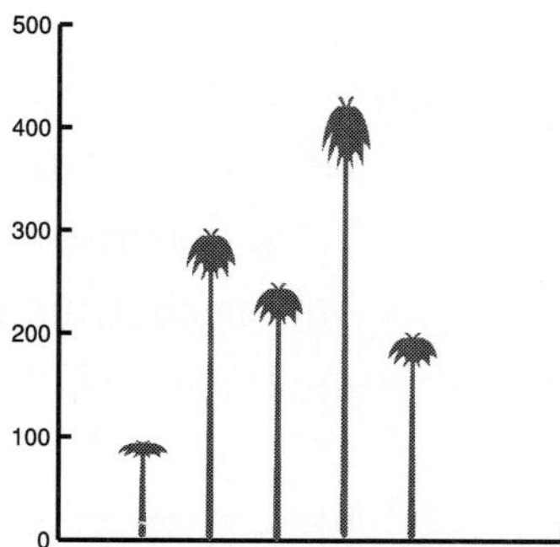

14. With the graph selected, go to the **Type->Font** menu and change the typeface to ATC Margarita Bold.

Draw a rectangle to enclose the graph as shown. Fill the rectangle: **Fill** = None, **Stroke** = 1pt. Black.

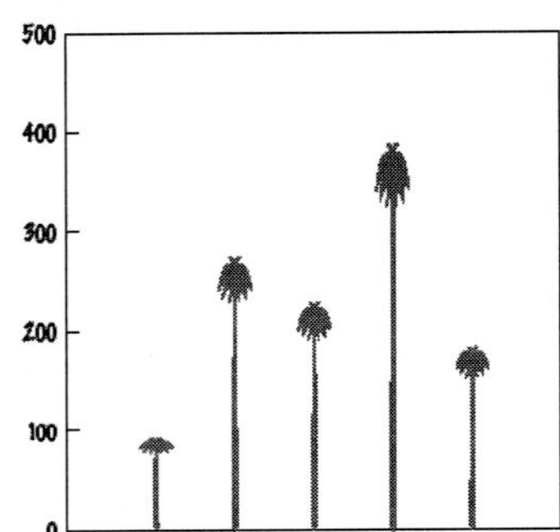

15. Select the graph and **Object->Ungroup** it. In the appearing warning message press **OK** to continue. It is necessary to **Ungroup** the graph to apply filters to the paths. Click on the numbers to select them and then **Object->Lock** them. **Edit->Select All.** Go to **Filter->Distort->Free Distort.**

16. In the **Free Distort** window, move the top right corner downward so that it looks as if it will match the guide. The guides are not shown in the **Free Distort** window.

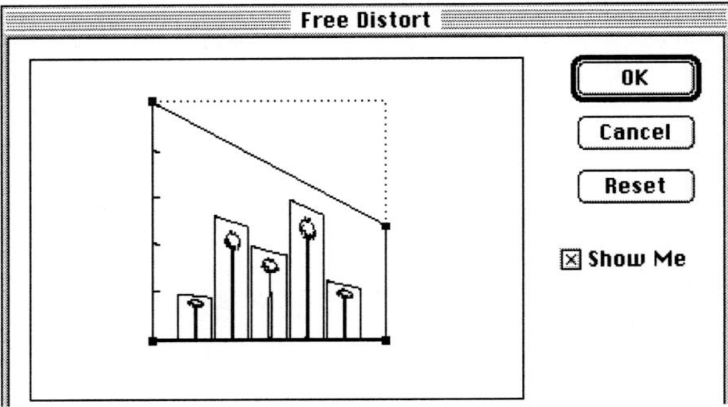

This process is trial and error. You must distort the paths, then click **OK**. In the document, if the distortion did not match the guide, go to **Edit->Undo** it, then go back to the **Free Distort** window. It will still be as you last moved it.

You can move the corner a little more, then click **OK**. Keep doing this until the guide is matched.

17. The Free Distorted graph should look like this. Press Shift-Command-L (Macintosh) or Shift-Control-L (Windows) to Unlock the type.

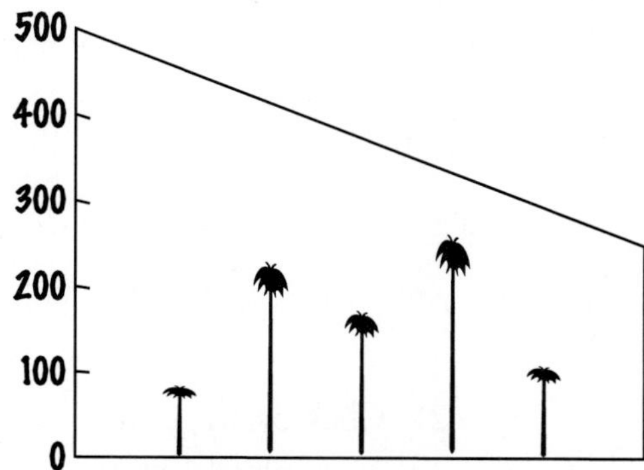

18. To draw the graph on the left side of the perspective grid, click on the Graph tool in the Toolbox. Begin drawing the graph box at the center point of the guide. End the box at the lower left corner of the guide.

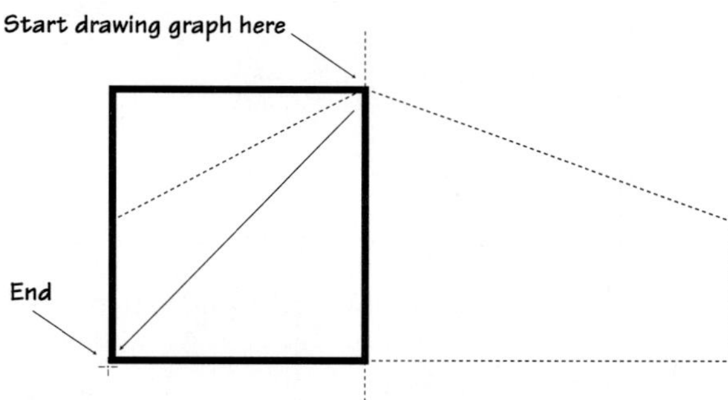

19. In the following **Graph Data** dialog box, type this information.

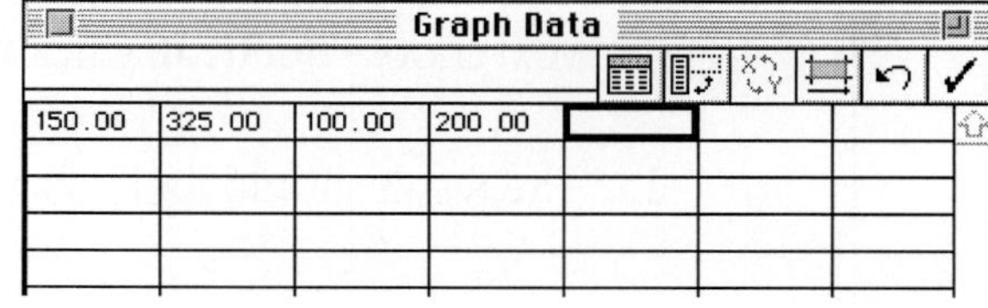

Close the **Graph Data** window, and **Save** the changes in the following warning window.

20. The graph should look like this.

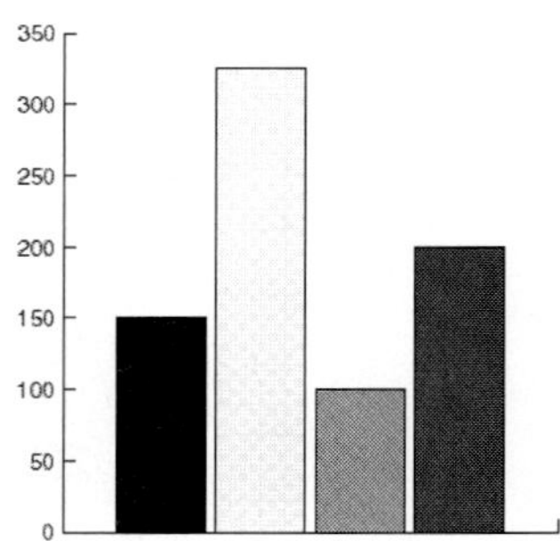

21. Click on the graph and go to **Object->Graphs->Column**. In the **Object ->Graphs->Column** dialog box, the Palm Pattern will appear in the window. Select **Palm Pattern** and click **OK**.

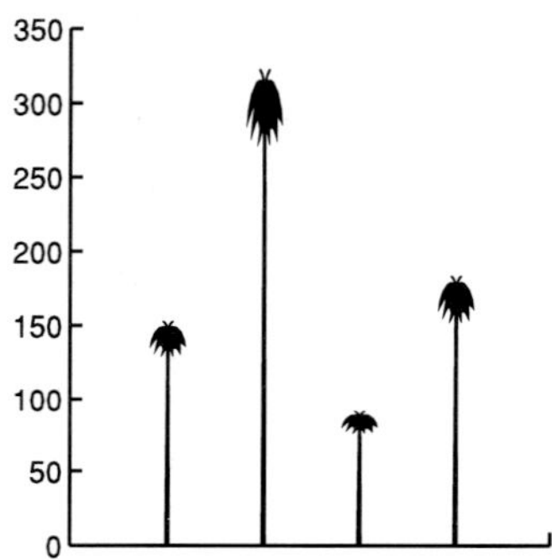

Draw a rectangle surrounding the graph, as you did with the other graph.

22. Select the graph then **Object->Ungroup** it. Click **OK** in the appearing warning window. Select the type and Delete it. Access the Reflect tool in the Toolbox. Hold the Option (Macintosh) or Alt (Windows) key and click the crosshair on the center point of the graph. In the **Reflect** dialog box, choose **Vertical.** Click **OK**.

23. The result should look like this.

24. Select all the paths of this graph and its rectangle. Go to **Filter->Distort ->Free Distort.** Move the top left corner downward to match the perspective guide.

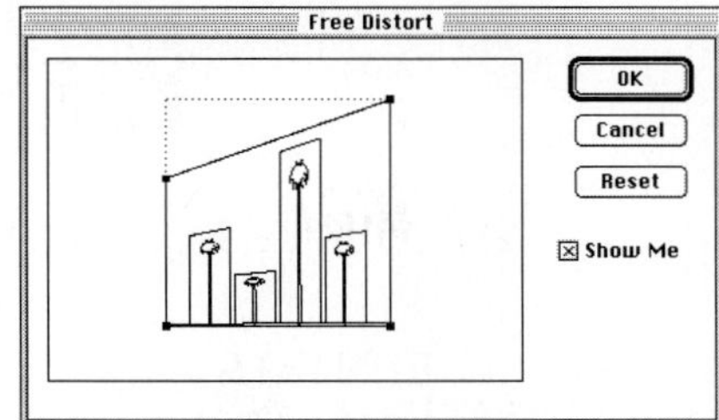

25. The result should look like this. Select the paths and **Object->Group** them. Go to **Object->Unlock All** to unlock the numbers text.

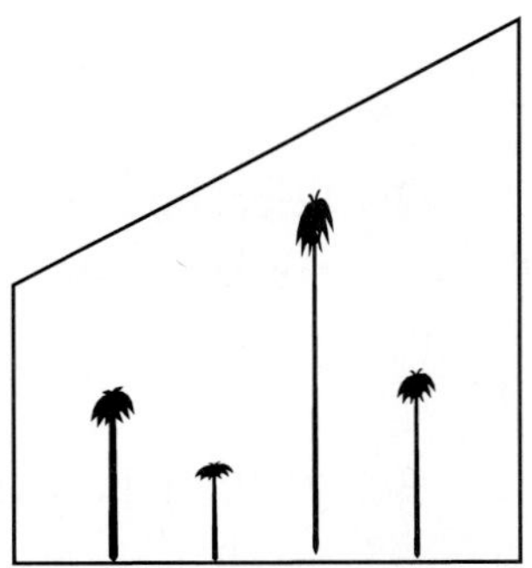

26. Move the left side graph into position so that the rules match the center lines next to the numbers.

    With the Direct Selection tool, hold Option (Macintosh) or Alt (Windows) and click on the "0" number text block. Position it under the center line.

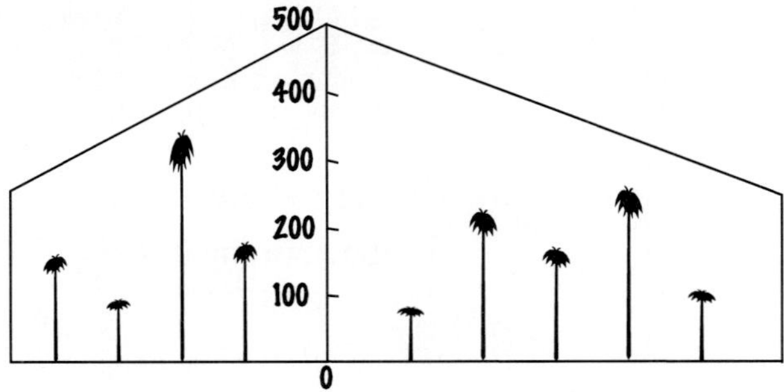

27. With the Direct Selection tool, click on the two rectangles. Paint them: **Fill** = Yellow & Orange Radial Gradient, **Stroke** = 1 pt. Black.

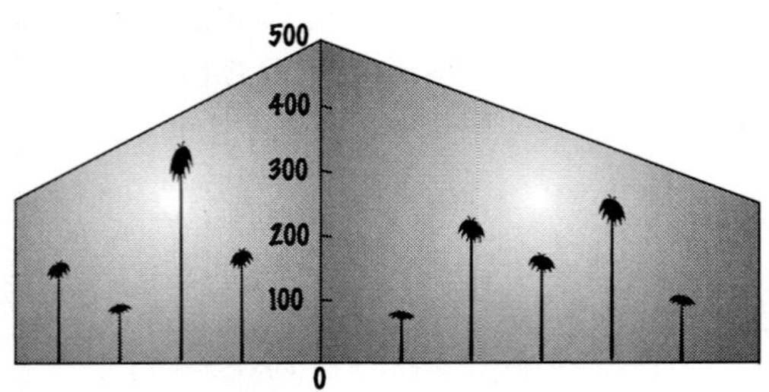

28. With the Type tool, type these words in one text block:

    RENTALS TIPS SALES PARKING

    Deselect the text block and click the Type cursor to create another text block. Type these words in the other text block:

    TAX RETAIL DRINKS ROOMS GIFTS

29. Select both text blocks with the Selection tool, and access the **Type Character** palette. Make the following settings: **Font** = ATC Sands , **Size** = 12 pt., **Leading** = Auto, **Tracking** = -20, **Horizontal scale** = 70%. Apply the settings.

30. Position the text blocks in place so that they align with the palm trees. It will be necessary to use the spacebar to add spaces before the words so as to fine-tune their positions under the appropriate trees.

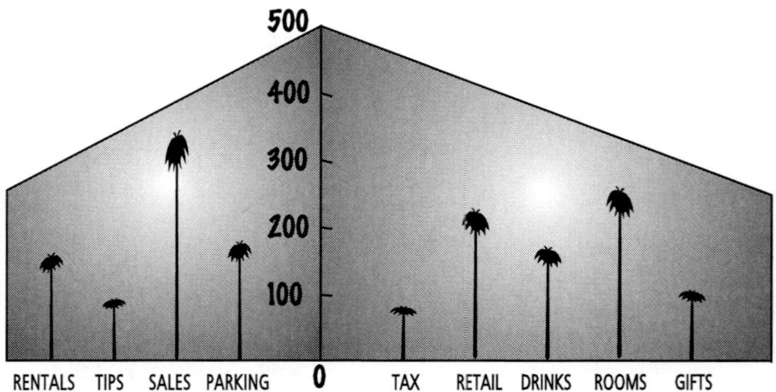

31. The perspective graph is complete. **Save As** the file in **Illustrator 7.0** format, naming it "Perspective Graph.AI." **Close** the document.

Project M: Java Jungle Goodies Ad

Setting General Layout with Objects

1. Create a **New** document.

2. Draw a rectangle with the dimensions: 4.25" x 5.5". This rectangle will be the border of the ad. Paint it: **Fill**=None, **Stroke**=1 pt. Black.

3. Center the border in the middle of the page. **Object->Lock** the border.

4. Using the Pencil tool, create the rough-drawn border that will surround the type and images. Paint the border: **Fill** = None, **Stroke** = 2.5 pt. Black.

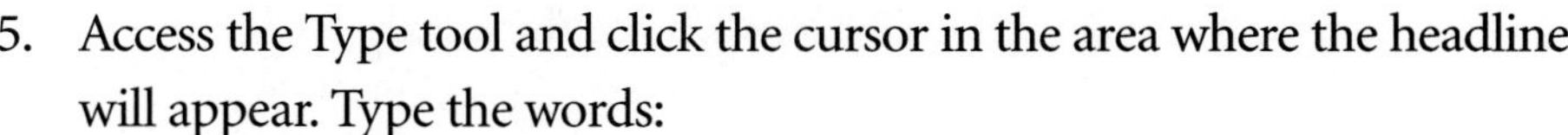

5. Access the Type tool and click the cursor in the area where the headline will appear. Type the words:

   Goodness!
What goes
great with
goodies

6. Highlight the text and go to the **Type->Character** palette. Make these settings: **Font** = ATC Holiday, **Size** = 72 pt., **Leading** = 43, **Tracking** = -20, **Horizontal scale** = 100%, **Alignment** = Center. Press Return (Macintosh) or Enter (Windows) to apply the settings.

7. Click on the Type tool in the Toolbox to deselect. Click the cursor on the page to create a new text block. Type a single question mark "?".

   Highlight the question mark and apply these settings. **Font** = ATC Holiday, **Size** = 83 pt., **Leading** = Auto, **Tracking** = -20, **Horizontal scale** = 100%.

   With the Selection tool, move the question mark into position, following the word "goodies." Select both text objects and go to **Type->Create Outlines. Object->Group** them. Leave them painted Black.

   Move the headline group into position on the layout. If necessary, **Scale** the headline to fit your layout.

8. Access the Type tool and click the cursor on the page to create a new text block. Type the words:

   Coffee Cointreau

   Highlight the type and go to the **Type->Character** palette. Make these settings: **Font** = ATC Holiday, **Size** = 30 pt., **Leading** = Auto, **Tracking** = -20, **Horizontal scale** = 100%. Press Return (Macintosh) or Enter (Windows) to apply the settings. Click on the Selection tool in the Toolbox. Go to **Type->Create Outlines.** Paint the outlines: **Fill** = White, **Stroke** = None. **Object->Group** the outlines.

9. Deselect the Cointreau text block. Click the Type tool cursor on the page to create a new text block. Type the words:

   French roast cafe with a touch of Cointreau.

10. Highlight the type and apply these settings in the **Type->Character** palette: **Font** = ATC Colada, **Size** = 11 pt., **Leading** = Auto, **Tracking** = -20, **Horizontal scale** = 70%. Click on the Selection tool in the Toolbox. Go to **Type->Create Outlines**. Paint the outlines: **Fill** = Black, **Stroke** = None. **Object->Group** them.

11. With the Pencil tool, draw the border that holds the Coffee Cointreau. Paint the border: **Fill** = Black, **Stroke** = None. Send the border to the back (**Object->Arrange->Send to Back**). Position the border so that it surrounds the Coffee Cointreau type. Select the type and the border. **Object->Group** them.

12. Position the Coffee Cointreau group to the lower left of the ad. Underneath this object, position the "French roast cafe with a touch of Cointreau" outlines.

13. Go to the Student Files folder and **Place** the file **Java Jungle Logo.EPS**. Move the logo into position in the lower right corner.

14. Go to the Student Files folder and **Place** the image **Dessert Tray.TIF.**

The photo will need to be Masked, which we'll do later. For now, merely move the photo into approximate position on the ad. With the photo selected, go to **Object->Arrange->Send to Back.**

15. With all elements in position, the ad should look similar to this, so far:

16. **Save As** the file in **Illustrator 7.0** format, naming it "Java Jungle Ad.AI."

Masking Objects

17. The photo of the dessert tray will need to be Masked. Use the Pen tool to outline the desserts and the plate in one closed path.

18. With the Direct Selection tool, adjust the curves to fit the contours of the tray and desserts (a.). Select both the photo and the masking path. Go to the **Object->Masks** menu and choose **Make** (b.).

a.

b

19. **Object->Group** the photo and mask. Scale the group 60%. Position this group into place in the ad.

20. **Save** the file. Keep the document open for the next exercise.

Using Filters on Raster Images

21. You will now make the dessert plate air-brush shadow. Draw an oval the size of the dessert plate. Move the oval off to the right of the page.

22. Paint it: **Fill** = 50% Black, **Stroke** = None.

23. Draw a rectangle surrounding the oval.
    Paint the rectangle: **Fill** = None, **Stroke** = None.

    The purpose of the rectangle is to give added room around the oval that the airbrush spray can extend into. Otherwise, if only the oval were rasterized, the spray would be cut off sharply at the edge of the oval.

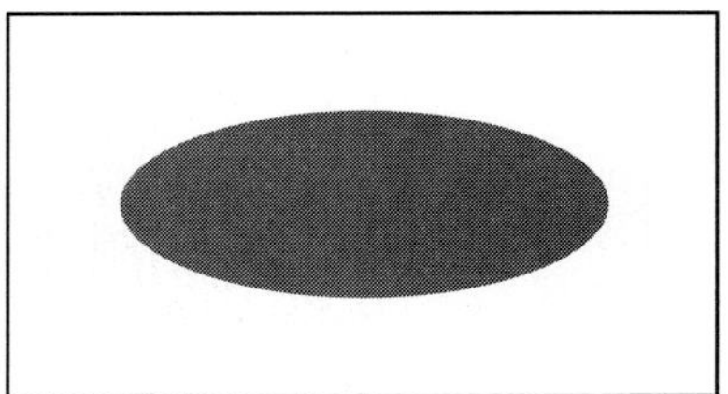

24. Select the two objects and go to **Object->Rasterize.** Make these settings.

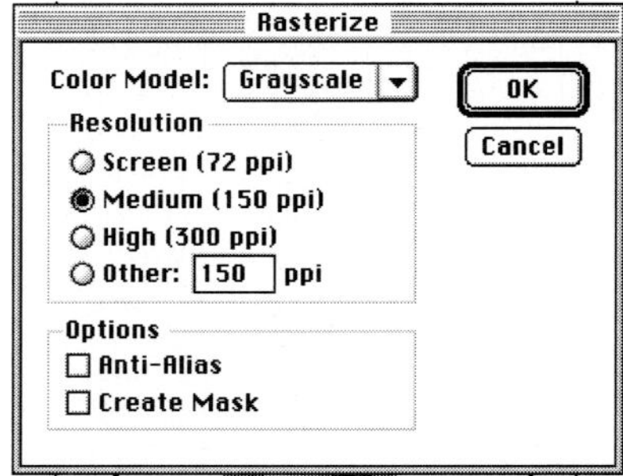

25. Select the Rasterized object. Go to **Filter->Brush Strokes->Spatter** filter.

26. Make these settings in the **Spatter** window. **Spray Radius** = 18, **Smoothness** = 1. Press **OK.**

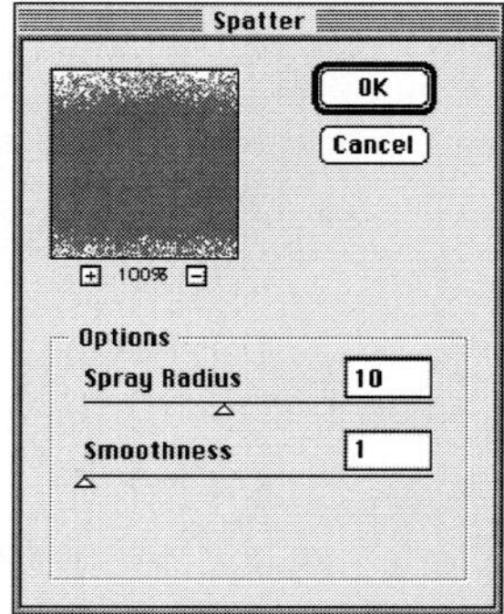

27. The Rasterized blend will now resemble a rough, airbrushed look. It will be used as a shadow under the dessert tray.

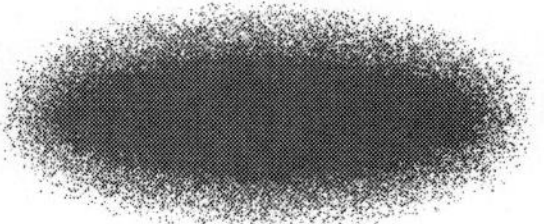

28. Move the shadow into position so that it is offset from the dessert tray. **Edit->Cut** the shadow. Select the dessert tray and **Edit->Paste In Back** the shadow of the tray.

29. **Save** the file. Keep this document open.

Using Gradients on Objects

30. **Open** the file **Java Jungle Cup.AI.** Zoom in on the cup (a.).

31. With the Direct Selection tool, hold the Option (Macintosh) or Alt (Windows) key and click on the black ellipse portraying the interior of the cup. Press the Delete key (b.).

32. Select the cup with the Selection tool. Go to **Object->Pathfinder** and choose **Unite**. An outline of the cup will remain (c.).

33. Paint the outline: **Fill** = Black, White Gradient, **Stroke** = None (d.).

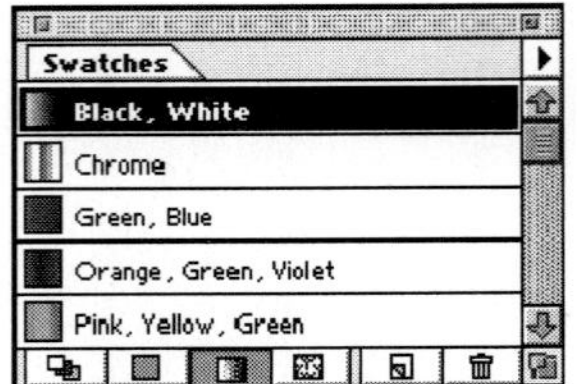

34. With the Gradient tool, start the crosshair in the upper left corner and drag down to the lower right (e.).

    The gradient direction will change in the cup outline (f.). Select the cup with the Selection tool. **Edit->Copy** it to clipboard.

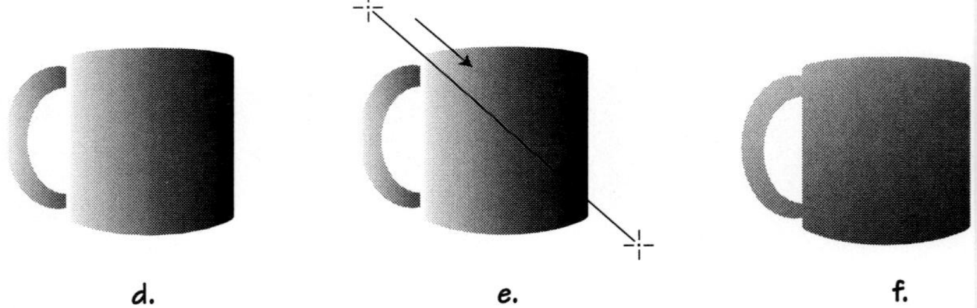

    Close this document without saving.

35. You will be back in the open document **Java Jungle Ad.AI.**

36. With the Zoom tool, drag a selection marquee around the Java Jungle logo area in the lower right corner of the ad.

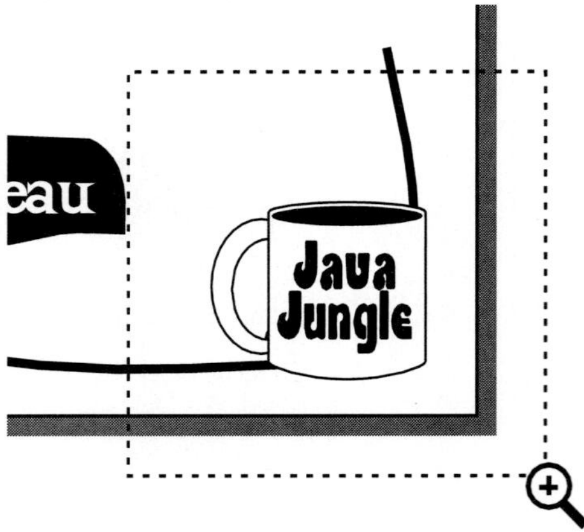

37. **Edit->Paste** the cup gradient shadow. Move the shadow so that it is positioned in front of the cup, offset to the lower left.

Edit->Cut the shadow.

38. Click on the Java Jungle logo to select it. Press Command-B (Macintosh) or Control-B (Windows) to **Paste In Back** the shadow behind the logo.

39. The ad is complete, and should look similar to this.

40. **File->Save** the file. **Close** the document.

Notes:

4/1

A job printed using four colors of ink on one side of the sheet, and one color of ink on the other.

4/4

A job printed with four colors of ink on both sides of the sheet. A full four-color project. See *process colors, subtractive color.*

Acetate

A plastic material used to block or expose specific portions of a layout through "windows" cut from the material by a stripper. The resultant "masks" are used to generate film separations for generating printing plates.

Achromatic

By definition, having no color; therefore, completely black or white or some shade of gray.

Acrobat

This program by Adobe Systems, Inc. converts any document from any Macintosh or Windows application to PDF format, which retains the page layout, graphics, color, and typography of the original document. It is widely used for distributing documents online because it is independent of computer hardware. The only software needed is a copy of Acrobat Reader, which can be downloaded free.

Adaptive Palette

A sampling of colors taken directly from an image, and used in a special compression process usually used to prepare images for the world wide web.

Additive Color Process

The additive color process is the process of mixing red, green, and blue light to achieve a wide range of colors, as on a color television screen. See *Subtractive Color.*

Adjacent Color

The eye will respond to a strong adjacent color in such a way as to affect the perception of the particular color in question. That is, a color having different adjacent colors may look different than it does in isolation. Also referred to as metamarism.

Adobe Systems Incorporated

A major software developer responsible for the creation of the PostScript page description language (see *PostScript*), used in almost all graphic arts environments. PostScript resides in a printer or Raster Image Processor (see *Raster Image Processor*) and is used to convert graphics from the screen to high-resolution output. Adobe also develops the highly popular Photoshop, Illustrator, PageMaker, and Premiere graphics and video applications, in addition to a range of others.

Airbrush

A tool driven by compressed air that applies a very fine spray of color to artwork to produce various effects. Its effects are simulated in digital illustration and imaging programs.

Algorithm

A specific sequence of mathematical steps to process data. A portion of a computer program that calculates a specific result.

Alley

The white space, or margin, between columns on a page.

Alpha Channel

An 8-bit channel of data that provides additional graphic information, such as colors or masking. Alpha channels are found in some illustration or graphics programs, and are used in video production.

ANSI

The American National Standards Institute. ANSI establishes and publishes industry standards in many fields including data transmission and graphics.

Anti-aliasing

A graphics software feature that eliminates or softens the jaggedness of low-resolution curved edges.

Apple Computer, Inc.

A computer manufacturer based in Cupertino, California. Apple was responsible for the development of the Macintosh computer and the first Postscript-equipped laser printer, which ushered in the "desktop publishing" revolution.

Archival storage

The process of storing data in a totally secure and safe manner. Archiving differs from backup in that it's meant to be used to restore entire systems or networks, rather than providing quick and easy access to specific files or folders.

Art

Illustrations and photographs in general; that is, all matter other than text that appears in a mechanical.

Artifact

By definition, something that is artificial, or not meant to be there. An artifact can be a blemish or dust spot on a piece of film, or unsightly pixels in a digital image.

Ascender

Parts of a lower-case letter that exceed the height of the letter "x". The letters b, d, f, h, k, l, and t have ascenders.

ASCII

The American Standard Code for Information Interchange, which defines each character, symbol, or special code as a number from 0 to 255 (8 bits in binary). An ASCII text file can be read by any computer, and is the basic mode of data transmission on the Internet.

ATM (Adobe Type Manager)

A utility program which causes fonts to appear smooth on screen at any point size. It's also used to manage font libraries.

Author's Alterations (A/As)

Changes made to the copy by the author after typesetting, and thus chargeable to the author.

Backing Up

The process of making copies of current work or work-in-progress as a safety measure against file corruption, drive or system failure, or accidental deletion. Backing up work-in-progress differs from creating an archive (see *Archiving*) for long-term storage or system restoration.

Backslant

A name for characters that slant the opposite way from italic characters.

Banding

A visible stair-stepping of shades in a gradient.

Banner

A large headline or title extending across the full page width, or across a double-page spread.

Baseline

The implied reference line on which the bases of capital letters sit.

Bézier Curves

Curves that are defined mathematically (vectors), in contrast to those drawn as a collection of dots or pixels (raster). The advantage of these curves is that they can be scaled without the "jaggies" inherent in enlarging bitmapped fonts or graphics.

Binding

In general, the various methods used to secure signatures or leaves in a book. Examples include saddle-stitching (the use of staples in a folded spine), and perfect-bound (multiple sets of folded pages sewn or glued into a flat spine).

Bit (Binary Digit)

The smallest unit of information in a computer, representing one of two conditions, ON or OFF; HIGH or LOW, etc. Eight bits comprise one byte. One byte can represent any text character.

Bitmap

A rectangular array of dots that, taken together, form an image. Bitmap file formats include: .BMP, .DIB, .GIF, .PCX and .TIFF (see *Raster Graphics*).

Bitmapped

An image formed by a grid of dots or pixels whose curved edges have discrete steps because of the approximation of the curve by a finite number of pixels.

Black

The absence of color; an ink that absorbs all wavelengths of light.

Blanket

The blanket, a fabric coated with natural or synthetic rubber wrapped around the cylinder of an offset press, transfers the inked image from the plate to the paper.

Bleed

Page data that extends beyond the trim marks on a page. Illustrations that spread to the edge of the paper without margins are referred to as "bled off."

Blind Emboss

A raised impression in paper made by a die, but without being inked. It is visible only by its relief characteristic.

Blow up

An enlargement, usually of a graphic element such as a photograph.

Body Copy

The text portion of the copy on a page, as distinguished from headlines.

Boldface

A heavier, blacker version of a typeface.

Bond

A sized (coated) writing paper used for business or personal stationery that normally has significant rag (cotton) content.

Border

A continuous line that extends around text; or a rectangular, oval, or irregularly-shaped visual in an ad.

Bounding Box

The imaginary rectangle that encloses all sides of a graphic, necessary for a page layout specification.

Brightness

1. A measure of the amount of light reflected from a surface. 2. A paper property, defined as the percentage reflection of 457-nanometer (nm) radiation. 3. The intensity of a light source. 4. The overall percentage of lightness in an image.

Bug

See *Logo*

Bullet

A marker preceding text, usually a solid dot, used to add emphasis; generally indicates that the text is part of a list.

Burn

1. To expose an image onto a plate. 2. To make copies of ROM chips or CD-ROMs. 3. To darken a specific portion of an image through photographic exposure.

Byte

A unit of measure equal to eight bits (decimal 256) of digital information, sufficient to represent one text character. It is the standard unit measure of file size. (See also *Megabyte, Kilobyte*, and *Gigabyte*).

Calibration Bars

A strip of reference blocks of color or tonal values used to check the registration, quality, density, and ink coverage during a print run.

Calibration

Making adjustments to a color monitor and other hardware and software to make the monitor represent as closely as possible the colors of the final printed piece.

Callout

A descriptive label referenced to a visual element, such as several words connected to the element by an arrow.

Camera Ready

A completely finished mechanical, ready to be photographed to produce a negative from which a printing plate will be made.

Cap Line

The theoretical line to which the tops of capital letters are aligned.

Caps and Small Caps

A style of typesetting in which capital letters are used in the normal way, while the type that would normally be in lower case has been changed to capital letters of a smaller point size. A true small-caps typeface does not contain any lower-case letters.

Caps

An abbreviation for capital letters.

Caption

The line or lines of text that identify a picture or illustration, usually placed beneath it or otherwise in close proximity.

CD-ROM

A device used to store approximately 600MB of data. Files are permanently stored on the device and can be copied to a disk but not altered directly. ROM stands for Read-Only Memory. Equipment is now available on the consumer market for copying computer files to blank CD-ROMs.

Character Count

The number of characters (letters, figures, signs or spaces) in a selected block of copy. Once used to calculate the amount of text that would fit on a given line or region when physically setting type.

Choke

See *Trapping*

Chooser

A part of the Macintosh operating system that permits selection of a printer or other peripheral device. Chooser is also used to access resources on a network.

Chroma

The degree of saturation of a surface color in the Munsell color space model.

Chromaticity Diagram

A graphical representation of two of the three dimensions of color. Intended for plotting light sources rather than surface colors. Often called the CIE diagram.

Cicero/Didot Point

The cicero is a unit of horizontal distance slightly larger than the pica, used widely in continental Europe. A cicero equals 0.178 inches, or 12 Didot points.

CIE (Commission Internationale de l'Eclairage)

An international group that developed a universal set of color definition standards in 1931.

CIE Diagram

See *Chromaticity Diagram*

Clip Art

Collections of predrawn and digitized images stored on disk that can be pasted into word processing and DTP documents.

Clipboard

The portion of computer memory that holds data that has been cut or copied. The next item cut or copied replaces the data already in the clipboard.

Cloning

Duplication of pixels from one part of an image to another.

CMS

See *Color Management System*

CMYK (Cyan, Magenta, Yellow, Black)

The process colors (subtractive primaries) used in color printing. The letter K stands for "Key," although it is commonly used to refer to the Black ink that is added to the three colors when necessary. When printing black text as part of a four-color process, only the black ink is used. A normal four-color separation will have a plate for each of the four colors. When combined on the printed piece, the half-tone dots of each color give the impression of the desired color to the eye.

Coated

Printing papers having a surface coating (of clay or other material) to provide a smoother, more even finish with greater opacity.

Cold type

Type produced by photographic or digital methods, as opposed to the use of molten metal as in the old Linotype machine.

Collate

To gather separate sections or leaves of a publication together in the correct order for binding.

Color Balance

The combination of yellow, magenta, and cyan needed to produce a neutral gray. Determined through a gray balance analysis.

Color Bars

See *Color Control Strip*

Color Cast

The modification of a hue by the addition of a trace of another hue, such as yellowish green, pinkish blue, etc. Normally, an unwanted effect that can be corrected.

Color Chart

A printed chart of various combinations of CMYK colors used as an aid for the selection of "legal" colors during the design phase of a project.

Color Control Strip

A printed strip of various reference colors used to control printing quality. This strip is normally placed outside the "trim" area of a project, as a guide and visual aid for the pressman.

Color Conversion

Changing the color "mode" of an image. Converting an image from RGB to CMYK for purposes of preparing the image for conventional printing.

Color Correction

The process of removing casts or unwanted tints in a scanned image, in an effort to improve the appearance of the scan or to correct obvious deficiencies, such as green skies or yellowish skin tones.

Color Gamut

The range of colors that can be formed by all possible combinations of the colorants of a given reproduction system (printing press) on a given type of paper.

Color Key

An overlay color proof of acetate sheets, one for each of the four primary printing inks. The method was developed by 3M Corporation and remains a copyrighted term.

Color Management System

A process or utility that attempts to manage color of input and output devices in such a way that the monitor will match the output of any CMS-managed printer.

Color Model

A system for describing color, such as RGB, HLS, CIELAB, or CMYK.

Color Picker

A function within a graphics application that assists in selecting a color.

Color Proof

A printed or simulated printed image of the color separations intended to produce a close visual simulation of the final reproduction for approval purposes.

Color Scanner

See *Scanner*

Color Separation

The process of splitting an image or PostScript into cyan, magenta, yellow, and black components for offset printing.

Color Sequence

The color order of printing the cyan, magenta, yellow, and black inks on a printing press. Sometimes called rotation or color rotation.

Color Space

Because a color must be represented by three basic characteristics depending on the color model, the color space is a three-dimensional coordinate system in which any color can be represented as a point.

Color Temperature

The temperature, in degrees Kelvin, to which a blackbody would have to be heated to produce a certain color radiation. (A "blackbody" is an ideal body or surface that completely absorbs or radiates energy.) The graphic arts viewing standard is 5,000 K. The degree symbol is not used in the Kelvin scale. The higher the color temperature, the bluer the light.

Color Transparency

A positive color photographic image on a clear film base that must be viewed by transmitted light. It is preferred for original photographic art because it has higher resolution than a color print. Transparency sizes range from 35mm color slides up to 8x10in. (203x254mm).

Colorimeter

An optical measuring instrument designed to measure and quantify color. They are often used to match digital image values to those of cloth and other physical samples.

Column rule

A thin vertical rule used to separate columns of type.

Comp

Comprehensive artwork used to present the general color and layout of a page.

Compose

To set copy into type, or lay out a page.

Compression

A digital technique used to reduce the size of a file by analyzing occurrences of similar data. Compressed files occupy less physical space, and their use improves digital transmission speeds. Compression can sometimes result in a loss of image quality and/or resolution.

Condensed Type

A typeface in which the width of the letters has been reduced. Condensed type can be a specific font, or the result of applying a percentage of normal width by a formatting command.

Continuous Tone

An image such as an original photograph in which the subject has continuous shades of color or gray tones through the use of an emulsion process. Continuous tone images must be screened to create halftone images in order to be printed.

Contrast

The relationship between the dark and light areas of an image.

Copy

Any material furnished for reproduction such as text or illustrations. As a verb, the computer command to copy data to the clipboard in preparation for pasting it to another location.

Copyfitting

Fitting a certain body of text to a given area by changing the font size, leading, justification, or some other parameter.

Copyright

Ownership of a work by the originator, such as an author, publisher, artist, or photographer. The right of copyright permits the originator of material to prevent its use without express permission or acknowledgement of the originator. Copyright may be sold, transferred, or given up contractually.

CorelDraw

A popular drawing program originally designed for the Windows environment, but now available as a Macintosh program. Corel is known to create files that can cause printing and/or output problems in many environments.

Creep

An unwanted movement of the blanket of an offset printing press that causes registration problems.

Cromalin

A single-sheet color proofing system introduced by DuPont in 1971 and still quite popular in the industry. It uses a series of overlaid colorants and varnish to simulate the results of a press run.

Crop Marks

Printed lines used for final trimming of a printed page.

Cropping

The elimination of parts of a photograph or other original that are not required to be printed.

Dash

A short horizontal rule of varying lengths used to indicate a pause or clause in a sentence; see *En-dash* and *Em-dash.*

DCS (Desktop Color Separation)

An EPS file format that creates one file for each of the four primary printing inks, and a fifth file that contains a thumbnail of the image. DCS files are used for building pages with layout programs; when the file is output, the small placement image is discarded, and the four high-resolution files are automatically substituted. This reduces the need to move large, high-resolution files around a network.

Default

A specification for a mode of computer operation that operates if no other is selected. For example, the default font size might be 12 point, or a default color for an object might be white with a black border.

Densitometer

An electronic instrument used to measure optical density. Reflective (for paper) and transmissive (for film) versions are available.

Density

The ability of a material to absorb light. In film, it refers to the opacity of a specific area of the image. A maximum density of 4.0 refers to solid black. Improper density in film images can result in washed-out or overly-dark reproduction.

Descender

The part of a lower-case letter that extends below the baseline (lower edge of the x-height) of the letter. The letters y, p, g, and j contain descenders.

Desktop

1. The area on a monitor screen on which the icons appear, before an application is launched. 2. A reference to the size of computer equipment (system unit, monitor, printer) that can fit on a normal desk; thus, desktop publishing.

Desktop Publishing (DTP)

Use of a personal computer, software applications, and a high-quality printer to produce fully composed printed documents. DTP is, in reality, an incorrect term these days. In the early days of Macintosh and PostScript technology, the term Desktop Publishing inferred that the materials produced from these systems was somehow inferior (as opposed to *professional* publishing). Now, the overwhelming majority of all printed materials – regardless of the quality – are produced on these systems, up to and including nationally famous magazines, catalogs, posters, and newspapers.

Dialog Box

A window in a computer application that – in most cases – presents an opportunity for the user to enter information relative to the process that they're executing. A dialog box might ask, for example, how many copies of a document you want to print, or what size a circle should be, or what color. Dialog boxes are an integral part of today's graphic user interfaces – both on the Macintosh and on Windows-based systems.

Digital Camera

A camera which produces images directly into an electronic file format for transfer to a computer.

Digital

The use of a series of discrete electronic pulses to represent data. In digital imaging systems, 256 steps (8 bits, or 1 byte) are normally used to characterize the gray scale or the properties of one color. For text, see *ASCII.*

Digital Proofs

Digital proofs are representations of what a specific mechanical will look like when output and reproduced on a specific type of printing press. The difference with a digital proof is that it is created without the use of conventional film processes and output directly from computer files.

Dingbat

A font character that displays a picture instead of a letter, number or punctuation mark. There are entire font families of pictographic dingbats; the most commonly used dingbat font is *Zapf Dingbats.* There are dingbats for everything from the little airplanes used to represent airports on a map, to telephones, swashes, fish, stars, balloons – just about anything.

Direct-to-plate

Producing printing plates directly from computer output without going through the film process.

Disk

A computer data storage device, either "floppy," "hard," or a high-capacity removable disk, that stores data magnetically.

Disk Operating System (DOS)

Software for computer systems that supervises and controls the running of programs. The operating system is loaded into memory from disk by a small program which permanently resides in the firmware within the computer. The major operating systems in use today are Windows95 and WindowsNT from Microsoft, the Macintosh OS from Apple Computer, and a wide range of UNIX systems, such as those from Silicon Graphics, SUN Microsystems, and other vendors.

Dithering

A technique used in images wherein a color is represented using dots of two different colors displayed or printed very close together. Dithering is often used to compress digital images, in special screening algorithms (see *Stochastic Screening*) and to produce higher quality output on low-end color printers.

Document

The general term for a computer file containing text and/or graphics.

Dongle

A security device that usually plugs into your keyboard or printer port, that allows copy-protected software to run on your system. Such protected software will only run on systems with the dongle present. This prevents a single copy of software from running on any but one machine at a time.

Dot Gain

The growth of a halftone dot that occurs whenever ink soaks into paper. This growth can vary from being very small (on a high-speed press with fast-drying ink and very non-porous paper) to quite dramatic, as is the case in newspaper printing, where a dot can expand 30% from its size on the film to the size at which it dries. Failure to compensate for this gain in the generation of digital images can result in very poor results on press. Generally speaking, the finer the screen (and therefore, the smaller the dot) the more noticable dot gain will be.

Double-page Spread

A design that spans the two pages visible to the reader at any open spot in a magazine, periodical, or book.

Double-Click

Two clicks of a mouse button in rapid succession that are interpreted as the command to open an application, file, or folder.

Downloadable Fonts

Typefaces that can be stored on disk and then downloaded to the printer when required for printing.

DPI (Dots Per Inch)

The measurement of resolution for page printers, phototypesetting machines and graphics screens. Currently graphics screens use resolutions of 60 to 100 dpi, standard desktop laser printers work at 600 dpi, and imagesetters operate at more than 1,500 dpi.

Dragging

The process of moving an object on the screen by clicking on it with the mouse, moving the cursor to another location, then releasing the button.

Drop Cap

A large initial cap, usually set down into the block or body of normal text. Excellent examples of ornate drop caps (called illuminated initials) can often be seen in manuscripts illustrated by hand in the Middle Ages.

Drop Shadow

A duplicate of a graphic element or type placed behind and slightly offset from it, giving the effect of a shadow.

Drum Scanner

A color scanner on which the original is wrapped around a rotary scanning drum. See *Scanner*.

DTP

See *Desktop Publishing*

Duotone

The separation of a black-and-white photograph into black and a second color having different tonal values and screen angles. Duotones are used to enhance photographic reproduction in two-, three-, or sometimes four-color work. Often the second, third, and fourth colors are not standard CMYK inks.

Dye

A soluble coloring material, normally used as the colorant in color photographs.

Dye Transfer

A photographic color print using special coated papers to produce a full color image. Can serve as an inexpensive proof.

Electrostatic

The method by which dry toner is transferred to paper in a copier or laser printer, and liquid toners are bonded to paper on some large-format color plotters.

Element

The smallest unit of a graphic, or a component of a page layout or design. Any object, text block, or graphic might be referred to as an element of the design.

Elliptical Dot Screen

A halftone screen having an elliptical dot structure.

Em Dash

A dash – often used in place of parentheses or commas to break a sentence – that is usually equal to the point size. For example, in 10 point type, an em dash would be 10 points wide. Formerly the width of a capital M in a particular font; this definition is still used by some type foundries.

Em Space

A space usually equal to the current point size; in 10 point type, an em space should be 10 points wide. Formerly the width of a capital M in a given font; this definition is still used by some type foundries. Hot lead typesetters often used this space as the standard distance for a paragraph indent.

Embedding

1. Placing control codes in the body of a document. 2. Including a complete copy of a text file or image within a desktop publishing document, with or without a *link* (see *Linking*).

Emulsion

The coating of light-sensitive material (silver halide) on a piece of film.

En Dash

A dash – often used in hyphenated word pairs – that is usually half the width of an em dash.

En Space

A space that is usually equal to half the width of an em space.

EPS (Encapsulated PostScript)

A file format used to transfer PostScript data within compatible applications. An EPS file normally contains a small thumbnail that's used to display the image when it's placed into position within a mechanical or used by another program. EPS files can contain text, vector artwork, and images.

Ethernet

A set of software protocols widely used in network communications.

Excel

A spreadsheet application produced by Microsoft; available separately or as part of Microsoft Office.

Exception dictionary

A file, used within a spell-checking or hyphenation process, that provides exceptions to standard spelling or justification rules.

Expanded Type

Also called extended, a widened version of a typeface design. Type may be extended artificially within a DTP application, or designed as such by the typeface designer. See also *Condensed Type*.

Export

To save a file generated in one application in a format that is readable in another application.

Extension

A modular software program that extends or expands the functions of a larger program. A folder of Extensions is found in the Macintosh System Folder.

Fill

To add a tone or color to the area inside a closed object in a graphic illustration program.

Film

Non-paper output of an imagesetter or phototypesetter.

Filter

In image editing applications, a small program that creates a special effect or performs some other function within an image.

Flat

A group of individual camera-ready pages mounted in the proper order and ready for photographing to produce a signature plate.

Flat Color

Color that lacks contrast or tonal variation.

Flatbed Scanner

A scanner on which the original is mounted on a flat scanning glass. See *Scanner*.

Flexography

A rotary letterpress process printing from rubber or flexible plates and using fast drying inks. Mainly used for packaging.

Floating Accent

A separate accent mark that can be placed under or over another character. Complex accented characters such as in foreign languages are usually available in a font as a single character.

Flop

To make a mirror image of visuals such as photographs or clip art.

Flush Left

Copy aligned along the left margin.

Flush Right

Copy aligned along the right margin.

Folder

1. The digital equivalent of a paper file folder, used to organize files in the Macintosh and Windows operating systems. The icon of a folder looks like a paper file folder. Double-clicking it opens it to reveal the files stored inside. 2. A mechanical device which folds preprinted pages into various formats, such as a tri-fold brochure.

Font

A font is the complete collection of all the characters (numbers, uppercase and lowercase letters and, in some cases, small caps and symbols) of a given typeface in a specific style; for example, Helvetica Bold.

Force Justify

A type alignment command which causes the space between letters and words in a line of type to expand to fit within a line. Often used in headlines, and sometimes used to force the last line of a justified paragraph, which is normally set flush left, to justify.

Four-color Process

See *Process Colors*

FPO

"For Position Only": a low-resolution graphic or simple box to designate the location of a graphic in the final file.

Frame

In desktop publishing, an area or block into which text or graphics can be placed.

FreeHand

A popular vector-based illustration program available from Macromedia.

Full Measure

A line set to the entire line length.

Galley Proof

Proofs, usually of type, taken before the type is made up into pages. Before desktop publishing, galley proofs were hand-assembled into pages.

Gamma Correction

1. Adjusting the contrast of the midtones in an image. 2. Calibrating a monitor so that midtones are correctly displayed on screen.

Gamma

A measure of the contrast, or range of tonal variation, of the midtones in a photographic image

Gamut

See *Color Gamut*

GASP

Acronym for Graphic Arts Service Provider, a firm that provides a range of services somewhere on the continuum from design to fulfillment.

GCR (Gray component replacement)

A technique for adding detail by reducing the amount of cyan, magenta, and yellow in chromatic or colored areas, replacing them with black.

GIF - Graphics Interface File

A CompuServe graphics file format that is used widely for graphic elements in Web pages.

G (Gigabyte)

One billion (1,073,741,824) bytes (2^{30}) or 1,048,576 kilobytes.

Global Preferences

Preference settings which affect all newly created files within an application.

Gradation

A smooth transition between black and white, one color and another, or color and no-color.

Gradient

A fill pattern that goes from dark to light or light to dark, or from one color or shape to another.

Grain

Silver salts clumped together in differing amounts in different types of photographic emulsions. Generally speaking, faster emulsions have larger grain sizes.

Graininess

Visual impression of the irregularly distributed silver grain clumps in a photographic image, or the ink film in a printed image.

Gray Balance

The values for the yellow, magenta, and cyan inks that are needed to produce a neutral gray when printed at a normal density.

Gray Component Replacement

See *GCR*

Gray Scale

An image containing a series of tones stepped from white to black that is used for monitoring tone reproduction.

Grayscale

An image composed in grays ranging from black to white, usually using 256 different shades of gray.

Greeking

1. A software technique by which areas of gray are used to simulate lines of text below a certain point size. 2. Nonsense text use to define a layout before copy is available.

Grid

A division of a page by horizontal and vertical guides into areas into which text or graphics may be placed accurately.

Group

To collect graphic elements together so that an operation may be applied to all of them simultaneously.

GUI

Acronym for Graphical User Interface, the basis of the Macintosh and Windows operating systems.

Guides

Lines created in layout application programs to assist in aligning various design elements.

Gutter

The white space between two facing pages. Sometimes used interchangeably with Alley to describe the space between columns on a page.

Hairline Rule

The thinnest rule that can be printed on a given device. A hairline rule on a 1200 dpi imagesetter is 1/1200 of an inch; on a 300 dpi laser printer, the same rule would print at 1/300 of an inch.

Halftone

An image generated for use in printing in which a range of continuous tones is simulated by an array of dots that create the illusion of continuous tone when seen at a distance.

Halftone Tint

An area covered with a uniform halftone dot size to produce an even tone or color. Also called tint or screen tint.

Hanging Indent

Formatting text so that the first line is not indented, and all subsequent lines within the paragraph are indented. Often used with bullets.

Hanging punctuation

Punctuation marks such as quotation marks that are set outside the text block; similar to a hanging indent.

Hard Copy

A tangible permanent image such as an original, a proof, or a printed sheet.

Hard Drive

A rigid disk sealed inside an airtight transport mechanism that is the basic storage mechanism in a computer. Information stored may be accessed more rapidly than on floppy disks and far greater amounts of data may be stored.

Hard Return

A manual line ending (created by pressing the Return or Enter key) that denotes the end of a paragraph.

Header

A fixed body of copy that appears at the top of each page of a section of a book. It may contain variable quantities such as page number, time, date, or file name.

Hide

A command in DTP applications that will render certain elements on the screen invisible, but will not remove them from the file.

High Key

A photographic or printed image in which the main interest area lies in the highlight end of the scale.

High Resolution File

An image file that typically contains four pixels for every dot in the printed reproduction. High-resolution files are often linked to a page layout file, but not actually embedded in it, due to their large size.

Highlights

The lightest areas in a photograph or illustration.

HLS

Color model based on three coordinates: hue, lightness (or luminance), and saturation.

HSV

A color model based on three coordinates: hue, saturation and value (or luminance).

HTML (HyperText Markup Language)

The language, written in plain (ASCII) text using simple tags, that is used to create Web pages, and which Web browsers are designed to read and display. HTML focuses more on the logical structure of a page than its appearance.

Hue

The wavelength of light of a color in its purest state (without adding white or black).

Hyperlink

An HTML tag that directs the computer to a different Anchor or URL (Uniform Resource Locator). The linked data may be on the same page, or on a computer anywhere in the world.

Hyphenation Zone

The space at the end of a line of text in which the hyphenation function will examine the word to determine whether or not it should be hyphenated and wrapped to the next line.

Icon

A small graphic symbol used on the screen to indicate files or folders, activated by clicking with the mouse or pointing device.

Illustrator

A vector editing application owned by Adobe Systems, Inc.

Imagesetter

A raster-based laser device used to output a computer page-layout file or composition at high resolution onto photographic paper or film, from which to make printing plates.

Import

To bring a file generated within one application into another application.

Imposition

The arrangement of pages on a printed sheet, which, when the sheet is finally printed, folded and trimmed, will place the pages in their correct order.

Indent

A typographical technique that lines up the beginnings or ends of lines at a position other than the preset margin.

Indexing

In DTP, marking certain words within a document with hidden codes so that an index may be automatically generated.

Indexed Color Image

An image which uses a limited, predetermined number of colors; often used in Web images. See also *GIF.*

Initial Caps

Text in which the first letter of each word (except articles, etc.) is capitalized.

Inline Graphic

A graphic that is inserted within a body of text, and may be formatted using normal text commands for justification and leading; inline graphics will move with the body of text in which they are placed.

Intensity

Synonym for degree of color saturation.

International Paper Sizes

The International Standards Organization (ISO) system of paper sizes is based on a series of three sizes A, B and C. Series A is used for general printing and stationery, Series B for posters, and Series C for envelopes. Each size has the same proportion of length to width as the others. The nearest ISO paper size to conventional 8-1/2 x 11 paper is A4.

ISO

The International Standards Organization.

Italics

A version of a typeface designed with letters slanted to the right.

Jaggies

Visible steps in the curved edge of a graphic or text character that results from enlarging a bitmapped image.

JPG or JPEG

A compression algorithm that reduces the file size of bitmapped images, named for the Joint Photographic Experts Group, an industry organization that created the standard; JPEG is a "lossy" compression method, and image quality will be reduced in direct proportion to the amount of compression.

Justification

The alignment of text along a margin or both margins..

Kelvin (K)

Unit of temperature measurement based on Celsius degrees, starting from absolute zero, which is equivalent to -273 Celsius (centigrade); used to indicate the color temperature of a light source.

Kerning

Moving a pair of letters closer together or farther apart, to achieve a better fit or appearance.

Key (Black Plate)

In early four-color printing, the black plate was printed first and the other three colors were aligned (or registered) to it. Thus, the black plate was the "key" to the result.

Kilobyte (K, KB)

1,024 (2^{10}) bytes, the nearest binary equivalent to decimal 1,000 bytes. Abbreviated and referred to as K.

Knockout

A shape or object printed by eliminating (knocking out) all background colors. See *Overprinting.*

L*a*b

The lightness, red-green attribute, and yellow-blue attribute in the CIE Color Space, a three-dimensional color mapping system.

Landscape

Printing from the left to right across the wider side of the page. A landscape orientation treats a page as 11 inches wide and 8.5 inches long.

Laser printer

A high quality image printing system using a laser beam to produce an image on a photosensitive drum. The image is transferred to paper by a conventional xerographic printing process. Current laser printers used for desktop publishing have a resolution of 600 dpi. Imagesetters are also laser printers, but with higher resolution and tight mechanical controls to produce final film separations for commercial printing.

Layer

A function of graphics applications in which elements may be isolated from each other, so that a group of elements may be hidden from view, locked, reordered or otherwise manipulated as a unit, without affecting other elements on the page.

Layout

The arrangement of text and graphics on a page, usually produced in the preliminary design stage.

Leading ("ledding")

Space added between lines of type. Usually measured in points or fractions of points. Named after the strips of lead which used to be inserted between lines of metal type. In specifying type, lines of 12-pt. type separated by a 14-pt. space is abbreviated "12/14," or "twelve over fourteen."

Leaders

A line of periods or other symbols connecting the end of a group of words with another element separated by some space. For example, a table of contents may consist of a series of phrases on separate lines, each associated with a page number. Promotes readability in long lists of tabular text.

Letterspacing

The insertion or addition of white space between the letters of words.

Library

In the computer world, a collection of files having a similar purpose or function.

Ligature

Letters that are joined together as a single unit of type such as oe and fi.

Lightness

The property that distinguishes white from gray or black, and light from dark color tones on a surface.

Line Art

A drawing or piece of black and white artwork, with no screens. Line art can be represented by a graphic file having only one-bit resolution.

Line Screen

The number of lines per inch used when converting a photograph to a halftone. Typical values range from 85 for newspaper work to 150 or higher for high-quality reproduction on smooth or coated paper.

Linen Tester

A magnifying glass designed for checking the dot image of a halftone. See *Loupe*.

Linking

An association through software of a graphic or text file on disk with its location in a document. That location may be represented by a "placeholder" rectangle, or a low-resolution copy of the graphic.

Linotype

A typecasting machine (now obsolete) that injected hot metal into a line of molds to produce lines of type. After printing, the type was melted and used again.

Linotype-Hell

The manufacturer of imagesetters such as the Linotronic that process PostScript data through an external Raster Image Processor (RIP) to produce high resolution film for printing.

Lithography

A mechanical printing process used for centuries based on the principle of the natural aversion of water (in this case, ink) to grease. In modern offset lithography, the image on a photosensitive plate is first transferred to the blanket of a rotating drum, and then to the paper.

Logo

A graphic element normally used as a design to represent a company or product.

Lossy

A data compression method characterized by the loss of some data.

Loupe

A small free-standing magnifier used to see fine detail on a page. See *Linen Tester*.

Lowercase

The uncapitalized letters of the alphabet; so named when type was composed by hand, and the small letters were in the lower part of the type case.

LPI

Lines per inch. See *Line Screen*.

Luminosity

The amount of light, or brightness, in an image. Part of the HLS color model.

LZW

The acronym for the Lempel-Ziv-Welch lossless data- and image-compression algorithm.

M, MB (Megabyte)

One million (1,048,576) bytes (2^{20}) or 1,024 Kilobytes.

Macro

A set of keystrokes that is saved as a named computer file. When accessed, the keystrokes will be performed. Macros are used to perform repetitive tasks.

Manuscript (MS or Mss)

The original written or typewritten work of an author submitted for publication.

Margins

The non-printing areas of page, or the line at which text starts or stops.

Mark up

To prepare copy for a compositor, setting out in detail all the typesetting instructions, or to denote corrections on a printed proof.

Mask

To conform the shape of a photograph or illustration to another shape such as a circle or polygon.

Masking

A digital technique that blocks an area of an image from reproduction by superimposing an opaque object of any shape.

Master Page

A page that holds repeating elements of a layout, such as guides or graphics.

Match Print

A color proofing system used for the final quality check.

Mechanical

A pasted-up page of camera-ready art that is to be photographed to produce a plate for the press.

Mechanical Dot Gain

See *Dot Gain*

Medium

A physical carrier of data such as a CD-ROM, video cassette, or floppy disk, or a carrier of electronic data such as fiber optic cable or electric wires.

Megabyte (MB)

A unit of measure of stored data equaling 1,024 kilobytes, or 1,048,576 bytes (10^{20}).

Megahertz

An analog signal frequency of one million cycles per second, or a data rate of one million bits per second. Used in specifying computer CPU speed.

Menu

A list of choices of functions, or of items such as fonts. In contemporary software design, there is often a fixed menu of basic functions at the top of the page that have pull-down menus associated with each of the fixed choices.

Menu-driven

Programs which allow the user to request functions by choosing from a list of options.

Metafile

A class of graphics that combines the characteristics of raster and vector graphics formats; not recommended for high-quality output.

Metallic Ink

Printing inks which produce an effect of gold, silver, bronze, or metallic colors.

Midtones or Middletones

The tonal range between highlights and shadows.

Mock-up

The rough concept or layout of a publication or design.

Modem

An electronic device for converting digital data into analog audio signals and back again (MOdulator-DEModulator.) Primarily used for transmitting data between computers over analog (audio frequency) telephone lines.

Moiré

An interference pattern caused by the out-of-register overlap of two or more regular patterns such as dots or lines. In process-color printing, screen angles are selected to minimize this pattern.

Monochrome

An image or computer monitor in which all information is represented in black and white, or with a range of grays.

Monospace

A font in which all characters occupy the same amount of horizontal width regardless of the character. See also *Proportional Spacing.*

Montage

A single image formed by assembling or compositing several images.

Mottle

Uneven color or tone.

Mss

See *Manuscript*

Multimedia

The combination of sound, video images, and text to create a "moving" presentation.

Network

Two or more computers that are linked to exchange data or share resources. The Internet is a network of networks.

Neutral

Any color that has no hue, such as white, gray, or black.

Neutral Density

A term that describes images or filters that are gray with no apparent hue.

Noise

Unwanted signals or data that may reduce the quality of the output.

Non-breaking Space

A typographic command that connects two words with a space, but prevents the words from being broken apart if the space occurs within the hypenation zone. See *Hyphenation Zone.*

Nonreproducible Colors

Colors in an original scene or photograph that are impossible to reproduce using process inks. Also called out-of-gamut colors.

Normal Key

A description of an image in which the main interest area is in the middle range of the tone scale or distributed throughout the entire tonal range.

Norton Utilities

A software product that provides programs for maintaining a computer's hardware or software; for example, locating and restoring a file that was accidentally "erased."

Nudge

To move a graphic or text element in small, preset increments, usually with the arrow keys.

Oblique

A slanted character (sometimes backwards, or to the left), often used when referring to italic versions of sans-serif typefaces.

OCR (Optical Character Recognition)

A special kind of scanner software that provides a means of reading printed characters on documents and converting them into digital codes that can be read into a computer as actual editable text rather than pure images.

Offset

In graphics manipulation, to move a copy or clone of an image slightly to the side and/or back; used for a drop-shadow effect.

Offset Lithography

A printing method whereby the image is transferred from a plate onto a rubber-covered cylinder from which the printing takes place (see *Lithography*).

OLE

Object Linking and Embedding, a software technique that permits linking an object in a document to its original file and enabling automatic updating. OLE applications may be OLE containers (able to accept OLE documents) or OLE servers (able to create OLE documents), or both.

Opacity

1. The degree to which paper will show print through it. 2. Settings in certain graphics applications that allow images or text below the object whose opacity has been adjusted, to show through.

OPI

Open Prepress Interface, a software device that is an extension to PostScript that replaces low-resolution placeholder images in a document with their high-resolution sources for printing.

Optical Disks

Video disks that store large amounts of data used primarily for reference works such as dictionaries and encyclopedias.

Orphan

The last line of a paragraph that appears alone at the top of a column or page.

Outline

A typeface in which the letters have outlines only and no fill.

Overlay

A transparent sheet used in the preparation of multicolor mechanical artwork showing the color breakdown.

Overprint Color

A color made by overprinting any two or more of the primary yellow, magenta, and cyan process colors.

Overprinting

Allowing an element to print over the top of underlying elements, rather than knocking them out (see *Knockout*). Often used with black type.

Page Description Language (PDL)

A special form of programming language that describes both text and graphics (object or bit-image) in mathematical form. The main benefit of a PDL is that makes the application software independent of the physical printing device. PostScript is a PDL, for example.

Page Layout Software

Desktop publishing software such as PageMaker or QuarkXpress used to combine various source documents and images into a high quality publication.

Page Proofs

Proofs of the actual pages of a document, usually produced just before printing, for a final quality check.

PageMaker

A popular page-layout application produced by Adobe Systems.

Palette

1. As derived from the term in the traditional art world, a collection of selectable colors. 2. Another name for a dialog box or menu of choices.

Panose

A typeface matching system for font substitution based on a numeric classification of fonts according to visual characteristics.

Pantone Matching System

A system for specifying colors by number for both coated and uncoated paper; used by print services and in color desktop publishing to assure uniform color matching.

Pasteboard

In a page layout program, the desktop area outside of the printing page area, on which elements can be placed for later positioning on any page.

PCX

Bitmap image format produced by paint programs.

PDF (Portable Document Format)

Developed by Adobe Systems, Inc. (and read by Adobe Acrobat Reader), this format has become a de facto standard for document transfer across platforms.

PDL

See *Page Description Language*

Perfect binding

A common method of binding paperback books in which the pages are glued directly to the binding.

Perspective

The effect of distance in an image achieved by aligning the edges of elements with imaginary lines directed toward one to three "vanishing points" on the horizon.

Photoshop

The Adobe Systems image editing program commonly used for color correction and special effects on both the Macintosh and PC platforms.

Pi Fonts

A collection of special characters such as timetable symbols and mathematical signs. Examples are Zapf Dingbats and Symbol. See also *Dingbats*.

Pica

A traditional typographic measurement of 12 points, or approximately 1/6 of an inch. Most DTP applications specify a pica as exactly 1/6 of an inch.

PICT/PICT2

A common format for defining bitmapped images on the Macintosh. The more recent PICT2 format supports 24-bit color.

Pixel

A picture element – the smallest dot or unit on a computer monitor or in a bitmapped image.

Plate

Paper, polyester, or metal sheet used in a printing press to transfer an image onto paper.

PMS

See *Pantone Matching System*

PMT

Photo Mechanical Transfer – positive prints of text or images used for paste-up to mechanicals.

Point

A unit of measurement used to specify type size and rule weight, equal to (approximately, in traditional typesetting) 1/72 inch.

Polygon

A geometric figure consisting of three or more straight lines enclosing an area. The triangle, square, rectangle, and star are all polygons.

Portrait

Printing from left to right across the narrow side of the page. Portrait orientation on a letter-size page uses a standard 8.5-inch width and 11-inch length.

Positive

A true photographic image of the original made on paper or film.

Posterize, Posterization

The deliberate constraint of a gradient or image into visible steps as a special effect; or the unintentional creation of steps in an image due to a high LPI value used with a low printer DPI.

Postprocessing Applications

Applications, such as trapping programs or imposition software, that perform their functions after the image has been printed to a file, rather than in the originating application.

PostScript

A page description language developed by Adobe Systems, Inc. that describes type and/or images and their positional relationships upon the page; the resulting file is processed by a RIP (see *Raster Image Processor*) into a format a laser printer or imagesetter can understand.

PPD

Acronym for PostScript Printer Definition file, the information that ensures that output remains within the capabilities of the selected output device.

PPI

Pixels per inch; used to denote the resolution of an image.

Prepress

All work done between writing and printing, such as typesetting, scanning, layout, and imposition.

Preferences

A set of defaults for an application program that may be modified.

Prepress Proof

A color proof made directly from electronic data or film images.

Primary Colors

Colors that can be used to generate secondary colors. For the additive system (i.e., a computer monitor), these colors are red, green, and blue. For the subtractive system (i.e., the printing process), these colors are yellow, magenta, and cyan.

Printer Command Language

PCL — a language, that has graphics capability, developed by Hewlett Packard for use with its own range of printers.

Printer fonts

The image outlines for type in PostScript that are sent to the printer.

Printer's Spreads

Pages arranged so that, when printed as spreads and assembled, the pages appear in the proper order. For example, the front and back covers are printed on a spread, the inside front and inside back covers are printed on another spread, etc.

Process Colors

The four colors (cyan, magenta, yellow, and black) that are combined to print a wide range of colors. When blended, they can reproduce many, but not all of the colors found in nature. See also *CMYK*.

Profile

A file containing data representing the color reproduction characteristics of a device determined by a calibration of some sort.

Proof

A representation of the printed job that is made from plates (press proof), film, or electronic data (prepress proofs). It is generally used for customer inspection and approval before mass production begins.

Proportional Spacing

A method of spacing whereby each character is spaced to accommodate the varying widths of letters or figures, thus increasing readability. Books and magazines are set proportionally spaced, and most fonts in desktop publishing are proportional. With proportionally spaced fonts, each character is given a horizontal space proportional to its size. For example, a proportionally spaced "m" is wider than an "i."

Pt.

Abbreviation for point.

Pull Quote

A phrase extracted from the copy and used as a graphic to break up a quantity of text visually, and to call attention to an important point.

QuarkXPress

A popular page-layout application.

Queue

A set of files input to the printer, printed in the order received unless otherwise instructed.

QuickDraw

Graphic routines in the Macintosh used for outputting text and images to printers not compatible with PostScript.

Ragged Left

See *Flush Right*

Ragged Right

See *Flush Left*

RAM

Random Access Memory, the "working" memory of a computer that holds files in process. Files in RAM are lost when the computer is turned off, whereas files stored on the hard drive or floppy disks remain available.

Raster

A bitmapped representation of graphic data.

Raster Graphics

A class of graphics created and organized in a rectangular array using bitmaps. Often created by paint software, fax machines, or scanners.

Raster Image Processor (RIP)

That part of an imagesetter that converts the page information from the Page Description Language into the bitmap pattern that is applied to the film or paper output.

Rasterize

Converting mathematical and digital information into a series of dots by an imagesetter for the production of negative or positive film or paper output

Ray Tracing

A software technique for rendering the surface of a reflecting object realistically by tracing the light rays from the source of illumination to the eye of the viewer.

Reader's Spreads

A two-page spread as seen by the reader after printing and collation; thus, the two pages may have been printed in separate locations on the signature.

Reference Marks

Symbols such as the asterisk (*), dagger, double dagger, section mark (§), and paragraph mark (¶) used in text to direct the reader to a footnote.

Reflective Art

Artwork that is opaque, as opposed to transparent, that can be scanned for input to a computer.

Registration

Aligning plates on a multicolor printing press so that the images will superimpose properly to produce the required composite output.

Registration Color

A default color selection that can be applied to design elements so that they will print on every separation from a PostScript printer. "Registration" is often used to print identification text that will appear outside the page area on a set of separations.

Registration Marks

Small crosshairs on film used to align the individual layers of film separations.

Resolution

The number of dots or pixels per inch of a monitor or output device.

Retouching

Making selective manual or electronic corrections to images.

Reverse Out

To reproduce an object as white, or paper, within a solid background, such as white letters in a black rectangle.

RGB

Red, Green, Blue, the additive primary colors used to create images on a computer monitor or television screen.

Rich Black

A process color consisting of sold black with one or more layers of cyan, magenta, or yellow.

Right Reading

A positive or negative image that is readable from top to bottom and from left to right.

Right-Click

Clicking the right mouse button on a Windows system, usually to reveal a pop-up menu. A Macintosh mouse has only one button.

RIP

See Raster Image Processor

River

An accidental and undesirable pattern of white space between words in text that appears to flow from one corner to another.

ROM

Read Only Memory, a semiconductor chip in the computer that retains startup information for use the next time the computer is turned on.

Roman Type

The primary serif typeface of a family.

Rosette

The pattern created when color halftone screens are printed at traditional screen angles.

Rotation

Turning an object at some angle to its original axis.

RTF

Rich Text Format, a text format that retains formatting information lost in pure ASCII text.

Rubylith

A two-layer acetate film having a red or amber emulsion on a clear base used in non-computer stripping and separation operations.

Ruler

Rulers displayed at two sides of the working space on a monitor that show measurements in units that can be selected in the set-up process.

Running Head

A line of type at the top of a page that repeats the same information. Also called header.

S/S (Same Size)

An instruction to the printer to reproduce at the same size as the original.

Sans Serif

Sans Serif fonts are fonts that do not have the tiny lines that appear at the top of and bottom of letters.

Saturation

The intensity or purity of a particular color; a color with no saturation is gray.

Scaling

The means within a program to reduce or enlarge the amount of space an image will occupy by multiplying the data by a scale factor. Scaling can be proportional, or in one dimension only.

Scanner

A device that electronically digitizes images point by point through circuits that can correct color, manipulate tones, and enhance detail. Color scanners will usually produce a minimum of 24 bits for each pixel, with 8 bits each for red, green, and blue.

Screen

To create a halftone of a continuous tone image (See *Halftone*).

Screen Angle

The angle at which the rulings of a halftone screen are set when making screened images for halftone process-color printing. The equivalent effect can be obtained electronically through selection of the desired angle from a menu.

Screen Frequency

The number of lines per inch in a halftone screen, which may vary from 85 to 300.

Screen Printing

A technique for printing on practically any surface using a fine mesh (originally of silk) on which the image has been placed photographically. Preparation of art for screen printing requires consideration of the resolution of the screen printing process.

Screen Shot

A printed output or saved file that represents data from a computer monitor.

Screen Tint

A halftone screen pattern of all the same dot size that creates an even tone at some percentage of solid color.

Script

A typeface designed to imitate handwriting.

SCSI

Small Computer Systems Interface, a standard software protocol for connecting peripheral devices to a computer for fast data transfer.

Selection

The act of placing the cursor on an object and clicking the mouse button to make the object active.

Self-Cover

A cover for a document in which the cover is of the same paper stock as the rest of the piece.

Serif

A line or curve projecting from the end of a letter form. Typefaces designed with such projections are called serif faces.

Service Bureau

A business that specializes in producing film for printing on a high-resolution imagesetter.

Set Solid

Type set with no extra spacing between the lines; for example, 12-pt. type with 12-pt. leading, or 12/12.

SGML

Standard Generalized Markup Language, a set of semantics and syntax that describes the structure of a document (the nature, content, or function of the data) as opposed to visual appearance. HTML is a subset of SGML (see *HTML*).

Sharpness

The subjective impression of the density difference between two tones at their boundary, interpreted as fineness of detail.

Sheet Fed

A printing press that prints single sheets of paper rather than from a continuous roll.

Shortcut

1. A quick method for accessing a menu item or command, usually through a series of keystrokes. 2. The icon that can be created in Windows95 to open an application without having to penetrate layers of various folders. The equivalent in the Macintosh is the "alias."

Show

The opposite of "Hide," a toggle command. For example, the tabs and paragraph marks in a text document can either be shown or hidden by clicking on an icon in the toolbar.

Sidebar

Supplementary text positioned at the side of a page.

Signature

A group of pages ganged together on a large, single sheet for printing, usually comprising an individual section of a publication.

Silhouette

To remove part of the background of a photograph or illustration, leaving only the desired portion.

Skew

A transformation command that slants an object at an angle to the side from its initial fixed base.

Small caps

A type style in which lowercase letters are replaced by uppercase letters set in a smaller point size.

Smart Quotes

The curly quotation marks used by typographers, as opposed to the straight marks on the typewriter. Use of smart quotes is usually a setup option in a word processing program or page layout application.

Snap-to (guides or rulers)

An optional feature in page layout programs that drives objects to line up with guides or margins if they are within a pixel range that can be set. This eliminates the need for very precise, manual placement of an object with the mouse.

Soft Font

See *Downloadable Font*

Soft or Discretionary Hyphen

A hyphen that is coded for display and printing only when formatting of the text puts the hyphenated word at the end of a line.

Soft Return

A return command that ends a line but does not apply a paragraph mark that would end the continuity of the style for that paragraph.

Spectrophotometer

An instrument for measuring the relative intensity of radiation reflected or transmitted by a sample over the spectrum.

Specular Highlight

The lightest highlight area that does not carry any detail, such as reflections from glass or polished metal. Normally, these areas are reproduced as unprinted white paper.

Spine

The binding edge at the back of a book that contains title information and joins the front and back covers.

Spot Color

A color not created by CMYK separations, usually specified by a Pantone swatch number. A spot color is printed by mixing given proportions of various inks in accordance with the percentages given by the Pantone number.

Spread

Two facing pages that can be worked on as a unit, and will be viewed side by side in the final publication.

Stacking Order

The order of the elements on a page, wherein the topmost item will obscure the items beneath it.

Standard Viewing Conditions

A prescribed set of conditions under which the viewing of originals and reproductions are to take place, defining both the geometry of the illumination and the spectral power distribution of the light source.

Standing Cap

A large capital letter sharing baseline with the adjoining text but rising above it. See *Drop Cap*.

Standoff

The distance between a graphic and the text that wraps around it. See *Wrap*.

Stat

Photostat copy.

Stet

Used in proof correction work to cancel a previous correction. From the Latin; "let it stand."

Stipple

Black and white line art where shading is accomplished by the placement of pinpoint dots.

Stochastic Screening

A method of creating halftones in which the size of the dots remains constant but their density is varied; also known as frequency-modulated (or FM) screening.

Stripping

The preparation and assembling of film prior to platemaking.

Stroke, Stroking

Manipulating the width or color of a line.

Stuffit

A file compression utility used in the Macintosh environment.

Style

A set of formatting instructions for font, paragraphing, tabs, and other properties of text.

Style Sheet

A file containing all of the tags and instructions for formatting all parts of a document; style sheets create consistency between similar documents.

Subhead

A second-level heading used to organize body text by topic.

Subscript

Small-size characters set below the normal letters or figures, usually to convey technical information.

Substitution

Using an existing font to simulate one that is not available to the printer.

Substrate

The paper or any other generally flat material upon which an image is printed.

Subtractive Color

Color which is observed when light strikes pigments or dyes, which absorb certain wavelengths of light; the light that is reflected back is perceived as a color. See *CMYK* and *Process Color*.

Superscript

Small characters set above the normal letters or figures, such as numbers referring to footnotes.

Swash Letters

Letters with extra flourishes usually used in logos, headlines, or as initial caps.

Swatch

A sample of a set of papers, inks, etc. that may be provided in physical form, or appear as a menu in a word processing or illustration application program.

Syntax

The rules that govern the structure of statements in a computer language, or in a language in general.

System Folder

The location of the operating system files on a Macintosh.

Tabloid

A paper size 11 inches wide and 17 inches long.

Tabular

Text set in columns or tables.

Tagged Image File Format (TIFF)

A common format used for scanned or computer-generated bitmapped images.

Tags

The various formats in a style sheet that indicate paragraph settings, margins and columns, page layouts, hyphenation and justification, widow and orphan control and other parameters.

Template

A document file containing layout and styles by which a series of documents can maintain the same look and feel.

Text Attribute

A characteristic applied directly to a letter or letters in text, such as bold, italic, or underline.

Text Block

A set of characters that may be manipulated as a group.

Text File

A file containing text in ASCII format that does not contain style formatting.

Text Type

Typefaces used for the main text of written material. Generally no larger than 14 point in size, and variable with the type of publication.

Text wrap

See *Wrap*

Text

The characters and words that form the main body of a publication.

Texture

1. A property of the surface of the substrate, such as the smoothness of paper. 2. Graphically, variation in tonal values to form image detail. 3. A class of fills in a graphics application that give various appearances, such as bricks, grass, etc.

Thin Space

A fixed space, equal to half an en space or the width of a period in most fonts.

Thumbnails

1. The preliminary sketches of a design. 2. Small images used to indicate the content of a computer file.

Tick Mark

A small mark at right angles to the axis of a graph that indicates the location of a certain measurement; such as tick marks indicating the numbers 1, 2, 3, etc.

TIFF

See *Tagged Image File Format*

Tight

A characteristic of text in which the characters are set very close together.

Tile

1. A type of repeating fill pattern. 2. Reproduce a number of pages of a document on one sheet. 3. Printing a large document overlapping on several smaller sheets of paper.

Tint

1. A halftone area that contains dots of uniform size; that is, no modeling or texture. 2. The mixture of a color with white.

Tip In

The separate insertion of a single page into a book either during or after binding by pasting one edge.

Toggle

A command that switches between either of two states at each application. Switching between Hide and Show is a toggle.

Tone

Any variation in lightness or saturation while hue remains constant.

Toolbox

An on-screen mouse-operated palette that allows the user to choose from a selection of tools available in computer application programs.

Tracking

Adjusting the spacing of letters in a line of text to achieve proper justification or general appearance.

Transfer Curve

A curve depicting the adjustment to be made to a particular printing plate when an image is printed.

Transparency

A full color photographically produced image on transparent film.

Transparent Ink

An ink that allows light to be transmitted through it.

Trapping

Compensating for potential gaps between two adjoining colors because of misregistration.

Trim

After printing, mechanically cutting the publication to the correct final dimensions. The trim size is normally indicated by marks on the printing plate outside the page area.

TrueType

An outline font format used in both Macintosh and Windows systems that can be used both on the screen and on a printer.

Type 1 Fonts

PostScript fonts based on Bézier curves encrypted for compactness that are compatible with Adobe Type Manager.

Type Family

A set of typefaces created from the same basic design but in different weights, such as bold, light, italic, book, and heavy.

Typesetting

The arrangement of individual characters of text into words, sentences, and paragraphs.

Typo

An abbreviation for typographical error. A keystroke error in the typeset copy.

Typographer

A specialist in the design of printed matter and generally an expert in type and letterforms.

Typography

The design and planning of printed matter using type.

U&lc

An abbreviation for UPPER and lower case. Also the name of a popular design publication.

UCR (undercolor removal)

A technique for reducing the amount of magenta, cyan, and yellow inks in neutral or shadow areas and replacing them with black.

Undertone

Color of ink printed in a thin film.

Unsharp Masking

A digital technique (based on a traditional photographic technique) performed after scanning that locates the edge between sections of differing lightness and alters the values of the adjoining pixels to exaggerate the difference across the edge, thereby increasing edge contrast.

Uppercase

The capital letters of a typeface as opposed to the lowercase, or small, letters. So called because when type was hand composited, the capital letters resided in the upper part of the type case.

Utility

Software that performs ancillary tasks such as counting words, defragmenting a hard drive, or restoring a deleted file.

Varnish Plate

The plate on a printing press that applies varnish after the other colors have been applied.

Varnishing

A finishing process whereby a transparent varnish is applied over the printed sheet to produce a glossy or protective coating, either on the entire sheet or on selected areas.

Vector Graphics

Graphics defined using coordinate points, and mathematically drawn lines and curves, which may be freely scaled and rotated without image degradation. Two commonly used vector drawing programs are Illustrator and FreeHand.

A class of graphics created using mathematically described geometric shapes that overcomes the limitations of bitmapped graphics.

Velox

Strictly, a Kodak chloride printing paper, but used to describe a high-quality black & white print of a halftone or line drawing.

Vertical Justification

The ability to automatically adjust the interline spacing (leading) to make columns and pages end at the same point on a page.

Vignette

An illustration in which the background gradually fades into the paper; that is, without a definite edge or border.

Visible Spectrum

The wavelengths of light between about 380 nm (violet) and 700 nm (red) that are visible to the human eye.

Watermark

An impression incorporated in paper during manufacturing showing the name of the paper and/or the company logo. A "watermark" can be applied digitally to printed output as a very light screened image.

Web Press

An offset printing press that prints from a roll of paper rather than single sheets.

Weight

1. The thickness of the strokes of a typeface. The weight of a typeface is usually denoted in the name of the font; for example, light, book, or ultra (thin, medium, and thick strokes, respectively). 2. The thickness of a line or rule.

White Space

Areas on the page which contain no images or type. Proper use of white space is critical to a well-balanced design.

White Light

Light containing all wavelengths of the visible spectrum.

Widow

First line of a paragraph that appears alone at the bottom of a column or page.

Window Shade

A type of text block used in certain applications, such as PageMaker. Windowshades have handles at the top and bottom which, when dragged with the mouse, will reveal or conceal text.

Wizard

A utility attached to an application or operating system that aids you in setting up a piece of hardware, software, or document.

Word Break

The division of a word at the end of a line in accordance with hyphenation principles.

Word Processor

A desktop publishing application program designed for creating and formatting text, but not for page layout.

Word Space

The space inserted between words in a desktop publishing application. The optimal value is built into the typeface, and may usually be modified within an application.

Word Wrap

In word processing, the automatic adjustment of the number of words on a line of text to match the margin and hyphenation settings, resulting in shifting a word to the next line as required.

Wrap

Type set on the page so that it wraps around the shape of another element.

WYSIWYG (pronounced "wizzywig")

An acronym for "What You See Is What You Get," meaning that what you see on your computer screen bears a strong resemblance to what the job will look like when it is printed.

X-height

The height of the letter "x" in a given typeface, which represents the basic size of the bodies of all of the lowercase letters (excluding ascenders and descenders).

Xerography

A photocopying/printing process in which the image is formed using the electrostatic charge principle. The toner replaces ink and can be dry or liquid. Once formed, the image is sealed by heat. Most page printers currently use this method of printing.

Zero Point

The mathematical "origin" of the coordinates of the two-dimensional page. The zero point may be moved to any location on the page, and the ruler dimensions change accordingly.

Zip

1. To compress a file on a Windows-based system using a popular compression utility. 2. A removable disk made by Iomega (a Zip disk) or the device that reads and writes such disks (a Zip drive).

Zooming

The process of electronically enlarging an image on a monitor to facilitate detailed design or editing.

Index

S

T

U

V

W

Z